Critical Essays on Charles Brockden Brown

Critical Essays on Charles Brockden Brown

Bernard Rosenthal

G. K. Hall & Co. • Boston, Massachusetts

Copyright © 1981 by Bernard Rosenthal

Library of Congress Cataloging in Publication Data
Main entry under title:

Critical essays on Charles Brockden Brown.

(Critical essays on American literature)
Includes bibliographical references and index.
1. Brown, Charles Brockden, 1771–1810—Criticism and
interpretation—Addresses, essays, lectures. I. Rosenthal,
Bernard, 1934–   . II. Series.
PS1137.C7   813'.2   80-27488
ISBN 0-8161-8255-8

This publication is printed on permanent/durable acid-free paper
MANUFACTURED IN THE UNITED STATES OF AMERICA

CRITICAL ESSAYS ON AMERICAN LITERATURE

This series seeks to publish the most important reprinted criticism on writers and topics in American literature along with, in various volumes, original essays, interviews, bibliographies, letters, manuscript sections, and other materials brought to public attention for the first time. Bernard Rosenthal's volume on Charles Brockden Brown is not only the most substantial collection of scholarship ever assembled on this important writer, it is an extraordinary addition to the field. It contains, along with early comments by Richard Henry Dana, William Hazlitt, Margaret Fuller, and John Greenleaf Whittier, nine original essays by Nina Baym, William J. Scheick, Sydney J. Krause, Cathy N. Davidson, Bernard Rosenthal, Emory Elliott, Paul Witherington, Charles E. Bennett, and Charles A. Carpenter. We are confident that this collection will make a permanent and significant contribution to American literary study.

JAMES NAGEL, GENERAL EDITOR

ACKNOWLEDGMENTS

I wish to express my deep appreciation to Sydney J. Krause for his generosity in letting me examine the materials on Brown at Kent State and for his scholarly advice. I am also grateful to him and his wife, Evy, for the courtesy and warm hospitality they extended to me during my stay in Kent, Ohio. Obviously, any errors in this collection are my own responsibility.

I am also grateful to Charles E. Bennett for his courtesy in letting me examine his transcription of Charles Brockden Brown's letter of October 24, 1795 to Joseph Bringhurst. Although I have made my own decisions regarding the transcription of the letter, I have benefited from Charles Bennett's knowledge. Again, any errors are my own responsibility.

CONTENTS

INTRODUCTION

It has been the fate of Charles Brockden Brown to be honored by critics more for what he helped begin than for what he achieved. If the idea of Brown as progenitor of American fiction eventually collapses for want of substance, the impulse to find him interesting for what he foreshadowed accords with the milieu in which Brown wrote. In his own day Brown's belletristic contemporaries made much of how America's literature would develop and who would be the first to write a native American literature worthy of national recognition and, always implicitly, of British approval. Brown himself, as in the preface to *Edgar Huntly*, contributed to the call for a body of literature that would be both worthy and distinguished by the special characteristics of America:

> The flattering reception that has been given, by the public, to Arthur Mervyn, has prompted the writer to solicit a continuance of the same favour, and to offer to the world a new performance.
>
> America has opened new views to the naturalist and politician, but has seldom furnished themes to the moral painter. That new springs of action and new motives to curiosity should operate,—that the field of investigation, opened to us by our own country, should differ essentially from those which exist in Europe,—may be readily conceived. The sources of amusement to the fancy and instruction to the heart, that are peculiar to ourselves, are equally numerous and inexhaustible. It is the purpose of this work to profit by some of these sources; to exhibit a series of adventures, growing out of the condition of our country, and connected with one of the most common and most wonderful diseases or affections of the human frame.
>
> One merit the writer may at least claim:—that of calling forth the passions and engaging the sympathy of the reader by means hitherto unemployed by preceding authors. Puerile superstition and exploded manners, Gothic castles and chimeras, are the materials usually employed for this end. The incidents of Indian hostility, and the perils of the Western wilderness, are far more suitable; and for a native of America to overlook these would admit of no apology. These, therefore, are, in part, the ingredients of this tale, and these he has been ambitious of depicting in vivid and faithful colours. The success of his efforts must be estimated by the liberal and candid reader.[1]

Brown's stated intentions are clear, although it is arguable whether or not his fiction, *Edgar Huntly* or other works by him, finally rests heavily on the "new views" found in America. If his use of the wilderness and of Indians in *Edgar Huntly*, and of urban plagues in *Arthur Mervyn* and *Ormond*, employ American settings, the heart of what Brown claims for himself is the wish to be a "moral painter," and such a task quickly transcends nationality.[2] Brown wrote his fiction from the premise of one not merely skeptical of Christianity but in large measure hostile to it for its danger to moral conduct.[3] At a time when his contemporaries clamored for an American literature—and perhaps Brown wrote his preface to *Edgar Huntly* merely to pacify or to capitalize on that sentiment—his own interests lay with problems more metaphysical than geographical.

In concerning himself more with the individual's relation to moral or spiritual matters, rather than with social arrangements, Brown adumbrated the kinds of literary concerns that eventually found expression in America's greatest early novelists, Hawthorne and Melville. Regarding these two writers, F.O. Matthiessen has written that they "were more concerned with human destiny than with every man in his humor."[4] The same might be said for Brown, who shared their literary isolation. For while historians of early American literature have been most interested in writers who explored "human destiny"—and one can easily add Emerson, Thoreau, and Whitman—the American public had other literary tastes. William Starbuck Mayo probably sold more books than Brown, Hawthorne, and Melville combined, and if Hawthorne's "scribbling women"[5] are added to the sales figures, one quickly sees how *quantitatively* insignificant the writers of "human destiny" were for our culture. While the concern for "human destiny" guarantees neither qualitative writing nor literary obscurity for a writer in his own time, it does help establish one basis for Brown's particular claim to attention in American literary history. Like Hawthorne and Melville, Brown examined issues that have remained germane long after the time in which they were written has passed.

Perhaps he was the first American novelist for whom such a claim can be made. That this distinction brought little financial reward seems clear enough, and Brown would have probably starved had his income depended on the sale of his novels.[6] What it did bring him was a limited recognition in his own day as a "serious" writer and a continuing recognition by literary historians as America's first important writer of fiction. Whether this justifies claims for him as our first "professional" writer may be debated, and even the basis for the claim is a little puzzling.[7] But beyond any reasonable doubt, Brown was the first American writer of fiction his countrymen claimed as meritorious. Without ever achieving a wide audience, or even having much direct influence on future writers,[8] Brown has found his place in American literary history as the beginner of its serious fiction.

This recognition appeared early, and, where it counted most for American literati, in England. He had, according to one mid-nineteenth century critic, "honorable distinction . . . awarded to him, as a novelist, by the British press, at a period when it was almost certain that every book with an American imprint would only be mentioned to be carped at . . . ."[9] This claim for Brown's favorable reception in England, in spite of some savage attacks on him, essentially holds up upon examination of the reviews he received, even though the initial response to Brown in England was mixed.[10] In some cases early reviewers favorable to one of his novels may have castigated others. This is nicely exemplified by a review of *Jane Talbot:*

> This novel [*Jane Talbot*] purports to have been written by the author of Arthur Mervyn and Edgar Huntly, but certainly this could scarcely have been collected from the perusal of the work itself. It is indeed something in his style and manner, but so very inferior in point of nervous language and vigour of imagination, that one can scarcely help suspecting that this is an awkward imitation by some other hand, and that he lent his name only. This author, we mean Mr. Browne, delights in pourtraying singular characters, but when these are well drawn and consistent with human nature, having the shades only strongly heightened, we generally read them with pleasure, and even with profit. The author appears to be friendly to the interests of religion and morality. But as to the present silly publication, we again assert that it can scarcely have been the work of the author whose name it bears.[11]

The most unambiguously negative response appears in a review of *Ormond* that presents five paragraphs of vilification, including the observation that *"if* a want of perspicuity, *if* a want of elegance in style, *if* a want of imagination, *if* a want of nature in the delineation of character, *if* a want of incident, *if* a want of plot and connection, and, finally, *if* a want of *common sense*, be excellencies in a novel, the author of *Ormond, Wieland, Arthur Mervyn,*&c. &c. has a fair claim to the laurel of preeminence in 'the temple of Minerva.' "[12] But a writer for the *Imperial Review* found merit in Brown, although like some other critics who would follow, he was offended by *Ormond*, perhaps because of its radical insinuations regarding the status of women and the use of rape as a literary topic. Unfortunately, the reviewer does not make the concerns clear enough. The reviewer does observe that various novels "have been published in America by Mr. Browne. The first, we believe, was Wieland, or the Ventriloquist, than which [sic] we never read a tale that more strongly excited our interest and curiosity. The first volume of Arthur Mervyn, which was published some time before the others, had a degree of merit which was very far from being equalled by the two succeeding ones. Ormond is a disgusting, and Edgar Huntly a tedious story. With respect to the merits of the present work, Jane Talbot, though we deem it far inferior to Wieland, we yet prefer it upon the whole to any of the other works of Mr. Browne."[13]

On the yet more favorable side, the reviewer in *Monthly Magazine* found "Mr. Browne's *'Arthur Mervyn'* . . . entitled to considerable praise,"[14] and another reviewer of *Arthur Mervyn* also commended the book but not without some reservation about Arthur's marrying a woman who retained neither youth nor virginity.[15] Later British reviews continued to show a mixed response to his work.

One lengthy review shows a generally favorable response, though tempered by reservations.[16] A scathing, one-sentence review elsewhere condemns *Wieland:* "A most improbable and horrid tale; and evidently written by one whose talents might have been better employed."[17] But another review appearing in the same year, 1811, praised him at length and offered a perceptive insight on Brown's concern in *Wieland* not merely with religious excess, but with the inherent danger of religion itself:

> The leading aim of the writer of this extraordinary performance seems to be to manifest the dreadful consequences which may result from not entirely subjecting the mind to the controul of moral feeling, and to the dictates of moral duty. To obey any supposed supernatural impulses, which are hostile to these; or even to pause for a moment on the possibility that such an impulse may be a communication from on high, is to enter on a career of crime, the end of which mocks all ordinary foresight or calculation. When the horridly operative principles of fanaticism are once set at work, religion, which should disarm their rage, serves only to redouble their force. The deluded wretch, while he is in the very act of opposing the moral commands of the deity, fancies himself the secret instrument of performing his [sic] will; the chosen agent through whom his decrees are to be consumated.[18]

The insight about religious delusion is not to be taken for the "enthusiasm" which so concerned earlier English and American clerics. Rather it reflects Brown's belief, at least at one time in his life, that obedience to morality and obedience to religion can be mutually exclusive.

The diversity of response among Brown's early British critics ultimately emerges as more orderly than might appear at first and not wholly inconsistent with the way he has been seen in America from the beginning of his career to the present. Brown's detractors saw chaos of narration, an inability to delineate characters, and a body of fiction that depended too heavily on improbable events. His admirers tended to grant these objections but felt that they were secondary considerations in responding to Brown's merits. One of his English admirers presented the case in a particularly useful way, in view of how Brown has ultimately been regarded in America. In 1824 the critic wrote:

Charles Brockden Brown was the first writer of prose fiction of which America could boast. In his style, and in his treatments of subjects, *he* also is unquestionably English. He grounded himself upon the manner of Godwin, and followed the grand and gloomy track of that celebrated writer. Like him, Brown's object was to take a single human heart, and strip and anatomize it nerve by nerve; to cast his victim amongst appalling scenes and stirring passions; and in this he has in a great degree succeeded. But Brown had no power over character: he dealt only with events; that is to say, with sickness, and death, and peril; with hair-breadth escapes from tigers and savages; with depths, and rocks, and the boundless wilderness. The hero of his tale was merely an object set up to connect these things, or make them probable.[19]

While universal agreement on this assessment may not prevail, one would be hard put to deny that the basic history of Brown criticism has not deviated much from the issues raised in this observation. The notion of Brown as our "first writer of prose fiction" appears almost as a litany in surveys of American literature, even if some literary historians have failed to emphasize the perceptive distinction made by the writer for the *Retrospective Review*. The statement is *not* that Brown is our first writer, nor even that he is the first writer to live by his pen. The key to the insight is the qualitative response. Brown is the first "of which America could boast," and in that phrase one may find the major basis for all arguments proposing Brown as our first writer of fiction, whether earning money or not.

The observation that Brown "is unquestionably English" offers a more tantalizing and less certain proposition. Whether one ultimately agrees with the view will depend on how the "Americanness" of a writer is defined, but surely Brown criticism has rarely strayed far from the belief that Godwin in some way fathered Brown's fiction. Nor have critics found much to quarrel with in the view that Brown was stronger on passion than on characterization. If the terms of this early assessment of Brown have been modified and refined, the principles enunciated have essentially governed critical response to Brown.

But the degree to which Brown's early critics were willing to praise him has not continued in American critical history. The same writer in the *Retrospective Review* offers a comparison of Brown with Cooper that quickly highlights how far modern criticism has diverged from some of the early assessments of Brown:

Mr. Cooper, the author of *The Pioneers*, is a young man of high and undoubted talent. There is a freshness and vivid beauty in some of his scenes, which may challenge competition with *any* writer of the present day. He is much more dramatic than Brown; but he has not the same power over the passions, and scarcely the same burning and impetuous strength of narration.[20]

This observation is from a writer who recognized and admired Cooper at the outset of his career and who had read *The Pioneers*, as good a novel as Cooper would ever write. So, in spite of the lavish praise he offers Cooper, or rather in view of it, the claims for Brown's strengths relative to Cooper's offer a significant insight into how highly Brown was once regarded by some of his readers.

Nor is this high esteem a mere quirk of one anonymous reviewer. As various scholars have noted, Brown appealed to, among other noteworthy figures, Keats, Peacock, Shelley, and, indeed, even to Godwin, with whom Brown is so often compared.[21] Keats referred to his "Powerful genius" and Peacock called some of Brown's novels "unquestionably works of great genius."[22] Also, according to Peacock, "nothing so blended itself with the structure of [Shelley's] interior mind as the creations of Brown."[23] More restrained, though acknowledging British enthusiasm for Brown, are the comments of William Hazlitt in 1829, some of which repeated earlier English reservations about Brown and some of which would be incorporated by later critics, whether through reading Hazlitt or through arriving at similar conclusions independently.[24]

Hazlitt's reservations about Brown do not detract from his clear recognition of him as a significant American writer, a recognition that came later for Brown in his own country. As Alexander Cowie has pointed out, Brown was translated into French and German, reprinted in England, but with the exception of *Edgar Huntly*, not reprinted in America during his lifetime.[25] This is not to imply that Brown received no recognition in America at all. Rather, the issue is a matter of degree. Certainly, Brown could boast that "to be the writer of Wieland and Ormond is a greater recommendation than I ever imagined it would be."[26] Moreover, the American reviews of his books were favorable, though scant.[27] Yet, the failure of his works to be reprinted in America reflects the general lack of interest in him, and one of Dunlap's stated hopes in writing Brown's biography was that it might "induce a lively regret that their subject was prevented by death from attaining that celebrity which his talents and acquirements must have gained for him, and of leaving to his country works of the highest importance both scientific and literary."[28] All the evidence that one can glean confirms Dunlap's recognition that Brown, whatever his merits, simply did not achieve wide notice in his own time.

This apparent fact became the basis for a legend about Brown that reached its ultimate bathos in George Lippard's "The Heart-Broken" (1848), an excerpt of which shows something of the wonderful proportions to which the retrospective sentimentalization of Brown could grow:

Nobody knew him. Nobody cared for him. He could wander along Independence Square, with hands behind his back, and his head bowed down. He would return home, and while that dear wife smiled sadly on him, and those lovely children gazed upon his pale forehead and earnest eyes, with a tender awe, he seized his pen and wrote all the day, scattering sheet after sheet from beneath his fingers, even until the night set in. Then, as the night without harmonized with the night within, he toiled away by the light of his dim lamp, until his pale face glowed with a beauty that was almost inspiration.

What became of these works?

They were published in England and America. In England they are read at this hour, by tens of thousands. Men of renown place them among their most treasured volumes; yes, men like Godwin or Bulwer, or even the crabbed Editor of a Scotch Review, hold this Philadelphia Novelist in high estimation, as a man of remarkable and original genius.[29]

But, Lippard tells us in much the same tone, he died forgotten and remains unknown.

Lippard's rhetorical excesses are obvious enough, and the wife and children with Brown at the time he wrote his novels represent pure invention. Nevertheless, Lippard's point that Brown had no popular recognition is accurate enough. This is true in spite of the fact that some notable Americans were finding kind words for Brown. Although Cooper denigrated Brown in his preface to *The Spy*, he had a flattering comment for him in *Notions of the Americans*.[30] Longfellow and Whittier both praised him, as did others.[31]

But the essential perception of Lippard, however exaggerated its tone and fabricated its facts, reflected what was by then a tradition of seeing Brown as a forgotten, neglected, but worthy American writer. Lippard made his plea in 1848 for the rescue of Brown from oblivion, but John Neal had urged the same cause in 1824 in an unsigned essay for *Blackwood's Magazine*.[32] The plea for recognition came as part of a larger essay assessing the merits of American writers, including Neal himself, but the piece was by no means mere puffery, since Neal's essay condemned as well as praised writers. In the review, Neal emerges as an early contributor to the legend of Brown as martyr to the cause of American letters. Brown appears as a poor, struggling author, underpaid for his literary productions and unappreciated by his countrymen. Perhaps the emphasis on inadequate recognition—in money and in applause—might be regarded as self serving, since Neal, a writer of fiction himself, certainly had reason to stimulate interest in the cause of novelists. But in spite of any charge of special pleading, and in spite of a prose style that scarcely encourages confidence in Neal's objectivity, his general assessment of the critical reception of Brown in America as contrasted with England remains reasonably valid:

> Some years ago, we took up CHARLES BROCKDEN BROWN; disinterred him; embalmed him; did him up, decently; and put him back again—(that is—one of us did so.)— Since then, poor Brown has had no peace, for his countrymen. We opened upon the North American creature—making him break cover; and riding after him, as if he were worth our while. *Then*—but never till then—(we were the first)—did they give tongue, on the other side of the Atlantic.—We puffed him a little. They have blown him up— 'sky-high.'—We went up to him, reverently—they, head-over-heels. We flattered him somewhat—for he deserved it; and was atrociously neglected. But they have laid it on with a trowel.—He would never have been heard of, but for us.—They are determined, now, that we shall never hear of anything else.—We licked him into shape: they have slobbered him—as the anaconda would a buffaloe (if she could find one)—till one cannot bear to look at him. We pawed him over, till he was able to stand alone—in his own woods—they—till he can neither stand nor go; till we should not know our own cub, if we saw him.[33]

Neal's hyperbole notwithstanding, his observations accurately convey the fact that Brown was more appreciated in England than in America, and that attempts to resurrect his literary reputation were not going well, and, in any case, were often excessive.

It was not until 1827 that Brown's novels were reissued in America, and on that occasion Richard Henry Dana, Sr. reviewed, in *The United States Review and Literary Gazette* the six-volume collection. By now the pattern reflected in Neal's essay and which would culminate in Lippard's excesses had taken hold, and Dana's essay offers the familiar regret regarding Brown's neglect. But Dana nevertheless presents a serious, balanced critique of Brown.[34]

While American critics worked at rescuing Brown from oblivion, they generally failed to offer useful insights into the cause of his neglect. Why, after all, should a writer of genius, though flawed, remain so ignored in his native country? This question, invariably raised, implicitly or explicitly, generally found its answer in the complaint that Americans simply did not have the confidence to recognize native talent. But the question itself generally missed the point that writers in America *were* finding popularity.[35] At least this was true by 1827, when Brown was finally reprinted in America. That other writers should succeed by 1827, while Brown, even reprinted, remained relatively ignored, simply refutes the notion that his lack of popularity rested on some unadulterated bias against American fiction by Americans. Surely, by 1827 Cooper and Irving—to say nothing of writers lesser known today—were finding a relatively wide audience. Brown was not.

A better clue to Brown's lack of an American audience may be discovered in a brief review that appeared in 1836 in *The Ladies' Companion*. Here, the writer makes a key distinction, one that has become standard today. Writers of fiction are divided into two groups, popular writers and "serious" writers. If the language framing this proposition differed in 1836 from its use today, the idea remains linked, and the reviewer's comments are almost as important for presenting the distinction at this early date as for helping to clarify the reason for Brown's failure to find an audience:

> It is a fact, to establish which needs not the labor of proof, that the mind does not receive as great pleasure from a work of the imagination, wherein the author has indulged in a philosophizing style, as from one characterized by elegant description, pleasing variety, and startling incident. Hence the unbounded preference given to those fictitious writings, which can move the feelings, and arouse the passions, without too heavy a tax upon the attention. Books, which possess essential requisites, are lauded by the critics, and as a natural consequence, are frequently perused by the reading community; while, on the contrary, those marked by gravity, and by less that affords amusement, are almost entirely overlooked. In the one, the mind is relieved from fatigue, and the cares of life— in the other, it finds new objects for reflection, and new principles and truths, by which to regulate the conduct. Whatever may be the talent displayed in works of the latter description, they are seldom read, since they are regarded as defeating the very objects of novel-reading. None, but the learned can peruse such works, and find pleasure. From them, the common reader derives little delight; but is compelled to follow the author in his wanderings through the mazes of philosophy and thought, and in his investigation of new truths.
>
> Mr. Brown appears, in his novels, to have indulged in such a style of writing. . . . Though we cannot but regret that his attention and talents, were not directed to some subject of more importance than novel writing, yet if proper thought be bestowed in the perusal of his works, we cannot leave them without being more instructed and wise.[36]

The old bias against fiction should not undermine the lesson to be learned from this reviewer. On the contrary, it accentuates the distinction between the "serious" writer and the popular one, since it presupposes that all fiction risks not being serious. The reviewer too has understood, whether one agrees with the premises of the review or the categorization of Brown, that Brown never could be a popular writer. He asks too much from the reader looking for sentimental romance. But, and here is where Brown's reputation keeps floundering, he remains too flawed to be fully accepted by "the learned." And recognizing Brown's failure to fit comfortably into either category offers the basis for the anomalous state of his reputation. Lacking some better way to categorize him, historians have decreed that he was at least "first." But it will not do, neither as history nor as criticism.

One comes back to the perceptive insight of the British critic who saw Brown as "the first writer of prose fiction of which America could boast."[37] Such an observation from a late eighteenth-century or early nineteenth-century reviewer, whether American or British, could be made only on behalf of a writer concerned with, in Brown's words, being a "moral painter." Fiction that did not have such a quality was suspect then, even as it is today, although to pursue that point is not appropriate here. But an examination of Brown as "moral painter" is.

In 1824 a writer in *European Magazine*, rejecting the notion that Brown was particularly American, saw the emphasis on what would one day be called "human destiny":

> Had the scene been laid in England, at the present day, a suspicion could never once enter our mind, either from their actions, their manners, or their language, that they were not genuine English characters. The fact is, that so far from having any thing peculiar in them, arising either from peculiarity of disposition, or peculiarity of national manners, they are such characters as might be placed in any age and in any clime, because they are actually such as are met with at all times, and in all countries. Brown is no describer of *manners*, and, indeed, he never attempts it. His power lies in describing the passions and secret workings of the heart, and as these passions can never be grafted on national manners, founded as they are in the very nature of man, they are the same in all ages and countries.[38]

The point of the reviewer is not necessarily that Brown is "English" rather than "American." It is instead that Brown did not choose as his main purpose anatomizing society. He is a writer who wishes to understand the individual. And while the concern for individual, as opposed to social, destiny is surely not exclusively an American preoccupation, one can scarcely escape the fact that with the exception of Cooper the writers of early nineteenth-century America who have achieved the greatest recognition are precisely those whose concerns were more with human destiny than with social arrangements.[39] In this sense, Brown often shows an affinity with the early nineteenth-century tradition of Emerson, Hawthorne, Melville, Poe, Thoreau, and Whitman. Placing Brown in the company of these writers does not imply a qualitative parity, but it does suggest a commonality of literary concern.

Flawed or not, all of Brown's fiction seeks to examine the spiritual or social conduct of the individual. *Wieland* poses the question of the relation between individual behavior and theological requirements. *Arthur*

Mervyn and *Edgar Huntly* examine individual conduct in more secular terms. And *Ormond*, in some way the opposite of *Wieland*, explores secular limitations as the other examines theological ones. *Clara Howard* and *Jane Talbot*, the most neglected of Brown's fiction, center much more on social arrangements than his other fiction does.

Although the break between *Clara Howard* and *Jane Talbot* from Brown's earlier fiction may be less marked than generally thought, these novels do show the beginnings of Brown's separation from his past examination of the kinds of metaphysical issues raised in a work such as *Wieland*. While Brown's critics have always understood that by 1803 the radical young man who had written *Alcuin* had emerged into the much more conservative editor of *The Literary Magazine and American Register*, his early religious radicalism was more pronounced than is usually indicated. Since Brown saw himself as a "moral painter," the premises of his morality, of his perception of the individual's relation to the Christian society in which he lived, ought not to rest with scholarly speculation when Brown has fully articulated these premises himself. He has done this, most dramatically, in a letter written to his friend Joseph Bringhurst in 1795, probably the same year that he began *Arthur Mervyn*. Given the timing of this letter, so close to the appearance of his major fiction, its carefully constructed arguments, whatever their validity, offer a major insight into Brown's theological premises, and even into his theory of fiction.[40] Although the theological implications of the letter most obviously bear on *Wieland* and the issue of religious fanaticism, it is difficult not to rethink his other fiction, at least if one has considered that work as in some way bearing on Brown's theological views. The letter does require some caution on the part of the reader, since Brown was a man of changing views, a tester of ideas, and a lover of debate. Yet it seems unlikely that he would trifle with his close and Christian friend on a subject of such gravity. Although it is reasonably safe to assume that Brown died a Christian, his major fiction appeared a few years after this letter. The letter to Bringhurst is offered as an autobiographical statement by a man very much concerned with "human destiny."

Letter to Joseph Bringhurst, October 24, 1795[41]
Dear Joseph
    I have just received your letter. I delivered the enclosed immediately. . . .
    I have advanced but little way in any useful tract: but have read far more than I have written. Another instance thou wilt suppose of my instability: by this time I ought to have finished the design that I had contemplated, but alas! it is very remote from a conclusion, and know not when I shall arrive at it. The epistolary and narrative forms of Composition have each their respective advantages, but I have no doubt about the superiority of the former if it were well executed, but the latter

is in itself, an easier task, though abundantly difficult, and one to which, I approach very near to the discovery, that my powers are absolutely inadequate. It being however easier than the other whatever I write with a view to the amusement of the world, will certainly be in the form of the narrative.

I listen with respect to your advice on the subject of Christianity, but, my friend, we are far from well understanding each other on this subject. How ambiguous is the meaning of that word! How difficult to ascertain its true meaning! You talk of it as if you thoroughly understood it. You are aware that there are a thousand sects in the world, who call themselves Christians, who differ *essentially* from each other in their practical and speculative creed, that there are sects who affirm the humanity of Christ, and deny the eternity of future punishment, and whose religion justifyes every freak of fickleness, and caprice of the passions. Have you determined which of these is the true? Are you qualified, by your present ignorance of languages and history, to decide those intricate and obscure questions? If *you* are, *I* am not.

Then the question between [us][42] is, not whether I condemn christianity, but whether I condemn your *system* of Christianity. What is it? You have more than once assured me that our morality agrees. If so I fight not against it. I am supporting and confirming it. If the moral precepts of Christ are good they are mine, because they are true, if bad nothing can induce me to esteem them good, and there can be no question about the propriety of endeavoring to exterminate pernicious and errionious doctrines, but that which, in truth, denominates any system of belief religious, and which probably makes a part of your end, relates to the *authority* of the law-maker and the *sanction* of the law. If Christ was no more than Pythagoras or Socrates, the acceptance of his doctrines, moral or metaphysical, must depend upon their intrinsic evidence, nor according to the common acceptation of that term, can his system be termed a Religion: but if he was of nearer kin than other men to the deity, and the effect of that relationship be, a readier submission to his injunctions, and if our compliance or non compliance with his instructions be rewarded or punished hereafter, the case is materially altered. Are these tenets Christianity, are they necessary parts of it? And in attacking these tenets, in reducing Christ to the rank of the Grecian Sages, do I assail the [bulwarks] of Christianity in your opinion? I suppose you will answer yes. If so I can make no scruple to answer all your questions in the affirmative. I really think Christianity, that is, the belief of the divinity of Christ and future retribution, have been pernicious to mankind? That it has and does destroy friendship and benevolence? That it has created war and engendered hatred, [entailed] inexpressible calamities on mankind—You tell me that these effects have flowed from the errors and ignorance of mankind, from their misconception of the gospel precepts which enjoin universal love and concord: the return of good for evil, and [succor] of the needy and beneficence to all, and that it is wrong to impute that to the doctrine which is to be imputed only to the ignorance or passions of its followers! I answer that these effects have flowed from the belief of the divinity of Christ and a belief of future retribution. It is for you to determine whether these be parts of Christianity. Whether the religion of Constantine and the Roman Empire: of the subjects of Charlemagne, the Crusaders: the men of Italy and Spain and France and Germany and Russia and G. Britain was and is Christianity or not. If these be not parts of Christianity then, in opposing these, I am only the friend of genuine christianity.

I am almost afraid of that angry and [contemptuous] frown which is at this moment [settling] on your brow. You imagine I overlook the most obvious distinctions, and exhibit the strongest example of absurdity and inconsistency: Your heart is eloquent in praise of boundless love and universal beneficence: This in your opinion is the christian doctrine, and you wonder how any can imagine these to be apologies for vice, and warrants of injustice. I despair of banishing this cloud. I write on this subject without that energy and perspicuity which are the surest means of conviction while they arise [merely] from the persuasion that it is practicable to impart conviction[.][43]

["]This divine teacher enjoins us to adhere to truth and do justly.[44] He that acts thus and who at the same time believes that he who thus enjoins is commissioned by God, shall be rewarded hereafter with happiness: he who acts contrary and denies this shall be punished hereafter with misery. The hope of future and blissful existence must be a powerful incitement to adhere to truth and do justly: the dread of future misery, equally lasting and exquisite, must be a cogent motive for abstinence from ill. What can be urged against this conclusion? Can any thing be nearer demonstration? And why would you endeavor to shake the confidence of men from a system of morality which enlarges all the amiable affections of the heart, consoles the afflicted and elevates the soul to the sublimest contemplations?"

This last, my friend, is a droll question. It would indeed be a subject of curiosity why one man should consume his time and pains in making others unhappy and unjust; but it would be a strange *question* to *ask*, because it implies a concession in the *questioned*, that he is really busy to an evil purpose. *I* for my *own* part cannot answer your enquiry: it poses me I must own. I can conceive no earthly reason why I *should* employ myself only in injuring mankind, but I am at no loss to justify the purpose which I, in reality, cherish, that of *confirming* the confidence of men in a System of morality which *renders boundless* the amiable affections of the heart, *annihilates* affliction, and *dedicates the soul exclusively and wholly* to the sublimest contemplations. *This purpose* you will not require from me laboriously to justify. I shall always receive, for doubtless I shall merit your applause, by endeavoring to enforce on mankind the observance of their duty, and by demonstrating the connection between their duty and their happiness. It is not the rational business of men to settle what is the creed of Moses, of Christ[,] of Mahomet[,] of Confucius, of Pythagoras or Solon.[45] It is indeed not without its use: it is, in a certain degree, properly the theme of historical curiosity, but the chief business is to ascertain the dictates of moral duty, by consulting his Understanding; and measuring the opinions of others, whatever may be their pretensions, by the standard of his own judgment,—You say I have mistaken the christian tenets. It is of little moment: I deny that religious sanctions are friendly to morality, I deny the superhuman Authority of any teacher: and a future retribution: were these affirmed by Jesus Christ or merely by you? It is indifferent: The truth is the same independently of any ones assertion or authority. The deity is said to have commanded men, through the mouth of one prophet, to hate their enemies and to shed the blood of him by whom blood has been shed, and through the mouth of another, to love their enemies and benefit those by whom we are injured: now in my opinion hatred and killing are just or unjust and that of consequence it is, or is not our duty to hate and kill as if it had never been enjoined in one case or prohibited in the other, and that truth is immutable.

But what is the extent of my mistake? Let us dismiss what have been termed the doctrinal points of Christianity: and discant to the practical.[46] [Have] I been guilty of mistake with respect to these? So far as others differ from you, you must esteem them in an error, that is they annex the sanctions of the Christian religion to modes of conduct and opinion to which you think it is inapplicable: in other words they err in their estimate of that which will entitle them to favor and reward from the deity, or which will expose them to his displeasure and punishment. This is an error of no little importance. Is it not my friend? Is it not with respect to these enormously pernicious[?][47] for bad actions, in these circumstances, will be as powerfully prompted as good actions would in other circumstances: I need not send your curiosity gadding into ancient times, and remote regions: I need not enumerate the errors (you will unquestionably deem them such) of the millions that have lived, and the millions that live at present: You have affirmed that the hope of eternal reward or the fear of eternal punishment are powerful motives to actions. Jesus Christ has annexed these sanctions to a certain mode of action: from unfortunate contingencies a part of mankind has mistaken the application and imagined rewards and punishments hereafter: prepared for those actions respectively, of which the real allotment is exactly different. It is not requisite to point out the consequences of this error. They are sufficiently and dreadfully manifest.

I fear my friend you will number me among the erring: I doubt whether my apprehensions of moral duty can be reconciled with any natural and obvious construction to be put upon all the precepts of Christianity. I mean the moral and practical precepts: With respect to some, indeed, I am sure they can not: but you will probably be of a different opinion. In some cases you will think my own tenets erroneous, and in others, easily [irreconcilable] with what you will esteem a just and natural construction of the language of the New testament. But I cannot help this difference between us: It will be an additional argument with me that religious sanctions are unfriendly to morality: The Construction of one of us only can be true, one of us must commit actions positively wrong: with the additional incitement that they are sanctioned by heaven: And what shall I think of the utility of motives which may operate with equal force with respect to opposite actions and which are infinitely more in danger of being applied erroneously than rightly, of inciting to evil than to good.

It is only when the precepts of Christ are rightly interpreted, that you will allow the utility of the hopes and fears which this religion imparts. By whomsoever they are misinterpreted, injury and not benefit must follow. The sanctions of a positive law being altogether arbitrary in their connection with practice.

"Do you admit then that the precepts of Christ constitute, when rightly understood, a System of true virtue, and that the christian promises are powerful incitements to virtue; Or do you still more liberally admit with Archdeacon [Paley] the necessity of a Revelation to point out to men their duty, and enforce their performance of it."[48]

I would speak with moderation, my good friend, upon this Subject. I know your opinions on this subject, and that such, in your eyes, is the importance of Religion that you find it difficult to tolerate reasoning, much less ridicule when aimed at religion. I should hurt you by uttering my real Sentiments on this strange concession of the necessity of revelation to enlighten our understanding or invigorate our fortitude.[49] A Concession on which your favorite authour has built all his arguments in defence of Christianity, and without which all that he has said is vague and superfluous.

But why have I dwelt thus long on this unprofitable subject? Your letter has betrayed me into it. Truth is, doubtless preferable to error. It is but a slight effort of virtue to desire or endeavor the Conversion of our friend. The obligation must be

equally incumbent on us both: yet there is unfortunately wanting in one or both of us the prevalence of that temper which
would make epistolary or conversational discussion a sure
means of discovering truth.

Reflexion is sufficient for all purposes: if the machine of
reflexion can once be set going: but to this, is not the belief of
the possible erroneousness of our present conclusions
necessary?[50] I cannot pretend to produce this doubt in you, and
yet I can not help desiring you to reflect upon the foundations
of your present opinions, and to give a deliberate and impartial
reperusal to one author, to whom, in my present mode of
thinking, I appeal, as to an Oracle.

I once thought as, possibly, you now think that religious
belief were desirable even if it were erroneous. I am now of a
different opinion, and believe that utility must always be coincident to truth.

I shall not scruple to practise that which I recommend to
you: profound and impartial reflexion upon these subjects. But
I can safely affirm that I can listen with candour and calmness
to the Advocate of religion, and that you cannot speak or write
upon a subject on which I can listen with more attention and
complacency. Too much cannot be said upon this subject and
if you have patience to enter into formal defences of that which
you perhaps think too clear to admit of a moments doubt
among ingenuous and impartial people I shall thank you for
it. . . .[51]

II

The brief review of Brown's critical reception and the thesis of him as
a writer concerned with "human destiny" are intended to offer a preface
to the critical selections which follow, but the reader need not accept this
thesis to benefit from the essays in this collection. Other approaches to
Brown are thoroughly presented. Additionally, Charles Carpenter's
bibliography in this collection updates the record of Brown scholarship
and greatly facilitates the search for critical opinion on him.

This collection contains original essays on Brown, and a word about
them is in order. They have not been chosen to justify the thesis of the
editor (except perhaps in the case of his own contribution), nor to support
or refute past criticism. Their appearance here represents an attempt to
include a diversity of opinion on Brown by outstanding scholars and a
commentary on all his completed fiction, taking into account previous
scholarship on the subject. Contributors include those who have achieved
special recognition as Brown scholars as well as those whose ac-
complishments have been primarily elsewhere. The balance has been intentional and for the purpose of presenting as wide a range as possible of
the latest critical thinking regarding Brown. As is appropriate for a writer
who has always received mixed critical reception, the views are diverse.

So also are the methodologies, ranging from traditional modes of scholarship to the employment of "post-modern" critical approaches. Obviously, none of these essays can be definitive. No work of scholarship ever is. But all of them offer the reader an examination of Brown's fiction that takes into account those views of the works that preceded it. Readers not thoroughly versed in Brown will find ready reference to earlier criticism. Those who have concerned themselves with Brown scholarship will recognize the thorough attention each of the writers has given to alternative readings of Brown, and if newer interpretations are accepted, the lines for much future scholarship will have been drawn.

III

Whether Brown will ever again receive the kind of high praise once bestowed upon him by the likes of Keats and Shelley, or by lesser individuals in the canon of literary history, is a matter for prophets and not for critics to address. But if the future cannot be predicted, at least the past can be understood. Those who appreciated Brown the most valued the passion with which he sought to comprehend and to interpret the place of the individual in a morally ambiguous world. Interested more in humanity regarded spiritually rather than socially or economically, Brown at his best penetrated the kinds of mysterious regions examined by those poets of England who valued him so highly. He made tentative explorations into interior regions that would be profoundly examined by the great romancers, Hawthorne and Melville. That he did not search deeper than he did seems more a function of aesthetic limitation than of inadequate will. But his impulse was toward Hawthorne's unraveling of the human heart and toward Melville's obsessive search for clarity in an ambiguous world. These concerns by our greatest writers have rarely been the subject of popular fiction, so it is not surprising that Brown never had a wide audience. Nor were his aesthetic achievements ever sufficient to force him into the company of writers whom people feel they ought to know and like. So Brown has remained an anomaly, a historical curiosity who persists in attracting attention as the beginner of something he never started. Yet if he was not the progenitor of the great Romantics who followed him, he was certainly, to use a nineteenth-century term, a kindred spirit.

BERNARD ROSENTHAL

Notes

1. Charles Brockden Brown, *Edgar Huntly* (Philadelphia: David McKay, 1887), pp. 3–4. The 1887 republication of Brown's fiction, more recently reprinted by Burt Franklin publishing company, has been the standard scholarly text in spite of numerous textual deficiencies. Brown's works are now being reedited under the general editorship of Sydney J. Krause and will be published by Kent State University Press. The project, begun under the

auspices of MLA's Center for Editions of American Authors, is now being completed under its successor, the Center for Scholarly Editions. As of this writing, only *Wieland* has appeared, although editions of the other works will be issued shortly. Once in print, the Kent State edition of Brown's works will properly become the standard scholarly text for Brown.

2. For another example of Brown on the topic of an American literature, see his note on his lost novel, *Sky-Walk* in *The Rhapsodist*, ed. Harry R. Warfel (New York: Scholars' Facsimiles & Reprints, 1943), pp. 135–36. An early perception of Brown's writing as not particularly American appears in a British review, *European Magazine*, 85 (January, 1824), 55–60. A portion of this review is quoted later in this introduction.

Brown's assessment of himself as a "moral painter" in his fiction contrasts sharply with William Dunlap's claim that Brown "considered all his fanciful works as mere matters of recreation and amusement." See William Dunlap, *The Life of Charles Brockden Brown* (Philadelphia: James P. Parke, 1815), 1:261. Although Dunlap was Brown's close friend and authorized biographer, his assessment has to be considered in the context of the times when the writing of fiction was generally regarded as suspect and as in need of some defense. Another mitigating factor stems from the complex history of Dunlap's biography, since he took much of what he wrote, including the above quotation, verbatim from Paul Allen's unfinished biography of Brown. The circumstances connected with Dunlap's biography, including pressures of time and economics requiring him to work from Allen's biography, make problematic the question of how much his close knowledge of Brown governed the biography he wrote. For discussions of the textual history of the Allen and Dunlap biographies, see Paul Allen, *The Life of Charles Brockden Brown*, ed. Charles E. Bennett (Delmar, New York: Scholars' Facsimiles & Reprints, 1975) and Paul Allen, *The Late Charles Brockden Brown*, ed. Robert E. Hemenway and Joseph Katz (Columbia, South Carolina: J. Faust & Co., 1976). The quotation cited above appears on p. 388 of both editions.

3. The matter is discussed subsequently in this introduction in conjunction with Brown's letter to Joseph Bringhurst, previously unpublished.

4. F.O. Matthiessen, *American Renaissance* (New York: Oxford University Press, 1941), p. 271.

5. Hawthorne's famous complaint about his inability to compete for popularity with the "d-------d mob of scribbling women" appears in a letter dated January 19, 1855. See Nathaniel Hawthorne, *Letters of Hawthorne to William D. Ticknor, 1851–1864* (Newark, N.J.: The Carteret Book Club, 1910), 1:75.

6. Just how much Brown actually did earn from his writings will probably never be known, but those who wrote about him in the early nineteenth century took for granted his failure to make much money from his fiction. Certainly it would have been difficult at the turn of the century for any American fiction writer to prosper at the task. A good insight into the economics of selling fiction is offered by John Neal, writing anonymously about Brown in *Blackwood's Magazine* in 1824. In a note to his "American Writers II," 16 (October, 1824), p. 422, Neal writes: "A few facts will shew what is reckoned 'munificent patronage' in America. Two hundred dollars (about 45 1.)—payable partly, or wholly, in books—the *best* of paper money by the way—are *now*, even to this hour, considered a good price, for a good novel, in two American volumes, (which make from three, to four, here.)" For a general study of the subject see William Charvat, *The Profession of Authorship in America, 1800–1870*, ed. Matthew J. Bruccoli (Columbus: Ohio State University Press, 1968).

7. One answer might be that Dunlap made a claim for Brown that simply stuck *(The Life of Charles Brockden Brown,* II, 12). An alternative explanation that warrants serious consideration would be that women writers who preceded Brown have been excluded from the honor of being first on the grounds of bias, as suggested by Nina Baym in footnote 1 of her essay in this collection. But men such as William Hill Brown, Hugh Henry Brackenridge, and Gilbert Imlay also published fiction before Brown did. That they did not live entirely by their pen is not wholly germane, since neither did Charles Brockden Brown. Because much biographical information about Brown remains unclear to this day, his method of supporting

himself, particularly during the mid and later part of the 1790s, is somewhat obscure. Harry Warfel, for example, observes that for "the winter of 1794-1795 . . . [n]ot a bit of biographical information survives. . . ." Warfel also examines the question of whether Brown was a teacher in 1794. See Harry R. Warfel, *Charles Brockden Brown* (Gainesville, Fla.: University of Florida Press, 1949), pp. 54, 44.

8. Influence is here distinguished from thematic similarity. For some cogent observations on the latter point see Donald A. Ringe, *Charles Brockden Brown* (New York: Twayne Publishers, Inc., 1966), p. 138. More than one critic has suggested possible specific instances of influence, as William Scheick does in this collection (see footnote 21 in his essay). D.L. Clark, "The Sources of Poe's *The Pit and the Pendulum*," *Modern Language Notes*, 44 (1929), 349-356, also argues for Brown's influence, and some claims have been made regarding Brown's initiation of wilderness and Indian themes. But specific cases of influence are rare, and the argument for furthering the use of Indians and the wilderness is tenuous at best. Cooper, who has a genuine right to such a claim, had little to praise in Brown's use of such topics. See note 30. For Alexander Cowie's observation that "Brown founded no school," see *The Rise of the American Novel* (New York: American Book Company, 1948), p. 108.

9. Anon., "Charles Brockden Brown," *American Whig Review*, 7 (March, 1848), 260.

10. The conclusions reached here about British response are based on a study of all Brown items listed by William S. Ward in his exceptionally valuable "American Authors and British Reviewers 1798-1826: A Bibliography," *American Literature*, 49 (1977), 1-21.

11. Anon., *Literary Journal*, 3 (May, 1804), 492.

12. Anon., *Antijacobin Review*, 6 (August, 1800), 451.

13. Anon., *Imperial Review*, 3 (November, 1804), 392.

14. Anon., *Monthly Magazine*, Supplement, 16 (January 25, 1804), 635.

15. Anon., *Critical Review*, s. 2, 34 (September, 1803), 119.

16. Anon., *British Critic*, s. 3, 2 (April, 1826), 53-78.

17. Anon., *Gentleman's Magazine*, 81 (April, 1811), 364.

18. Anon., *Critical Review*, s. 3, 22 (February, 1811), 162-163.

19. Anon., *Retrospective Review*, 9 (1824), 317.

20. *Ibid.*, 323.

21. For example, see Ringe, pp. 16, 141; Cowie, p. 99; and Van Wyck Brooks, *The World of Washington Irving* (New York: E.P. Dutton & Co., Inc., 1944), pp. 24-25. Associations of Brown with Godwin have been made from his earliest reviewers to contemporary critics. If the nature of Brown's indebtedness to Godwin can be debated, there can be no reasonable doubt of its existence. The connection is perhaps most easily seen by comparing *Arthur Mervyn* to *Caleb Williams*. For Godwin's subsequent appreciation of Brown, see Cowie, p. 99.

22. John Keats, *The Letters of John Keats 1814-1821*, ed. Hyder Edward Rollins (Cambridge, Mass.: Harvard University Press, 1958), p. 173; Thomas Peacock's comment is cited by Earnest Marchand in his introduction to *Ormond* (New York: American Book Company, 1937), p. xliv.

23. Peacock's comment is cited by Arthur Hobson Quinn, *American Fiction, An Historical and Critical Survey* (New York: Appleton-Century-Crofts, Inc., 1936), p. 37. For reasons that are not clear David Lee Clark seems skeptical of Peacock's reliability regarding Shelley's views on Brown. See *Charles Brockden Brown: Pioneer Voice of America* (Durham, North Carolina: Duke University Press, 1952), 173, 295. Whatever the basis for Clark's caution, the case for Shelley's interest in Brown is overwhelming. Even Mary Shelley observes that he was reading *Edgar Huntly* in 1814. See *Mary Shelley's Journal*, ed. Frederick L. Jones (Norman, Oklahoma: University of Oklahoma Press, 1947), p. 26. Mary Shelley herself was reading Brown, although not always with appreciation. Her comment on *Clara Howard (Philip Stanley* in the English edition) is witheringly succinct: "very stupid," p. 27.

24. "Sermons and Tracts. . . . By W.E. Channing," *Edinburgh Review*, 50 (October, 1829), 125–144.

25. Cowie, p. 99. *Edgar Huntly* first appeared in 1799 and was reprinted in 1800 with "The Death of Cicero, a Fragment" appended to the end of Volume III. See also Clark, p. 295 for Brown's reputation in France and Germany.

26. Dunlap, II, 99.

27. No checklist as useful as Ward's exists for early American reviews of Brown, although Warfel, p. 139 and 110 ff. is valuable.

28. Dunlap, I, 2.

29. George Lippard, "The Heart-Broken," *The Nineteenth Century*, 1 (January, 1848), 22.

30. Cooper wrote in his preface to *The Spy* (1821) that "although the English critics not only desire, but invite works that will give an account of American manners, we are sadly afraid they mean nothing but Indian manners; we are apprehensive that the same palate which can relish the cave scene in Edgar Huntly, because it contains an American, a savage, a wild cat, and a tomahawk, in a conjunction that never did, nor ever will occur—will revolt at descriptions in this country . . ." (New York: Wiley and Halstead, 1822), p. vi. But Cooper was kinder in *Notions of the Americans* (1828): Brown, "who curbed his talents by as few allusions as possible to actual society, is distinguished for power and comprehensiveness of thought. I remember to have read one of his books (Wieland) when a boy, and I take it to be a never-failing evidence of genius, that, amid a thousand similar pictures which have succeeded, the images it has left still stand distinct and prominent in my recollection. This author (Mr. Brockden Brown) enjoys a high reputation among his countrymen, whose opinions are sufficiently impartial, since he flattered no particular prejudice of the nation in any of his works" (London: Henry Colburn), 2, 145–146. For a more recent edition see Robert E. Spiller, intro. (New York: Frederick Ungar Publishing Co., 1963), 2, 111. Cooper's assertion about Brown's popularity may have been contrived for a book conceived in part for the purpose of defending America's reputation to England. The possibility also exists that Cooper really believed Brown was popular, since he may have been among Cooper's friends, the kinds of educated elites to whom Brown appealed.

31. For Longfellow see Lawrance Thompson, *Young Longfellow* (New York: The Macmillan Company, 1938), 44–45. Whittier's essay is reprinted in *The Prose Works of John Greenleaf Whittier*, Vol. 7 (Boston: Houghton, Mifflin and Company, 1889), 391–395. The essay originally appeared in the weekly newspaper, *The National Era*, June 1, 1848. Often cited is Hawthorne's reference to Brown in "The Hall of Fantasy" (1843). See *Mosses from an Old Manse*, ed. William Charvat, Roy Harvey Pearce, and Claude M. Simpson (Columbus, Ohio: Ohio State University Press, 1974), p. 174. In the same volume see also "P's Correspondence," p. 380.

32. John Neal, "American Writers II," *Blackwood's Magazine*, 16 (October, 1824), 415–428.

33. Neal, p. 423.

34. "The Novels of Charles Brockden Brown," 2 (August, 1827), 321–33.

35. See Nina Baym, *Woman's Fiction: A Guide to Novels by and about Women in America, 1820–1870* (Ithaca, New York: Cornell University Press, 1978) and Henri Petter, *The Early American Novel* (Columbus, Ohio: Ohio State University Press, 1971). It must be conceded that pinning down the issue of popularity awaits a better methodology than any literary historian has yet employed. For some valuable comments on this problem, see Baym, 300–01.

36. Anon., "The Novels of Charles Brockden Brown," *The Ladies' Companion*, 4 (January, 1836), 135.

37. See note 19.

38. *European Magazine*, 55–56. This excerpt appears in a review of Brown's *Carwin*,

the Biloquist, and other American Tales and Pieces (1822). Of all Brown's fiction reviewed in England from 1800 to 1826 no work received more uniformly high praise. Since the work comprises uncompleted fiction by Brown this response seems mysterious, and no speculation can be offered here for the phenomenon except perhaps that of random occurrence.

39. For a full examination of the premises behind this classification, particularly Cooper's exclusion here, see Bernard Rosenthal, *City of Nature* (Newark: University of Delaware Press, 1980).

40. Joseph Bringhurst, Jr. was a close friend of Brown's. See Clark, p. 24 and Warfel, p. 30. Both Clark and Warfel have occasional references to Bringhurst in their biographies of Brown but no detailed discussion of him.

41. Omitted from the letter here are comments, at the beginning and the end, regarding matters on another subject. The letter came to my attention while examining Daniel Edward Kennedy's massive, unpublished study of Brown. This study is currently housed at Kent State University, and I am deeply grateful to Sydney J. Krause for allowing me to examine it. For permission to publish the letter, I gratefully acknowledge Bowdoin College, which has this and other manuscript letters by Brown in its holdings. Dianne M. Gutscher, Special Collection Librarian and Arthur Monke, Librarian, have been extremely helpful in giving me access to this manuscript and in acting expeditiously to permit its publication here.

For the most part my transcription accords with Kennedy's, but in some cases I have departed from his text. In a few instances I have bracketed words or punctuation to indicate a Kennedy transcription which seems probable but not certain. Unless otherwise indicated, all brackets are mine. Significant variations from Kennedy's reading are footnoted. No changes have been made in Brown's spelling, capitalization, or punctuation, although some of my readings differ from Kennedy's.

42. Kennedy's insertion.

43. Kennedy has "connection" instead of "conviction," and Brown has no period.

44. The bracketed quotation is mine. Quotation marks appear at the end of the paragraph, although Kennedy does not transcribe them. Apparently Brown is paraphrasing—and possibly copying—arguments presented by Bringhurst. He does this in one other instance in the letter.

45. Commas after "Christ" and "Mahomet" do not appear in Brown's letter. Kennedy's insertion of them is a silent emendation of his.

46. Kennedy has "descend" instead of "discant."

47. The punctuation in the letter is not clear, and Kennedy has a comma instead of a question mark. The question mark appears more likely to me from the markings on the letter and from the context, even though the word "for" is not capitalized.

48. The quotation marks enclosing this paragraph clearly appear in the text, although Kennedy does not transcribe them. The brackets around "Paley" are mine, although the letter appears to read "Papley" and is transcribed as such by Kennedy. I have found no record of an Archdeacon Papley, and it seems almost certain that Paley was intended, since the arguments to which Brown is responding are consistent with Paley's. Kennedy apparently intended to make the correction, since he has a handwritten note as follows: "Paley's *View of the Evidences of Christianity* was published Dublin 1794 and in Philadelphia 1795" (ms. p. 703). For a valuable guide to Paley and his historical context see D.L. LeMahieu, *The Mind of William Paley* (Lincoln, Nebraska: University of Nebraska Press, 1976). Chapter 5 of this book, "Ethical and Political Thought," is particularly germane for its discussion of ideas to which Brown was responding, although the Brown connection does not appear in the book because it is not LeMahieu's topic.

49. Kennedy has "conception" instead of "concession," as he also does in the sentence that follows.

50. Kennedy has "insufficient" instead of "sufficient."

51. Kennedy has "ingenious" instead of "ingenuous."

REVIEWS AND
EARLY CRITICISM

"The Life of Charles Brockden Brown: together with selections from the rarest of his printed works, from his original letters, and from his manuscripts before unpublished (1815). By William Dunlap."

Anonymous*

Little remains to be said on the subject of literary biography. The usual complaint is that the life of a man of letters is almost necessarily wanting in incident, and when the writer has made this general apology for a meagre narrative, he too often feels at liberty to be as deficient in every thing as may suit his ignorance, indolence, or want of discrimination. He is unable perhaps to collect such facts in the life of a scholar as are commonly called remarkable, and hence infers that there is nothing in it worthy of public notice. Perhaps he is able to collect a few anecdotes, which he records with a proper regard to the order in which they occurred, but without shewing their connexion with the character of the man. It seems as much a matter of course to place a memoir at the beginning of his works, as a stone and epitaph over his remains, and they generally tell us the same thing,—how much we honour and how little we know of him. It is hardly possible that a faithful, judicious history of a literary man should not be full of amusement and important instruction; but it cannot be made so by relating only what is common to him and every one else, or what would be equally interesting if told of another. Most of the events of his life, (if they may be called such,) in which we are concerned, pass within himself rather than abroad. We would see how his experience affected his judgments, purposes and feelings; we want to know, principally, the history of his mind; what gave him a strong, un-

*Reprinted from *North American Review*, 9 (1819), 58–77. In spite of its title, the essay reviews Brown much more than Dunlap. Perhaps this was inevitable, since Dunlap's biography offers relatively little on Brown's life and relies heavily on printing Brown's own writing.

The review was apparently written by E.T. Channing or Gulian C. Verplanck. For a discussion of authorship, see Charles A. Carpenter's bibliography, p. 228.

conquerable inclination to a certain pursuit, what retarded his progress or enabled him to subdue difficulties, what influenced him in the selection of his subjects and in his peculiar views of them, and what were the little incidental aids to the accomplishment of some great work, which appears to have grown up as silently and independently as the oak under the open sky. We want his conversation when most unguarded and unconstrained, for we would see his character and power when there was no effort, nor disguise, nor anxiety about the effect of his opinions upon his fame or upon society. We would know his character thoroughly, for it may serve to explain and qualify his opinions, weaken our false confidence in him, or animate and strengthen our just attachment, give the practical force of example to instruction, and that peculiar attraction to his opinions which every thing possesses that belongs to one whom we understand and love.

The man of letters, in one sense, may always be his own biographer, if he writes from honest feeling and conviction only, without any attempt to pass for what he is not; for his character will then be wrought into his opinions, and we shall at least be familiar with the man, though not with his history. But this is not enough—we want his history; and no one can write it so well as himself, if he has but an ordinary share of honesty. His opportunity of close self-inspection, his secret knowledge of what has formed his character—trifles perhaps in our eyes, but in fact the only important incidents of his life; his strong sense of the danger of indulging too much in habits of speculation and abstraction, that solitude is sometimes filled with worse temptations than the city; his remembrance of his anxieties and indifference, his disappointments and triumphs, and it may be of his indignant misanthropy when the world misjudged or slighted him;—all these are his and his only. And if they are fairly used and disclosed to us, his narrative will be a lesson of morals, of character, of intellectual philosophy; not a formal and abstract one, but living and practical; what we hear from him has been passed through; the heart warmed it before it was told, and we derive its good instruction for ourselves, from a discriminating view of all the details. And even where his self-love tempts him to hide or extenuate, his anxiety may betray as much as a confession, and throw further light upon his character.

If he has left no memoir of his life, a judicious biographer will present us with his journals, letters, conversation, and especially record the events and occupations to which he recurred most frequently, as having had a decisive influence upon his happiness, ambition or ways of thinking. His literary history will also be preserved as far as possible; all his projects, failures, and success, his mode of life, his rivalries, friendships and antipathies; even the price he obtained for a work, and the editions it passed through, with or without his alterations. Some of these facts are always interesting as they affect or illustrate his character; and the rest may be so from their connexion with a great man, and for the light they may throw upon the literature or distinguished characters of his age.

The work before us contains little that is new, of any value, except a few of Brown's letters, and some extracts from his journal, which occupy but a very small place. The selections fill nearly the whole book, and all of any consequence had been already published. The Life appears to be only an apology or pretence for republishing these, and it is certainly a very poor one. But Brown himself would be the last man to complain of this. He never seems to have laboured with a view to do justice to his powers; he left his fame to accident, and would not have expected a friend to do more for it, after his death, than he had done while living. His life appears to have been always desultory, and his mind never under steady discipline. His feeble health withheld him from the common amusements of children, and this drove him to books and his own thoughts for companions and diversion. Diligent study wore down the little strength he had, and then we find him alone in the fields, seeking health from exercise, but in fact acquiring a love of solitude and habits of abstraction, till he became, for a season at least, 'an eccentric, isolated being loathing the common pursuits and topics of men.' His mind was always active and curious, acquiring largely but irregularly and with no distinct object in view. His literary ambition seems to have been above his opportunities and situation, and sometimes discovers an ignorance of his powers and uncertainty in his taste. For a large part of his short life he appears as a sad enthusiast, a sceptical inquirer, a dissatisfied observer, a whimsical projector of better things for society than he could ever bring to pass, or in a calm moment wish to realize, even if his own views had been completely carried out; turning his mind to various pursuits with rash eagerness; planning epics, studying architecture, forming literary associations, discussing legal questions with his fellow students, and abandoning the profession of his choice before he had felt either its vexations or excitements, or even framed a tolerable excuse for his conscience or an answer to the persuasions of his friends. Such was his hurried, mingled, undirected life. From all that surrounded and excited him, he shrinks within himself to mourn in secret. 'As for me, I long ago discovered that nature had not qualified me for an actor on this stage. The nature of my education only added to these disqualifications, and I experienced all those deviations from the centre, which arise when all our lessons are taken from books, and the scholar makes his own character the comment. A happy destiny indeed brought me to the knowledge of two or three minds which nature had fashioned in the same mould with my own, but these are gone. And, O God! enable me to wait the moment when it is thy will that I should follow them.'

Such strong sensibility as his could not be safe unless all his powers had acted together, and in its diseased state it absolutely prevented this. He wanted something from without to draw his attention from himself, and make him a sober, practical thinker; he needed regular employments that always tended to something, and produced some visible effect; he had yet to learn what man was made of and why he was placed here, and that the same world which offended the sensitiveness of the weak, was a fine school for character and might be a nursery for the tenderest feeling. He tells us with what rapture he communed with his own thoughts in the gloom of woods, and 'peopled it with the beings of his fancy, till the barrier between himself and the world of spirits seemed burst by the force of meditation;' but it was in vain that he promised himself that he could come back to society, to the concerns of life and his appropriate duties, to converse with the world in its own language and upon its favourite subjects.

From the slight view which is given of Brown's character in these volumes (and we know it only from this source) we should judge him to have been, nothwithstanding his infirmities, a friend worthy of all trust; one who could never be spared, and least of all abandoned. His sufferings neither repelled nor wearied. He was a sincere and unobstrusive sufferer. It was a principle with him to conceal what he endured. 'I sincerely lament that I ever gave you reason to imagine I was not happy. The discovery could not take away from the number of the wretched, but only add to it. When I cannot communicate pleasure, I will communicate nothing. Do I wish friendship only to make myself a burden? Let me share in your joys and sorrows, and bear all my misfortunes myself.' We may call this an error, for why should sympathy be unavailing? But with him it was the fruit of a generous spirit. There was no coldness, nor misanthropy, nor repining in his intercourse with the world. He did not refuse pity because he was above it, but he could not endure to wear in the presence of others the wretched singularity of a broken, dissatisfied spirit; to be marked out as one who could only spread clouds over his home and the hearts that loved him.—His mind was perfectly fair, quick to discern and urge what was best for his friend, even though he should give counsel which reproached himself. He was humbled by his weakness, but he was unwilling to rise in his own estimation from the good opinion of others, till he felt that he deserved it. His self-diffidence, however, reminded him that he might not be the fairest judge of his own conduct, and though he might dread approbation, he knew the worth of it.

His life was pure, but he says that frail health had made him an exile from temptation, that his virtue was under the protection of nature; he is grateful for his infirmities, and thinks he loved intellectual glory because he had no resource but in intellectual pleasure. A gentle, subdued spirit appears in his whole character. He expected little from the world, but seems every day growing more and more prepared for its ills, more zealous to do something in its service, and more willing to trust in its reasonable promises. His life was short, but a few years before his death it was active and happy. His importance was increasing, and his claims to the remembrance of after times were secured. His character was unchanged in death. The following affecting account of his last hours was communicated by his wife to the biographer.

> He always felt for others more than for himself; and the evidences of sorrow in those around him, which could not at all times be suppressed, appeared to affect him more than his own sufferings. Whenever he spoke of the probability of a fatal termination to his disease, it was in an indirect and covered manner, as "you must do so or so when I am absent," or "when I am asleep." He surrendered not up one faculty of his soul but with his last breath. He saw death in every step of his approach, and viewed him as a messenger that brought with him no terrors. He frequently expressed his resignation; but his resignation was not produced by apathy or pain, for while he bowed with submission to the divine will, he felt with the keenest sensibility his separation from those who made this world but too dear to him. Towards the last he spoke of death without disguise, and appeared to wish to prepare his friends for the event which he felt to be approaching. A few days previous to his change, as sitting up in the bed, he fixed his eyes on the sky, and desired not to be spoken to till he first spoke. In this position and with a serene countenance, he continued some minutes, and then said to his wife, "when I desired you not to speak to me, I had the most transporting and sublime feelings I ever experienced. I wanted to enjoy them, and know how long they would last."

Brown died in 1809 at the age of thirty nine. For ten years before his death he had been an indefatigable author by profession, at first in New York and afterwards in Philadelphia, his native city. During this period he conducted and was principal contributor to three periodical works, of which we have seen at least fifteen volumes. To these we must add his political pamphlets, his unpublished manuscripts and his six novels. Wieland, Ormond, Arthur Mervyn, and Edgar Huntly are the earliest and best known, and to these we shall confine our remarks. Clara Howard and Jane Talbot, his two latest tales, are so very inferior to and unlike the others, that they require no particular notice.

Brown owes his reputation to his novels. He wrote them indeed principally for his amusement, and preferred publishing them when unfinished to labouring upon them after they had lost their interest to himself: they are proofs or signs of power rather than the result of its complete and steady exertion; but they shew the character of his mind and will justify our curiosity to examine it. In attempting this, we do not feel as if we were bringing forward a deserving but neglected author; he has received honourable notice from distinguished men abroad, and his countrymen discerned his merits without waiting till a foreign glory had shone on and revealed them. Still he is very far from being a popular writer. There is no call, as far as we know, for a second edition of any of his works. He is rarely spoken of but by those who have an habitual curiosity about every thing literary, and a becoming pride in all good writing which appears amongst ourselves. They have not met with the usual success of leaders in matters of taste, since, with all their admiration, they have not been able to extend his celebrity much beyond themselves. Some will explain this by saying that he wrote too rapidly, or that his subjects are too monstrous or at least too extraordinary for common sympathy. But the thoughts of great minds, when earnestly at work, are rarely improved by deliberation and change, and a powerful imagination can imprison us with any thing that is not spiritless, or incapable of suggesting something like reality to the mind. No reader would leave Wieland unfinished notwithstanding its self-combustion and ventriloquism, nor Edgar Huntly because of its sleep-walking. If we do not return to them, it is to avoid suffering, and not that they want fascination, and a terrible one, if we are willing to encounter it more than once.

Some have ascribed his want of popularity to his placing the scenes of his novels in our own country. What are the embarrassments from this cause, which the American novelist must be prepared for, and how far has Brown overcome or avoided them?—Our busy streets, and the commodious apartments of our unromantic dwellings are, it is thought, very unsuitable for the wonders and adventures which we have been accustomed to associate exclusively with the mouldering castles and unfrequented regions of older countries. Our cities are large, but new, and they constantly suggest to us the gainful habits and the secure homes of a recent and flourishing population; the labouring and happy are seen every where and not a corner or recess is secret. The deserted street at midnight produces no awful sense of solitude or danger, and the throng that passes us by day would scarcely suggest the thought that any one was alone in the crowd, buried in contemplation and perhaps brooding over mischief in darkness. We hear of crimes, but they usually appear so vulgar and selfish, so mean or cruel, that the imagination almost sleeps under abhorrence or disgust; we regard them as public evils, and think it enough to leave them to the benevolent reformer and the laws of the land. We hear of conspiracies and circumvention, but they are directed at our gains or good name and put us upon our guard; we think of the injury and its prevention, more than of the terrible power, dark purposes and inextricable toils of the contriver. The actions we esteem great, or are prepared to witness and encourage, are the useful rather than the heroic, such as tend to make society happier, not such as disturb or darken it. Our pride, good sense and warmest wishes are satisfied, but the imagination is not kindled, nor could it lend any lustre to what we approve. The writer then who frames a story to call forth extraordinary and violent interest, and lays the scene amongst ourselves, must encounter the difficulty of creating an illusion, where his events and characters are broad exceptions to all we witness or should expect, and where our imaginations are kept from wandering, and from deceiving us into a faint conviction of reality, by the mention of some place or circumstance which is too stubbornly familiar and unpoetical for any thing but common incidents and feelings. We are speaking of that kind of tale-writing in which Brown delights, the romantic; and we have ascribed the difficulty of succeeding in it here, not to the entire absence of romantic incident, situation and characters, but, which is just as unfortunate for the writer, to the want in his readers of romantic associations with the scenes and persons he must set before us, if he makes a strictly domestic story.

But there is another and an extremely popular kind of fictitious writing, which makes the fable subservient to the developing of national character, or of the manners, usages, prejudices and condition of particular classes. Besides truth, spirit and a nice discrimination of peculiarities in the sketches of individuals, a single picture is widely applicable, and gives us much knowledge of the state of society at the time, and what is still higher, an increased and nearer knowledge of mankind. These sketches are not caricatures, merely grotesque delineations of strange individuals, such as amuse or distress us chiefly for their total separation from the crowd to which we belong. They represent classes; they shew us some peculiar operation of familiar principles, in men who received their natures from our common author, and their distinctive characters from limited external influences. A source of sympathy is thus opened between the remotest nations; we read with delight of those who are separated from us by their institutions and manners as well as climate, not that they are represented as beings formed of another mould and with different capacities from ourselves, but because they resemble us in every thing except that distinguishing character and those prevailing tastes which are ascribable to the peculiar circumstances in which they are placed. We love to see the common world moulding the mind a thousand ways, and multiplying our studies and pleasures without lessening our sympathy and attachments.

How far may this kind of fictitious writing be expected to succeed among us? This cannot depend upon the genius only of authors; at least, mere invention is out of the question. The object is to present what exists, to appeal to men's observation and daily experience. We might possibly be more delighted with a merely poetical creation, than with a history of living men and a sketch of ordinary society, but these would lose all their attraction and value, when they profess to describe realities, while in fact they are occupied principally with an imaginary world.—Our state of society at present offers very imperfect materials for a novel, of the kind which has just been alluded to. If we admit that there is here a *lower class*, its peculiarity would not be found in character so much as in vulgarity of manners and narrowness of opinion; and a foreigner would be as little delighted as ourselves with the most lively record of corrupt speech, of coarse or indelicate customs, of sturdy insolence towards the rich, and indifference or contempt for those who consented to be poor, where competency was so easy and so privileged. If such a sketch should be true, it would be so only of individuals, whose influence is scarcely felt amongst ourselves, and whose peculiarities would give strangers very little knowledge of the effect of our institutions or pursuits upon our opinions and character.

We come next to a large and invaluable order, composed of sensible, industrious, upright men, whose whole experience seems at war with adventure, and whose chief distinction is in their unmolested happiness, and perfectly independent modes of living. They are exactly fitted to make society secure and prosperous, and to teach us the importance of good habits and principles; with more firmness and efficiency than variety, sprightliness or vehemence in their characters; free from wild superstitions; not much in the habit of forming poetical associations with the objects they are most familiar with; using, occasionally, highly picturesque expressions, without betraying the feelings in which they originated; affected by many sober and rooted prejudices, which are inseparable perhaps from strong, unpolished character and are even its protection, but such as might appear to more advantage in a book that was only to make us wiser, than in one designed also for our diversion. With such a class of men, we should find more instruction than entertainment, more to gratify our kind feelings and good sense than to fill our imaginations. To visit them in their own homes would please us more than to read of them in a novel; they might offer little to call forth discrimination and acute remark, but a great deal of general happiness and virtue for a good mind to approve and imitate.

If we should look for what are called the higher classes of society, the wealthy, fashionable and ostentatious, whose manners, parade and intrigues in the older countries have given birth to some of the finest modern tales; we might be in a great measure disappointed. We should, indeed, find splendor, luxury and refinement, and possibly an incomplete imitation of foreign fashions; but little of the exclusive spirit of an established order, which owed its existence to something peculiar in our state of society, and had secured respect for its claims from those who are most impatient of superiority and all separate pretensions. More years, practice and affluence might be necessary to render the class more distinct, character more various, peculiarities more graceful and easy, vice and folly more finished and creditable, and affectation less insupportable than uncouth sincerity.

No doubt, it is impossible to give a just account of society, whatever be its state, without affording some entertainment, or at least knowledge. Man is always our best study, and our most fruitful subject whether we hate or love him. If a writer would be a despot, with power never to be shaken or questioned, let him become the fearless and exact historian or painter of real life. If he would be the most efficient moral teacher, let him tell men what they are and what is thought of them; let him take us from the crowd where there is too much motion for thought, where each is countenanced and sheltered by the other, with an example on all sides for his follies or vices, and where the very sense of fault dies because there is none to condemn; let him shew us our conduct in a silent picture, when there is nothing to dim our perceptions, or mislead our judgments, when the music has ceased which put us all in the same motion, attracted us to one object, and made every man happy without a thought of the cause or the manner. We may then learn the real spirit and business of society, with much to laugh at and something to lament as well as approve. In every class amongst ourselves there are fine subjects for the moral and satirical observer, which have already called forth much grave and light rebuke, and many short, lively sketches of domestic manners, national customs and individual singularities. But our common every-day life hardly offers materials as yet for a long story, which should be full of interest for its strong and infinitely various characters, fine conversation and striking incident, for conflicting pretensions and subtile intrigues in private life, and which should all appear to be exactly in the ordinary course of things, and what every one would feel to be perfectly true, without being obliged to verify it by particular and limited applications. And genius is not apt to employ itself upon subjects where it feels embarrassed by the want of materials. It does not indeed court novelties, as if it thought nothing else would do, nor shun what common minds might think unpromising or impossible. It follows its own wishes, and chooses what it can manage to advantage; what provokes its energy and is yet within its controul.

Brown had the courage to lay the scenes of his stories at home, but no one will charge him with a disgusting familiarity. He has not even attempted to draw a peculiar American character; he seeks for many of his most important persons abroad, or among those who had lived and been educated abroad, where the character had been formed and opinions decidedly fixed, under better influences perhaps for his purposes than existed or at present could be expected to exist here, while many things in our situation and prospects would offer a good field for a new and striking exhibition of his characters. The scene is rarely in common life or for ordinary events. Sometimes he begins with a simple, domestic narrative, as in Ormond, which has no very distinct reference to our state of society, but which exhibits merely, though with great spirit, the unwearied solicitude of a daughter for a weak, sinful and helpless father, the victim of a young impostor whom he had received to his confidence. We are constantly expecting something more important, though without an intimation what it will be. At length some terrific being—little less than omnipotent, of strong mind and feelings, utterly and deliberately perverted—is introduced, and thence forward rules the destinies of every one else, without exhibiting very definite purposes, or adopting any distinct plan of operations. His power is usually of a moral kind; he establishes an inquisition to put the mind to torture; looks, tones, persuasions, threats and dark insinuations are his instruments. Our chief interest is not in the events, nor at all dependent upon the conviction that we ever saw the place or the man. We are not thinking of accustomed modes of living or our ordinary experience, but are held captive by the force of character, the intensity of intellectual suffering, the unrelenting perseverance of a bad spirit disappointed. A spell is thrown over our imaginations, and our belief is at least strong enough for sympathy.

Sometimes the events are placed so far back, that they belong to a somewhat different race from ourselves, at least with different pursuits, pleasures and dangers; but we are not in a strange country; what was then a wilderness is now covered with our own flourishing settlements; the savage and beast of prey are scarcely heard of; the wild, adventurous character of the recent settler has become softened by regular and secure industry, and we feel as if we were reading of our antiquities.

Sometimes the author takes advantage of a recent event amongst ourselves, as in Wieland, which is too shocking to receive any aid from exaggeration, or to lose any interest from its notoriety. A father is tempted by apparent communications from above to murder his family. The rapture and exultation with which he contemplates his triumph over his fond weakness in obedience to heaven, very often reach the sublime. This is equalled perhaps by his utter prostration when he learns that he has been deceived. The author connects this event with just such beings as should be concerned in it; he makes it illustrative of character and dependent upon it; and though it might appear rare and monstrous enough for a lie instead of a wonder, he contrives by the earnestness and argumentative cast of reflection, the depth, sincerity and torture of feeling, the suitableness of every circumstance and the apparent inevitableness of all that occurs, to chain us to a more revolting narrative than perhaps ever before made the smallest pretensions to truth.

Sometimes his stories rest chiefly upon recent events of public concern. We refer particularly to the pestilence that has more than once wasted our principal cities; and here he is so willing to confine himself to mere truth, that he proposes to make his narrative of practical use, by preserving such incidents as appeared to him most instructive amongst those which fell under his own observation. He enters the city; the streets are still, the dwellings deserted or occupied by the sick. There is such terrible distinctness in his description of the calamity, so much of vulgar suffering which cannot be relieved, and of disgusting, selfish inhumanity in the timid, too rarely contrasted with a generous self-exposure, that we are sometimes oppressed and sickened; the reality seems too near. But in connexion with this, there is sufficient horror and wildness for the imagination. We feel that all this suffering is crowded into one spot, where the poor and wretched are almost alone amongst the deserted mansions of the wealthy and in the scenes of recent gayety. The victim is left in a dark, closed dwelling, as if to die in his tomb, with no one near but the safe plunderer. The day and night are equally still—there are no sounds but of the dying and the hearse. The fugitive, whom we thought secure, perishes in a purer air; and to make our sense of hopelessness and desolation still more complete, we see the sun shining as brightly and the grass-walks as fresh in the morning, as if the happy were there to enjoy them.

We can offer only these few remarks upon the course Brown has followed in the selection of his subjects and the use of his materials. Though his scenes lie at home, yet in his four principal tales, we can say with some confidence, that there is little which is too humble and familiar for interest, or so monstrous and unusual that he has not been able to recommend it sufficiently to our belief for all his purposes.

We have alluded to the singular or improbable character of his persons and incidents; and it is the first thing that presents itself on reading his four principal tales. He selects minds that are strangely gifted or influenced, as if for the pleasure of exploring some secret principles of our nature, disclosing new motives of conduct, or old ones operating in a new direction; and especially that he may have an opportunity, the necessity of which we are to admit, of accounting at large for every thing that is resolved upon or done; as if he had discovered springs of action which could not be understood in the usual way, by our observation of their effects, but only from a minute, philosophical discussion of impulses and motives by the parties concerned, after a cool, thorough self-inspection, and a detailed enumeration of rapid and subtile thoughts which incessantly gleamed across their minds in the storm. In the language of one of his characters, 'I cannot be satisfied with telling you that I am not well, but I must be searching with these careful eyes into causes and labouring to tell you of what nature my malady is. It has always been so. I have always found an unaccountable pleasure in dissecting, as it were, my heart, uncovering, one by one, its many folds, and laying it before you as a country is shown in a map.' This scrutiny into the feelings is given with such an air of probability and conclusiveness, or at least sincerity, that we are disposed to admit the existence of the most extraordinary beings, and then their opinions, purposes, conduct, and influence over others are quite satisfactorily explained, without supposing any other despotism over the will but that which is to be found in the power of involuntary thoughts.

But this accounting for every thing is often excessively irksome. A ludicrous importance is given to trifles; the vast mind is seen busied, amazed and anxious about incidents or intimations that are wholly inadequate to the concern they give or the effects which are traced to them, and which ordinary men would be ashamed to notice. What would be nothing elsewhere is every thing here. The feelings not only appear to obey the impulse they receive and tend unerringly to their object, but in a state of excitement and tumult, they are excellent philosophers; they shew the mind's perfect consciousness of all that is passing within; they appear to prescribe their own operations, pass through anticipated changes, and remember that they are afterwards to render an account of themselves. The reader would be better pleased if the mind's rapid conclusions were given, and an opportunity left for his own sagacity to account for them from observation of the whole character.

Brown's principal characters are designed chiefly for our imaginations and ingenuity. They study and delineate themselves with exemplary diligence and fidelity. This is not done that they may grow better, or give us a moral lesson; they are perfectly satisfied with the study, and succeed in engaging us to watch them. They are of a contemplative turn, forever hunting for materials of thought rather than motives to action, not so much from irresolution or speculative indolence, as from a love of thinking and feeling deeply at all times, and associating every thing around them with their own minds. They defer as far as possible the day when the deed shall be done which is to deprive them of something to brood over; they are anxious to operate upon the minds of others rather than upon their conduct, to keep them in suspense, and divert them from the purpose which they themselves have inspired, as soon as they see it ripening into action. They would envy no man the calm assurance and prompt determination, which spring from a general consciousness of good intentions and a quick insight into the subject of his thoughts. They have a perverse love of perplexity and doubt, and of needless though not vulgar difficulties; and to gratify this, a false and bewildering consequence is given to their own most common feelings and the most obvious conduct in others. They have not been enough exposed to the world to acquire a contempt for their singularities; they feel as if they were very peculiar and must attract as much attention as they bestow upon themselves, and especially that mischief must lurk in every thing which appears mysterious to them. Then they plunge into solitudes and heap conjectures upon conjectures about endless possibilities. 'Thought is first made a vehicle of pain,' and then life is not worth enduring; but they live on, for to die would be as fatal as torpor to the wild dreamer, and a disposition to make evils supportable would be just as bad.

But the time for action at last comes—we could not anticipate what would be done, nor comprehend why any thing should be done—there is all at once a rushing and thronging of incidents; the bright heavens are suddenly darkened; a strange accumulation of unforeseen ills falls upon a single deserted being. His innocent actions are most ingeniously misconceived or misrepresented; he is made the blind instrument of all the woe he suffers or inflicts; his sad delusions are made use of to draw him to the most atrocious deeds; the means of vindication to the injured or of correction to the erring are always near but never possessed. It is of no consequence to the author whether you were prepared by the early view of a doubtful character for his conduct afterwards; whether he fulfils his promise or breaks it. He chooses to make men as intense in action as they were before in reflection. He conjures up at once a terrible scene for mighty agents; if one perishes, he supplies the place by infusing new strength and other purposes into him who remains. And the attention is so much engrossed, the imagination is so filled by what is passing now, that we care not for its connexion, if there be any, with the past or future; we want no more, and least of all such explanations as are sometimes given. We seem to have had a disturbed dream; we suddenly reached the precipice, plunged, and awoke in falling, rejoiced that it was an illusion and that it has passed away.

A writer so engrossed with the character of men and the ways in which they may be influenced; chiefly occupied with the mind, turning every thing into thought, and refining upon it till it almost vanishes, might not be expected to give much time to descriptions of outward objects. But in all his tales he shews great closeness and minuteness of observation. He describes as if he told only what he had seen in a highly excited state of feeling, and in connexion with the events and characters. He discovers every where a strong sense of the presence of objects. Most of his descriptions are simple, and many might appear bald. He knew perhaps that some minds could be awakened by the mere mention of a water-fall, or of full orchards and cornfields, or of the peculiar sound of the wind among the pines.—We have alluded to the distinctness and particularity with which he describes the city visited with pestilence; the dwelling-house, the hospital, the dying, the healed, all appear before our eyes; the imagination has nothing to do but perceive, though it never fails to multiply and enlarge circumstances of horror, and to fasten us to the picture more strongly by increasing terror and sympathy till mere disgust ceases.—The most formal and protracted description is in Edgar Huntly, of a scene in our Western wilderness. We become acquainted with it by following the hero night and day, in a cold, drenching rain-storm, or under the clear sky, through its dark caverns, recesses and woods, along its ridges and the river side. It produces throughout the liveliest sense of danger, and oppresses the spirits with an almost inexplicable sadness. Connected with it are incidents of savage warfare, the disturbed life of the frontier settler, the attack of the half-famished panther, the hero's lonely pursuit of a sleep-walker, and his own adventures when suffering under the same calamity. The question is not how much of this has happened or is likely to happen; but is it felt; are we for the time at the disposal of the writer, and can we never lose the impression he leaves? Does it appear in its first freshness when any thing occurs which a busy fancy can associate with it? Does it go with us into other deserts, and quicken our feelings and observation till a familiar air is given to strange prospects? If so, the author is satisfied. To object that he is wild and improbable in his story is not enough, unless we can shew that his intention failed or was a bad one.

Brown delights in solitude of all kinds. He loves to represent the heart as desolate; to impress you with the self-dependence of characters, plot-ting, loving, suspecting evil, devising good, in perfect secrecy. Sometimes, when he would exhibit strength of mind and purpose to most advantage, he takes away all external succour, even the presence of a friend who might offer at least the support of his notice and sympathy. He surrounds a person with circumstances precisely fitted to weaken resolution by rais-ing vague apprehensions of danger, but incapable of producing so strong an excitement as to inspire desperate and inflexible energy. The mind must then fortify itself, calmly estimate the evil that seems to be ap-proaching, and contemplate it in its worst forms and consequences in order to counteract it effectually.—He is peculiarly successful in describ-ing a deserted house, silent and dark in the day-time, while a faint ray streams through the crevices of the closed doors and shutters, discovering in a peculiar twilight that it had been once occupied, and that every thing remained undisturbed since its sudden desertion. The sentiment of fear and melancholy is perhaps never more lively, nor the disturbed fancy more active than in such a place, even when we are strangers to it; but how much more, if we have passed there through happiness and suffer-ing, if the robber has alarmed our security, or if a friend has died there and been carried over its threshold to the grave. The solemnity of our minds is unlike that which we feel when walking alone on the sea-shore at night, or through dark forests by day, for here there is no decay, nothing that man had created and which seems to mourn his absence: there is rap-ture as well as awe in our contemplations, and more of devotion than alarm in our fear.

Brown's mind is distinguished for strong, intense conception. If his thoughts are vast, he is still always master of them. He works with the greatest ease, as if his mind were fully possessed of his subject, and could not but suggest thoughts with freedom and rapidity. In the most monstrous and shocking narrative, he writes with the utmost sincerity, as if he laboured under a delusion which acted with a mischievous but un-controllable power. He never, indeed, shews a desire to complete a story, nor draws a character so much for what it is to effect in the end, as for the development of mind. The present incident is perhaps fine in itself, and answers the author's purpose, and gives room for the display of great strength; but it has little or no connexion with others. With the greatest solicitude to tell us every thing that passes in the mind before a purpose is formed, he is very careless as to any continuity or dependence in the events which lead to or flow from that purpose. He sometimes crowds more into one day than we should have expected in many, and at others leaps over so large an interval as to make the narrative improbable to all who are not in the secret. His characters cannot be relied upon: not-withstanding their strength and apparently stubborn singularities, they accommodate themselves readily to the author, sometimes losing all the importance with which they were at first invested, and at others accomplishing something beyond or opposite to what was expected, and almost what we can believe to be within the compass of human power in the agent or weakness in the sufferer. This incompleteness of views and inconsistency of characters is not owing to carelessness or haste in the writer; he had never determined how things should end, nor proposed to himself any prevailing object when he began, nor discovered one as he advanced. We generally close a story with a belief that as much more might be said. He was engrossed by single, separate scenes, such as invention suggested from time to time; and while we can account from this fact for our feeling little solicitude about the story as a whole, we must at the same time form a high estimate of an author's power, who can carry us through almost disconnected scenes without any considerable failure of interest. He seems fond of exciting and vexing curiosity, but when he fails of satisfying it, it is more, we believe, from forgetfulness than design.

There is very little variety in his writings; at least in those where his genius is most clearly discerned. He loves unusual, lawless characters, and extraordinary and tragic incident. There should not be a moment of calm brightness in the world, unless as it may serve to heighten the effect of approaching gloom and tempest. The innocent are doomed to suffer, as if virtue were best capable of enduring and shone most conspicuously in trial, or at least drew the largest sympathy. This suffering is of the mind; bodily pain and death appear but moderate and vulgar evils, and rather a refuge than punishment for the triumphant criminal, who has rioted in mischief till he is weary, and willing to die for repose since his work is ended. In these sad views of life, which make society worse than the wilderness and men's sympathy and promises little better than a mockery, there is no apparent design to mislead the world, or covertly condemn its opinions and awards, but merely to take a firm hold of the heart, by appeals to its pity, terror, indignation or wonder. He wants the universality and justice of a fair observer of the world. He thinks too much in one way, and that a narrow one. His views are of one kind, and shew that he thought more than he observed.

His style is clear, simple and nervous, with very little peculiarity, and not the slightest affectation or even consciousness of manner; rarely varying to suit the subject, or to distinguish conversation from narrative or description. It uniformly bears marks of a serious, thoughtful mind, remembering its excitement and suffering rather than experiencing them. There are, now and then, some attempts at playfulness and humour, but they are wholly unsuccessful, and sometimes ludicrous and offensive. There are few striking sentences which the reader would unconsciously retain for the beauty of their structure, or any peculiar terms; we have the thought without the expression. We should not pronounce Brown a man of genius, nor deny him that distinction, from his style. It might have been acquired by care and study, but it is the result only and never betrays the process. There is no attempt at what is too vaguely called fine writing; no needless ornament, no sacrifice of spirit and energy from a weak ambition of harmony or finish, no use of a strictly poetical term to excite the imagination, when another and a simpler one will convey the meaning more definitely. He uses words merely to express his own thoughts, and not to multiply our associations. He never allows them to outstrip, or, which is nearly the same thing, to take the place of feeling and truth. He appears to be above the common temptation to exhibit tokens of more passion than is felt, merely on account of 'the imaginary gracefulness of passion,' or to decorate scenes with borrowed beauties till they have lost every thing which could distinguish them, or even persuade us that we were in our own world.

It has been our object in these remarks, to point out some of Brown's prominent defects and excellences. We never intended to make an abstract of his stories; and such extracts as we could admit would do little justice to the author.—His readers will observe every-where that he was an ardent admirer of Godwin, though not his slave. Godwin himself has pronounced him a writer of distinguished genius and acknowledged himself in his debt.—The uses and evils of criticism can no longer be felt by him; the dead are beyond our judgment. It is for the living that their opinions and genius should be inquired into; and it is hardly less dishonourable to let the grave bury their worth than consecrate their errors.

"Carwin the Biloquist, and other American Tales and Pieces (1822)"

Anonymous*

This is a collection of the authors unfinished pieces. The editor informs us, that "unlike most other writers, his modes of thinking, the system of ratiocination with which he invests his characters, and the peculiarities arising from the state of society in which his scenes are laid, are more the objects of our admiration or attention than the incidents or themes of his fictions." Hence he concludes, that "the incomplete state in which some of these posthumous pieces have been left, is therefore the less to be regretted." We should draw a different conclusion from these premises, granting them to be true; but this is more than we honestly can; and as there is only one lecture more in the preface, we shrewdly suspect that the editor wrote the preface without ever reading the work. We may be wrong, it is true, but he who suspects cannot help himself. Very few can be implicit believers where they perceive a reason for doubting, and the reason of our scepticism, in the present instance, is simply this. We have read these tales from beginning to end, and we are certain that we have never read any work in which there are less allusions to the state of society. In fact there are no allusions to it at all, nor is there in the characters themselves, the least tincture of that species of peculiarity which arise from a peculiarity of manners in the state of society. Had the scene been laid in England, at the present day, a suspicion could never once enter our mind, either from their actions, their manners, or their language, that they were not genuine English characters. The fact is, that so far from having any thing peculiar in them, arising either from peculiarity of disposition, or peculiarity of national manners, they are such characters as might be placed in any age and in any clime, because they are actually such as are met with at all times, and in all countries. Brown is no describer of *manners*, and, indeed, he never attempts it. His power lies in describing the passions and secret workings of the heart, and as these passions can never be grafted on national manners, founded as they are in the very nature of man, they are the same in all ages and coun-

*Reprinted from *European Magazine*, 85 (January, 1824), 55-60.

tries. The character of "Carwin the Biloquist" is not formed when his history concludes: we only know he had a thirst for knowledge, and a restless ambition. These are not new traits in the human character; nor is there any thing more novel in the character of "Stephen Calvert," "Jessica," or the "Scribbler." It does not follow from this, that they are uninteresting characters: on the contrary, the most interesting characters are those where human nature is alone depicted. It is true that human nature is often whimsical, and often produces whimsical characters, whose eccentricity or peculiarity of disposition is altogether independent of the state of society; but Brown's characters do not belong to this class. He is far from being a Quixotic writer. Stephen Calvert is described a slave to his passions: so are a great portion of the world. Except what was the natural consequence of this propensity, we find nothing else peculiar in the character of Calvert, and as for the Scribbler, he is one of those characters that are met with every day, for there is nothing in him sufficiently characteristic to excite our sympathy.

Neither do we believe with the writer of this preface, that the incidents or themes of Brown's fictions are less *interesting* than the "modes of thinking or the systems of ratiocination with which he invests his characters," because the *interest* of the latter depends entirely on the *interest* we take in the characters themselves. Whatever excites our *interest* in any character, excites a proportionable *interest* in every incident of his life, and therefore the *interest* which we take in the incidents related in this work must always be proportioned to the *interest* we take in the characters themselves, whether this be produced by their "modes of thinking" or by any modes or means which are placed within the reach of the novelist. To suppose that an incident can be interesting in itself, abstracted from the person to whom it happens, is to suppose what is contradicted by the experience of every day. If we read of a battle in some remote part of the globe, in which some thousands were lost, the electric thrill of commiseration never awakes our dormant sympathies, because we had no previous acquaintance with, and consequently no previous *interest* in the ill-fated sufferers. An incident or event, then, may be very important, but creates no *interest* at the same time, while the most trifling incident will become highly *interesting*, if we only feel an *interest* in those who are concerned. We cannot then be *interested* in Brown's characters without being proportionably *interested* in every incident of their lives; and yet we are told, that the little *interest* we take in the incidents, render "the incomplete state of these posthumous pieces the less to be regretted." The fact, however, is the contrary, for if the loss of the incidents is not much to be regretted, it proves the characters of whom these incidents are related must be extremely uninteresting, and, therefore, their loss is as little to be regretted as that of the incidents themselves. When we look at the matter more closely, however, we shall find, that it is the loss of the incidents that entirely cause our regret; for the moment we become fully acquainted with the peculiarities of a person's character and his mode of reasoning, we can guess pretty nearly how he will act and reason on every future occasion, if we only know the situation in which he is placed. It is our ignorance of this situation, or of the future incidents of his life, that we, therefore, regret, because there is no possibility of guessing at future incidents, or the future fate of a man from what is passed. This is so true, that after perusing a considerable portion of a novel, and getting acquainted with the characters, we frequently pass over many of their reasonings to get at the incidents. We guess what they are going to say, from the situation in which they are placed, but we cannot, without a spirit of prophecy, tell what is to happen them next, and, therefore, we hurry on to get acquainted with it. The reason, therefore, why the editor thinks the incomplete state of these pieces, is *less* to be regretted, appears to us to be the very reason why they are to be regretted *most*. When he talks of the incomplete state of *some* of these pieces, he seems not to know that they are all incomplete, and what is worse, that, except Stephen Calvert, they all break off at the very point where our expectations are raised to the highest, and where we hope for an explanation of all the mystery through which we had been hitherto led. Stephen Calvert, it is true, explains at the conclusion, a considerable portion, though not the entire, of the mystery which precedes; but in all other respects, it is as imperfect as any of the rest; for the story is a five act drama, of which only the first act is given here. The story was written by Calvert himself after he quitted the world, and became a recluse on the banks of the *Mechigan*. We consequently know nothing of this interesting hermit, from the end of the first act down to the period of his seclusion from society; nor is the entire mystery removed, that preceded the conclusion of the first act, for it is impossible to ascertain whether Miss Neville was guilty of some of the charges attributed to her or not, though there are stronger reasons for believing her innocent. Indeed we must say, that for our own parts, few can regret more than we do, the incomplete state of these pieces, particularly the story of Carwin and Jessica. The mysterious character of Dudloe, and the mysterious life of Colden, excite the highest expectations, and the most intense interest; but what appears most surprising to us is, that these pieces should break off exactly where the mystery was on the point of being developed. Can it be supposed, that the author would have written so much, and begun so many pieces before he finished either, or that it gave him any satisfaction to mortify his readers, by dropping the subject at the very crisis where further information was most eagerly sought after, and most anxiously expected. At any rate, we know the thing did not happen by chance. A novelist who engages in several pieces, before he concludes either, must necessarily leave some in a greater state of forwardness than others. As all these pieces, then, break off abruptly at the same critical juncture, it is obvious that the author never intended to complete them; or that those who became the subsequent depositaries of these papers lopped off the remaining part, judging they would be more interesting by discontinuing the subject where expectation was at its highest. Perhaps they judged right with regard to those readers who cannot enter into the spirit of an author, and who believe he can get out of the greatest difficulty with as much ease as he got himself into it; for such readers attach a sort of omnipotence to men of genius, and believe they can effect any thing they undertake. Feeling they can do nothing themselves, and perceiving the ease with which former writers have resolved those gordian knots of fiction, which were perfectly inexplicable to them, and which, in fact, they thought it impossible to explain satisfactorily, from being complete sceptics, they become implicit believers, and imagine that a noble writer can give satisfactory reasons for the most unaccountable line of conduct which their fictitious characters can pursue. Thus it is that extremes meet. The most pertinacious pyrrhonists become the completest dupes, if their sceptical principles be once shaken; and the most unhesitating believer becomes the most confirmed sceptic, if the absurdity of one article of his faith be once satisfactorily demonstrated to him. Men of strong minds and enlarged perceptions avoid both these extremes. They perceive more clearly the real magnitude of the difficulties in which a writer has placed himself; and if these difficulties be not absolutely insurmountable, they perceive some at least of the resources by which they may be overcome; but as they know, that a fool may advance positions which the ablest logician can never prove, so also do they know, that a novelist may make any of his characters pursue a line of conduct so perfectly at variance with the opinions which we are led to entertain of him, that the most inventive genius can never reconcile them with each other. In such a case, if the story be dropped in the middle, before any explanation takes place, it is fair to conclude, that he could assign no sufficient reasons for the mysterious manner in which he has conducted himself. We make these observations in reference to Dudloe. The author insinuates in one or two places, that he was a deep designing man, and yet, we think, that a man may be very deeply versed in the intrigues of life, without being able to reconcile the tenor of his conduct with speculative cunning. As for Carwin himself, on whom alone he could have practised his designs, and whom he so liberally patronized, we are infinitely less interested in him than in Dudloe. Our interest in the latter arises from a desire to know what possible object he could have in view; but with regard to Carwin, who is the hero of the piece, we know too little of his character to feel any interest in his fate. His real character is far from being developed when the story is dropped: we can hardly tell what he might turn out to be, and, therefore, we are the less interested in whatever might have happened him. He seems to have somewhat of Gil Blas in him, at the opening of his career. He has the same thirst for knowledge, but if possible, a greater ignorance of the purposes to which his knowledge might be applied. Indeed it is difficult to reconcile the idea which we are led to entertain of his literary acquirements, and the spirit of curiosity by which he was actuated, with his total ignorance of the world. His genius was by no means of a sublime character, he sought rather to know what was curious than what was great and elevated, and a genius of this character, is, we believe, seldom slow in getting acquainted with such matters as are best calculated to promote his interests. Carwin, however, with these qualifications, and with no slight portion of the cunning of Gil Blas, is still perfectly ignorant of any means by which his interests can be promoted. We think the idea of sending him to Spain to get acquainted with the world, is rather unhappy. France or Italy would have served his purpose better. The story, however, cannot be read without the strongest interest; but this interest, as we have already observed, arises from our desire to penetrate into the deep designs of Dudloe. Unhappily our curiosity is baffled, for the story drops exactly where we expected to have all our perplexities resolved.

The story of Stephen Calvert takes up a considerable portion of the first and third volumes, and the entire of the second, and yet it forms only one-fifth of the plot which the author had sketched out. Calvert is a much more interesting character than Carwin. His prevailing passion is an attachment to the fair sex, and yet he is not what the French call *homme gallant*, for he has too much native modesty and timidity to disclose his affections, even when they are of the most honourable kind. How long he preserved this hallowed feeling we cannot tell: we only know it did not forsake him during the first act, where the story drops; but we are inclined to think, that a longer intercourse with the world, indurated its delicacy and restraining influence. To this supposition we are led by the following passage in which the author accounts for his seclusion from the world.

> For this solitude and labour, I was induced to change my habits of corruption and idleness by a just estimate of benefits and evils. I tried the world, and found it too abundant in temptation and calamity for me safely to remain in it. Some men gifted with extraordinary endowments, or fortified by an auspicious education, may preserve their integrity in every scene; but, as to me, experience has taught me, that I can be safe only in withdrawing from temptation, and can escape from guilt and remorse only by interposing deserts between me and the haunts of mankind.

There are men whose reason is clear and unclouded, whose feelings are delicate and refined, whose souls are in unison with the finer harmonies of nature, and whose discrimination of things are piercing and acute, but who, with all these redeeming and subliming qualities, rush headlong into the snares of the stupid, and the machinations of the crafty. The impetuosity of passion extinguishes, for the moment, the sunshine which is kindled within them, and tramples on the dictates which its intelligence prescribes. Their intentions are good, and yet they abandon the guidance of their better will. Vice can assume no disguise in which they cannot recognize her, nor throw any veil over her turpitude which they cannot unmask; and yet with a rooted and unalterable abhorrence of vice, they resign themselves to its sway, and abandon that virtue which they admire and esteem. Such was Calvert: he saw clearly, in the first instance, the evil of pursuing a certain line of conduct; and immediately after sought for arguments to convince himself that this evil was imaginary. Thus he became the slave of passion, a vane that yielded to the softest zephyr. No wonder that he should at length get tired of the world, and embrace the only means which were left him of avoiding its snares. To set vice at defiance, is to yield to its dominion: to fly from its habitation, is to trample on its seductions. He who can read Calvert without interest, has little of human nature in him. The character of Sidney is finely contrasted with that of Calvert. Both of them are endowed by nature with honesty of principle and the love of virtue, and yet no two characters can be more dissimilar. Calvert is the slave of passion, Sidney the stern, unbending disciple of reason. He seems placed above the reach of every influence which tends to seduce the mind from the love of virtue: and yet he is not an interesting character, simply because he has no character at all. He who betrays a total want of passion, may be properly said to possess no character, because the character of a man is determined by some peculiar propensities or aversions which distinguish him from the generality of mankind. These propensities and aversions, however, can find no place in a man void of passion, and, therefore, he cannot be said to possess a character at all. Without a character, however, there can be no interest, for though we may admire the man who always acts right, from a sense of duty, not from the impulse of any internal emotion, we can neither love nor hate him, and without love or hatred there can be no interest. Calvert, therefore, with all his imperfections, is infinitely more interesting than Sidney, and we are not surprised that Louisa should be more in love with his faults than with Sidneys virtues.

The story of Jessica is simply told, and the first indications of love beautifully pourtrayed. Jessica is in love with Colden, a strange mysterious wight, of whom neither she nor any one else could make any thing. We are, indeed, at a loss ourselves to know what the author intended to make of him; all he has condescended to tell us of him is, that he had lately come to America from Europe; that he boarded at a family of the Phillipsons; that their leaving the city obliged him to seek new quarters; that he was recommended by the Phillipsons to Jessica's brother, as a proper person to procure him a quiet domestic family to board with; that the brother introduced him to his mother and sister, with whom he boarded till the story drops; that he paid liberally for his board, though his fare was of the simplest description, consisting of a pint of milk in a tin porringer, with a cut or two of brown bread, morning, noon, and night; and his bed a blanket laid on a sacking bottom; that he avoided society except during meal hours, and even seldom spoke a word unless spoken to; that his intellectual acquirements appeared extensive, his appearance prepossessing, his eyes piercing and intelligent, but wandering and unsettled; and his countenance generally shaded with a cast of melancholy; that Jessica, who had a little before refused the hand of a man of fortune, fell in love with him; that she was extremely desirous of engaging Colden in conversation at meal hours, but wanted resolution to commence it; that at length she resolved to ask him, why leaving the Romish religion and turning Protestant, should be so criminal as to deserve burning alive; that she asked the question at length after considerable stammering, and some encouragement from Colden, who perceived her agitation of mind; that Colden, however, so far from being pleased with the question, started half up, cast a dreadful look at her, uttered not a syllable, paused for a moment, and hurried out of the room; that Jessica's feelings were so overpowered by this scene, that she wandered across the fields towards the Hudson, and sat under an old tree, on the edge of a hill that overlooks Wantseys Marsh, where she remained till it was an hour after dark, forgetful of herself, forgetful of every thing but Colden's strange behaviour, when a figure suddenly came up, and accosting her in a tone of surprise, said "Jessy Arnot, is it you?" that with some difficulty he made her confess the cause of her remaining there at so late an hour; that Colden acknowledged himself to be a faulty wretch, in acting as he did, but that it was an infirmity which could not be accounted for; that after humbling himself to Jessica, he accompanied her till they reached Broadway, where he parted with her, saying, "you know the way now: my path leads me differently."

Here the story breaks off; but the peculiarities of Colden's character cannot be conceived from this sketch, nor can they be satisfactorily explained after perusing the original piece. What was there in Jessica's question that could terrify him: it is evident from the whole tenor of his conduct, and the intelligence that occasionally beamed in his countenance, that he was not a religious enthusiast. He could not, therefore, be offended with Jessica's question, as it proved her no advocate for an exclusive system of belief. Did he suspect her passion for him, did he hope, from the agitated and stammering manner in which she began to ask the question, that she was going to acknowledge her flame, and did his conduct arise from disappointment in this surmise? This seems the most probable supposition, and yet how could he expect such a confession from a girl whom he treated so coldly, and with whom he never exchanged a word beyond the common salutations of the day. With the exception of the Scribbler, we should wish to see all those pieces completed, and all those mysteries resolved by a master hand. The subject would be worthy the author of Waverly, for however powerful he may be in unfolding and analyzing the secrets of the heart, and the impulses and influences by which it is diversely governed, the completion of Carwin, Calvert, and Jessica would give ample exercise to his genius.

"The Novels of Charles Brockden Brown"

Richard Henry Dana, Sr.*

Twenty odd years have been allowed to pass before even an imperfect edition of the works of fiction of our long unrivalled novelist is given to the public. Yet nearly the whole of that time Brown has been alone; for no one approached the height he rested on, till the author of the "Pioneers" and "Pilot" appeared. Like his own Clithero, he lay stretched in moody solitude, the waters of the noisy world rolling blindly on around him, and a wide chasm open between him and his fellow men. In 1815, Mr. Dunlap gave us a life of him; an ill arranged and bulky work, yet too meagre where it should be particular and full. To this, however, we are indebted for all we know of Brown's life; and we owe to it also an article on Brown, which appeared in the North American Review for 1819; an article which, we fear, has left us little to say.

Mr. Dunlap's Life of our author was not of a character to be much read; and it was, after all, perhaps, in this case, as it has been in some others, chiefly to England that Brown was indebted for his coming into general notice at home. It is true that his stories were to be found amongst the shabby editions of works which go to make up a circulating library, and that some of them were occasionally read; but excepting his personal acquaintance, few or none knew or cared whether he was an Englishman or a Laplander; whether he was living, whether he had died a natural death, or was one of the many Browns who are regularly hanged. Even when an American edition at last appears, it is recommended to public notice by extracts from a London paper, congratulating Brown's countrymen that Boston was to give them an edition of the works of a man of whom they might well be proud. We hope we are giving no offence. We would merely suggest to the zealous that whenever a man of genius appears amongst us, we should give him cordial welcome and support, and hearty praise; and not be so wanting in patriotism as to let foreigners be the first to take him by the hand.

This edition of Brown is in six conveniently sized volumes, very neat in appearance, though not quite so accurately printed as we could have wished. The notice of him, at the beginning, gives not a single new fact,

*Reprinted from *The United States Review and Literary Gazette*, 2 (August, 1827), 321-333.

or peculiarity in his character, that we recollect. The publisher might as well have set his printer to compiling a notice out of Dunlap, as have brought such an one as this all the way from Philadelphia. We wish, too, he had taken advice before making his selection. No edition of Brown's works should be published without the Memoirs of Carwin, and those of Stephen Calvert. It is true, Brown did not live to finish them; but to those who feel something like a personal attachment to our author,—and what good man ever reads him without feeling it?—this gives them a near and peculiar interest; it connects us with him in his sickness, it brings us to the side of his deathbed, and helps us watch in spirit the passing of his exalted and solemn soul into the other world. Had any sacrifice been necessary, which we very much doubt, "Clara Howard" should have been omitted, for it has all Brown's defects, with little or none of his power. Notwithstanding these deficiencies, we hold the public to be under great obligations to the publisher; and hope he will be fully rewarded for his praiseworthy undertaking.

To the speculative mind, it is a curious fact that a man like Brown should of a sudden make his appearance in a new country, in which almost every individual was taken up in the eager pursuit of riches, or the hot and noisy contests of party politics; when every man of talent, who sought out distinction, went into one of the professions; when to make literature one's main employment, was held little better than being a drone; when almost the only men who wrote with force and simplicity were some of the leaders amongst our active politicians; when a man might look over our wide and busy territory, and see only here and there some self-deluded being dabbling in a dull, shallow stream, which he fancied running clear and strong to the brim with the waters of Helicon.

Did not the fact that Brown produced such works at such a time show clearly the power of genius over circumstances, we might be inclined to attribute to his loneliness of situation something of the solitariness, mysteriousness, and gloom, which surround all he wrote. But these come not of outward things. The energies of his soul were melancholy powers, and their path lay along the dusky dwelling-places of superstition, and fear, and death, and woe. The soul of such a man takes not its character from the world, but takes out from the world what suits its nature and passes the rest by; and what more it needs, and what it cannot find abroad, it turns for inward, and finds or creates it there. "My existence," says Brown, "is a series of thoughts, rather than of motions. Ratiocination and deduction leave my senses unemployed. The fulness of my fancy renders my eye vacant and inactive. Sensations do not precede and suggest, but follow and are secondary to the acts of my mind." So strong was this cast of his mind, and so single was it in its purpose, that of all men of imagination we know of none who appear from their writings to have looked so little at nature, or to have been so little open to its influences. With the exception of Mervyn's return to Hadwin's, and his last journey thence, and the opening of Carwin, with one or two more slight instances, he seldom attempts a description of natural scenery, or, where he labors it most, is confused and indistinct, as, for instance, in Edgar Huntly. It is amidst shut-up houses, still, deserted streets, noisome smells, and pestilence, and death, and near the slow, black hearse, and the dead man's grave, that his calling lies; and he has no time to turn aside to breathe the fresh, clear air of the country. He seems, in fiction, as intent upon his purpose as Howard ever was in real life; he who could spare no time from hospitals and prisons, for palaces and statues and pictures. This may be thought a serious deficiency in Brown's genius; yet it is curious to see how sometimes a defect takes somewhat the appearance of an advantage. This very want of variety has given such an air of truth to what he is about, showing such an earnest singleness of purpose, that perhaps no writer ever made his readers so completely forget that they were not reading a statement of some serious matter of fact; and so strong is this impression, that we even become half reconciled to improbabilities, which so vex us in fiction, though often happening in daily life. This enables us to bear, too, better with his style; for, along with something like a conviction that the man who had vivacity of genius enough for such inventions, could never have delivered himself with such dull poverty and pedantry of phrase, we at last are almost driven to the conclusion that however extraordinary it may be, it is nevertheless a fact; for the man "never could have made it," and that things must have happened pretty much as he tells us they did.

If Brown was remarkable for having appeared amongst a people whose pursuits and tastes had, at the time, little or no sympathy with his own, and in a country in which all was new, and partook of the alacrity of hope, and where no old remembrances made the mind contemplative and sad, nor old superstitions conjured up forms of undefined awe; he is scarcely less striking for standing apart, in the character of his mind, from almost every other man of high genius. He is more like Godwin than like any other; but differs from him in making so many of his characters live, and act, and perish, as if they were the slaves of supernatural powers, and the victims of a vague and dreadful fatality. Even here his character for truth is maintained; and his invisible agencies mingle with the commonest characters, and in the most ordinary scenes of life. It is true that these mysterious agencies are all explained away; yet such a hold do they take upon our minds, that we cannot shake off the mystical influence they have gained over us; and even those who have practised the deceptions, seem to have done it not so much from a love of deception as from a hankering after something resembling the supernatural, and an insane sort of delight in watching its strange and dreadful force over others; both he that is wrought upon, and he that works, seem, the one to suffer and the other to act, as under some resistless fate. Brown's fatal power is unsparing, and never stops; his griefs and sufferings are not of that kind which draws tears and softens the heart; it wears out the heart and takes away the strength of our spirits, so that we lie helpless under it. A power of this kind holds no associations with nature; for in the gloomiest, and the wildest, and barrenest scenes of nature, there is something enlarging, and elevating, something that tells us there is an end to our unmixed sorrow, something that lifts us above life, and breathes into us immortality—God is there! No! it is surrounded by man and the works of man—man in his ills, and sins, and feebleness; it is there alone that we can feel what is the bitterness and weariness of unmixed helplessness and woe.

So much was gloominess the character of Brown's genius, that he does not, like other authors, begin his story in a state of cheerfulness or quiet, and gradually lead on to disappointment and affliction. Some one writes a letter to a friend who has asked him for an account of his suffering life. It hints at mysteries, and sorrows, and remorse—sorrows and remorse to which there can be no end, but in the rest of the grave. He has already passed through years of miseries, and we come in and go on with him to the end of his story; but they have not ended there; and we leave him praying that death may at last bring peace to his sick and worn heart. There is woe behind us, and woe before us. The spirit cries, with the Apocalyptic angel, seen flying through the midst of heaven, in vision by John, "Woe, woe, woe, to the inhabiters of the earth!"

We know that it has become fashionable of late years, to hold sorrow as the chiefest of sins, and the melancholy story-teller as the great seducer of men from their duties and the highest of all virtues—gaiety of heart. But proneness to melancholy is not the evil of our times. We live too much abroad for that; day time and evening, we are running at large with the common herd, or are gathered into smaller flocks and folds, called societies. No one is seen ruminating alone in the still shade of his own oak or willow. The thoughtful observer, too, must have remarked, that those who are most apt to be talkative upon the duty of cheerfulness and the danger of strong excitement, are mainly those, the depths of whose feelings a fishing-line might fathom, those who have no dark, mysterious, unsounded places; and yet if a breeze but ruffle their placidity, one would think from the outcry, that the mighty sea itself was heaving and tossing into fury and foam. Besides, why all this alarm? If one author is melancholy, there are hundreds who are cool and wise, or cheerful, or full of fun. Be under no concern; neither college, nor the bar, nor the exchange, is in danger of being changed into an Arden, nor our literati, lawyers, nor merchants likely to become so many melancholy Jaqueses. We have no room to go further into the subject here. To treat it rightly, we must look deeper than men are apt to look into human nature, and we have no time for that now.

But why need any man have such gloomy views, and write in so melancholy a strain always? The answer is, this was according to Brown's temperament, and whenever he tried to thwart it, he utterly failed. Of humour, Mr. Dunlap says, he "had no portion in himself, nor any adequate conception of it in others." And Brown, himself says, "My powers do not enable me to place the commonplace characters around me in an interesting or amusing point of view." He falls off even in the cheerful, and grows heavy.

This variety which people so unhesitatingly ask for, as if no one could think of denying them; and as if it were as "good cheap" as common business talent, is in itself a mark of high quality of genius. "Pray, Sir," one might say to Mackenzie, "I have been reading your 'La Roche' and your 'Man of Feeling,' and have been crying so! and am *so* sad!—do make me laugh now, will you?" "My dear Sir, I would gratify you with all my heart, were it in my power," replies Mackenzie, "but it is not. If you wish to laugh, you must go see the Dean, or there is Shakspeare, he will make you laugh or cry, just as you please! No; he will not make you cry; he is 'too deep for tears,' but he will make you 'as sad as night,' whenever you wish it."

Brown's genius not only wanted variety; it seemed to be without even pliability. It was as ungainly and stiff when put out of its ordinary track, as is an honest yeoman, when he sets himself to some act of gentlemanly courtesy, and for his pains, gets praised for his excellently obliging disposition, and ridiculed for his awkward way of showing it.

With the exception of Constantia, in "Ormond," and Louisa, in the unfinished tale of "Stephen Calvert," there is very little to interest us in the females. Perhaps we should include the Hadwins. Constantia is an excellent girl, and goes through her sufferings, and the hard offices that poverty and sickness lay upon her, with all patience and perseverance. But it was not necessary, though "entire affection hateth nicer hands," to tell us that the beautiful Constantia "washed the foul linen;" or when she tended the sick man, how she administered the medicine and watched its two-fold operation. There is a great deal which must be done by us poor mortals for one another, which it is best to say as little about as possible. But Louisa is the most finely conceived of the female characters. Undersized, thin, awkward, sallow complexioned, and O! most fatal of all to love, rough-voiced, still she is lovely. Yet she, too, must needs offend us. Brown wishes to show her frankness, and therefore when Calvert intimates something about an early marriage, ye gods! what follows? "My intimations were understood before they were fully expressed. They obtained not a dubious acquiescence, but a vehement assent. It was unwise to defraud herself of the happiness of wedlock by the least delay. Next week was a period preferable to the next month; to-morrow was still more to be desired. Nay, she would eagerly concur in ratification of this contract on that very night. Domestic arrangements might follow with as much convenience and propriety as precede." "Why tolerate a longer delay, or pass through more forms than were absolutely indispensable?"

O! Mr. Tremaine, thou "Man of Refinement!" which way wouldst thou have looked, and how wouldst thou have felt at such a time, and what wouldst thou have done? We tell thee what thou wouldst not have done; thou wouldst not have burnt thy fingers and scalded thine arm for such a *coming* fair one. But the parson is missing; and the next day, in consequence of a conversation with a friend, Louisa tells Master Calvert that the marriage must be put off for five years in order to give his character time *to settle*. In truth, we scarcely recollect any full drawn, and complete gentleman or lady, by an American author; and as for the nice art, love-making:—"Once, on a sudden meeting," Stephen Calvert is made to say, "she so far overstept the customary boundaries, as to wrap me in her arms and kiss my cheek. No self-reproof or blushful consciousness ensued this act of unguarded tenderness, though indeed it took place without a witness." Would he have had her kiss in company? And for our own parts, we think a little "blushful consciousness" would not have made it any less winning.

Strange things happen. Constantia has a friend, Sophia, who goes to Italy, has a lover, Courtland, and marries him; and the very next day this platonic lady sends him to England, and sets off herself for America, in search of her friend; and not finding her as soon as she wished, resolves, after a very flattering manner to Mr. Courtland, that she will die of grief—that she will never know joy again this side the grave. These things are strangely out of nature. Besides, Mr. Brown's lovers, as a matter of course, relate to their friends their love dialogues; and the love-letters go the rounds of the family as regularly as the daily paper. Such conduct in the fair sex is extremely annoying to us sensitive gentlemen. But we have more serious charges to make against them.

There is a Mrs. Jane Talbot, who has no liking for her husband, and loves another man, and yet is virtuous; sits till after twelve o'nights with him, while her husband is absent, and yet is virtuous; and when the husband dies, the experienced widow writes letters to this same friend after a manner as girlish as one in her teens, though not always with the same delicacy. There is another, married too, and living apart from her husband, and she has a friend and midnight visits, ah, and tender embraces also, and she, too, is virtuous. Now we have no doubts of the strength of female virtue, but a chain-cable will give way, put but enough upon it. There is not an oftener needed prayer than that,—Lead us not into temptation. These are but a few instances of this kind of improprieties in Brown's stories. Pure and delicate minds in real life never fall into them, nor will a woman of principle be apt to place herself in a situation which may have an equivocal appearance.

We believe Brown to have been one of the purest of men. The intellectual so predominated in him, and he seems so to have loathed the sensual, that perhaps he was not aware of the strength of certain temptations over others. More than this, Brown had his system, or rather was caught by a system of that day, which held all distinctions in society to be but old abuses, the restraints of marriage unworthy free and rational beings;—when senate and bar-room alike rang with the bold and shallow *philosophy*, as it was termed, of atheists, deists, and equality men. "Freethinkers," says Wollaston, (though he himself has been suspected on one point) "are half-thinkers." No one can now read the works of the time we speak of without feeling the truth of this remark, and being amazed at the effect they produced and the noisy notoriety they attained to. It is easy for every age to see the errors of any time but its own. We now have our systems; they may not be nearly as full of danger, but they are almost as full of folly as those of past ages. Brown lived to reason himself out of his errors, and settled down, as every man of fair mind and good affections will be likely to do, into a christian; but these mistakes did not quit him without doing a lasting injury to his good taste.

We have said that even the want of variety, and the defects of style in Brown have in some measure helped to the impression of the truth of his stories. But he makes this impression in a better way also, by his circumstantiality, his careful mention of a thousand little particulars. His personages, too, before undertaking the simplest act, go through a process of reasoning; we have all the *pros* and *cons* that can be started; and though the reasoning has too often more of show than substance, still, this being the way in which the larger part of the world reasons, we are more and more convinced of the truth of his relations. He certainly has this striking characteristic of genius, the power of making his characters living and breathing men, acting in situations which are distinctly and vividly presented to our minds. To be sure, he must needs turn philosopher, and be prodigiously profound on small matters. Formal questions are put about the course to be taken, when every body sees there is but one course, and that "as plain as way to parish church." It is dark; one of his heroines has occasion to go to her chamber for a manuscript which she wishes to read. Common folks would take it for granted, without any serious ratiocination, that the first thing would be to get a light. But softly and slowly,—there is nothing like exercising our reason on all occasions.

> To do this it was requisite to procure a light. The girl had long since retired to her chamber; it was therefore proper to wait upon myself. A lamp, and the means of lighting it, were only to be found in the kitchen. Thither I resolved forthwith to repair; but the light was of use merely to enable me to read the book. I knew the shelf and the spot where it stood. Whether I took down the book, or prepared the lamp in the first place, appeared to be a matter of no moment. The latter was preferred, and, leaving my seat, I approached the closet in which, as I mentioned formerly, my books and papers were deposited.   Vol. i. p. 78.

Again, Constantia not only washes the clothes of the family, but makes them too; and hear this, ye of the goose and shears!

Clothing is one of the necessaries of human existence. The art of the tailor is scarcely of less use than that of the tiller of the ground. There are few the gains of which are better merited, and less injurious to the principles of human society. She resolved therefore to become a workwoman, and to employ in this way, the leisure she possessed from household avocations. To this scheme she was obliged to reconcile not only herself but her parents. The conquest of their prejudices was no easy task, but her patience and skill finally succeeded, and she procured needlework in sufficient quantity to enable her to enhance in no trivial degree the common fund.

Vol. vi. pp. 22, 23.

Brown's style is rather remarkable. The structure of his sentences is for the most part simple, but his words! they remind one of the witty M.P.'s reply, when asked what was doing in the house; "Lord Castlereagh is airing his vocabulary this morning, that's all." To use the happy phrase of that lord, "the fundamental feature" of the style is a most pains-taking avoidance of the Saxon, wherever it is possible, and a use of words of Latin origin in such combinations as they were never put into before. Dudley's leaving New York is spoken of as "this evasion." "Her decay was eminently gradual." Constantia scarcely "retrieving her composure." "Retrieved reflection;" "extenuate the danger;" "extenuate both these species of merit;" "preclude the necessity;" "exclude from my countenance;" "resume her ancient country;" "immersed in perplexity;" "obvious to suppose;" "obvious to conclude;" "unavoidable to conclude;" "copious epistle;" "copiously interrogated;" "copious and elegant accommodation;" "my departure was easy and commodious;" "the barrier that severs her from Welbeck must be as high as heaven and insuperable as necessity;" "a few passengers likewise occurred, whose hasty," &c. No one who has once read the description of Carwin as he is first introduced, can ever forget it. Yet we are told, "shoulders broad and square, breast sunken, his head drooping, his body of uniform breadth, supported by long and lank legs, were the *ingredients* of his frame." The ingredients of a pudding!

Brown is much more remarkable for putting his thoughts into the form of questions than Godwin ever was, yet *to ask* and *to question* are scarcely to be met with through the whole six volumes, but instead of these, we have *interrogated, interrogations*, and even *interrogatories*. It is true that the kind of writing we speak of does not show itself equally in all his stories; some few of them are tolerably free from it.

This perverted taste is much to be regretted; for after the excitement of a first reading (when less attention is paid to the style of a powerful story), we are perpetually feeling the incongruity between the strong characters and passions and terrific scenes, and the language in which they are presented to us. The distinguished novelists of this day must by and by suffer from defect in style, while the beauty and truth of language of our old dramatists will help to the increased pleasure they give the more they are studied. Brown himself has beautifully said, "The language of man is the 'intercourse of spirits,' the perfect and involuntary picture of every fixed or transient emotion to which his mind is subject." We wish he had remembered this, and left his passions and thoughts to speak their own tongue.

Though Brown's style is never rich and idiomatic, in some of his writings we find it clear and simple; and it is probable that it never would have been so wide of good English as we generally find it in his stories, had he received what is called a public education. It is often amusing to hear some very clever men who have never received such an education, talk about colleges and college learning. They have most magnificent notions upon the subject; and it is a hard matter to persuade them that they can write better sense, and put it into better language too, than the greater part of those who have been entered and graduated regularly. You may confess that such a course of instruction is of great benefit to the industrious, and no loss to the idle, even, that at college something is absorbed by every brain which is capable of being imbued at all with what is intellectual. This is not enough to allow. There is to these men an undefinable charm and change wrought within that circle into which they have never entered; and they conclude that they have little to do except to bear their inferiority like good christians. They must try something, however, which shall gloss over this inferiority; and they accordingly set themselves industriously to forming modes of talking and writing, such as never came from tongue or pen, learned or vulgar. They are made to suffer for all this; for what really grew out of self-distrust and humility, is commonly set down to affectation and pedantry. This is the best solution we can give of the cause of Brown's style, as great a man as he was.

We cannot quit Brown without one word upon the inward struggle he endured in deciding between the strong tendencies of his genius, and what he seemed half persuaded, notwithstanding his scruples, to have been his duty. He was educated for the bar, and obtained some distinction in his club for his management of the fictitious cases proposed there. We would say in passing, that we believe, after all, these clubs are not the places to determine a man's powers; and notwithstanding some eminent men first distinguished themselves in these mock contests, we have great doubts whether it is not quite as well for a man to fight his first battle on the field where nothing is allowed but keen steel and naked points. Physical and intellectual dexterity and power are very different things, and obtained by very different means. At any rate, Brown's time came, and then he hesitated, and then his friends talked, or by their marked silence pained him yet more. Unsatisfied in his own mind, and those whose good opinion he fain would have had being against him, he became harassed and dejected. There was something working within, the nature and power of which he did not then enough understand to follow without scruple. He still doubted; and when at last he did resolve, he felt not the relief and vigor of a resolved man; for he feared it might be the yielding of weakness, not the resolution of strength. It was his good fortune that the waking, instinctive energy of genius at length prevailed. Instead of living as only one of the multitude of keen and clever men at the bar, and then dying and being forgotten, he is going down with the history of our country as the earliest author of genius in our literature. Already this distinction is something; but it is to be yet greater. The writers of genius who may come up amongst us, instead of taking from his good name, will but bring to it fresh honor and reverence, for he will be called the father of all of them.

Let this struggle in the sensitive temperament of Brown, be a caution to parents and friends. A little more, and he would have gone to a still earlier grave, a disappointed and scarcely noted man. If a young man's bent be a strong one, so it be innocent, point out the hardships of the course he would take, if you will, but let him follow it. The father talks of his experience, as if one man's experience would serve alike for all. We are not all made after one pattern, or this would be no longer a world of trial and effort, of great failure and glorious success.

There are men, very kind men too, who would do good service to a man of genius, but then they must do it to suit themselves, not him. It is taken for granted that he is fantastic and wayward, merely because, as he differs in his intellectual powers, so does he in temperament and sympathies from the world at large. He must be made a useful citizen, however. Pegasus must be yoke-mate with donkey, or be turned out to shift for himself. Perhaps he submits; but, as every one might suppose, donkey proves the more serviceable beast, works and grows fat, while Pegasus is breaking down. Nor is this all. If the man of genius declines these well meant offers, he is sensible that he is looked upon as one who will not let you do him good if you would; and to the weight of his troubles and sorrows is added the feeling, that those who care most about him, mingle disappointment and disapprobation with their concern. This is a sad and comfortless thought to visit a mind, which, from its very nature, must dwell much alone and needs much of sympathy to take it from its solitude. There is, perhaps, no class more envied than men of genius; and it is natural enough that they should be, when estimated by their productions, and it is true, also, that they have times of high aspirations, and scenes of intellectual beauty and grandeur seen but dimly and at a distance by others; yet could the world see into their whole souls, it would hardly envy them so.

It may be thought that we have dwelt too long upon the faults of Brown, and that we are of an ungracious temper for so doing. We have taken no delight in this part of our work, for we reverence his genius and feel an affection for so kind and good a man. If we speak with all our hearts of what is excellent in a great man, we shall do him little harm by pointing out his defects, while at the same time we are doing good to multitudes. We are not of those who would pull down a stone upon the head of him who is but just raising a structure for his own fame; nor of those who are glad to see the barren sands drifting over the foundation which another was beginning to lay. Brown has built up his eternal pyramid, and laid him down to rest in it.

"Sermons and Tracts. . . . By W. E. Channing"

William Hazlitt*

Of the later American writers, who, besides Dr Channing, have acquired some reputation in England, we can only recollect Mr Washington Irving, Mr Brown, and Mr Cooper. To the first of these we formerly paid an ample tribute of respect; nor do we wish to retract a tittle of what we said on that occasion, or of the praise due to him for brilliancy, ease, and a faultless equability of style. Throughout his polished pages, no thought shocks by its extravagance, no word offends by vulgarity or affectation. All is gay, but guarded,—heedless, but sensitive of the smallest blemish. We cannot deny it—nor can we conceal it from ourselves or the world, if we would—that he is, at the same time, deficient in nerve and originality. Almost all his sketches are like patterns taken in silk paper from our classic writers;—tho traditional manners of the last age are still kept up (stuffed in glass cases) in Mr Irving's modern version of them. The only variation is in the transposition of dates; and herein the author is chargeable with a fond and amiable anachronism. He takes Old England for granted as he finds it described in our stock-books of a century ago—gives us a Sir Roger de Coverley in the year 1819, instead of the year 1709; and supposes old English hospitality and manners, relegated from the metropolis, to have taken refuge somewhere in Yorkshire, or the fens of Lincolnshire. In some sequestered spot or green savannah, we can conceive Mr Irving enchanted with the style of the wits of Queen Anne;—in the bare, broad, straight, mathematical streets of his native city, his busy fancy wandered through the blind alleys and huddled zig-zag sinuosities of London, and the signs of Lothbury and East-Cheap swung and creaked in his delighted ears. The air of his own country was too poor and thin to satisfy the pantings of youthful ambition; he gasped for British popularity,—he came, and found it. He was received, caressed, applauded, made giddy: the national politeness owed him some return, for he imitated, admired, deferred to us; and, if his notions were sometimes wrong, yet it was plain he thought of nothing else, and was ready to sacrifice every thing to obtain a smile or a look of approbation. It is true, he brought no new earth, no sprig of

*Reprinted from *Edinburgh Review*, 50 (October, 1829), 125–28. The essay continues to p. 144 of the *Edinburgh Review* but ceases to focus on Brown.

laurel gathered in the wilderness, no red bird's wing, no gleam from crystal lake or new-discovered fountain, (neither grace nor grandeur plucked from the bosom of this Eden-state like that which belongs to cradled infancy); but he brought us *rifaciméntos* of our own thoughts—copies of our favourite authors: we saw our self-admiration reflected in an accomplished stranger's eyes; and the lover received from his mistress, the British public, her most envied favours.

Mr Brown, who preceded him, and was the author of several novels which made some noise in this country, was a writer of a different stamp. Instead of hesitating before a scruple, and aspiring to avoid a fault, he braved criticism, and aimed only at effect. He was an inventor, but without materials. His strength and his efforts are convulsive throes—his works are a banquet of horrors. The hint of some of them is taken from Caleb Williams and St Leon, but infinitely exaggerated, and carried to disgust and outrage. They are full (to disease) of imagination,—but it is forced, violent, and shocking. This is to be expected, we apprehend, in attempts of this kind in a country like America, where there is, generally speaking, no *natural imagination*. The mind must be excited by overstraining, by pulleys and levers. Mr Brown was a man of genius, of strong passion, and active fancy; but his genius was not seconded by early habit, or by surrounding sympathy. His story and his interests are not wrought out, therefore, in the ordinary course of nature; but are, like the monster in Frankenstein, a man made by art and determined will. For instance, it may be said of him, as of Gawin Douglas, 'Of Brownies and Bogilis full is his Buik.' But no ghost, we will venture to say, was ever seen in North America. They do not walk in broad day; and the night of ignorance and superstition which favours their appearance, was long past before the United States lifted up their head beyond the Atlantic wave. The inspired poet's tongue must have an echo in the state of public feeling, or of involuntary belief, or it soon grows harsh or mute. In America, they are 'so well policied,' so exempt from the knowledge of fraud or force, so free from the assaults of *the flesh and the devil*, that in pure hardness of belief they hoot the *Beggar's Opera* from the stage: with them, poverty and crime, pickpockets and highwaymen, the lock-up-house and the gallows, are things incredible to sense! In this orderly and undramatic state of security and freedom from natural foes, Mr Brown has provided one of his heroes with a demon to torment him, and fixed him at his back;—but what is to keep him there? Not any prejudice or lurking superstition on the part of the American reader: for the lack of such, the writer is obliged to make up by incessant rodomontade, and facemaking. The want of genuine imagination is always proved by caricature: monsters are the growth, not of passion, but of the attempt forcibly to stimulate it. In our own unrivalled Novelist, and the great exemplar of this kind of writing, we see how ease and strength are united. Tradition and invention meet half way; and nature scarce knows how to distinguish them. The reason is, there is here an old and solid ground in previous manners and opinion for imagination to rest upon. The air of this bleak northern clime is filled with legendary lore: Not a castle without the stain of blood upon its floor or winding steps: not a glen without its ambush or its feat of arms: not a lake without its Lady! But the map of America is not historical; and, therefore, works of fiction do not take root in it; for the fiction, to be good for any thing, must not be in the author's mind, but belong to the age or country in which he lives. The genius of America is essentially mechanical and modern.

Papers on Literature and Art

Margaret Fuller*

We see we have omitted honoured names in this essay. We have not spoken of Brown, as a novelist by far our first in point of genius and instruction as to the soul of things. Yet his works have fallen almost out of print. It is their dark, deep gloom that prevents their being popular, for their very beauties are grave and sad. But we see that Ormond is being republished at this moment. The picture of Roman character, of the life and resources of a single noble creature, of Constantia alone, should make that book an object of reverence. All these novels should be republished; if not favorites, they should at least not be lost sight of, for there will always be some who find in such powers of mental analysis the only response to their desires. . . .

We rejoice to see these reprints [*Ormond* and *Weiland*] of Brown's novels, as we have long been ashamed that one who ought to be the pride of the country, and who is, in the higher qualities of the mind, so far in advance of our other novelists, should have become almost inaccessible to the public.

It has been the custom to liken Brown to Godwin. But there was no imitation, no second-hand in the matter. They were congenial natures, and whichever had come first might have lent an impulse to the other. Either mind might have been conscious of the possession of that peculiar vein of ore without thinking of working it for the mint of the world, till the other, led by accident, or overflow of feeling, showed him how easy it was to put the reveries of his solitary hours into words and upon paper for the benefit of his fellow men.

"My mind to me a kingdom is."

Such a man as Brown or Godwin has a right to say that. It is no scanty, turbid rill, requiring to be daily fed from a thousand others or from the clouds! Its plenteous source rushes from a high mountain between bulwarks of stone. Its course, even and full, keeps ever green its banks, and affords the means of life and joy to a million gliding shapes, that fill its deep waters, and twinkle above its golden sands.

*Reprinted from *Papers on Literature and Art* (1846; New York: Fowlers and Wells, 1852), pp. 142–50.

Life and Joy! Yes, Joy! These two have been called the dark masters, because they disclose the twilight recesses of the human heart. Yet their gravest page is joy compared with the mixed, shallow, uncertain pleasures of vulgar minds. Joy! because they were all alive and fulfilled the purposes of being. No sham, no imitation, no convention deformed or veiled their native lineaments, checked the use of their natural force. All alive themselves, they understood that there is no joy without truth, no perception of joy without real life. Unlike most men, existence was to them not a tissue of words and seemings, but a substantial possession.

Born Hegelians, without the pretensions of science, they sought God in their own consciousness, and found him. The heart, because it saw itself so fearfully and wonderfully made, did not disown its Maker. With the highest idea of the dignity, power and beauty of which human nature is capable, they had courage to see by what an oblique course it proceeds, yet never lose faith that it would reach its destined aim. Thus their darkest disclosures are not hobgoblin shows, but precious revelations.

Brown is great as ever human writer was in showing the self-sustaining force of which a lonely mind is capable. He takes one person, makes him brood like the bee, and extract from the common life before him all its sweetness, its bitterness, and its nourishment.

We say makes *him*, but it increases our own interest in Brown that, a prophet in this respect of a better era, he has usually placed this thinking royal mind in the body of a woman. This personage too is always feminine, both in her character and circumstances, but a conclusive proof that the term *feminine* is not a synonym for *weak*. Constantia, Clara Wieland, have loving hearts, graceful and plastic natures, but they have also noble thinking minds, full of resource, constancy, courage. The Marguerite of Godwin, no less, is all refinement, and the purest tenderness, but she is also the soul of honour, capable of deep discernment and of acting in conformity with the inferences she draws. The man of Brown and Godwin has not eaten of the fruit of the tree of knowledge and been driven to sustain himself by sweat of his brow for nothing, but has learned the structure and laws of things, and become a being, rational, benignant, various, and desirous of supplying the loss of innocence by the attainment of virtue. So his woman need not be quite so weak as Eve, the slave of feeling or of flattery: she also has learned to guide her helm amid the storm across the troubled waters.

The horrors which mysteriously beset these persons, and against which, so far as outward facts go, they often strive in vain, are but a representation of those powers permitted to work in the same way throughout the affairs of this world. Their demoniacal attributes only represent a morbid state of the intellect, gone to excess from want of balance with the other powers. There is an intellectual as well as a physical drunkenness, and which no less impels to crime. Carwin, urged on to use his ventriloquism, till the presence of such a strange agent awakened the seeds of fanaticism in the breast of Wieland, is in a state no more foreign to nature than that of the wretch executed last week, who felt himself drawn as by a spell to murder his victim because he had thought of her money and the pleasures it might bring him, till the feeling possessed his brain that hurls the gamester to ruin. The victims of such agency are like the soldier of the Rio Grande, who, both legs shot off and his life-blood rushing out with every pulse, replied serenely to his pitying comrades that "he had now that for which the soldier enlisted." The end of the drama is not in this world, and the fiction which rounds off the whole to harmony and felicity before the curtain falls, sins against truth, and deludes the reader. The Nelsons of the human race are all the more exposed to the assaults of fate that they are decorated with the badges of well-earned glory. Who, but feels as they fall in death, or rise again to a mutilated existence, that the end is not yet? Who, that thinks, but must feel that the recompense is, where Brown places it, in the accumulation of mental treasure, in the severe assay by fire that leaves the gold pure to be used sometime—somewhere.

Brown, man of the brooding eye, the teeming brain, the deep and fervent heart; if thy country prize thee not and has almost lost thee out of sight, it is that her heart is made shallow and cold, her eye dim, by the pomp of circumstance, the love of gross outward gain. She cannot long continue thus, for it takes a great deal of soul to keep a huge body from disease and dissolution. As there is more soul thou wilt be more sought, and many will yet sit down with thy Constantia to the meal and water on which she sustained her full and thoughtful existence, who could not endure the ennui of aldermanic dinners, or find any relish in the imitation of French cookery. To-day many will read the words, and some have a cup large enough to receive the spirit, before it is lost in the sand on which their feet are planted.

Brown's high standard of the delights of intellectual communion and of friendship correspond with the fondest hopes of early days. But in the relations of real life, at present, there is rarely more than one of the parties ready for such intercourse as he describes. On the one side there will be dryness, want of perception or variety, a stupidity unable to appreciate life's richest boon when offered to its grasp, and the finer nature is doomed to retrace its steps, unhappy as those who having force to raise a spirit cannot retain or make it substantial, and stretch out their arms only to bring them back empty to the breast.

"Fanaticism"

John Greenleaf Whittier*

There are occasionally deeds committed almost too horrible and revolting for publication. The tongue falters in giving them utterance; the pen trembles that records them. Such is the ghastly horror of a late tragedy in Edgecomb, in the State of Maine. A respectable and thriving citizen and his wife had been for some years very unprofitably engaged in brooding over the mysteries of the Apocalypse, and in speculations upon the personal coming of Christ and the temporal reign of the saints on earth,—a sort of Mahometan paradise, which has as little warrant in Scripture as in reason. Their minds of necessity became unsettled; they meditated self-destruction; and, as it appears by a paper left behind in the handwriting of both, came to an agreement that the husband should first kill his wife and their four children, and then put an end to his own existence. This was literally executed,—the miserable man striking off the heads of his wife and children with his axe, and then cutting his own throat.

Alas for man when he turns from the light of reason and from the simple and clearly defined duties of the present life, and undertakes to pry into the mysteries of the future, bewildering himself with uncertain and vague prophecies, Oriental imagery, and obscure Hebrew texts! Simple, cheerful faith in God as our great and good Father, and love of His children as our brethren, acted out in all relations and duties, is certainly best for this world, and we believe also the best preparation for that to come. Once possessed by the falsity that God's design is that man should be wretched and gloomy here in order to obtain rest and happiness hereafter; that the mental agonies and bodily tortures of His creatures are pleasant to Him; that, after bestowing upon us reason for our guidance, He makes it of no avail by interposing contradictory revelations and arbitary commands,—there is nothing to prevent one of a melancholic and excitable temperament from excesses so horrible as almost to justify the old belief in demoniac obsession.

Charles Brockden Brown, a writer whose merits have not yet been

*Reprinted from *The Prose Works of John Greenleaf Whittier*, vol. 7 (Boston and New York: Houghton, Mifflin and Company, 1889), 391–95. The essay originally appeared in the weekly newspaper, *The National Era*, June 1, 1848.

sufficiently acknowledged, has given a powerful and philosophical analysis of this morbid state of mind—this diseased conscientiousness, obeying the mad suggestions of a disordered brain as the injunctions of Divinity—in his remarkable story of *Wieland*. The hero of this strange and solemn romance, inheriting a melancholy and superstitious mental constitution, becomes in middle age the victim of a deep, and tranquil because deep, fanaticism. A demon in human form, perceiving his state of mind, wantonly experiments upon it, deepening and intensifying it by a fearful series of illusions of sight and sound. Tricks of jugglery and ventriloquism seem to his feverish fancies miracles and omens—the eye and the voice of the Almighty piercing the atmosphere of supernatural mystery in which he has long dwelt. He believes that he is called upon to sacrifice the beloved wife of his bosom as a testimony of the entire subjugation of his carnal reason and earthly affections to the Divine will. In the entire range of English literature there is no more thrilling passage than that which describes the execution of this baleful suggestion. The coloring of the picture is an intermingling of the lights of heaven and hell,—soft shades of tenderest pity and warm tints of unextinguishable love contrasting with the terrible outlines of an insane and cruel purpose, traced with the blood of murder. The masters of the old Greek tragedy have scarcely exceeded the sublime horror of this scene from the American novelist. The murderer confronted with his gentle and loving victim in her chamber; her anxious solicitude for his health and quiet; her affectionate caress of welcome; his own relentings and natural shrinking from his dreadful purpose; and the terrible strength which he supposes is lent him of Heaven, by which he puts down the promptings and yearnings of his human heart, and is enabled to execute the mandate of an inexorable Being,—are described with an intensity which almost stops the heart of the reader. When the deed is done a frightful conflict of passions takes place, which can only be told in the words of the author:—

> I lifted the corpse in my arms and laid it on the bed. I gazed upon it with delight. Such was my elation that I even broke out into laughter. I clapped my hands, and exclaimed, 'It is done! My sacred duty is fulfilled! To that I have sacrificed, O God, Thy last and best gift, my wife!'
>
> For a while I thus soared above frailty. I imagined I had set myself forever beyond the reach of selfishness. But my imaginations were false. This rapture quickly subsided. I looked again at my wife. My joyous ebullitions vanished. I asked myself who it was whom I saw. Methought it could not be my Catharine; it could not be the woman who had lodged for years in my heart; who had slept nightly in my bosom; who had borne in her womb and fostered at her breast the beings who called me father; whom I had watched over with delight and cherished with a fondness ever new and perpetually growing. It could not be the same!

The breath of heaven that sustained me was withdrawn, and I sunk into *mere man*. I leaped from the floor; I dashed my head against the wall; I uttered screams of horror; I panted after torment and pain. Eternal fire and the bickerings of hell, compared with what I felt, were music and a bed of roses.

I thank my God that this was transient; that He designed once more to raise me aloft. I thought upon what I had done as a sacrifice to duty, and was calm. My wife was dead; but I reflected that, although this source of human consolation was closed, others were still open. If the transports of the husband were no more, the feelings of the father had still scope for exercise. When remembrance of their mother should excite too keen a pang, I would look upon my children and be comforted.

While I revolved these things new warmth flowed in upon my heart. I was wrong. These feelings were the growth of selfishness. Of this I was not aware; and, to dispel the mist that obscured my perceptions, a new light and a new mandate were necessary.

From these thoughts I was recalled by a ray which was shot into the room. A voice spoke like that I had before heard: "Thou hast done well; but all is not done—the sacrifice is incomplete—thy children must be offered—they must perish with their mother!"

The misguided man obeys the voice; his children are destroyed in their bloom and innocent beauty. He is arrested, tried for murder, and acquitted as insane. The light breaks in upon him at last; he discovers the imposture which has controlled him; and, made desperate by the full consciousness of his folly and crime, ends the terrible drama by suicide.

Wieland is not a pleasant book. In one respect it resembles the modern tale of *Wuthering Heights:* it has great strength and power, but no beauty. Unlike that, however, it has an important and salutary moral. It is a warning to all who tamper with the mind and rashly experiment upon its religious element. As such, its perusal by the sectarian zealots of all classes would perhaps be quite as profitable as much of their present studies.

ORIGINAL
ESSAYS

The Matter and Manner of Charles Brockden Brown's *Alcuin*

Cathy N. Davidson*

I

Charles Brockden Brown's *Alcuin, A Dialogue* (1798) has long been regarded as one of its author's minor works and was not even published as a complete text until 1971.[1] The book was also early condemned, and some of Brown's contemporaries maintained that it should never have been published at all. For example, Brown's first biographer, Paul Allen, dismissed the arguments in this early dialogue as "dangerous novelties" and "ingenuous sophistry."[2] He also insisted that *Alcuin* was not representative of the moral, conscientious Brockden Brown whom he had known.[3] It was, instead, an aberration, an authorial slip that required some explanation or excuse: "Hence the ardour with which he speaks, unless the peculiarity of his character is known, unless his warm and sublimated fancy, his intense feelings are taken into consideration, will need an apology." Brown happily outgrew, Allen retrospectively maintained, his early radicalism, and "those plunging tenets and dangerous doctrines which he advanced in his first entry into public life, [became] gradually contracted as he mingle[d] with men and observe[d] human manners."[4] Allen even had to justify his own intention to bring before the public the previously unpublished Parts III and IV of *Alcuin:* "It was deemed proper to give a full and front view of such speculations, to show the arguments which ingenuous sophistry might urge against any existing establishment, and at the same time, how little mankind will be benefitted by the substitute recommended as a cure for such evils."[5] Furthermore, Allen implies that Brown himself might have come to recognize the true nature of his first production and so chose "silence," "guardedness," and "expressive caution" instead of loosing on the unwary world the remainder of a dangerous dialogue.[6]

*I wish to thank Professors Sydney J. Krause and S. W. Reid for making available to me the resources of the Kent State University Bibliographical and Textual Center, where the first complete, scholarly edition of *Alcuin* (which will appear as part of Volume VI of the CEAA/CSE Bicentennial Edition of Brown) is currently being prepared.

As circumstance would have it, Allen did not publish the final half of *Alcuin* either. That task fell to William Dunlap when he was commissioned to rework the materials in Allen's unfinished biography. Yet Dunlap probably shared his predecessor's misgivings, for he retained in his *Life of Charles Brockden Brown* essentially all of Allen's apologies.[7] Those misgivings also mark a change in Dunlap's estimation of *Alcuin*. In the 1790s Brown's fellow member of the New York Friendly Club had praised the dialogue.[8] But by 1815 when he completed his biography, Dunlap had renounced his earlier radicalism and felt compelled to condemn *Alcuin* in order to salvage the good name of his former friend.[9] These representative readers of the late eighteenth and early nineteenth century and perhaps even the older author himself all found it necessary to question or condemn *Alcuin*.[10]

But such reservations, like the work itself, surely reflect the changing tenor of the time in which these men all wrote. If *Alcuin* expresses the early idealism and something of the progressive (albeit confused) mood of the country in the years after the Revolutionary War and the signing of a new Constitution, the subsequent criticisms of *Alcuin* equally represent a mood of conservatism and retrenchment that followed quickly upon the heels of early revolutionary ardour.[11] Thus, if *Alcuin*, Brown's earliest major work and one of the most eloquent of the late eighteenth-century American discussions on the rights of women, is important in literary history as a "first," it is equally important in social history as a "last." Brown's initial publishing venture coincided with the end of an era and the climax of discussion on the "woman question." The publication of *Alcuin* came just as Americans began to regard that whole problematic subject with increasing suspicion and to view advocates of equality with moral indignation and even contempt. Brown himself, in 1803 and at the age of only 32, renounced his previous works and insisted that he "should enjoy a larger share of my own respect, at the present moment, if nothing had ever flowed from my pen, the production of which could be traced to me."[12] *Alcuin* was surely one of the former works that he then disavowed, for the issues debated in that dialogue were no longer considered to be the proper concerns of a respectable magazine editor and literary figure.

Much had changed between 1797 (when Brown was finishing *Alcuin*) and 1803 (when he penned his early palinode). As a number of commentators have noted, the prominence of equalitarian sentiments towards women in the last three decades of the eighteenth century constituted a fledgling feminism and even something of a political "movement."[13] Abigail Adams could voice her famous request that her husband "remember the ladies" in the new government. A number of Americans seriously debated the various aspects of the "woman question"—the advantages or disadvantages of female education; the form such education should take; what woman's role should be in the family, the society, and the political system. Prominent Americans such as Thomas Paine, Benjamin Rush, and Judith Sargent Murray addressed these issues. Almanacs, newspapers, and the majority of early American novels presented to the public different theories on woman's proper nature and proper place. Brown's interest in women's rights was hardly singular. He had, however, the misfortune to begin his career by joining in on a debate that would effectively end within months after his own contribution to the controversy was published. That debate, fueled in America by the publication of Mary Wollstonecraft's *A Vindication of the Rights of Woman* in 1792, foundered with the American publication of *Memoirs of Mary Wollstonecraft Godwin, Author of "A Vindication of the Rights of Woman"* in 1799.

Godwin's publication of his late wife's *Memoirs* was misguided to say the least. An account of the famous feminist's extramarital entanglements, of her bearing an illegitimate child, and of her belated marriage to Godwin could hardly serve the purpose Godwin intended and win converts to Wollstonecraft's cause. Rather, in both England and America the reaction to the book was immediately and violently negative.[14] "Wollstonecraftism," previously employed to describe even American feminism, at once became a term of contempt and, after 1799, typically described a woman of loose morals rather than a social theorist of libertarian principles. Anyone who championed women's rights was consequently morally suspect. Certainly this was one reason why Brown's first biographers felt compelled to testify to the author's moral rectitude and respect for matrimony. In *Alcuin* Brown had obviously drawn from both Godwin and Wollstonecraft. The serialization of *Alcuin* in the *Weekly Magazine* even bore the title, "Rights of Woman," which made the connection to Wollstonecraft unequivocal and irrevocable. Of course, we do not know positively why Brown did not publish the latter half of *Alcuin*.[15] Elihu Smith's untimely death in 1798 was surely one factor. But the publication the following year of Wollstonecraft's *Memoirs* may have been another. Any author aspiring to professional status at the very turn of the eighteenth century could hardly profit from being labeled a follower of the English feminist.[16]

Few desired that dubious distinction. After 1799 most prominent thinkers and writers disavowed any interest in women's rights. Novelists, most of whom overtly addressed the female reader and who wrote primarily about women characters, were particularly ready to deny any guilt by association. At least four novels written soon after the publication of the *Memoirs* actually denounced Wollstonecraft directly and by name.[17] But most writers simply avoided the language of women's rights and ignored the issue. Or, like the author of *Jane Talbot* and *Clara Howard*, if they portrayed capable women, these women were concerned with cultivating domestic virtues, not advocating political emancipation. For the most part, though, the issues raised in books like *Alcuin* simply were no longer issues for the readers of the early nineteenth century. This disregard persisted until about the third or fourth decades of that century when women like Catherine Beecher, Margaret Fuller, Elizabeth Oakes Smith, and Elizabeth Cady Stanton again began to raise questions about women's situation and women's prerogatives. But they then did so with terms appropriate for women in their "sphere." The language of those proper feminists bore little resemblance to the indignant tone of the Godwins.[18]

It is not surprising that the full text of *Alcuin*, all four parts, was first published as a complete volume in 1971. The language and tone found in Wollstonecraft, in Godwin, and—to a lesser extent—in Charles Brockden Brown was not widely heard again in America until the advent of the recent feminist movement. Thus Mrs. Carter, a proponent of female rights in *Alcuin*, can strike a particularly contemporary note. Consider, for example, how she images the dehumanization of women that she sees all around her: "Lawmakers thought as little of comprehending us in their code of liberty, as if we were pigs, or sheep" (p. 29). [19] Later she is equally graphic: "I am a woman. As such, I cannot celebrate the equity of that scheme of government which classes me with dogs and swine" (p. 33). The dog comparison explicitly invokes a concept of marriage that required a woman to promise "unlimited obedience": "She will be most applauded when she smiles with most perseverance on her oppressor, and when, with the undistinguishing attachment of a dog, no caprice or cruelty shall be able to estrange her affection" (pp. 24–25). Even when the imagery is human, it still conveys a dehumanized state. Succinctly put, so far as Mrs. Carter is concerned, "females are slaves" (p. 25).

But her rhetoric, however modern it may seem, still addresses the questions commonly considered in numerous late eighteenth-century debates: the need for female education; the alleged moral superiority of women; the division of labor along gender lines and the relative hardships of man's versus woman's work; the justice of barring women from the professions; woman's legal handicaps and especially her loss of property and autonomy after marriage; the very character of marriage; the advisability of divorce; the advantages and disadvantages of common property; the basic nature of each sex and what the concomitant social order should be. Of course many of these questions, by their very nature, remain largely unanswered today and are again a matter of general concern. If the caprice of political and social change made *Alcuin* an embarrassment in 1803 or 1815, another change in social climate has made it, belatedly, acceptable once more. Ironically, the biographers' apologies themselves now require sociological explanation and apology. Finally *Alcuin* can stand—or fall—on its own.

II

I have thus far discussed *Alcuin* only as a piece of polemical writing which arose from the political and social debates that took place during the last part of the eighteenth century and which is, in many ways, representative of those debates. But that is only half the story. As I shall now argue at some length, *Alcuin* anticipates Brown's later novels and is consequently at least as noteworthy for its manner as for its matter. To begin with, the dialogue technique approximates the conversational tone and the pseudoepistolary form Brown would later employ in his fiction. *Alcuin* also provides an early illustration of how Brown could shape his narrative to serve the two separate ends of moral didacticism and psychological realism. Brown, it should be recalled, defined himself as a "story-telling moralist" and even as a "moral painter."[20] Later he would strike a more effective balance between story and moral. But even in *Alcuin* we can see how Brown begins to fit his method to his meaning by manipulating points of view and thereby suggesting complex interrelationships between a character's psychology and the same character's moral pronouncements. Finally, in *Alcuin* we see early signs of novelistic dialogue, of Brown's ability to portray realistic interactions between characters, to explore the emotions implicit in those encounters, and to employ a language appropriate to the situations described. But despite such adumbrations of things to come, *Alcuin* is no masterpiece. This is one case where the sum of the parts is more significant than the limitations of the whole, and we can profitably give credit to separate successful aspects of *Alcuin* without conferring "major" status on the entire production. Sometimes, indeed, the successes are simply the obverse of more obvious faults, which is exactly what one would expect from an apprentice writer still working out his basic techniques.

Let us look, for example, at the opening of the dialogue. It definitely drags. Some six pages of text precede the first spoken words, the inelegant opening question, "Pray, Madam, are you a federalist?" This sudden and somewhat presumptuous query hardly presages a dialogue that will center on the question of the rights of women. Yet such stalling has a purpose.[21] What will become the dialogue begins as a monologue in which we learn a good deal about the character of one of the participants. We see Alcuin through his own eyes. He is an overworked, underpaid school teacher who reflects upon his occupation with a combination of self-pity and redeeming irony: "My trade preserves me from starving and nakedness, but not from the discomforts of scarcity, or the disgrace of shabbiness. Money, to give me leisure; and exercise, to give me health; these are all my lot denies: in all other respects, I am the happiest of mortals" (pp. 7–8). But this character soon shows himself to be more limited than he thinks he is.

Alcuin would emulate his eighth-century namesake and be a philosophical teacher who leads others to truth. More accurately, he is only an aspiring philosopher who is also something of a dilettante, something of a pedant, and something of an idle dreamer. His imagination allows him to contemplate the hardly original yet "seducing suppositions of, 'if I were a king,' or, 'if I were a lover' " (p. 7). His imagination also allows him to people his mental world with the characters of his "fancy." But, he apologizes, his quotidian life limits that peopling: "like some other dealers in fiction," his "stock" of characters is "slender" because his "experience" of other human beings is slight (p. 9). Unfortunately, his lowly profession and his poverty, attested to by his shabby garb, prevent him from fully enjoying the "pleasures of society." Furthermore, since he finds books "insipid" and "hate[s] a lecturer," he particularly laments the fact that he can seldom enjoy discourse with other intellectuals. Conversation, he maintains, is the most useful and pleasurable way to pass one's time. In short, Brown portrays Alcuin as a budding intellectual yearning for the opportunity to encounter similarly enlightened souls. Only such a character would engage in the long debate that constitutes *Alcuin*. So the meandering beginning might be an artistic fault but, if it is a flaw, it is one that shows the author to be as concerned with the logic of the controlling structure as he is with the logic of the contained debate.

The controlling structure is rooted in the nature of the participants in the dialogue. Both Alcuin and Mrs. Carter must be complex yet believable characters. To achieve this end Brown attempts to show in each different and conflicting qualities. Thus Alcuin is an intriguing combination of the naive and malleable Arthur Mervyn, the rational Henry Pleyel, the romantic Philip Stanley, and, in Parts III and IV, even anticipates the visionary radicalism of Henry Colden. These qualities of naivete, rationality, romanticism, and incipient radicalism keep the dialogue in motion—frequently in the "careless, and unfettered," the "fugitive and brilliant" (p. 9) manner that Alcuin himself sees as a necessary attribute of interesting conversation. But equally important to the progress of the dialogue are the differences between the busy young man and the widow, Mrs. Carter. Unlike the overworked Alcuin, Mrs. Carter "was always at home" (p. 4). She tends house for her brother who—like Alcuin—is too occupied supporting himself and presumably his sister to cultivate conversation. Again like Alcuin, this physician-brother aspires to the higher pursuits of the mind. He is a would-be " man of letters" but one who "finds little leisure from the engagements of a toilsome profession" (p. 4).

Once more seemingly extraneous information serves a valid function. These details establish the crucial social difference between this widow and her brother, between Alcuin and the widow. Men of talent, teachers and doctors, are seemingly wasted in their tedious professions, while a housekeeper, who initially is thought to have no particular merit, has the leisure to conduct an intellectual "lyceum." Brown thus indicates some of the circumstances and the prejudices of the participants before the debate begins. Because of this prolegomenon, the reader can better understand not only the social framework of the argument but the more underlying psychological considerations (jealousy, envy, bitterness) that partly motivate supposedly rational discourse. The touch of the later novelist is obvious in this early work.

Still another contrast is delineated before the promised debate. Alcuin is shown to be not only inexperienced but rather gauche. This awkward young schoolmaster who yearns to mingle in intellectual society comically anticipates, in his anxiety lest he give offense, the J. Alfred Prufrock of another era. Uncertain as to what manners make the enlightened man, he "pondered . . . the mighty task of hitting on a right movement at entrance, and a right posture in sitting, and on the perplexing mysteries of tea-table decorum" (pp. 6–7). In contrast, Mrs. Carter, "the superintende[nt] of the teatable" (p. 4), capably dispenses tea and cake and ices. She presides regally over her "empire of cleanliness and order" (p. 5). But the self-conscious schoolteacher with his threadbare jacket and worsted stockings still dismisses the older lady's role as "mistress of the ceremonies" by seeing her as some lower laborer such as a "waiter at an inn, or the porter of the theatre" (p. 5). We have difference in sex, difference in age, and now a presumed difference in social status. Inadvertently, Alcuin shows himself to be as much a snob of the spirit as he *assumes*, with no evidence, that Mrs. Carter will be a snob of the more expected order.

She is not. The subsequent dialogue demonstrates that Mrs. Carter does not at all correspond to Alcuin's comforting presuppositions. Despite the lamentable educational system for women, this woman is well read. Despite her being barred from politics, she is politically astute and soon shows that Alcuin's initial question—"Are you a federalist?"—was petty in the extreme. While he wonders which party she supports, she questions not only the party system but the whole system of government that perpetuates discriminations based on class, gender, and race.

Alcuin desired a modestly obliging auditor with the "docility to listen" (p. 4) to his advanced opinions. The self-important schoolmaster encounters an intelligent, articulate woman who can teach him a lesson or two. Yet these debaters are not so different as one might expect. Like Alcuin, Mrs. Carter appreciates the opportunity to engage in rational exchange, for she especially wants to be taken seriously. As she tells Alcuin, despite the stream of intellectuals through her household, she has never previously been invited to participate in a serious political discussion. Alcuin's class apparently bars him from associating with society's most enlightened members. Mrs. Carter's sex bars her. So Mrs. Carter is intellectually angry, while Alcuin is socially uncouth. How appropriate that his brash question—one an eighteenth-century gentleman would never put to a lady—finally initiates the dialogue on the rights of women.

Like Alcuin, Mrs. Carter also prefigures a number of the characters in Brown's later fiction. She resembles both Clara Wieland and Achsa Fielding, rational, capable, and unconventional women who impress us with their verbal dexterity. Similar to Constantia Dudley in *Ormond* and Mary Wilmot in *Clara Howard*, she aspires to high moral standards. But despite her abilities, she seems trapped in her lyceum. As a perpetual superintendent of the tea table, she can well lament her lack of opportunity to experience the possibilities of social freedom. Ironically, she even aspires to the lowly opportunities that Alcuin claims he despises. Yet it is obvious that Alcuin, for all his rhetoric, would hardly exchange places with her. Indeed, he would not happily allow her to enter his "demeaning" profession.

Alcuin's naivete—perhaps hypocrisy is the more accurate word—is revealed graphically at the end of the first half of the dialogue (the portion published during Brown's lifetime). We remember that Alcuin initially envied Mrs. Carter's leisurely life and complained of his own tedious occupation. When Mrs. Carter, however, maintains that women would be happier if they were financially independent and further argues that this independence is impossible when women are barred from all professions and made to be the "property" of their fathers and husbands, Alcuin objects. In that protest Brown captures the paternalistic and patronizing tone of the "haves" who seem to know precisely what is good for the "have nots," and who know this far better than the "have nots"—misguided souls who would surely not complain if they really knew what they were asking for. Alcuin goes on to eulogize woman's "real" role as "household deity," as mother "pressing a charming babe to her bosom," and as "my companion in the paths of love, or poetry, or science" (p. 40). The tone here is remarkably different from the earlier tone with which he dismissed Mrs. Carter as a mere functionary, the lowly housekeeper. He now extolls her present status—the status quo—so that he can condemn by contrast the role to which she aspires. As lover, wife, and mother, a woman is exalted; as secretary, lawyer, judge, or senator, she is ludicrous. Alcuin ends his argument with another variation of that same theme. Mrs. Carter should be happy that she does not have to endure the sordid deceitfulness of the world of men. Woman's exclusion from the crass world of work allows her to be ultimately superior to man, not inferior as Mrs. Carter argues. Again Brown deploys the circular logic that terminates debate by begging the question. In this sense, Alcuin, like such later villains as Carwin or Ormond, exhibits not intelligence but the perversion of intelligence. Alcuin, of course, is no Ormond. He is harmless. But he can argue with the duplicity of the later villains. Changing terms, twisting the meaning of words so that "inferior" and "superior" both mean their opposite, Alcuin makes the worse cause seem the better and so shows himself to be more a sophist than a philosopher.

III

Only a small circle of the author's friends were treated to the remainder of the dialogue in which we see that Alcuin's argument at the end of Part II is by no means Brown's last word on the subject. It is not even Alcuin's last word. Once more Brown the novelist transcends Brown the polemicist and stays true to his characters by having them stray from their first line of argument. Part II ends with the participants in the dialogue polarized. But in Parts III and IV the initial positions of these two characters are reversed. They are reversed, however, in a manner which portends the type of synthesis that regularly occurs in Brown's novels. The debate abandoned in stalemate is taken up a week later. Yet Alcuin, in the intervening time, has changed his tune entirely. He insists that he has spent his week in the "paradise of women." He has more likely spent it rehashing his conversation with Mrs. Carter and trying to imagine a society founded on the principles that he believes she upholds. To atone for any previous social backwardness, he will now show her how advanced his views can be. The result, however, is not Mrs. Carter's utopia but William Godwin's (as presented in the first edition of the *Enquiry Concerning Political Justice*).[22] And at this point we can better understand why Brown earlier portrayed Alcuin as a dreamer of limited vision who indulged his imagination mostly on the basis of borrowed fantasies.[23] He has borrowed the wrong fantasy.

Alcuin proudly relates his vision of an ideal social order, whereupon Mrs. Carter tuts him for his visionary fancy. "Fancy," however radical, changes none of the real conditions to which she objected. So she has a "hearty aversion" (p. 44) to such "mysteries," which "perhaps, may be poetry, but though pleasing [they] had better be dispensed with" (p. 48). She is not the utopian dreamer that he imagined her to be. Suspecting that he has nothing concrete to propose, she wishes "merely to obtain the sum of [his] information" (p. 48). In brief, her pragmatic common sense turns the debate completely around. Again Brown effectively exploits the dramatic possibilities of the dialogue form. The erstwhile stodgy and conservative schoolmaster is now filled with zeal and expects others to accede immediately to the new truths he thinks he has discovered. The woman who could so intelligently articulate the injustices of her society has seemingly become staid and officious. She wants the facts, only the facts.

Alcuin does not comply with Mrs. Carter's request. For some twenty pages he recounts his visionary explorations in the paradise of women. While he does so, monologue only masquerades as dialogue, dialogue between Alcuin and his utopian guide. Yet Alcuin, even in this "interior dialogue," still remains true to the character we saw in Parts I and II. And it is here, I would suggest, that Brown achieves one of his most subtle narrative effects. We have previously had two Alcuins—the indulgent self-portrait that Alcuin draws of himself and the somewhat less flattering picture presented by Brown. Now we encounter a third picture, the visionary Alcuin who participates in the interior dialogue that Alcuin the character, at this point describes. Alcuin, recounting the dialogue with his imaginary guide, details the experience that has rendered him, he believes, radical. But Brown knows better. He has the Alcuin whom Alcuin portrays correspond to the same Alcuin who we, as readers, have seen all along. Within the Godwinian fantasy a rather priggish and often astonishingly obtuse young man fumblingly attempts to understand a society in which he can discern none of the "normal" gradations of class, gender, race, occupation—precisely those discriminations the justice of which was debated in Parts I and II. This Alcuin is only a tourist in the utopia that he would claim as his own.

Alcuin also undergoes a common experience for the tourist. At times neither he nor his guide to the visionary world through which he travels can understand the other, so different are their basic assumptions. For example, Alcuin simply cannot believe that, in the paradise of women, sexual differences do not somehow correspond to social differences: "As far as I could discover they were distinguished by no peculiarities of manners or dress" (p. 49). His guide, on the other hand, finds in Alcuin's description of America "monstrous" gender distinctions that have been pursued, the guide maintains, to the point of "common madness": "One would imagine that among you, one sex had more arms, or legs, or senses than the other. Among us there is no such inequity" (p. 61). In Alcuin's insistence that some sexual bias must exist he also finds evidence that this schoolmaster is really a very slow learner who requires an explanation of the physiological differences between the sexes. At least three times he is ready to launch into a brief lecture on the birds and bees in answer to Alcuin's questions about how the envisioned society distinguishes male from female: "You question me as to the existence of that concerning which it is impossible for you to be ignorant. You cannot at this age be a stranger to the origin of human existence" (p. 65). There are other similar exclamations of incredulity voiced by both parties, all of which demonstrate that even though Alcuin put together this paradise, he remains, on a deeper level, uncomfortably within it—the initiate uninitiated.

His implicit reservations are succeeded by Mrs. Carter's explicit ones.[24] She resoundingly rejects his paradise of women: "A class of reasoners has lately arisen, who aim at the deepest foundation of civil society. Their addresses to the understanding have been urged with no despicable skill. . . . The journey that you have lately made, I merely regard as an excursion into their visionary world" (p. 68). She is not at all pleased by the way the schoolmaster has embraced what was earlier her cause, for he has pursued her ideas, she suspects, not to their logical conclusion but to their reductio ad absurdum. In short, she is even less of a Godwinian than Alcuin. One can support the rights of women, she implies, without overthrowing American republicanism. One can be a reformer, she insists, without being a radical. After her remarks, we hear no more of paradise.

Perhaps this is because the subject of paradise finally impinges on the subject of sexuality, and neither Alcuin nor Mrs. Carter can be comfortable with this topic. As Nancy Rice has pointed out, one of Brown's effective novelistic touches is to have his two supposedly rational participants in the debate both act like blushing adolescents as soon as discussion leads to the question of sexuality.[25] They fidget, bluster, and equivocate, both too fastidious to want to overstep the bonds of propriety—even for the sake of enlightened discourse. Mrs. Carter tries to assure Alcuin that she can consider such things calmly. But she cannot. Instead, she launches into a polemic on the virtues of marriage, now sounding even more conservative than previously.

The remainder of the dialogue is something of a mishmash, with each of the two participants—by turns—sounding sometimes less, sometimes more conservative than the other. Thus Mrs. Carter righteously upholds the sanctity of matrimony as an institution until Alcuin recalls her earlier invectives against marriage. She then repeats some accusations from the first half of the debate, especially the charge that marriage "renders the female a slave to the man" and "leaves the woman destitute of property" (p. 71). Whereupon Alcuin also reverts to his original position, to his former debating tactics, and advances the unlikely counterclaim that marriage does not leave the wife without possessions but rather makes her husband "nothing but a steward" of her property (p. 72). This is the same question-begging we witnessed earlier, and the reader senses that the debate is finally winding down to its conclusion.

Alcuin, in the privacy of his own home, could envision one standard version of the late eighteenth-century radical's utopia. But telling of that vision he cast himself as a doubting—and dull—sceptic, and soon returns, in his second exchange with Mrs. Carter, to his role of stodgy schoolman and slippery logician. Mrs. Carter, on the one hand, advances far-reaching criticisms of eighteenth-century sexual inequality but, on the other, she also remains true to her social class and never considers anything so radical as abolishing marriage or ignoring sexual differences. So the debate is sometimes cumbersome and unclear precisely because the characters of its participants are maintained. Alcuin's subsequent behavior is consistent with his first appearance. He is someone whose fancy is far more unfettered than his principles and behavior. Thus he early could rail against class prejudice and then self-consciously and self-pityingly lament his worsted stockings and unpowdered locks, just those amenities of class he pretended to be above. Similarly, Mrs. Carter demands radical changes yet is appalled at radicalism. (One can almost hear her intone, "I'm not a women's libber, but . . .").

On that ambiguous note the debate soon ends. The two conclude an argument in which Godwinian principles have been repudiated by embracing a Wollstonecraftian definition of marriage articulated by Mrs. Carter:[26]

> Marriage is an union founded on free and mutual consent. It cannot exist without friendship. It cannot exist without personal fidelity. As soon as the union ceases to be spontaneous it ceases to be just. This is the sum. If I were to talk for months,

I could add nothing to the completeness of this definition.
(p. 88)

These, the last words of *Alcuin, A Dialogue*, seem to please both parties. They, and we, have come a long way from the opening question of "Are you a federalist?"

IV

Just where we end up is, however, another question. As I have already suggested, Alcuin's paradise of women does not necessarily represent Brown's early views on the problem of the rights of women. Although Godwin's utopia is utilized, nowhere in *Alcuin* is it affirmed. Indeed, neither participant in the debate agrees with Godwin, and any other conveniently available radical utopia would have served Brown's purposes as well as Godwin's ideas did. Such observations suggest that Brown employed the dialogue form to explore ideas, not to advance or to substantiate them. More to the point, the dialogue form itself virtually precludes our seeking in *Alcuin* Brown's own theories. As I have shown, most of the ideas suggested are either mutually contradictory or they are abjured by their original proponent. Is Brown lurking behind the conservative schoolmaster we see in Parts I and II or behind the revolutionary Godwinian visionary we partly see in Parts III and IV? Does he share the views espoused by the sharp-tongued reformer Mrs. Carter in the first half of the dialogue or does he identify with the more moderate Mrs. Carter who briefly defends propriety in the second half? If ideas are espoused in somewhat bigamous fashion by Alcuin or Mrs. Carter, that does not necessarily wed them also to Brown. What is important in the dialogue is not so much the circumventions around the loci of debate but the skill with which Brown presents developing—and backtracking—thought and delineates the two characters who discuss ideas, who advance, retreat, reformulate, revise, reconsider, and in other ways engage in real discourse. Within the confines of the dialogue form, Brown creates believable characters who are not totally predictable: who have distinguishing self-doubts, small hypocrisies, personal blind spots, petty jealousies, and uncertain convictions.

For all its clumsiness, repetition, and more than occasional dullness, *Alcuin* thus anticipates better things to come. As Paul Witherington has suggested, one theme runs throughout all of Brown's fiction, through works as superficially disparate as *Wieland* and *Clara Howard*. That overall theme is the search for values and the questioning of values in a rapidly changing world.[27] I would suggest that *Alcuin* explores the same territory. Not a tract but a true dialogue, *Alcuin* neither propounds nor refutes Godwin and Wollstonecraft. Brown can present conflicting or internally contradictory positions without feeling obliged to resolve fully the issues raised, and he certainly does not affirm one extreme. In this respect, his literary achievements do not fully range from the radical *Alcuin* to the highly conservative *Jane Talbot*. Instead, my reading of *Alcuin* supports critics such as Warner Berthoff and David H. Hirsch who maintain that all of Brown's works explore a kind of middle way, a synthesis which ideally arises from the confrontation of extremes.[28] Even in *Alcuin*, each character is countered by the other and the dialogue ends with a definition that itself can seem another stalemate and a starting point for future debate. Brown apparently seeks some synthesis between the rhetorics of revolution and reaction, between the dramatic happenings in France in the late 1790s and the disturbing tendency of Americans to ape British manners and mores, between the political philosophies (if such a term apply) set forth in the edicts of Carnot and those of Peter Porcupine (both of which are mentioned in the first portion of *Alcuin*).[29] What Robert E. Hemenway and Joseph Katz observe of the fiction also applies to the first dialogue: "Charles Brockden Brown always was torn between a drive for social responsibility and an imagination that persistently envisioned alternative behaviors."[30] *Alcuin* seems to be precisely this balancing act between responsibility and radicalism. That balancing act necessarily leaves many major questions unanswered, which is perhaps just what the author intended. For in *Alcuin*, Brown begins his long consideration of the ways in which human beings can interact and communicate (or fail to communicate); of the strengths and weaknesses of both radicalism and conservatism, rationality and sentimentalism, intellect and emotion—a debate he continued, in various forms, throughout all of his later major work.

Notes

1. Charles Brockden Brown, *Alcuin: A Dialogue*, ed. Lee R. Edwards (New York: Grossman, 1971). Edwards's "Afterword," pp. 92–93, provides a concise survey of the publishing history of *Alcuin*.

2. Paul Allen, *The Life of Charles Brockden Brown*, ed. Charles E. Bennett (Delmar, New York: Scholars' Facsimiles and Reprints, 1975), pp. 107 and 105. Another reprint of Allen's biography, this one under the title of *The Late Charles Brockden Brown*, has also recently appeared, edited and with a fine introduction by Robert E. Hemenway and Joseph Katz (Columbia, S.C.: J. Faust, 1976). For the relation of Allen's biography to William Dunlap's, traditionally thought of as Brown's first biography, see the introductions to the editions cited in this note.

3. For example, Allen assures the reader that "none entertained higher ideas of the sanctity" of marriage than Brockden Brown (p. 106).

4. Allen, p. 71.

5. Allen, p. 105.

6. Allen, p. 107.

7. William Dunlap, *The Life of Charles Brockden Brown: Together with Selections from the Rarest of his Printed Works, from the Original Letters, and from his Manuscripts Before Unpublished* (Philadelphia: James P. Parke, 1815). Dunlap, it should be noted, was compelled by his printer to use many of Allen's unpublished plates. This fact might have prompted him to retain as his own reservations he did not fully share. Yet in other cases in

which he disagreed with Allen, Dunlap either insisted on printing his own views or substantially altered, through small changes in wording, his predecessor's meaning. It is therefore likely, even on the basis of the text itself, that Dunlap meant what he printed regarding *Alcuin*.

8. In August of 1797 Dunlap read portions of *Alcuin* and remarked, in his diary, that "there is much truth philosophical accuracy and handsome writing in the essay" [sic]. See *Diary of William Dunlap, 1766–1839*, ed. Dorothy C. Barck (New York: New York Historical Society, 1931), p. 133.

9. Thus Oral Sumner Coad, in *William Dunlap: A Study of His Life and Works and of His Place in Contemporary Culture* (New York: The Dunlap Society, 1917), observes that Dunlap "had undergone a change of heart since the days of Godwinian heresy. He had given up his radicalism as had Brown several years before his death" (p. 100).

10. One important exception among Brown's acquaintants was Dr. Elihu Hubbard Smith. Smith enthusiastically sponsored the publication of Parts I and II of *Alcuin* and, when he read the remaining portions in April of 1798, stated: "They merit my applause." Smith, however, died that same year, before he could decide whether to publish Parts III and IV of the dialogue. See *The Diary of Elihu Hubbard Smith (1771–1798)*, ed. James E. Cronin (Philadelphia: American Philosophical Society, 1973), p. 439.

11. Probably the best discussion of the way Brown's writing reflects the uncertain climate of America's 1790s is William Hedge's "Charles Brockden Brown and the Culture of Contradictions," *EAL*, 9 (1974), 107–42. See also David Lee Clark, *Brockden Brown and the Rights of Women*, Univ. of Texas Bulletin, No. 2212 (Austin: Univ. of Texas Press, 1922), pp. 31–44.

12. Charles Brockden Brown, "The Editor's Address to the Public," *The Literary Magazine and American Register*, 1 (October 1803), p. 4.

13. An overview of this debate can be found in Mary Sumner Benson's *Women in Eighteenth-Century America* (New York: Columbia Univ. Press, 1935). See also the first chapter of Barbara J. Berg's *The Remembered Gate: Origins of American Feminism* (New York: Oxford Univ. Press, 1978).

14. See R. M. Janes, "On the Reception of Mary Wollstonecraft's *A Vindication of the Rights of Woman*," *Journal of the History of Ideas*, 39 (April–June, 1978), 293–302; Patricia Jewell McAlexander, "The Creation of the American Eve: The Cultural Dialogue on the Nature and Role of Women in Late-Eighteenth-Century America," *EAL*, 9 (1975), 252–66; and Marcelle Thiebaux, "Mary Wollstonecraft in Federalist America: 1791–1802," in *The Evidence of the Imagination: Studies of Interactions between Life and Art in English Romantic Literature*, ed. Donald H. Reiman, et. al. (New York: New York Univ. Press, 1978), pp. 195–245.

15. David Lee Clark, in *Charles Brockden Brown: Pioneer Voice of America* (Durham: Duke Univ. Press, 1952), p. 125, suggests that Parts III and IV of *Alcuin* went unpublished because they received so little public notice, at which point Brown decided his real talents were for novel writing. Harry R. Warfel, in *Charles Brockden Brown: American Gothic Novelist* (Gainesville: Univ. of Florida Press, 1949), p. 82, states that the final two parts were not published "because of unfavorable comments." More recently, in "Charles Brockden Brown's Pursuit of a Realistic Feminism," Diss. Ball State 1971, Judith Ann Cunningham theorizes that Brown himself censored the final portions of *Alcuin* since by 1798 he had already "lost many of his radical ideas" (p. 132).

16. As early as August 1, 1799 (only sixteen months after the publication of *Alcuin*, Parts I and II), a reviewer ("L.M.") in Brown's *The Monthly Magazine and American Review*, pp. 330–35, eulogized the Wollstonecraft he or she had earlier known, but was "shocked, and even disgusted" by the *Memoirs*.

17. Wollstonecraft is denounced in Benjamin Silliman, *Letters of Shahcoolen, a Hindu Philosopher, Residing in Philadelphia* (Boston, 1802); Helena Wells, *Constantia Neville; or,*

The West Indian (London, 1800); and two books by Sarah [S.S.B.K.] Wood, *Dorval, or the Speculator* (Portsmouth, N.H., 1801) and *Amelia; or, The Influence of Virtue* (Portsmouth, N.H., 1802).

18. See Susan P. Conrad, *Perish the Thought: Intellectual Women in Romantic America, 1830–1860* (New York: Oxford Univ. Press, 1976); Nancy F. Cott, *The Bonds of Womanhood: "Woman's Sphere" in New England, 1780–1835* (New Haven: Yale Univ. Press, 1977); and Kathryn Kish Sklar, *Catharine Beecher: A Study in American Domesticity* (New Haven: Yale Univ. Press, 1973).

19. Donald A. Ringe, in a review in *EAL*, 8 (1974), 310–12, points out some of the textual deficiencies of Edwards's edition of *Alcuin*. Nevertheless, since this is currently the only complete text we have of the four parts of *Alcuin*, my quotations are taken from Edwards's edition, with page references indicated parenthetically throughout my essay.

20. Brown refers to himself as a "story-telling moralist" in his letter "To the Editor" accompanying the extract of "Sky Walk" published in the *Weekly Magazine*, March 24, 1798, pp. 228–31, and reprinted in Harry R. Warfel, *The Rhapsodist and Other Uncollected Writings* (New York: Scholars' Facsimiles and Reprints, 1943), p. 135. In his address "To the Public" at the beginning of *Edgar Huntly* (1799; rpt. Port Washington, N.Y.: Kennikat Press, 1963), Brown calls himself a "moral painter" (p. 3).

21. Warfel, in *Charles Brockden Brown*, notes that *Alcuin* "begins as fiction, and only after some vacillation does it settle into the dialogue form" (p. 82). Clark, in *Brockden Brown and the Rights of Women*, condemns the "fourteen dreary pages of introduction" but also notes that the "very dullness and narrow outlook of this prologue . . . stand in striking contrast to the liberal views that follow" (p. 38). I would suggest that Brown intended this contrast for quasi-fictional purposes.

22. Alcuin's paradise most resembles the concepts set forth in Book VIII, chapters v–ix of the First Edition (1793) of William Godwin's *Enquiry Concerning Political Justice and its Influence on Morals and Happiness*. See F.E.L. Priestley's edition of the text (1798; rpt. Toronto: Univ. of Toronto Press, 1946), II, 495–519 and textual notes on III, 218–224. (Priestley's is a photographic facsimile of the third corrected edition with variant readings of the first and second editions.) Godwin subsequently (and apparently after his marriage to Wollstonecraft) considerably modified his view of marriage.

23. Alcuin, who we see from the outset as a rather weak character, here acts true to form. He not only adopts Mrs. Carter's position but, like an overzealous convert, he even goes her one better and maintains it more vociferously than she, In this respect, Alcuin foreshadows Arthur Mervyn who, as a number of critics have noted, is ever eager to snap up the ideas and sentiments of others. See especially Michael Davitt Bell, " 'The Double-Tongued Deceiver': Sincerity and Duplicity in the Novels of Charles Brockden Brown," *EAL*, 9 (1974), 156–58 and p. 163, n. 28 and n. 29.

24. Jane T. Flanders, in "Charles Brockden Brown and William Godwin: Parallels and Divergencies," Diss. Wisconsin 1965, pp. 98–99, suggests that Alcuin's "paradise of women" is set up almost as a straw man for Mrs. Carter to refute, thereby allowing Brown to refute Godwin's views especially as they pertain to marriage.

25. Nancy Rice, "Alcuin," *Massachusetts Review*, 14 (1973), 807–09.

26. The concluding definition of marriage could be derived not only from Wollstonecraft's *A Vindication of the Rights of Woman* but also from her earlier work, *Thoughts on the Education of Daughters* (London: Joseph Johnson, 1787), in which she asserts, at length, that "love, unsupported by esteem, must soon expire" (p. 83).

27. Paul Witherington, "Brockden Brown's Other Novels: *Clara Howard* and *Jane Talbot*," *NCF*, 29 (1974), 257–71.

28. For example, Charles C. Cole, Jr., "Brockden Brown and the Jefferson Administration," *Pennsylvania Magazine of History and Biography*, 72 (1948), 253–63, contends that Brown, while writing his novels, changed from a radical Jeffersonian to a conservative

Federalist. But two essays by Warner Berthoff refute, from different standpoints, the "conversion" theory of Brown's life and letters. Cf. "'A Lesson on Concealment': Brocken Brown's Method in Fiction," *PQ*, 37 (1958), 45–57; and "Brockden Brown: The Politics of the Man of Letters," *Serif*, 3 (1966), 3–11. David H. Hirsch presents a similar view in "Charles Brockden Brown as a Novelist of Ideas," *Books at Brown*, 20 (1965), 165–84, as did a very early commentator on Brown, G. C. Verplanck, in his essay "Charles Brockden Brown," *North American Review*, 9 (1819), 58–77.

29. In the opening pages of Part I, Alcuin mentions that the "edicts of Carnot, and the commentary of *that profound jurist*, Peter Porcupine, had furnished ample materials of discussion" (p. 9, italics added). Brown here provides another clue to Alcuin's politics, since Peter Porcupine (William Cobbett) was one of America's most vocal royalists, almost fanatically anti-republican and anti-French. The French "edicts of Carnot," on the other hand, warned against dangerous royalists who threatened to disrupt the progress of the fledgling American government towards full political and cultural autonomy. See Clark, *Brockden Brown and the Rights of Women*, pp. 34–36.

30. "Introduction" to *The Late Charles Brockden Brown*, p. iv. Ellen L. J. Hoekstra, in "The Characterization of Women in the Novels of Charles Brockden Brown," Diss. Michigan State 1975, concludes that the fate of Brown's major characters shows that "reason unsupported by experience is insufficient, and . . . that reason unsupported by social convention is dubious" (p. 84).

A Minority Reading of
Wieland

Nina Baym

Charles Brockden Brown entered American literary history, via William Dunlap's two-volume eulogizing biography, *The Life of Charles Brockden Brown* (Philadelphia: James P. Parke, 1815), as the first author in this nation who tried to support himself solely by writing. He published five novels in four years (1798–1801) and, when these failed to attain the quick popularity he required for self-support, turned to political pamphleteering and magazine editing. In these latter modes he apparently succeeded in maintaining himself and his family until his early death, at the age of 39, in 1810. Brown's lack of financial success as a fiction writer has been interpreted by later generations of scholars as a sign of America's cultural immaturity: we were not yet ready to support a serious novelist. But his lack of success needs to be put in a somewhat wider perspective. No *novelist*, on either side of the Atlantic, had at that date succeeded in supporting him- or herself *solely* by writing novels, because authorship as a paying profession in general was then only nascent and because the novel was not yet recognized as a dominant, serious literary form.

These reminders may help us to avoid the sentimental fallacy of assuming that Brown would have succeeded better had he been a less serious author. E.g., "Americans simply had no great appetite for serious literature in the early decades of the Republic—certainly nothing of the sort with which they devoured Parson Weems' notorious cherry-tree biography of the nation's father . . . or, say, the ubiquitous melodramas of beset womanhood, 'tales of truth' like Susanna Rowson's *Charlotte Temple* [1791] and Hannah Foster's *The Coquette* [1797]."[1] We need hardly argue that the absence of seriousness in the two works cited does not speak to its presence in the works of Brown. Although there is scattered testimony to the powerful impression that Brown made on some important later writers, both British and American (Keats, J. F. Cooper), there is no real evidence that his novelistic aims were very high. His letters, as Dunlap presented them, indicate no concern with any aspect of his fiction other than its salability. The "seriousness" of Brown's work, nonetheless—as the quotation above exemplifies—is an article of faith among his twentieth-century critics. By "serious," these critics refer to a

87

presumed purpose of utilizing fiction as a means of developing themes and ideas.

Thus defined, the quality of seriousness in Brown's fiction calls for the discovery and exposition of the controlling ideas in his novels; and to these tasks the modest yet enthusiastic Brown revival has devoted itself. A survey of these ideas produces, however, a list of truisms: "universal" banalities and late eighteenth-century conventionalisms. In *Wieland*, for example, Brown is said to be defending—or attacking—rationalism; showing that our senses are liable to err, that we are not always in control of our will; tempering Deism with fate; decrying fanaticism. In his gothicism is discerned a commentary on the darker aspects of the human psyche.[2] Except that an analysis of most fiction for its idea content leads to a similar set of conclusions, one hardly sees a case for Brown's intellectual distinction in the ideas which the criticism has identified in his work. Perhaps, however, ideas are not what Brown's fiction (or fiction in general, no matter how "serious") is really about. It was not his ideas that Keats or Cooper remembered.[3]

Yet, the intense didactic bias in the Brown scholarship may be attributed in part to a distrust of his literary gift and achievements. At face value, it seems highly unlikely that five novels composed more or less simultaneously by a neophyte with no definite plan for any of them, will possess much literary merit. Indeed, only a genius of the first order could possibly produce good work under such conditions. Brown's method of composition throws doubt, at the very least, on the seriousness of his commitment; so does the rapidity with which he abandoned fiction for more rewarding forms of writing. And the fact is that although Brown's novels show command of some segments of the novelistic repertory of his day, they equally evidence carelessness, haste, forgetfulness, and changing intentions. Nor can they be put forward for their expansion of the boundaries of novelistic form or technique. Little wonder, then, that the academic critic, already prone to interpret novels by exposing their substructure of ideas, takes such an approach to Charles Brockden Brown.

Still, Brown's novelistic works are self-evidently fictions before they are works of exposition, deriving their impetus and direction not from the development of an argument but from the sequence of a narrative. What is wanted in the criticism is an acknowledgment of their flawed nature and an analysis which, nevertheless, directs itself more specifically to their literary qualities and their literary problems.

The flaw in Brown's *Wieland* is basic and central: there is a continuous sacrifice of story line and character—hence, long-term coherence—for the sake of immediate effect. As the narrative progresses, indeed, a second plot, designed to maximize the opportunities for such effects, overtakes and ultimately obliterates the main story. These effects involve the creation of a type of terror which is significantly different from the sort of terror inspired by the main story. In two words, the main story is tragic, the supervening tale is gothic. As the plot advances, the tragedy recedes to the background where its vague presence imparts to the gothic some resonance and power beyond its otherwise trivial and transient impact. Yet this supervening foreground, while drawing strength from the tragedy, prevents access to that tragedy, diverts the reader from it.

The basic shape of all stories runs something as follows: an actor at point A wants to get to point B (or stay at point A, for a variant) but encounters obstacles which make this goal difficult to attain. The reader is enlisted in the actor's behalf (hence the term protagonist) and is motivated to pursue the narrative to its end, in order to find out whether the actor will succeed. Each new event in the story is attached to the ongoing narrative by the implicit question: how will this event affect the actor's ultimate success or failure?[4] When the protagonist faces a sequence of relatively discrete obstacles, the plot is known as episodic; if all obstacles cohere in a single being—the antagonist—we have a classical, unified plot. The novel proper, as opposed to the picaresque (an earlier historical form), has a unitary plot. The effects of which it is capable are limited only by the author's skill in expanding the narrative in ways that contribute to the story line while pleasurably diversifying, complicating, and prolonging it.[5] As a matter of technical necessity, the protagonist must be identified very early in the action. If he is not, the reader will not know how to read the work. The identification of the antagonist, however, may be deferred; but eventually all characters in a story may be placed in the camp of the antagonist or the protagonist, as helpers or hinderers.[6] Considerable suspense and surprise may be produced through concealment of the proper placement of a character relative to the protagonist; plots of secret aid, or of deception and betrayal, are among the world's most common and most popular.

While protagonists are usually individuals, a group, a family, a tribe may also have protagonist's status. This is the case in *Wieland*, where the protagonist is identified at the beginning as the entire Wieland family unit. "I acknowledge your right to be informed of the events that have lately happened in my family," states the narrator in the novel's first paragraph (p. 5), directing our attention to the family group as the focus of events. This group consists of Clara, who is also the narrator; her older brother Theodore; his wife Catharine; their four children; Catharine's brother Pleyel (a probable spouse for Clara); and a family companion, Louisa Conway.[7] In that unit Theodore Wieland, usually simply called Wieland, titular head and mainstay of the family, is the chief actor. To him, in effect, the role of protagonist is delegated. It is only as he acts as a representative of his family that his acts have any significance. The obstacles to this family are to be understood in terms of their goal, which is to live together as a harmonious and self-enclosed group, enjoying the pleasures of a leisurely existence and of civilized, rational discourse. They represent, or appear to represent at the novel's beginning, a kind of enlightenment ideal of social happiness. Since they seem so happy, we know that they will be threatened. In fact, as the narrator's account of family history which comprises the first two chapters goes to show, the group is shadowed by a calamitous past in which the threat to their happiness is both contained and predicted.

The father and founder of the family, who had emigrated from Germany and established himself in America on the banks of the Schuylkill River, was a melancholy man of a fanatically religious turn of mind. He built an eccentric temple on his grounds where he worshiped his exacting God in solitude according to his own private rites. In that temple he died terribly and mysteriously (perhaps by spontaneous combustion) after becoming obsessed by the conviction that he had refused to carry out a divine command and was going to be punished for his disobedience. His wife died soon after, leaving the Wieland children to the ministrations of a capable aunt in the city (presumably Philadelphia).

As the story opens the family is back on the banks of the Schuylkill (the aunt, victim perhaps of Brown's haste, is never mentioned again). The terrible past has been repudiated; the temple has been converted into a summer house and furnished with the paraphernalia of the enlightenment—a bust of Cicero, a harpsichord. "This was the place of resort in the evenings of summer. Here we sung, and talked, and read, and occasionally banqueted. Every joyous and tender scene most dear to my memory, is connected with this edifice. Here the performances of our musical and poetical ancestor were rehearsed. Here my brother's children received the rudiments of their education; here a thousand conversations, pregnant with delight and improvement, took place; and here the social affections were accustomed to expand, and the tear of delicious sympathy to be shed" (p. 24).

One cannot say much for Brown's acuity as a psychologist in thus permitting the children to overlook, entirely, the way in which they are feasting on the spot where their father was struck down by his malady; but his story intentions are clear. The transformation of the temple from the house of gloom to the house of joy, the abode of the solitary to the domicile of the social, the locus of the irrational to the symbol of Reason, cannot but suggest the possibility of reversal, of the resurgence of the forces which the temple originally represented and contained. The threat to the family lies within its own depths, in the strain of madness and melancholia now successfully (so it appears) exorcised. The reader necessarily asks, will not this madness recur? If it does, whom will it strike? And what actions will it produce?

Since the narrator begins her tale alluding to catastrophe, the reader knows for a certainty that the madness has recurred. And before long the reader knows in whom it has manifested itself. Clara's inadvert exclamation (p. 21) "O my brother!" implies as much, and she soon indicates how like the brother is to the father: "There was an obvious resemblance between him and my father, in their conceptions of the importance of certain topics, and the light in which the vicissitudes of human life were accustomed to be viewed. Their characters were similar, but the mind of the son was enriched by science, and embellished with literature" (p. 23). Theodore Wieland, as embodiment both of the enlightened family and its irrational destroyer, is both protagonist and antagonist, a tragic hero with a fatal flaw: reason marred by madness.

Three questions then present themselves to the reader: how will Wieland succumb to his madness? What form will it take to express itself? What will happen to him afterwards? The answers to the second and third questions are, I think, discernible to a perceptive reader with some literary experience. The father's mania consisted in hearing voices; so will the son's. The voice or voices commanded him to do something so terrible that, devout as he was, the father refused to do it; the voices will levy a like command on the son and the son will obey. Because we know that the family is going to be destroyed, and because we can imagine what a command so dire must have been, we suppose that Wieland will become the literal destroyer of his family. Subsequently a proper dénouement requires that he become aware of his delusion and kill himself in disgust. The analog or prototype for this story most accessible to Brown would be *Othello*.[8]

The ultimate source of the character's behavior lies within him, in the failing that Aristotle named but did not account for. Precisely the inexplicability of the flaw leads to the effect of awe which the protagonist's career creates in the audience. It is from that mystery, as a mystery, that the story derives its power. The success of the story, so single-minded as it is, will depend on the handling of Wieland himself with respect to the remaining unanswered question: how the mania will develop in him. The audience must be made to hang on every step of the progression, suspended in that profound alembic of pity and fear with which a tragic fall is experienced. In such a story the basic mystery is the only mystery; all else is the mounting suspense of the inevitable. The stages of Wieland's decline into mania would have to be represented through incidents which would make his alteration visible, or through psychological analysis of his changing mental state. Given the models available to Brown in his day and age, we would expect him to take the former course unless he was a very great innovator, well in advance of his time.

The structure of visible alteration is, additionally, mandated by the selection of a first-person narrator, and is initiated in the opening chapters of *Wieland*. If one operates at a sufficient distance from the actual events of the novel, the structure might appear to be realized in its chapter organization. Chapters 1 and 2 establish the mood, the tragic anticipations, the family background. Chapters 3–5 present the family's present state of happiness, with foreshadowings of catastrophe. Chapters 6–15 constitute the rising action, the deteriorating of Wieland's grip on reality. Chapters 16–20 relate the climax, which is Wieland's murder of his wife and children. Chapters 21–25 contain falling action, Wieland's repeated but unsuccessful attempts to kill Clara and Pleyel. Chapter 26 is the dénouement in which Wieland, on the point of murdering Clara, is made aware of his delusions and commits suicide. Chapter 27 is a clumsy epilogue in which Clara and Pleyel are united and the Conway subplot (see above p. 89, and n. 7) is reconstituted and dispatched; putting this chapter aside, the outline looks like a tidy structure, at least at first glance.

But the summary suggests a disproportion if Wieland's deterioration is the focus. In such a situation the dénouement ought to come very soon after the murders, as is the case in *Othello*; for Brown to use six chapters detailing Wieland's thwarted attempts to murder his sister and Pleyel is to digress significantly. The only way to spend six chapters on these attempts is to protract the story along the lines of its capacity to titillate, for the only question that would keep a reader attached to the story during this interval is: will Wieland succeed in killing his two intended victims?

Even more to the point, the chapters that ought to constitute "rising action" in the sense defined above—chapters 6 to 15—do not do so. In fact, Wieland virtually disappears from the tale at precisely the point when he ought to become its unremitting focus. He does not appear again until the reader is given a brief transcription of his testimony during his trial, in a segment of Chapter 19. In Chapter 6 Brown introduces Carwin, a subsidiary character who is the agent—the inadvertent agent, as it turns out—initiating Wieland's decline. But we never see that decline. Instead, Carwin becomes the focus of the narrative's attention, a great red herring who, brought to the forefront of the fiction through Clara's obsession with him, produces a differently organized novel and quite different effects from those which the opening chapters might have led readers to expect.

In the first sentence of Chapter 4—"Six years of uninterrupted happiness had rolled away, since my brother's marriage" (p. 26)—we sense the beginnings of tragedy. Midway in the chapter, a series of events begins which throws all the characters into perplexity. Different members of the family hear, over a period of time, a voice or voices which do not seem explainable by natural causes. Voices of unknown persons erupt from places where no person can be; known voices are heard when their owners are manifestly elsewhere. The mystery of these disembodied voices, heard by all, sets up an ambience in which a person who is prone to hearing voices might well become disoriented. Thus the voices set the stage for Wieland's mania and may be instrumental in encouraging it. It is not so much that these voices will cause his madness as that, when his madness begins to develop, he will be unable to withstand it because these various prior episodes will have weakened the defenses of his reason.

There is a nice irony here, in that these mysterious voices will turn out to have natural causes after all—Carwin is a ventriloquist with a taste for making mischief—while Wieland's madness will not.[9] There is another nice irony in Carwin's status as the only character in *Wieland* who is not a member of the family; he is readily assumed to be the villain because he is an outsider while the locus of crime is deeply within the group.

Carwin thus enters the novel in a minor though significant function. His small evil is to set in motion the terrible train of events. The disproportion between the banality and meanness of the agent and the horror of the final result could have been emphasized to show the tremendous gulf between the outer, orderly world and the inner turbulence of the unfathomable mind through the analogous disparity between cause and effect. Having thus introduced the ventriloquist as initial cause, Brown had to keep him in the story while concealing his agency—keep him in the story so that, ultimately, the early voices can be accounted for, but conceal his agency so as to enhance the mystery. The challenge to literary art lies in the manner in which Carwin is to be taken up into the story line, made to seem natural in the plot. Some of the wide range of possibilities available to the storyteller are foreclosed by the earlier commitment to a first-person narrative. For example, private exchanges between Wieland and Carwin cannot be represented. Even granting this limitation, Brown might have handled Carwin variously. The one kind of development not permitted would be one which made Carwin too important a character, because if this were to happen Wieland would lose his commanding role and the tragic effects would be blunted.

But Brown, in defiance (or ignorance?) of story logic, chose to bring Carwin into the novel's center, where, for much of the action, the ventriloquist replaces Wieland as the object of narrative attention. It seems almost as if his function becomes precisely to divert the reader from the true center. As in a detective story, we must see everyone *except* the murderer. Through Clara's obsession with Carwin—she is certain from the start that he is her family's evil genius—he effectively usurps the antagonist's role. Whether he meant to or not, Brown invented a second plot whose action moves from ignorance to discovery. Clara is like a detective protagonist, wanting to know what is happening to the family and who is responsible for it. Carwin, a minor character in Wieland's story, is truly the antagonist in this one, because his behavior presents the obstacles that prevent Clara from discovering the truth. Fixed on Carwin, she doesn't see the changes in her brother. She assumes that Carwin is the murderer at the climax because she has eliminated any other possibility. But fixed on Clara, Brown's narrative *also* fails to see Wieland's change. He is taken off stage a rational man and brought back a demented maniac.

The novel's change of direction proclaims itself in the opening of Chapter 6, when Clara introduces Carwin. "I now come to the mention of a person with whose name the most turbulent sensations are connected.

It is with a shuddering reluctance that I enter on the province of describing him. . . . My blood is congealed: and my fingers are palsied when I call up his image" (p. 49). Let us remember that Clara is not telling her tale as it happens, in the mode of an epistolary novel. She is recollecting it. As a character she now knows that Carwin is not the villain she mistook him for. Yet she (or the author who manipulates her) brings him to the reader's attention with a heated vocabulary inconsistent with the narrator's knowledge at the time she tells the story. Apparently, Brown is not attempting to characterize Clara but simply to use her as a register for melodramatic effects. Reader attention is arrested at those surface events which, though "thrilling," will prove susceptible of explanation. We have no access to the state of Wieland's mind; the question is no longer how he becomes a murderer, but who the murderer is. Substituted for the pity and awe of the tragic are the excitement and shock of the early whodunit, the gothic thriller. Ultimately, then, *Wieland* draws its dynamic neither from its transcendence of gothic nor its expansion of the mode to cover new literary territory, but just the reverse. *Wieland* does open such possibilities, but quickly retreats from them. It is gothic and sensational to the core. Like many aspiring writers in the early years of the republic, Brown's literary purpose seems to be little more than to domesticate the currently popular genres.

I imply above that, as an inexperienced writer, Brown might have found Carwin too difficult a technical problem and allowed him, through ineptness, to take a central role he was not supposed to have. But it might well be supposed instead that it was Wieland who posed the insuperable technical difficulties to a novice (especially given the choice of the first-person narrator), tragedy being so much more difficult to achieve than melodrama, and gothic machinery being so easily imitable. The suggestion of spontaneous combustion as the cause of the elder Wieland's death indicates a weakness for such machinery early on in Brown's treatment, and certainly after Chapter 6 scenes are developed and drawn out for their maximum sensational value. Carwin permits such treatment; Wieland would not. Yet it is the trace of that tragic story which provides the darkening power that stays with readers and—for those whom it moves—makes the novel memorable.[10]

The introduction of Carwin was consistent with Clara's function as narrator but required a dramatic alteration in her "character." Nothing in the early chapters of the novel suggests to the reader that there is any serious defect in Clara's ability to perceive her world, and insofar as she is given a character it seems to be one consistent with her enlightened philosophy. Occasional references throughout the narrative allude to her perfections in unironic terms. For example, this effusion from Pleyel in Chapter 13:

Here, said I, is a being, after whom sages may model their

transcendent intelligence, and painters, their ideal beauty. . . . I have marked the transitions of your discourse, the felicities of your expression, your refined argumentation, and glowing imagery; and been forced to acknowledge, that all delights were meagre and contemptible, compared with those connected with the audience and sight of you. I have contemplated your principles, and been astonished at the solidity of their foundation, and the perfection of their structure. . . . I have seen by what skilful arrangements you facilitate the performance of the most arduous and complicated duties; what daily accessions of strength your judicious discipline bestowed upon your memory; what correctness and abundance of knowledge was daily experienced by your unwearied application to books, and to writing. (pp. 121–22)

But if Clara is to be the source of error and remain a character, she must become an unreliable narrator; and if the story is to turn gothic she must be an easily impressed, fearful, being. Such a role—which Brown imposes on her—is not at all consistent with the traits she is said to possess. Essentially, character goes by the board for Clara as it does for Carwin. Clara serves only as the vantage point from which events are misapprehended and experienced in their fullest capacity to shock and to terrify—a capacity beyond what the events if rightly understood would be reasonably able to produce.

Although the many inconsistencies in Brown's presentation of Clara have prompted some critics to devise complex neurotic personalities for her (see, e.g., Krause & Reid, pp. xix–xxi), these personalities (integrating incest wishes, sexual repression, hyperrationality, paranoia, defensiveness, emotional rigidity) are not compatible with the descriptions of her that other characters in *Wieland* offer. Simply, Clara is not a character in any traditional sense. She is not even a function in Propp's sense, since she has no role with respect to the action except to misreport it. She is, however, a function with respect to the story's telling. She is the screen imposed between Wieland and the reader, the result of narrative strategies calling for the greatest degree of inaccuracy coupled with—leading to—the greatest degree of sensational effect. Without her, Carwin could not reach the reader in the grossly distorted manner that he does. Clara is thus a trick played upon the reader, who, giving credence to her account, participates in her terrors. Her errors repeatedly lead to fresh shocks, fresh fears, fresh amazements; her frightened focus produces Carwin's sensational effects. *Wieland*'s superficiality, then, is intentional. Hoax is its motif.

Let us document these assertions by following Clara in the production of sensational effects in one segment of the novel only—to trace the workings of the melodrama throughout would create a critical work many times longer than the novel itself. I shall use for this purpose the closet episode in Chapter 9, because of its appeal in psychological readings of *Wieland*.

In the opening pages of Chapter 9 a family gathering has not materialized because Pleyel has not arrived. Alone in her room later that night, Clara imagines possible catastrophes that might have befallen him. Her brooding leads to general speculations on human life and death, and then to her father. Recalling a memoir of his life that he had left (a document mentioned only on this occasion), she resolves to take it from her closet and reread it. The book, we quickly see, has no function other than to maneuver Clara to the closet; and her long deliberation over whether to get the book first and then a candle, or a candle first and then the book, leads up to the result that the ensuing events take place in the dark (she chooses to get the book first). All this associationist machinery for such small results—to propel the heroine toward her closet in the dark—indicates the novice writer rather than the experienced psychologist. Unless, of course, Brown's interest is not in Clara's mind but in the reader's mind: for the reader, impressed with all this machinery, will wonder what it is working toward, and be prepared for mystery connected with the closet.

The reader is not to be enlightened without an exquisite prolonging of the anxieties and tensions generated by the machinery. "Leaving my seat, I approached the closet in which, as I mentioned formerly, my books and papers were deposited. . . . Suddenly the remembrance of what had lately passed in this closet occurred." (In Chapter 6, she had heard voices in the closet plotting—as she misunderstood them—her murder.) "I was, as then, alone, and defenseless. . . . My steps faultered, and I stood a moment to recover myself. I prevailed on myself at length to move towards the closet. I touched the lock, but my fingers were powerless; I was visited afresh by unconquerable apprehensions. . . . I receded a few steps. . . . It would be difficult to depict, in words, the ingredients and hues of that phantom which haunted me. . . . I returned to the closet, and once more put my hand upon the lock" (pp. 84–85).

This passage, condensed from five long paragraphs in the narrative, cannot but inform the reader that terror lies ahead. Even a very dense reader—for Brown's technique is hardly subtle—ought to be in a state of apprehension about the closet corresponding to Clara's own. And the anxiety is justified. "O! may my ears lose their sensibility, ere they be again assailed by a shriek so terrible! Not merely my understanding was subdued by the sound; it acted on my nerves like an edge of steel. It appeared to cut asunder the fibres of my brain, and rack every joint with agony. . . . 'Hold! Hold!' were the words of this tremendous prohibition, in whose tone the whole soul seemed to be rapt up, and every energy converted into eagerness and terror" (p. 85).

Clara retreats—again—from the closet. "Shuddering, I dashed myself against the wall." There follow two pages combining an account of her physical sensations, by no means understated—"Surprize had mastered my faculties. My frame shook, and the vital current was congealed. I was conscious only to the vehemence of my sensations"—with her attempt to interpret the experience (pp. 85–86). The lengthening intensifies the suspense—quantity translates into a qualitative change in the nature of the experience. Association leads Clara to conclude that it was Wieland in the closet, a false presumption which will produce fresh terrors when the true incumbent is revealed.[11]

Once more Clara approaches the closet and this time encounters physical resistance. The door will not open. She experiences terror and fear anew: "The frantic conception that my brother was within, that the resistance made to my design was exerted by him, had rooted itself in my mind. You will comprehend the height of this infatuation, when I tell you, that, finding all my exertions vain, I betook myself to exclamations. Surely I was utterly bereft of understanding" (p. 88). In this "crisis of [her] fate" she addresses the unknown something or someone in the closet, "the door swung upon its hinges and"—but not yet are we to know the secret—"displayed to my view the interior of the closet. Whoever was within, was shrouded in darkness. A few seconds passed without interruption of the silence. I knew not what to expect or to fear" (p. 89). After another like paragraph a figure emerges and reveals himself after yet four paragraphs more as Carwin.

Since she expected Wieland, this apparition comes as a great surprise, and leads her to imagine a host of new perils. "What motive but atrocious ones could guide his steps hither? I was alone. My habit suited the hour, and the place, and the warmth of the season. All succour was remote. He had placed himself between me and the door" (ibid). Nothing transpires, however, beyond a speech of frightful menace from Carwin: thrills, but no actual harm—the semblance of terror without its realization. The scene has been squeezed for all the sensation it can yield, short, of course, of a truly horrible outcome which a modern gothicist like Alfred Hitchcock would not spare.

This scene also provides the motive (just as the closet scene in Chapter 6 and the summerhouse sequence in Chapter 7 motivate the mistakes in this episode) for Clara's mistaken conclusion that Carwin is the murderer when she finds her sister-in-law dead in her—Clara's—bed. Naturally she assumes that Carwin has made an attempt on her life and killed Catharine by mistake, though she never seems to wonder what Catharine was doing in her bed to begin with. This mistake permits the drawn-out revelation of the true murderer's identity. Each mistake Clara makes leads her plausibly to the next, so that her story achieves a specious, ungrounded, consistency. Diverted from its original task of conveying Wieland's madness, the novel is experienced as a continuous sequence of mysterious events, systematically misread by a narrator motivated to make sense of her world. Then the truth bursts upon her—and through her, upon us—with an effect the opposite of tragedy. We encounter not the inevitable but the entirely unexpected, that which the plot has rigorously prevented us from seeing.

The revelation of Wieland's agency in the murder of his family creates simple shock instead of pity and awe. His identity is produced with the maximum of prolongation and tease:

> "You gather from this," said [my uncle],[12] "that Carwin is the author of all this misery?" "Is it not," answered I, "an unavoidable inference?" . . . "Good heaven!" I exclaimed; "what say you? Was not Carwin the assassin? Could any hand but his have carried into act this dreadful purpose?" . . . I besought him to say who this criminal was, and what the instigations that compelled him. My uncle was silent. I urged this inquiry with new force. I reverted to my own knowledge, and sought in this some basis to conjecture. I ran over the scanty catalogue of the men whom I knew; I lighted on no one who was qualified for ministering to malice like this. (pp. 161–62)

Clara continues in this manner until the end of the chapter (Chapter 18), which produces only the transcript of the unnamed murderer's courtroom confession. "My uncle left me alone. My curiosity refused me a moment's delay. I opened the papers, and read as follows" (p. 163). Although Clara cannot delay, the reader is halted at this point by the end of the chapter. Suspense is thus prolonged to intensify the effect of the first words of Chapter 19: "Theodore Wieland, the prisoner at the bar, was now called upon for his defense" (p. 164).

The remaining chapters, which comprise almost a quarter of the length of the novel, draw out the question of whether Wieland, now totally insane (as his boastful account of the killings at his trial has shown), will succeed in escaping from prison to kill Clara and Pleyel. Superhumanly, he escapes two times, but is caught. And when Clara goes off to her house (abandoned since the night of the killings) alone, for no clear reason, we know that the story is being engineered toward a final confrontation. Since the narrator has survived to tell the tale, suspense now centers on the question of how Wieland will be prevented this third and last time. And here, neatly, Brown brings back Carwin who first confesses his innocence to Clara and then employs his ventriloquist powers to prevent Wieland from killing her and to free him from his delusion. This freeing leads directly to Wieland's suicide, the tragic dénouement. But Wieland, in these last chapters, is a mere monster; not a trace of the tragic hero remains.

During the middle section of the book, when Wieland's mania would, in the nature of things, be germinating, Clara's occasional reports of him depict the serious, kindly, rational brother she has always known. This reportage, whatever its intention, helps deflect our attention from

Wieland in order to make the revelation of his agency all the more shocking. During the middle section the reader is engulfed by Clara's fears and fantasies as they are aroused by mysterious events which come increasingly to focus on Carwin. These events, as I have observed, are managed in a fashion designed to exploit their capacity to produce sensational effects. The forward motion of the plot is achieved by the way in which each of Clara's mistakes overlaps with the next. The structure of her reasoning, beginning from false premises and making continual reference to wrong facts, is nonetheless—grotesquely—logical.

Although Clara and Carwin do not take over the novel until Chapter 6, before which time Clara has seemed a reliable narrator who is going to tell us about her family tragedy, *Wieland* is consistent from the very first in its invitation to be read as melodrama. It begins with promise of horrors, shocks, and thrills at the very edge of the credible. Hence, we may feel confirmed in our suspicion that Brown's ultimate handling of the story represented his talent and inclination better than the story he had seemed to be planning to tell.

Even before the story begins, the "Advertisement" sets the tone. Of course, the Advertisement was composed after the novel was finished[13] and might represent Brown's attempt properly to frame the reader's attitude to the story that he had actually written rather than the one he had planned. Asserting his (obligatory) moral purpose in the first paragraph, Brown adds that "the incidents related are extraordinary and rare. Some of them, perhaps, approach as nearly to the nature of miracles as can be done by that which is not truly miraculous" (p. 3). References to the "extremely rare," the "uncommon," the "apparently impossible" iterate his point. The lexicon exerts itself in synonyms for the extreme and outlandish.

And Clara's opening paragraphs echo those later composed sentiments which they now follow. Volunteering to write her story only at the request of some friends, to whom she leaves the eventual disposition of the narrative, she strikes the melodramatist's note at once: "The storm that tore up our happiness, and changed into dreariness and desert the blooming scene of our existence, is lulled into grim repose; but not until the victim was transfixed and mangled; till every obstacle was dissipated by its rage; till every remnant of good was wrested from our grasp and exterminated" (pp 5–6). The vocabulary promises terrible events. The elusive syntax, confusing references, and chaotic metaphors may indicate carelessness or ineptness, but they also mime the whirlwind which they promise. Even more curiously but appropriately, they effectively conceal the precise identity of the actors in this story, just as Brown's reference in the advertisement to his "principal person" with his extremely rare powers implies rather than discloses a secret.

"How will your wonder," Clara continues, "and that of your companions, be excited by my story! Every sentiment will yield to your amazement. If my testimony were without corroborations, you would reject it as incredible. The experience of no human being can furnish a parallel: That I, beyond the rest of mankind, should be reserved for a destiny without alleviation, and without example! Listen to my narrative, and then say what it is that has made me deserve to be placed in this dreadful eminence, if, indeed, every faculty be not suspended in wonder that I am still alive, and am able to relate it" (p. 6).

The reader is unambiguously instructed to receive the narrative as the channel for experiences the like of which he or she has never known before. Few are the works that could deliver on such a promise; yet, in Wieland's story there are events both awful and bizarre enough to make good, to some extent, the extravagant guarantee. Yet, the events to which Clara is referring prove to be nothing more than the concatenation of tricks that Carwin performs with his ventriloquist abilities. Only works of gothic irony persistently fall so far below their promises as *Wieland*, then, actually does, palming off on the reader (with the collusion of the narrator, who, since she narrates retrospectively, knows better) as marvels hoaxes which are little more than parlor tricks. In the low gothic mode, however, it is very important that events be produced by trickery; the reader depends on it. When we enter a chamber of horrors we do not expect to meet real ghosts. We expect to be entertained by their simulacra. The horror we feel is counterfeit horror.

The Advertisement tells us which kind of gothic we will be reading when it assures us that everything will be explained away at the end, attributed to natural causes: "It is hoped that intelligent readers will not disapprove of the manner in which appearances are solved, but that the solution will be found to correspond with the known principles of human nature" (p. 3). But remember, Wieland's madness is not solved, nor are any principles known in human nature advanced to account for it. Brown actually protects the reader from extreme events in *Wieland* (one might contrast Poe to see the point better) and offers instead the pretense of them, permitting emotions to be indulged without risk but also (I think) cutting out the possibility of catharsis.

There is, even so, a sense in which the two plots of *Wieland*— Wieland's story and the Clara-Carwin story—have more than a coincidental relation to one another derived from their sharing the same set of characters and their deployment in each of the figure of Carwin, the ventriloquist, for special effects. Both the gothic and the tragic stories are founded on the opposition of the values of reason and unreason. In Wieland's story, this opposition appears capable of a rich and diverse development: family, home, peace, education, civilization, moderation, control, intellect, nature in contrast to solitude, primitive emotions, extremism, violence, the supernatural, the unnatural, embodied in one complex character. In the Clara-Carwin story the opposition is much simpler: logic versus sensation, and restricted to the surface of events where characterization is superfluous. But this restriction was probably in

keeping with Brown's idea of what he wanted to do in fiction. The restriction also probably produced a work that was better suited to—or more
representative of—his abilities and his imagination than the tragic story
of Wieland. As a first effort, *Wieland* is an interesting and promising
book—more interesting and more promising than a first like *Fanshawe*,
though not more so than *Typee*. It would seem time, however, to stop
castigating the young Republic for its failure to be serious when it did not
make the work into a best seller. The failure of seriousness is at least as
great on Brown's part.

Notes

1. *Wieland & Memoirs of Carwin* by Charles Brockden Brown (Kent State Univ. Press,
1978), Introduction by Sydney J. Krause and S. W. Reid. This paperback edition reprints the
1977 authoritative text (see n. 2) but lacks the apparatus and supplies a different introduction,
from which this quote is taken. Page references to *Wieland* will parenthetically refer to the
Kent State University text, identically paginated in the two editions.

The quoted assertions bear some thinking about. They are too quick to equate literature
with fiction. And, according to Lyle Wright's bibliography, *American Fiction, 1774–1850*
(San Marino: The Huntington Library, 1979), only 27 works of fiction were published in the
United States between 1774 and 1797; no type of fiction, then, could properly be called "ubiquitous." To be sure, five of these 27 were written by Mrs. Rowson; surely to her, then,
should go the title of America's first professional author of fiction! Is there, perhaps, some an-
drocentricity in the idea of "seriousness?" here put forward?

2. E. g., David Lee Clark, *Charles Brockden Brown, Pioneer Voice of America*
(Durham, N. C.: Duke Univ. Press, 1952), pp. 168–69, describes *Wieland* as "a sermon
against credulity and religious fanaticism"; Larzar Ziff, "A Reading of *Wieland*," *PMLA*, 77
(1962), 51–57, counters by finding in the novel a quasi-calvinist pessimism about human
possibility which he takes as the work's justification, purpose, and message. Richard Chase,
The American Novel and its Tradition (New York: Anchor Press, 1957), puts Brown at the
head of the "tradition" for his use of melodrama to present abstract ideas and the dark side of
human consciousness. "Brown," he writes (p. 29), "was the first writer of fiction in this country to use melodrama significantly," i.e. to mean something. Werner Berthoff's "A Lesson in
Concealment: Brockden Brown's Method in Fiction," *PQ*, 57 (1958), 45–67, though not
specifically about *Wieland*, describes Brown's method as the dramatization of ideas to study
their modulations as embodied in different life situations. Nothing less than the full work will
suffice to express the theme; the full work is nothing more than the theme expressed. Donald
Ringe's excellent *Charles Brockden Brown* (Twayne, 1966), while full of perceptive literary
commentary, nevertheless justifies analysis of *Wieland* (as well as Brown's other works) by attempting to show that it is an "important intellectual document" (p. 42) because it illuminates
"the central error in the rationalist theory . . . its failure to take sufficiently into account that
all men, no matter how rational, possess fallible minds and powerful passions" (p. 33). Alexander Cowie's Historical Essay in the scholarly Kent State edition of *Wieland* states that "the
religio-philosophical rationale of *Wieland* is essentially a deistic one modified by
'fate'. . . . This is not a pitiless book, but it is a comfortless one. . . . For Brown the world
can appear a harsh place, but he seems to imply that however bleak the fate visited on individuals, it must be endured with fortitude" (*Wieland & Memoirs of Carwin, The Novels
and Related Works of Charles Brockden Brown*, Vol. I (Kent State Univ. Press, 1977), pp.
334, 338. In further references this volume will be cited as *KSU*.

Cowie also sees value in Brown's psychological insights, a view put forth earlier in
William Manly's "The Importance of Point of View in Brockden Brown's *Wieland*," *AL*, 35
(1963), 311–21. It is also found in Robert D. Arner's yearly review essays of the period in

American Literary Scholarship, an Annual (Durham: Duke Univ. Press) See especially *ALS/76*, p. 89. It is seen again in Krause & Reid, pp. xix–xxii; and David Lyttle, "The Case Against Carwin," *NCF* 26 (1971), 257–69 (a Freudian reading). Leslie Fiedler's scattered comments on *Wieland* in *Love and Death in the American Novel* (New York: Criterion, 1960) are widely quoted by other critics but when closely examined (e.g., Carwin is called a Richardsonian seducer, p. 149; the novel is said to be narrated by filtering the experiences through the perceptions of the "male protagonist," Wieland, p. 99) suggest that Fiedler did not have the book firmly in mind when he wrote. These essays taking a psychological approach transform the psychological insights described into Brown's "ideas" about human nature and then make these ideas the theme of the work.

3. See introduction to this collection, pp. 6 and 7.

4. These theoretical remarks derive loosely from an amalgamation of Aristotle's *Poetics*; the Chicago Aristotelians (especially R. S. Crane et. al., *Critics and Criticism*, Chicago: University of Chicago Press, 1952); V. Propp, *Morphology of the Folktale* (Austin: University of Texas Press, 1977); Roland Barthes, *S/Z* (New York: Hill and Wang, 1974); Barthes, "An Introduction to the Structural Analysis of Narrative," *NLH*, 6 (1975), 237–72; Jonathan Culler, *Structuralist Poetics* (Ithaca: Cornell Univ. Press, 1975); Seymour Chatman, *Story and Discourse* (Ithaca: Cornell Univ. Press, 1978); and the less current but extremely useful, clear, and practical manuals of fiction writing such as Clayton Hamilton, *The Art of Fiction* (New York: Odyssey, 1939) and Arthur Sullivant Hoffman, *The Writing of Fiction* (Boston: The Writer, Inc., 1934).

5. Sub-plots constitute another mode of lengthening the novel, but are generally evaluated according to how successfully or convincingly or naturally the novelist works them into the fabric of the major plot line.

6. This observation departs from Propp-inspired orthodoxy, wherein there are several functions allotted to minor characters rather than simply two. Culler feels that the various functional categorizations of characters (*actants* in Greimas's phrase) are all artificial; yet, to perceive all characters as falling into two categories is quite consistent with the binary thinking of structuralist critics.

7. Louisa is introduced to the narrative with considerable rhetorical fanfare, heralding a sub-plot. This sub-plot, however, never materializes. Brown's forgetfulness is clumsily repaired in the last chapter of *Wieland*, though most critics find the cure worse than the disease. The writing of *Wieland* certainly was not helped by its being set in proof almost as quickly as the author composed it (see Joseph Katz, "Analytical Bibliography and Literary History: The Writing and Printing of *Wieland*,"*Proof*, 1 [1971], 8–24; and the Textual Essay in *KSU*, pp. 353–58).

8. I won't claim influence here, though Brown clearly knew Shakespeare. He footnotes, for example, *Macbeth* (p. 203) and it is reasonable to assume that he read others of the tragedies. Pleyel's readiness to disbelieve Clara and distrust her—while clearly functional to the plot—suggests an *Othello* motif.

9. Brown noted in his "Outline" for *Wieland* that the Carwin character (there named "Moncrieve") would act "merely to encite surprize & sport with credulity" (*KSU*, p. 429). The outline, of course, proves nothing about the novel, since it is not internally coherent and since Brown clearly deviated from it in many particulars.

10. When the early appreciations named the source of felt power in *Wieland*, it was the family tragedy and Theodore Wieland; and more recent evaluations confess, though reluctantly, that Carwin is an impediment rather than a strength in the finished work. See the Historical Essay in *KSU*, pp. 340–48.

11. In a few other instances Clara imagines, but dismisses the thought, that her brother is a sinister figure. Critics have tended to build a quasi-Freudian interpretation of her character on this fact. But these imaginings function effectively in the plot because they are simultaneously foreshadowings *and* mistakes which lead to surprise and reversal.

12. Just as the aunt who raised the young Wielands disappears from the tale without a trace, her function completed, so this uncle appears without preparation and functions as Clara's confidant and mentor between the climax and the dénouement.

13. Textual Essay in *KSU*, pp. 349, 354.

The Voices of *Wieland*

Bernard Rosenthal

Nina Baym's "A Minority Reading of *Wieland*" forcefully demonstrates the structural problems of *Wieland* as seen from the perspective of the contemporary critical theories applied to it. While one might wish, for the sake of Brown's reputation, that modern approaches lack validity for a late eighteenth-century writer of fiction, the fact is that one finds even harsher charges leveled at *Wieland* in Brown's own time.[1] The most virulent complaints of the earlier critics centered on the perceived gimmickry of Brown, such as the use of spontaneous combustion. But hostile critics reserved their greatest disdain for Brown's trick of ventriloquism as a device for unraveling the mysteries of the tale. If one may indeed sympathize with a reader's disappointment at finding the solution to a mystery as nothing more than a parlor stunt gone wrong, the irony remains that the power of the novel as seen by Brown's friendly critics depends on the existence of some natural phenomenon to explain a misguided belief in supernatural agencies. In one sense, then, the division of opinion over Brown's artistry hinges on the success or failure of his use of voices. Regarded as the mere solution to a mystery, ventriloquism surely must disappoint most readers. But I want to argue that Brown's employment of ventriloquism, as well as his alleged use of spontaneous combustion, had purposes having little to do with the solving of mysteries. Brown had a polemic message, the danger of morality based on revealed religion; and he employed a literary methodology that suggested rather than explained, a methodology that in the hands of a literary genius like Hawthorne would be perfected and would receive the label of "Romance."[2] As Hawthorne often does, Brown turns to an event from the past to set a shadow of gloom upon the present. In *Wieland*, the dark spell originates from an earlier religious discovery.

The tale has scarcely begun when the elder Wieland happens upon "a book written by one of the teachers of the Albigenses, or French Protestants."[3] Declining the opportunity to dwell on the lurid associations connected with the Albigenses, Brown perhaps relied on popular beliefs about them to suggest the motif of religious fanaticism central to *Wieland*.[4] Thought to be an offshoot of Manichean theology, the Albigenses were conflated in popular thought with the Cathari and the Camisards.[5] Among the beliefs attributed to them were the views that Satan and the

God of the Old Testament were one, that marriage was sinful and should be renounced, and that a select group known as "perfecti" belonged to a higher class of men worthy of salvation. One need not dwell long on these ideas to find associations with the demented killer of his family in Brown's novel.

If such a religion would seem bizarre to a person from Brown's theological culture, so much the better for his purposes. The intrinsic danger of religion, not merely theological excess, might be demonstrated more emphatically. To follow any scripture rather than to follow rational morality risked surrendering sober, wise judgment to the elder Wieland's "empire of religious duty" (p. 9). The excesses of a man slaughtering his family in response to divine revelation likewise demonstrated the inherent danger of human conduct rooted in religious duty. The issue here is not merely one of religious excess, but rather of a fundamental perception regarding revealed religion as inherently leading to such excess, whether in the purported beliefs and actions of the Albigenses or in the murder of Wieland's family. In his letter of October 24, 1795, to Joseph Bringhurst, Brown had set forth an intellectual premise on revealed religion that would be played out in the fiction of *Wieland*.[6]

In Brown's novel, the elder Wieland takes his new religion to America, prospers, does missionary work, builds a temple, and lives bound in guilt for having failed to execute a divine injunction. Whether the elder Wieland had been commanded to slay his family is problematic. Brown, in Clara's narrative, writes that the "duty assigned to him was transferred, in consequence of his disobedience, to another, and all that remained was to endure the penalty" (p. 9). Brown does not assert that the injunction was passed to the son, but no ambiguity exists as to the son's compulsion to obey a command he believed to be divine. Nor does Brown leave ambiguous the text that originally impels the elder Wieland, the words " 'Seek and ye shall find' " (p. 8)—good, orthodox Christianity of a kind that trusts the individual to learn from the Bible and to obey the commandments derived from religious study.[7]

By following this advice, the younger Wieland embarks on a course resulting in the slaughter of his family. Brown prepares the reader for so terrifying an act through inviting speculations on the supernatural resulting from the strange death of the elder Wieland. Although the book never does explain what happened to him, the label of "spontaneous combustion" has stuck to the event from the earliest readings to the present. A more skillful writer like Hawthorne would learn the trick of romance whereby alternative explanations are offered for an event that belongs to imaginative understanding rather than to literal translation. For example, does any reader of *The Scarlet Letter* believe that witches flying overhead attract the attention of Mistress Hibbins? Do readers fail to understand that such an event, otherwise ludicrous, in Hawthorne's hands conveys the sense of the demonic that haunts Hester? Unfortunately, readers often miss Brown's early employment of what Hawthorne would call "Romance" and take literally what is merely a suggestion in a footnote (p. 19), this, even though the words "spontaneous combustion" never appear in Brown's novel.[8]

On the night of his death, the elder Wieland goes to the temple. His wife first thinks a pistol has been fired (p. 16). Her brother rushes to the scene to find some extraordinary light, but no flame (p. 17). Wieland's "body was scorched and bruised. His right arm exhibited marks as of having been struck by some heavy body" (p. 18). His clothing is in ashes, but his hair and his slippers are unaccountably intact. Now at this point in the story, Wieland the religious fanatic has every reason to explain his experience as divine retribution. Stories from him about avenging angels, or even spontaneous combustion, would be quite in character. At least this would be the case if something more secular had not happened. Yet Wieland's own explanation belongs neither to mysteries of religion nor of science.[9] Here is the dying man's testimony:

> By his imperfect account, it appeared, that while engaged in silent orisons, with thoughts full of confusion and anxiety, a faint gleam suddenly shot athwart the apartment. His fancy immediately pictured to itself, a person bearing a lamp. It seemed to come from behind. He was in the act of turning to examine the visitant, when his right arm received a blow from a heavy club. At the same instant, a very bright spark was seen to light upon his clothes. (p. 18)

This is Wieland's testimony, which Brown never does clarify. If the victim is to be believed, the fire that burned him fell first on his clothes and did not come from within as it would in spontaneous combustion. The elliptical reference to such an explanation is from Clara, who was not there. Moreover, Wieland claims to have been hit by a club. Granted that Clara's uncle feels "that half the truth had been suppressed" (p. 18), neither it nor the other half is ever told. The reader has only the word of the victim who essentially says a light shone, a club hit him, and a spark ignited his clothing. A rational hypothesis would not be hard to construct. Only the "sudden vanishing" of the cloud at the approach of the uncle seems contrary to reasonable explanation. As for the rest, it lends itself to speculations about an intruder with a lamp who attacked Wieland, hit him on the arm and deliberately or accidently ignited his clothing with the lamp's fire. The blow on the arm is a detail of the story to which Brown never returns. Nor does Clara, as she incorporates the mystery at the temple into the family myth of something unnatural having happened to the father. Clara asks the questions early that will engage the reader throughout. "Was this the penalty of disobedience? this the stroke of a vindictive and invisible hand? Is it a fresh proof that the Divine Ruler interferes in human affairs, mediates an end, selects and commissions his agents, and enforces, by unequivocal sanctions, submission to his will?" (p. 19). Clara follows these questions with the speculation hinting at spontaneous combustion, but the latter possibility will play no further role in the novel. The former will become its center. And Clara, not the rational person some readers have wanted her to be, will to the end have almost as much faith in divine voices as does her tormented brother.[10]

The initial event having left its legacy of supernatural intimations to the six-year-old Clara and to her brother, it is scarcely to be wondered that they become susceptible to the tricks of ventriloquism that Carwin plays. After an idyllic childhood, only vaguely haunted by the horrendous past, the children enter adulthood with marriage for Wieland and hints of romance with Pleyel for Clara. Amidst a life uninterrupted by labor, the foursome live in their almost Arcadian world until a voice is heard calling Wieland back from the temple. The reader subsequently learns that Carwin had played the trick of ventriloquism, initiating a series of deceptions that accounts for all of the voices except for the ones that command Wieland to kill his family. Whether this voice emanates from Carwin, as early critics assumed it did, will be examined subsequently. But setting that voice aside, the reader receives an acceptable—though unsatisfying to many—explanation for all the others.

Acceptable, that is, if certain assumptions are granted: Clara is a reliable narrator as is Carwin and both may be believed. Granting the validity of Clara's experiences with voices and Carwin's confession, all mysteries except the central one are explained by ventriloquism. By the central mystery, I mean the one involving the elder Wieland's death and the younger Wieland's subsequent behavior independent of Carwin's tricks. For when Carwin has completed his explanations, the reader is left with some puzzles that cannot be explained merely on the basis of Wieland's presumed madness. The unaccountable blow on the arm of the elder Wieland offers one problem.

Another intriguing puzzle arises from Clara's discovery of the murdered Catharine's body. What is one to make of Clara's initial response?

> To die beneath his [Clara is assuming Carwin as the murderer] grasp would not satisfy thy enemy. This was mercy to the evils which he previously made thee suffer! After these evils death was a boon which thou besoughtest him to grant. (p. 151)

Readers need not have prurient imaginations to take for granted that Clara can be suggesting nothing other than rape. Does she see something that she will not narrate? Or does Brown raise the specter in order to encourage the false lead that Carwin was guilty?[11] Certainly nothing in Wieland's account suggests that he raped his wife before murdering her, and Brown never returns to clarify this issue.

A third unaccountable mystery involves the light Clara sees in her bedroom window as she approaches her house just prior to discovering Catharine's body. She sees the light, and then "after flitting to and fro, for a short time, it vanished. I turned my eye again toward the window, and perceived that the light was still there; but the change which I had noticed was occasioned by a change in the position of the lamp or candle within" (p. 145). When she reaches her room, she posits, as she often does, supernatural causes, encouraged this time by the mystery at the foot of the stairs. "Neither lamp nor candle was to be found," she narrates (p. 149). A person comfortable with rational explanations might simply have assumed that the bearer of light has merely departed the room taking the lamp or candle. But Clara's mind does not run toward the rational. Nor is Clara a discerning auditor in hearing Carwin's explanation. " 'A light stood on the table' " in her room, Carwin says (p. 213). He makes no comment as to whether he ever touched or moved it, except to say that he turned it out and quickly left the room upon hearing Clara's approach. Now it would certainly be reasonable if Carwin had walked around the room holding the light he had discovered and even fled with it to see his way out. But why put out a light and then take it with him? It makes no sense; or, to be more conservative, it invites questions from Clara that are never asked. Indeed, from the account given there is no reason to believe that Carwin ever moved the light, and thus the mystery of the moving light in Clara's room is never resolved.

Without considering whether other unaccountable events occur in the story, one may contemplate the implications of the three unexplained episodes: the blow on the arm, which nothing in the story contradicts; the hinted rape of Catharine, which creates a contradiction between Wieland's account and Clara's; and the light in the bedroom, which poses Carwin's credibility against Clara's. If one grants that these incidents create narrative problems for the reader, it seems reasonable to assume that Brown either hurried past these incidents and simply left aesthetic flaws or that they are consistent with some as yet undiscussed explanation. I would like to offer a hypothesis for the latter view. For it seems to me that these three minor anomalies are symptomatic of the ambiguity that suffuses Brown's novel; that they fit his pattern of showing how untrustworthy the senses are, particularly—for Brown, I believe, was writing a polemic novel—regarding *all* varieties of religious experience.[12] He was testing in fictional form the argument he offered his friend Bringhurst. The hypothesis of the dangers of all morality based on religious forms, not merely religious excess or religious fanaticism, was being played out in a novel that *required* anomalous and unexplained occurrences. While the line between controlled ambiguity and aesthetic inconsistency may indeed be thin, Brown does seem to strive for the former. A better writer might have achieved his end more convincingly, but even Melville has not escaped from readers of *Pierre* who mistake ambiguity for a variety of literary sins. And Brown did not write at that level of genius.

Still, the patient reader will find the purposes of *Wieland* to be clear and the ambiguities and anomalies integral to the polemic against morality based in religious thought.

As indicated earlier, the tragedy of *Wieland* finds its roots in the religious conversion of the elder Wieland. That he chooses a bizarre theology—at least by the standards of his culture—merely highlights the danger of all religion. The man who will follow a "good" voice of God rather than his own moral senses will be capable of following any voice. For all the reader knows, Wieland was struck dead in the temple by a human intruder, or struck on the arm by one and then set on fire, externally ignited, if Wieland's own account is to be believed. But scarcely does the event occur, when Clara, not her father, raises the question of divine retribution (p. 19).

Theodore Wieland from the outset shares his father's religious temperament and habits. Unlike Clara, he studies theology and worries about "preparation and provision" (p. 23) for the next life in a way consistent with the religious mode rejected by Brown in his letter to Bringhurst. Clara herself does not look for faith based "in the weighing of proofs, and the dissection of creeds" (p. 22), although as subsequent events show she is much given to a belief in the supernatural and to explanations of events not rooted in rational thought. The advocate of rational thought is Pleyel. "Pleyel was the champion of intellectual liberty, and rejected all guidance but that of his reason" (p. 25), which may be open to debate but which is at least generally true. Catharine seems to have no thoughts on anything. Her primary function in the novel is to give Theodore something to murder and Carwin a voice to imitate.

In response to the first voice heard, the one calling Theodore back from the temple, Pleyel suggests "a deception of the senses" (p. 34), while Theodore flatly rejects such an explanation (p. 36). Clara fears that Pleyel's view might be right (p. 35), but she essentially reserves judgment. And very soon thereafter, a switch in perceptions occurs, which shatters the symmetry of Theodore as the voice of religion, Pleyel as the voice of reason, and Clara as inclined toward the latter and fearing the former (p. 35). For the second voice, announcing the death of Pleyel's fiancée, quickly ends the reliance on rational causes. Pleyel, without questioning the source of the voice, simply accepts the idea that she is dead. And Clara makes clear her belief in the supernatural. "That there are conscious beings, beside ourselves, in existence, whose modes of activity and information surpass our own, can scarcely be denied" (p. 45). She assumes that the voice heard by Theodore and Pleyel is supernatural but benign (p. 46). She will generally believe this about the voice throughout the book. And if Clara needed confirmation on the validity of the voice, she received it upon learning that Theresa, Pleyel's fiancée, was indeed dead (p. 48). That this subsequently proved to be untrue is consistent with Brown's method of unexplaining events almost as rapidly as he explains them, a technique most extensively and explicitly employed in *Arthur Mervyn,* where, as Emory Elliott shows, the reader receives two versions of reality with little basis for choosing between them.[13]

At this point in the story, immediately after the second voice, Carwin is introduced. The reader should not ignore Clara's account of him as monstrous (p. 49), particularly when considering that the lines are written after all the facts had been heard.[14] Clara regards Carwin as responsible for "the evils of which it is but too certain that [he was] the author" (p. 50). And the third experience with voices, the sounds of murderers in her closet (including the voice of one who claims he will deserve " 'perdition' " if he commits " 'more' " than murder [p. 58]), certainly does little to mitigate Clara's harsh judgment of Carwin. But the fourth voice, the one calling for someone to assist Clara (p. 59), further confirms her views that an outside agency with benevolent intentions is at work (pp. 59–60). Since this is a retrospective telling, it accounts only for her feelings at the time, but subsequent events will show that in spite of Carwin's confession, in spite of her hatred for him, she does not abandon the belief in an outside agency that would seem untenable in view of the explanations subsequently given by Carwin. At least if Carwin clarifies everything. But he does not.

Consider the fifth voice. Clara, asleep in her summer house, dreams of her brother's leading her to an abyss. Suddenly, a voice calls and a hand grasps her. The voice, according to his confession, is Carwin's (p. 204). The hand, unmentioned in the confession, presumably belongs to the dream. Clara, awakened by the voice, hears the sound "of him who had proposed to shoot, rather than to strangle" (p. 63), the voice recalled from her bedroom closet. It cautions Clara away from the summer house and threatens her father's fate, presumably learned by Carwin from Clara's maid. At this point, a key incident occurs. Clara "perceived a ray flit across the gloom and disappear. Another succeeded, which was stronger, and remained for a passing moment" (p. 63). Clara's response to what she sees invites alternative choices for the reader of *Wieland:*

> The first visitings of this light called up a train of horrors in my mind; destruction impended over this spot; the voice which I had lately heard had warned me to retire, and had menaced me with the fate of my father if I refused. I was desirous, but unable, to obey; these gleams were such as preluded the stroke by which he fell; the hour, perhaps, was the same—I shuddered as if I had beheld, suspended over me, the exterminating sword. (p. 64)

The original account of Wieland's death in the temple had left the reader with only one mystery not accountable by some rational explanation—even if one resorted to the spontaneous combustion unsupported by Wieland's dying testimony. This was the mystery of the light. Now Clara sees the same light. Granted that the appearance of the original light came to her through second-hand description. Nevertheless, her own senses, distraught though they may be, see a light like that which preceded the destruction of her father. If the light is indeed the same, speculations of Carwin's presence in the temple when her father was murdered are invited. If the similarity of lights represents only Clara's runaway imagination, is there any reason to believe it runs away here only? In other words, if Clara is so taken in by her imagination at this point that the reader cannot believe her, then why trust her observations or her history elsewhere? But if she is right about the light, then Carwin may have had something to do with the death of her father. Brown does not pick up this idea, although in the true spirit of later "romancers" he suggests possibilities, he uses that which cannot be taken literally to tell truths otherwise untellable. He has, in a sense, discredited Clara and Carwin even as he eventually explains every event between them. To not tell and tell is the essence of romance.

Clara comes to believe that occurrences have been explained. "It was only by subsequent events, that I was fully and incontestibly assured of the veracity of my senses" (p. 65). Yet the evidence of her own tale has contradicted her, and since the reader only knows the tale through her the mysteries of plot really never do become clarified. Nor should they, any more than Melville should have clarified the meaning of his whale, or Hawthorne the true state of Mistress Hibbens's witches. As with Melville and Hawthorne, Brown uses extraordinary, inexplicable events to arrive at truths in fiction.

Because Brown was writing a book about the dangers of religion in view of the unreliability of human senses, he could not let go of the strategy that swung expectations back and forth between natural and supernatural causes. If he does not pursue fully the possibilities of Carwin's culpability in the murder of Clara's father, he nevertheless sends his heroine back and forth between reliance on the natural and the supernatural for explanations, and in suggesting the former he keeps suspicion focused on Carwin. When Clara has safely escaped the summer house, she tries to make sense of events that have occurred. Her thoughts are of human rather than supernatural explanations. She believes the voice that warned her away from the summer house to be human (p. 66), and she very clearly raises the possibility that this may be the same voice that was behind the death of her father. "Was then the death of my father, portentous and inexplicable as it was, the consequence of human machinations?" (p. 66). Only readers sucked into Brown's vortex of the supernatural could believe otherwise, and this has included quite a few of them. Perhaps it is necessary to emphasize here that I am not building a case for the conviction of Carwin. Whether he was even old enough to have been the murderer of Wieland is not clear from Brown's story. But I am trying to emphasize how easily the reader may overlook "human machinations" as causes for apparently inexplicable events and that searching for spontaneous combustion as a cause may suggest an irony that Brown could not have anticipated in writing his book about the dangers of religion. Could he have ever guessed how fully science would replace religion as a new theology, that just as people in his generation looked for miracles in the supernatural world, another generation would seek them in the natural one? The scientific paradigm that emerged in the nineteenth century and which has dominated the twentieth century simply overwhelmed his point about "human machinations." The idea needs to be retrieved in the reading of *Wieland,* and the person examining Brown's book must select from three and not two possibilities in considering the story's central mystery.[15]

Carwin himself, when first apprized by the Wielands and Pleyel of the family tragedy, pleasantly surprises Clara by not ridiculing their story and by encouraging the belief in divine voices although he claims his own experience has always found stories so attributed to be ultimately explainable in human terms (p. 74). Indeed, Carwin toys with the group by actually giving them the explanation of ventriloquism for all the voices so far heard, except at the summer house. That voice is not discussed at all, presumably because Clara has not told anyone of it in response to its warning of dire consequences. Not certain whether the voice was natural or supernatural, she listens nevertheless. But in apparently telling the truth, Carwin finds an audience of skeptics. In response to Carwin's general discussion of similar occurences, Wieland insists on "the probability of celestial interference" (p. 75), while Pleyel holds to the "testimony . . . of his senses" (p. 75). Clara apparently swings back to belief in the supernatural, since she allies her opinions with her brother's (p. 75). And when Carwin offers specific speculations regarding the voices heard by the group, they find his thoughts "insufficient to impart conviction to us" (p. 76). Carwin has offered the simplest and most plausible of explanations, but none of them, particularly Clara and Wieland, can believe in events unshrouded by mystery.

Clara's temptation toward her brother's sensibility of explanations by supernatural causes, as well as her obsession with her father's death, must not be scanted. Clara's thoughts turn often toward her father's death, as they do just before the closet scene in her bedroom, where, expecting to find her brother she finds Carwin instead (p. 83). Much has justifiably been made of this closet scene and its relation to Clara's dream of her brother's luring her to the abyss.[16] Its invitation to psychological criticism and its introspective search for the nature of human senses as well as its intrinsic drama have contributed to the interest in it. I simply want to emphasize something simple and obvious here. Clara assumes that the voice warning her away from the closet, as well as the same voice she had earlier heard, is "divine" (p. 89). Like her brother, she believes in voices from other worlds.

Carwin plays on the belief when discovered in the closet. Clara has opened the door, in defiance of the voice warning her away, and has discovered Carwin. What is a man to say when thus exposed in a woman's closet? Writing on the edge of farce, but never crossing over into it, Brown has him demand explanations of her! " 'What voice was that which lately addressed you?' " (p. 89) he asks in the first words that pass between them in this bedroom encounter. Or, more accurately, the first words, since Clara actually says nothing. Carwin does all the talking, pretending, if we are to believe his later confession, that the voice was not his but a " 'sound . . . beyond the compass of human organs' " (p. 90). Affirming that the voice belongs to his " 'eternal foe' " (p. 90), Carwin emphasizes that he is helpless before that power.[17] As if Clara is not sufficiently confused, the fast-talking Carwin then argues that there would be no harm done in any case if he executed his illicit designs, since only her " 'prejudices' " make them injurious (p. 90). Clearly, Clara has no wish to engage in social discourses about chastity to say nothing of divine voices. Her only response to Carwin's verbal counterattack upon being discovered is to wonder at her own frame of mind. "I used to suppose that certain evils could never befall a being in possession of a sound mind," she narrates (p. 90). The reader may want to question how sound her mind is at this point.[18]

Carwin might have left after his attack on chastity as a " 'chimera still worshipped' " (p. 90), for Clara was in no mood to do anything but stand and wonder. But Carwin makes a final verbal assault before lapsing into self-pity and leaving. He tells Clara that he cannot harm her. " 'The power that protects you would crumble my sinews, and reduce me to a heap of ashes in a moment, if I were to harbour a thought hostile to your safety' " (p. 91). Now Carwin has just told her that he contemplated taking " 'away the spoils of [Clara's] honor' " (p. 90), and the reader has some sorting of information to do. Did Brown forget what he had just written? Did Carwin forget what he had just said? Was Clara incapable of catching the obvious flaw? But most importantly, how does one assess Carwin's "heap of ashes," a phrase that so clearly evokes the death of Wieland? On the latter question, one might speculate that Carwin, knowing the fate of Wieland, has played on it to terrorize her. Or one may guess that he too is mad and believes in avenging spirits. Or that he is sane and believes in them.

The point of these questions is not to argue their answer. Such matters in a well-executed romance do not trouble the reader, and if it is true that Brown attempts in *Wieland* the elliptical style of romance that finds fulfillment in Hawthorne and Melville, the flaw is not in the inconsistencies but in the level of execution. The terrible events are not the spoken ones, but those hinted at. The terror of the chapter resides not in threats of ravishment or murder, but in the possibility that we live in a world where unnamed powers can reduce us to "a heap of ashes." And both the burning Wieland and Carwin's evocation of the event encourage the gloom that pervades Brown's novel; they hint at the "blackness" Melville saw in Hawthorne.[19] As Clara observes: "Something whispered that the happiness we at present enjoyed was set on mutable foundations. Death must happen to all. Whether our felicity was to be subverted by it to-morrow, or whether it was ordained that we should lay down our heads full of years and of honor, was a question that no human being could solve" (pp. 54–55). In a book that advocated reliance on this world and the understandings to be derived from it for one's actions, the next world could only emerge as a dangerous illusion and not as a consoling thought. Whether wrought by a human intruder, by some natural phenomenon, or even by divine ordination, the death of Wieland prefigured Clara's fears, articulated perhaps in the "heap of ashes" image. Carwin presumably lied in playing with Clara on the story of her father's death. But in the lie he told the truth.

Clara's thoughts do not entertain the possibility of a world unregulated by higher powers. Like her father and her brother, she tries to guess at the intentions of supernatural forces, to read divine minds. In sorting out her experience with Carwin at the closet, she continues to refer to a "divinity" (p. 96) that spoke to her. Moreover, she affirms that "to yield to my fears is to deserve that they should be realized" (p. 96). This observation is doubly ironic, since it describes what happens to her brother who does yield, even as it also describes the realization of her own fears whether she yields to them or not. For the nightmare of her brother as monster is spurned by her as a cause for serious anxiety, yet the terrible dream materializes, even if Clara's abyss is not literal.

But before Clara's nightmarish confrontation with her brother occurs, Brown unfortunately turns his attention to the deviltry that voices play in Clara's love life. Perhaps because conventions of the day required it, Brown integrated into his tale of madness and cosmic ambiguity the courting of Clara and Pleyel. If this aspect of *Wieland* does little to enhance the sustained power of the tale, it does bring to an everyday level the consequences of relying merely on appearances. Maybe the part of Brown who saw himself as a "moral painter" felt obliged to work this lesson into a situation familiar to readers of novels addressed to the misunderstandings of lovers.[20] More probably, he anticipated an audience that expected a love motif, and he gave them one along with a set of voices to precipitate the misunderstanding between Clara and Pleyel. As the explanations and accusations emerge, the story loses its central focus on the mystery of the past and its intimations of terror in the future. It also loses some consistency in story line that will not be explained by suggestions of the romantic mode. For example, as Pleyel gives his long account of why he has lost faith in Clara's virtue, she actually reflects on Carwin's powers in setting up the misleading situation. But this occurs at a point in the book prior to her knowledge of Carwin's ability (p. 133). And, shortly after, with no suspicion that he has been duped and with every reason to believe that Clara is at the summer house (having just spoken with her there, or so he thinks), Pleyel goes to Clara's bedroom to confirm the fact that she is not there (p. 135).

However, Brown picks up the thread of his story once more when he places Clara back in her bedroom in response to Carwin's note. Clara, questioning her own wisdom in returning to meet her would-be ravisher, contemplates her belief in the protection of voices and assumes them supernatural (p. 147). But shortly afterward she qualifies her narrative. Just after hearing the voice calling her back from her room and seeing a glimpse of a face, she observes: "I now speak as if no remnant of doubt existed in my mind as to the supernal origin of these sounds; but this is owing to the imperfection of my language, for I only mean that the belief was more permanent, and visited more frequently my sober meditations than its opposite" (p. 148). This is a telling statement, since the reader might otherwise think that early references to "divine" sounds were figurative. They were not. Clara is removing whatever ambiguity may have existed about her own belief in supernatural voices. If she sometimes departs from that belief, more often she holds to it. Whether Brown wanted to suggest that a more rational Clara might have helped avert tragedy can only be a matter of speculation. The story really does not make this point. It simply gives the reader the true state of Clara's mind on the issue of divine commandments in preparation for her encounter with Wieland as the high tragedy of the story unfolds with unresolvable ambiguity.

Upon seeing Clara in her room, Wieland soon becomes distracted by a commandment he receives. Neither Clara nor the reader has any evidence of voices, so the presumption must be that Wieland is now simply mad or that divine voices actually speak to him. Assuming the latter as implausible, one infers the former. Brown gives us no reason to do otherwise, and since no voice is heard to urge on the killing of Clara, one would think that Carwin is exonerated from a direct link to the other murders. Yet Wieland's account of his actions offers the reader the third alternative as stated earlier by Clara's uncle: " 'Carwin, perhaps, or heaven, or insanity, prompted the murderer . . .' " (p. 161). That Wieland is insane by the time he threatens Clara seems uncontestable. But the matter of his other murders is not so clear. As Wieland tells his story of the event precipitating the murder of his family, a sudden light came upon him.[21] The reader has seen something of this light in the temple of the elder Wieland and at Clara's summer house. The possibility of its human sources cannot be ruled out, nor is it necessarily only in Wieland's mind. Upon opening his eyes after the burst of light, Wieland still sees it, " 'but, anon, a shrill voice from behind called upon me to attend' " (p. 167). Whether the voices heard by madmen are always "shrill" is uncertain at best. But there is no reasonable doubt that Carwin at times speaks that way, at least if we believe his confession that the earlier voices were his. Wieland himself has heard three voices previously, once when alone and going to the temple, once with Pleyel, and once at his house when the voice called for assistance to Clara. The first two voices Wieland heard came as the sound of Catharine. The third had no association with anyone he knew. In its anonymity the most striking characteristic was "piercing shrillness" (p. 59), perhaps similar to the "piercing" voice Clara heard in approaching the closeted Carwin (p. 147). This third voice, with its "shrillness," was heard by others besides Wieland. So the sound at that time is not a trick of his imagination.

Is it wholly unreasonable to assume that the "shrill" voice commanding him to murder his family might be identical to the "shrill" voice heard earlier? It is not, and the idea that Carwin, a confessed liar, created the voice commanding murder remains a possibility, if not the certainty that early critics of *Wieland* assumed.[22] The indescribable sight that Wieland next sees argues for his madness, but this is not inconsistent with the notion that Carwin's "shrill" voice might have commanded the murders. Again, I want to emphasize that the issue is not Carwin's guilt or innocence. Rather it is the ambiguity of the event; it is Brown at his best, I believe, controlling the narrative so that the reader, unable to guess the source of this voice—coming from inner madness, outer chicanery, or even divinity—can scarcely dismiss the plausibility of Wieland's lapse into insanity, particularly with his predilection toward divine injunctions. Under the best of circumstances, Brown seems to be saying, rational conduct in this world is not easily maintained. Add the dimension of reliance on religion, and abandoning the norms of civilization becomes an event only awaiting the circumstances that will precipitate it.

Brown will not let the reader escape this association, nor will he allow one to see the issue merely as religious *excess*. It is reliance on religion per se that allows the situation. The unpenitent Wieland defends himself, like Carwin in the closet, not by apologizing for his actions, but by accusing. " 'You say I am guilty. Impious and rash! thus to usurp the prerogatives of your Maker! to set up your bounded views and halting reason, as the measure of truth!' " (p. 176). This is precisely the issue Brown debated with Bringhurst. Does not religion, by its nature, preclude our relying on our own reason? And who can predict the consequences when we abandon the rules of this world for the communications of another? The soundness of Brown's argument on this point of theology may be contested, as Bringhurst obviously did. But its soundness is not the issue. It is its application to *Wieland*.

Nor will Brown allow us the comfort of seeing the whole matter as an aberration of Wieland's, since Clara's uncle tells the story of her grandfather plunging to his death in response to voices from a dead brother (pp. 178–79). This does not invite the explanation of congenital madness in the Wieland family, since the grandfather here is on the maternal side. And Clara, ever wavering between natural and supernatural explanations, casts her lot with the latter as she tries to absorb what she has experienced.

> My opinions were the sport of eternal change. Some times I conceived the apparition to be more than human. I had no grounds on which to build a disbelief. I could not deny faith to the evidence of my religion; the testimony of men was loud and unanimous: both these concurred to persuade me that evil spirits existed, and that their energy was frequently exerted in the system of the world. (p. 180)

This is Clara relying on religion and not reason. Whereupon she proceeds to divide the world of spirits into benign and malign agencies. Their existence is a matter of certainty and not speculation for Clara. "That conscious beings, dissimilar from human, but moral and voluntary agents as we are, some where exist, can scarcely be denied" (p. 181). And this leads her to the mystery she cannot fathom. "Carwin was the miscreant whose projects were resisted by a minister of heaven. How can this be reconciled to the stratagem which ruined my brother? There the agency was at once preternatural and malignant" (p. 181).

The "answer" to this will appear as the disappointing ventriloquism which historically has seemed so unsatisfactory to critics of *Wieland*. But if the solution hinges on gimmickry, the issue posed is as old as Christianity. Why does a benevolent heaven allow evil voices? Wieland's father had found his answer in the Albigensian heresy as popularly understood—the division of the world into a Manichean scheme of good and evil, a god for each. Clara seems to believe her father's heresy as she juggles events into this dualistic scheme. Then, suddenly, she finds a "new channel" of thought (p. 181). Clara reasons that "there was truth in this [Wieland's] appeal" to God (p. 181), "and nothing but unerring proof of divine approbation could sustain his mind in its present elevation" (p. 181). Put another way, the "new channel" emerges in the recognizable form of the Christian synthesis whereby the duality of good and evil becomes subsumed under the unity of heaven's just purposes. In this "new channel," Clara has left the Albigensian heresy and has acknowledged the Christian requirement to accept the will of heaven. Consequently, for the moment at least, she takes the side of her brother! No "transformation" in a book carrying that subtitle proves more remarkable. Such is the power of reasoning from heaven's word.[23]

Attempts to persuade Clara that her brother is simply mad do not succeed. She reverts to uncertainty as to whether he is "a faithful servant of his God, the victim of hellish illusions, or the dupe of human imposture . . ." (p. 187). Clara wants to visit him, but her uncle opposes the plan in part with the argument that a visit from her might restore him to sanity and thus shake "his confidence is divine approbation and future recompense" (p. 187). Although his true reason for discouraging the visit is to protect Clara, he speaks the truth in warning about the fatal consequences of shattering his religious belief. Wieland has committed his life to religion, and he has based his morality on the promise of future reward, a central belief of Christianity and an issue fundamental to the dialogue between Brown and Bringhurst. The wisdom of Clara's uncle would be justified in the fate of Wieland as would Brown's argument to Bringhurst.

But before this climatic scene emerges, the reader is taken once more into the ambiguity of Clara's perceptions about Carwin, whom she can never see properly because her vision is through a prism of spirits. Thus the reader can never fully know just what role Carwin had, since he can be understood only through the distorted understandings of Clara.

For reasons never clarified by Brown, the tide of Clara's reasoning begins to shift toward focusing blame on Carwin—this, even before his confession and on the basis of no appropriate information. Terrorized by the thought of being hunted to death by Wieland, who does so in heaven's name and in the cause of virtue, Clara leaps at the prospect of somehow focusing her search for causes on Carwin. "In this paroxysm of distress, my attention fastened on him as the grand deceiver; the author of this black conspiracy; the intelligence that governed in this storm" (p. 190). By the time she meets Carwin, once more in her bedroom, she assumes that he somehow "urged" (p. 196) Wieland on to his crimes. That she has no basis for this insinuation is beside the point. More germane is that for the moment she surrenders her belief in his guilt for two reasons: Carwin's denial even of having heard of the murders and her own recollection of the voice that previously saved her from Carwin (p. 196). Clara simply will not abandon her belief in the supernatural. With none to blame, and having faced horror beyond her capacity to comprehend or even to fit into some consoling scheme, she asks only to be left to her own despair.

But Carwin has come to confess. Readers of *Wieland* have readily accepted that confession of ventriloquism, even if they have often regretted Brown's inability to do better. Clara is less easily convinced. Bluntly, she asserts that "his tale is a lie, and his nature devilish" (p. 216). Her response bears careful consideration. Upon first hearing Carwin's claim that it was his voice and face she heard and saw, Clara arrives at a plausible response. "But if Carwin's were the thrilling voice and the fiery visage which I had heard and seen, then was he the prompter of my brother, and the author of these dismal outrages" (p. 197). The reader may recall that earlier scene, one which indeed comes close to the method of Hawthorne. Clara says upon seeing the face that "the lips were stretched as in the act of shrieking; and the eyes emitted sparks, which, no doubt, if I had been unattended by a light, would have illuminated like the corruscations of a meteor" (p. 148). It is a tableau hinging on an "if," but as true to reality as the "A" in the sky of *The Scarlet Letter* that tells the truth, even if its reality rests in the illusion of the romancer's art. The "fiery visage" Clara has seen invites inconclusive speculations on its association with the death of Wieland and the precipitation of his son's murders. On the basis of her own senses, Clara has every right to doubt Carwin.

Carwin's story has less mystical problems. He insists to Clara that he did not cause Catharine's death, "yet had I not rashly set in motion a machine, over whose progress I had no controul, and which experience had shewn me was infinite in power?" (pp. 215–216). Maybe. But how would he know? By his own testimony he has claimed that he did not even know Wieland was a " 'lunatic' " (p. 196); he had no idea of his involvement in Catharine's murder until Clara told him on the very occasion of the conversation now transpiring. Brown is inconsistent or Carwin is lying. " 'The perpetrator of Catharine's death was unknown to me till now; nay, it is still unknown to me' " (p. 216). This is Carwin speaking almost immediately after admitting that he had " 'set in motion a machine' " (p. 215). How one responds to this clear contradiction no doubt depends on how one responds to Brown as an artist. While I readily grant that he writes careless lines and has inconsistencies of narrative, he was in my opinion too good a writer to make this kind of slip up, to inadvertently juxtapose such contrary evidence. The flaw is in Carwin's story and not in Brown's artistry. Clara does not reason it all out, but she understands "a lie" when she hears it here.[24]

What then of the rest of Carwin's story? Some perhaps is true; some perhaps false. Brown's point is that the event is beyond comprehension; his explanation is for an audience that must have answers, while his "moral" is that where no answers exist, one must not insist upon false ones. Neither Clara nor the reader really can decide whether Carwin prompted Wieland to his murders. If *Wieland* is a successful "Romance" directed to another point, the resolution of such a detail does not matter. Certainly, though, one can understand the belief in Carwin's guilt by those who wish to solve such problems. When Wieland tries to hear voices with Carwin and Clara in the room, there are none (p. 218). Only when Carwin leaves the room does a voice sound, this time to save Clara from Wieland.

Before the story's final voice rescues Clara, she finds herself alone with her brother; the nightmare of the summer house has been transformed into the reality of Wieland in her bedroom ready to send her to the abyss of death. Brown masterfully weds this pathetic, tragic moment to the "moral" he wants to teach. " 'I have acted poorly my part in this world,' " Wieland tells his sister, apparently doubting for the moment the righteousness of his acts. " 'What thinkest thou? Shall I not do better in the next?' " (p. 224). Here Brown relentlessly fixes on the issue he had debated with Bringhurst. What kind of morality can we expect if it is contingent on rewards and punishments in an afterworld? For all his misery, Wieland remains faithful to future judgments for present conduct. He does not reject this religious construct; he merely seems to acknowledge that he may not have followed heaven's rules after all. " 'The cup is gone by,' " he says, " 'and its transient inebriation is succeeded by the soberness of truth' " (p. 224). But only the "truth" that he may have been deceived. He does not question the morality of rewards and punishments.

Indeed, he shakes himself free of the tormenting doubt to affirm his purity on the grounds that " 'I believed that my God was my mover!' " (p. 224).

How does Clara react to this from the murderer of Catharine and her children? With admiration and with doubt over the capacity of her own reason or anyone's reason to judge wisely. But this must not be seen as an attack by Brown on reason or on its limitations. Rather it is an attack on reason rooted in beliefs of the supernatural. It is also of course not a condoning of Wieland's actions. But in the ambiguity of admiration for her "heroic brother" (p. 225) and the horror of what has happened, Clara can resort only to cursing Carwin.

Wieland is more certain in his beliefs, his wavering faith having returned. He claims that his silent prayers had after all been answered, and that he understands Carwin to be evil. But Carwin's evil has been commissioned by God, and that is sufficient for Wieland. To Carwin, Clara appeals for help, and the voice that subsequently saves her is presumably his. But Clara, after Wieland's suicide concludes the tragic sequence, has gone beyond concerns of whose voice belonged to whom.

> Talk not to me, O my revered friend! of Carwin. He has told thee his tale, and thou exculpatest him from all direct concern in the fate of Wieland. This scene of havock was produced by an illusion of the senses. Be it so: I care not from what source these disasters have flowed; it suffices that they have swallowed up our hopes and our existence.
>
> What his agency began, his agency conducted to a close. He intended, by the final effort of his power, to rescue me and to banish his illusions from my brother. Such is his tale, concerning the truth of which I care not. (p. 233)

The reader does well to be guided by Clara's final assessment (at least before the tacked-on chapter).[25] The questions of Carwin's reliability, of how the elder Wieland died, and of other matters belong to truths of fiction rather than to truths of life. Her lack of concern for the "truth" is in the spirit of romance where the details of narrative matter less than the implications behind them. For the "truth" has been told, and the monstrousness of a world that abandons the reason Brown believed in has been revealed.

The remainder of *Wieland*, the chapter apparently coming as an afterthought on Brown's part, has pained his admirers who understandably wish he had left well enough alone. An aspect of the story, the Louisa Conway motif that had been touched upon and dropped is here picked up and explained in the form of a tale of seduction and murder that bears little need for critical analysis. One may speculate that Brown felt obliged to tie up a loose end, or perhaps that he wanted to give his audience something brighter and more conventional, something to make the book more marketable. These must remain speculations.

But one observation about this chapter must be made. Brown returns in it to his moral lesson and ties the Maxwell story to the Wieland tale by observing that "it will not escape your notice, that the evils of which Carwin and Maxwell were the authors, owed their existence to the errors of the sufferers" (p. 244). That is, what applies in religious conduct applies in social conduct also. However extraneous the chapter may appear, it manages to take the moral of a religious tale and show its application to that of a conventional seduction story. Neither the Stuarts nor the Wielands ever did understand the correct moral obligations that this world requires of us, and the final sentence of the book implicitly applies to the Stuarts as well as to the Wielands and to the Bringhursts. "If Wieland had framed juster notions of moral duty, and of the divine attributes; or if I had been gifted with ordinary equanimity or foresight, the double-tongued deceiver would have been baffled and repelled" (p. 244). Here is no argument for atheism, since it acknowledges "divine attributes." But it is an argument for understanding that the voice of God must be obeyed only as it is consistent with human morality based in reason.

Brown was a man of the eighteenth century, so of course his assumptions about the efficacy and power of reason are tied to beliefs then held about the ways in which people learn and sense their world. The critic who seeks to understand Brown's premise need not accept it or the morality that the book attacks. But the critic is obliged to come to terms in some way with the ambiguities and contradictions of the tale or to acknowledge *Wieland* as an unsatisfactory novel. Read as a book hinging on the gimmick of ventriloquism, it indeed disappoints the reader. As a story that explores the limits of understanding, the ambiguity of perception, it justifies some of its most extravagant praise. At its best *Wieland* captures the wonder of romance and transforms improbabilities into vehicles for conveying truths otherwise beyond the capacity to tell. The theme of illusion and reality, so central to the writings of Hawthorne, Melville, and Poe, found its first American expression in *Wieland*. It was expressed well.

Notes

1. *Wieland* seems to have gone unnoticed in England when first published. Subsequently, reviews were mixed with particularly savage ones in *The Ladies' Monthly Museum*, n.s., 9 (December, 1810), 338–39 and *Gentleman's Magazine*, 81 (April, 1811), 364. Both reviews were anonymous. Others were mixed, and the only genuinely enthusiastic review appeared anonymously in *Critical Review*, s. 3, 22 (February, 1811), 144–63. Brown seems to have fared better in America. See Harry Warfel, *Charles Brockden Brown* (Gainesville: University of Florida Press, 1949), pp. 110–11.

2. I use the term here in the sense that Hawthorne does in his preface to *The House of the Seven Gables*. For an important consideration of Brown and Romanticism see Sydney J. Krause, "Romanticism in *Wieland*: Brown and the Reconciliation of Opposites" in *Artful Thunder*, ed. Robert J. DeMott and Sanford Marovitz (Kent: Kent State University

Press, 1975), pp. 13–24. See also Robert Strozier's suggestive essay, "*Wieland* and Other Romances: Horror in Parentheses," *Emerson Society Quarterly*, No. 50 (1st quarter, 1968), pp. 24–29. For associations with Hawthorne and others, see Donald A. Ringe, *Charles Brockden Brown* (New York: Twayne Publishers, Inc., 1966), pp. 42–43.

3. *Wieland*, ed. Sydney J. Krause and S. W. Reid (1798; Kent: Kent State University Press, 1977), p. 8. Subsequent citations from *Wieland* are from this edition and indicated parenthetically in the text.

4. Brown's outline for *Wieland* is published in the Kent State edition (pp. 420–41) and contains a notation to "See Chambers Cyclopaedia" for reference to Wieland's religious faith (p. 427), specifically in connection with the Savoyard sect. I have examined the 1788 and the 1741 editions of *Chambers' Cyclopedia* and have found no reference to the Savoyard sect in either one. However, the entry for "Albigenses," taken here from the 1788 edition, warrants notation: "The Romanists tax the *Albigenses* with abundance of heterodox opinions; as, for instance, that there are two Gods, the one infinitely good, and the other infinitely evil; that the good God made the invisible world, and the evil one that which we live in; with the rest of the Manichean tenets.

"But this seems to be one of those pious frauds allowed particularly in that church, which esteems it a kind of merit to blacken heretics, and those whom they chuse to call so." Ephraim Chambers, *Cyclopedia: or, An Universal Dictionary of Arts and Sciences*, vol. 1 (London, 1788). The 1741 entry differs in some details, particularly in its assertion that the Albigenses "maintained marriage unlawful" (vol. 1). Both emphasize the dualism cited above as "Manichean tenets," and both suggest that the Albigenses may not have necessarily held the views ascribed to them by their persecutors. No mention is made in the 1741 edition of the third name associated with Wieland's religion, the Camisards, although a brief and relatively insignificant entry appears in the 1788 edition. Although I cannot verify whether Brown followed up his stated intention in the outline to check this source, the entry cited regarding the Albigenses is similar to that appearing in other sources and does offer a reliable indication of the connotations carried by reference to that sect. The reliability of these perceptions regarding the Albigenses is not germane to Brown's use of the name. Its attraction seemed to be in the popular beliefs about the Albigenses.

5. Scholars of Brown have tended to scant the sources of *Wieland*'s theology and their implications for the novel. Some notable exceptions, however, may be found. David Brion Davis, *Homicide in American Fiction, 1798–1860: A Study in Social Values* (Ithaca: Cornell University Press, 1957), p. 88 makes the connection between "religious fanaticism" and *Wieland*'s interest in the Albigenses. Various critics have made passing references to the Manichean aspects of *Wieland*, particularly Richard Chase in *The American Novel and Its Tradition* (Garden City; Doubleday and Company, 1957), p. 38. The most serious and extensive examination of the Manichean aspect of *Wieland* may be found in Carl Nelson, "Brown's Manichean Mock-Heroic: The Ironic Self in a Hyperbolic World," *West Virginia University Philological Papers*, 20: 26–42. For an especially suggestive note on the Camisards and the use of voices, see Bruce E. Kirkham, "A Note on *Wieland*," *American Notes and Queries*, 5 (1967), 86–87.

6. See introduction to this collection, pp. 11–16. The notion that *Wieland* treats religious excess is so commonplace in the critical canon that no special citation is needed here. I am, of course, distinguishing between religious excess and reliance on revealed religion per se, the idea Brown attacks in his letter to Bringhurst. The idea that Theodore Wieland's problem stems from misguided religion rather than religion itself may be found, for example, in James E. Mulqueen, "The Plea for a Deistic Education in Charles Brockden Brown's *Wieland*," *Ball State University Forum*, 10 (1970), 77. In a different approach Larzar Ziff asserts that "stigmatizing religious fanaticism is inadequate because Wieland's training is singularly free from any sectarianism." "A Reading of *Wieland*," *PMLA*, 77 (1962), 54. While Ziff is clearly correct in pointing out that Wieland belongs to no special sect, Brown is explicit in associating the younger Wieland's approach to theology with that of his father,

who does follow a sect. See *Wieland*, p. 23. For the view that "Brown was testing theological ideas," see Warfel, p. 97.

In emphasizing as I do the association of *Wieland* with Brown's theological concerns, I do not mean to imply that the story has no other textual or intellectual sources. Much has been written about influences on *Wieland*. For a particularly suggestive essay regarding possible links to the German poet C.M. Wieland, see John G. Frank, "The Wieland Family in Charles Brockden Brown," *Monatshefte*, 42 (1950), 347–53.

7. The reference to "Seek and ye shall find" is noted by A. Carl Bredahl, Jr. in an essay that treats the lines from another perspective. "Transformation in *Wieland*," *Early American Literature*, 12 (1977), 177–92. The specific reference to the injunction appears on p. 179.

8. The association with "spontaneous combustion" appears from the earliest critical reception of *Wieland* to contemporary criticism, as, for example, in John Cleman's essay, valuable for its addressing the issue of ambiguity, "Ambiguous Evil: A Study of Villains and Heroes in Charles Brockden Brown's Major Novels," *Early American Literature*, 10 (1975), 190–219. The assumption has been questioned by David Ketterer, *New Worlds for Old: The Apocalyptic Imagination, Science Fiction, and American Literature* (New York: Anchor Books, 1974), p. 173. The best comment to date on the issue of "spontaneous combustion" in *Wieland* appears in Mulqueen, p. 72.

9. Although seeing "spontaneous combustion" as one of Brown's exceptions, John Cleman perceptively observes that "the instances of non-human evil, or harm not the result of human action, are rare in Brown's major novels, and the examples that do appear are never left without a sense of the human connection," p. 193. For one of the rare recognitions of alternative possibilities to spontaneous combustion, see Ringe, pp. 143–44, n. 10.

10. The association of Clara with reason is a traditional one in critical responses to *Wieland*, with various commentators observing that her reason unguided by sound religious principles is insufficient. For a refreshing recognition of the degree to which Clara departs from reason, see Michael Bell, "The Double-Tongued Deceiver: Sincerity and Duplicity in the Novels of Charles Brockden Brown," *Early American Literature*, 9 (1974), p. 148.

11. In his splendid historical essay on Brown in the Kent State edition of *Wieland*, Alexander Cowie, in arguing that Clara holds "latent incestuous longings" for her brother, addresses in a note Brown's willingness to write about sexual topics: "It would seem to be an anomaly that Brown, an almost prudish person by most tokens, should have made so much comment, in his publications, on sexual freedom and sexual aberrations, including, in *Stephen Calvert*, a reference to a relationship between man and wife in which the husband exhibits 'propensities . . . that have not a name which' the wife 'can utter' " (*Wieland*, p. 332). Although the note is somewhat misleading in that the reference is actually to the husband's homosexual relationships, Cowie's point remains germane. Brown, of course, also deals with the issue of rape elsewhere in his fiction. For the incident in *Stephen Calvert* cited by Cowie, see William Dunlap, *The Life of Charles Brockden Brown* (Philadelphia: James P. Parke, 1815), II, 400.

12. The issue of sensory experience has perhaps elicited more discussion in criticism of *Wieland* than any other subject. I cite only two of the many perceptive comments on this topic. See the introduction by Robert E. Hemenway and Joseph Katz to Paul Allen, *The Late Charles Brockden Brown* (Columbia: J. Faust & Co., 1976), p. liv; and J.V. Ridgely, "The Empty World of Wieland," in H. Kenneth Baldwin and David K. Kirby, eds. *Individual and Community: Variations on a Theme in American Fiction* (Durham: Duke University Press, 1975), p. 3.

13. See pp. 142–163 of this collection.

14. The matter of Clara's retrospective narration causes numerous uncertainties as to whether a given perception by her is one as seen from the present looking back or as seen at the time of the occurence. Ringe has given some attention to this matter, pp. 45–47, although a full analysis of the subject awaits a separate essay devoted to that topic.

15. Critics perceptive enough not to accept the death of the elder Wieland as a clarified event have tended to see two choices—theological or scientific—for the reader rather than three. For example, see Joe Lee Davis, John T. Frederick, and Frank Luther Mott, eds. *American Literature, An Anthology and Critical Survey* (New York: Charles Scribner's Sons, 1948), I, 232.

16. See, for example, the introduction by Sydney J. Krause and S.W. Reid to the paperback edition of the Kent State text, *Wieland, or The Transformation* (Kent: Kent State University Press, 1978), pp. xix–xx. This paperback reprint embodies the same pagination as the 1977 hardback *Wieland* Kent State text, although it does not have all the critical apparatus. It is not only the best paperback of *Wieland*, but also the only textually reliable one. For a view of the closet scene "as a metaphor for the entire action of this strange tale," see William H. Manly, "The Importance of Point of View in Brockden Brown's *Wieland*," *American Literature*, 35 (1963), p. 319.

17. The idea of the double personality used so successfully later by Poe, as in "William Wilson," seems suggested by Brown, but not explored.

18. Bredahl, p. 189, observes that Clara's confusions eventually bring her to the brink of suicide, as he compares her state of mind with her brother's. Frank, p. 253, sees her as faring much better, "since she shows the victory by reason and deism."

19. Herman Melville, "Hawthorne and His Mosses" (1850), in Edmund Wilson, *The Shock of Recognition* (New York: Farrar, Straus and Cudahy, 1955), pp. 187–204. See also the very perceptive observations by Pamela J. Shelden about the vision of the world that emerges from *Wieland*. "The Shock of Ambiguity: Brockden Brown's *Wieland* & the Gothic Tradition," *Literary Arts Journal*, 10 (1977), 17–26. See also Ziff, p. 52.

20. In his "Advertisement" for *Wieland*, Brown refers to "moral painters" in connection with his own intentions. See *Wieland*, p. 3.

21. Although nothing in the story suggests anything false to me about the confession, I do call attention to the fact that Wieland's confession comes to Clara from her uncle who received the transcription from an unidentified person; this confession, of course, along with the rest of the tale, comes to the reader through the perception of Clara. Those concerned with the reliability of narration in *Wieland* may want to scrutinize further this matter. See p. 163.

22. One must not, of course, rule out the possibility that a demented Wieland merely chose for his delusion a voice he had heard earlier. The question of whether Carwin commanded the murders is an old one. Most of the early critics, particularly those disliking the book, took Carwin's guilt for granted. A few examples of opinion in the twentieth century, presented chronologically, reflect the modern range of views on this subject. Martin S. Vilas sees "pure malice" from Carwin and holds him responsible for the voice: *Charles Brockden Brown: A Study of Early American Fiction* (Burlington: Free Press Association, 1904), p. 21. According to Ziff, "Wieland's homicidal actions result, finally, from causes which are inexplicable scientifically," p. 54. Arthur Kimball argues that to ask whether the villain is Carwin or the insanity of Wieland is to ask the wrong question; he also offers a useful survey of opinion on the subject. See *Rational Fictions: A Study of Charles Brockden Brown* (McMinville: Linfield Research Institute, 1968), pp. 44–49. Bell writes that "Wieland's insanity . . .turns out to have arisen from his own mind and not from Carwin's deceptions . . ." (p. 144). Ridgely takes the view "that the voice which Wieland heard was *not* that which had addressed [Clara] and the others on previous occasions" (p. 10). Finally, Robert. W. Hobson points the argument back toward earlier views in raising "the possibility that Carwin's influence on Wieland is more direct than Mr. Cambridge will allow. Indeed, it appears that Carwin may be as guilty of murder as Wieland." See "Voices of Carwin and Other Mysteries in Charles Brockden Brown's *Wieland*," *Early American Literature*, 10 (1975), 307–09.

23. William Hedges has called attention to Clara's "idolizing Wieland as Christlike" in response to his "supreme sacrifice" resulting from obedience "to orders he took to be divine." "Charles Brockden Brown and the Culture of Contradictions," *Early American Literature*, 9

(1974), p. 121. This response by Clara that Hedges notes warrants careful consideration on two grounds. It very clearly emphasizes how thoroughly Clara's thought is conditioned by religious predispositions. It also invites associations of Wieland with the "perfecti," cited in my essay's opening discussion of the Albigenses. Of the many notions attributed to this group, a particularly significant one held that Satan, the Old Testament Jehovah, created the material world and that most individuals are beyond redemption because they were Jehovah's creatures. According to Appleton's *American Cyclopaedia*, however, "there is also a higher class of men, whose souls are the fallen angels, and for the redemption of whom the God of light sent the angel Jesus, who taught them that they were of a higher nature, and that by despising everything material they could emancipate themselves from the prince of this world." Those in this group were presumably the "perfecti." See Appleton's *American Cyclopaedia*, ed. George Ripley and Charles A. Dana (New York: D. Appleton and Company, 1873), vol IV, 116. While I can identify no specific source in which Brown might have found such information, the view described here was an old one and widely available in Brown's day. His specific association early in the story of the elder Wieland's discovery of Albigensian theology, along with the younger Wieland's affinity with his father's theology, surely offers a possible theological frame of reference for Wieland's destruction of his attachments to the world. Certainly, Clara sees him as above and apart from other mortals. "Infatuated wretch that I was!" she exclaims. "To set myself up as a model by which to judge of my heroic brother!" (p. 225). Note also on the same page: "A new soul appeared to actuate his frame, and his eyes to beam with preternatural lustre."

Those interested in pursuing the subject of Manichean theology, of which the Albigensian heresy represented a late historical form, should begin with Hans Jonas, *The Gnostic Religion: The Message of the Alien God and the Beginnings of Christianity*, second edition, revised (Boston: Beacon Press, 1963).

24. For another perspective on Carwin, see David Lyttle, "The Case Against Carwin," *Nineteenth Century Fiction*, 26 (1971), 257–69.

25. For a history of this chapter, see Alexander Cowie's comments in *Wieland*, pp. 322–23.

The Problem of Origination in Brown's *Ormond*

William J. Scheick*

"Such is the motley and ambiguous condition of human society, such is the complexity of all effects, from what *cause* soever they spring, that none can tell whether this destructive pestilence was, on the whole, productive of most pain or most pleasure,"[1] opines Sophia Westwyn Courtland, the narrator of Charles Brockden Brown's *Ormond* (1799). Her observation warrants attention not only because it emphasizes an ambiguity concerning good and evil pervasive in the book[2] but also because it suggests a problem concerning the origins of experiences undergone by the characters, a problem embodied in both the plot and the narrative manner of the romance. In spite of its hasty composition, resulting in several inconsistencies in plot and characterization,[3] *Ormond* includes a goodly number of sustained themes, the most fundamental of which, I suggest, pertains to the apparently undisclosed cause or origin of one's reactive experiences in the world.

In *Ormond* the physical world, a place known to mankind only in response to its effects, exhibits a Hobbesian mechanism. Effect is everything, determining the tendency of the human mind to posit the existence of anterior cause. When we apply a Lockean adaptation of Hobbesian thought, we observe that time and again in the romance people experience a sequence of events without knowing anything about how the series began and that in the process they evince a "passive power," the ability to receive change. In the Lockean system, however, the mind is also accorded an "active power," the capacity for asserting will and thereby effecting change in itself.[4] Within this distinction between passive and active power lies an epistemological quandary identical to that informing *Ormond*: if the mind manifests a capacity for producing change in itself—that is to say, for self-origination—is there then real, precedent, determinative, extrinsic causality for how that mind behaves and for what that mind knows? Even if such causality exists in fact, does not its undisclosed nature in effect render it an absence? But, conversely and

* This essay was read at the University of Texas at Austin, on November 29, 1978, and appears here for the first time by permission of the author, who wishes to acknowledge the generous advice of R. James Kaufmann.

paradoxically, does not the absence or apparent absence of anterior external principle in turn become a cause necessitating the mind's self-origination? Whether a precedent extrinsic cause in the universe is present or is absent (in fact or in effect), self-origination in the mind is, then, vexingly not free from determination in some sense. Self-origination remains essentially, as Hume observed (capitalizing on a lapse in Locke's remarks on the imagination), illusory or fictive; yet—and this is significant—it amounts to a fiction which, in relation to inscrutable or absent (in fact or or in effect) precedent origins, becomes reality for us, defining and determining our experiences not only in the mind but also in the world. As Jacques Derrida has explained in another, but applicable context: "Everything begins with reproduction. Always already: repositories of a meaning which was never present, whose signified presence is always reconstituted by deferment, nachträglich, belatedly, supplementarily."[5] Concern with sources, as Michel Foucault has also observed, characterizes human reality:

> It is always against a background of the already begun that man is able to reflect on what may serve for him as origin. For man, then, origin is by no means the beginning—a sort of dawn of history from which his ulterior acquisitiveness would have accumulated. Origin, for man, is much more the way in which man in general, any man, articulates himself upon the already-begun.[6]

Admittedly such thoughts are abstruse, and we need to be cautious in applying them to *Ormond*, lest we create another and unintended fiction. But like his other important romances, *Ormond* reflects Brown's fascination with the implications of eighteenth-century rationalism,[7] particularly with Lockean psychology, and this interest includes the problem of the origin of behavior and knowledge in the mind. If *Ormond* provides no systematic approach to the subject, it nonetheless probes the matter to the extent that, despite difficulties arising from Brown's hasty composition of the text, concern with origination informs the central meaning of the work.

One clue to the significance of this theme surfaces in the repeated emphasis upon the orphan condition of so many of the characters in the romance. This pattern is introduced as early as the third paragraph of the first chapter, where we learn that Constantia Dudley's mother was an orphan (p. 5); and in the same chapter Craig (Mansfield?), a bastard who fabricates his family origins, presents himself as essentially orphaned. Lucy, whom the Dudleys take into their home, is also an orphan, a "child without friend or protector" (p. 20), as were Martinette de Beauvois and her brother, Ormond. Helena Cleves becomes Ormond's mistress as a consequence of her father's death, which "left her without provision" (p. 99) as if she were an orphan. The analogy applies as well to Constantia, who undergoes one loss after another—first the death of her mother, then the removal of her closest friend, then the murder of her father—leaving her bereft of family and of the comfort it provides as a tangible objectification of her origins.

In *Ormond* the image of the orphan serves as a metaphor for the psychological condition of Americans, who at the time of the publication of the romance had recently gained their independence from the colonial family and had now, as a consequence of that break from their origins, to struggle with the problem of identity—a plight depicted excellently a little later in Washington Irving's *The Sketch Book* (1819–1820). But in *Ormond* the metaphor signifies more, as will its thematic role in nineteenth-century fiction. In *Ormond* it epitomizes the general human dilemma concerning origination. The orphan stands alone, often without success (Helena commits suicide), sometimes with a self-generated, tenuous strength (Constantia exerts will against circumstance). So long as a person in *Ormond* defines himself primarily in relation to the family (in the largest sense) into which he is born, he can displace questions pertaining to the source of his knowledge and behavior by focusing on the comforting extrinsic biological reference provided by his parents; for in Lockean terms, one is born *tabula rasa*, his behavior and knowledge determined principally by environment. Such biological reference encourages a dependent disposition oriented toward the past. Should security founded on this trust in natural causality be shattered, either by a literal or a figurative orphaning of an individual, he is forced to confront himself henceforth as apparently self-originating; he enters the world, as if through a second birth, with a new awareness of independence in a present at once ever rich in potentiality and ever fraught with metaphysical uncertainty. Now concern with causality, in the sense of exterior limiting natural forces, metamorphoses into interest in *motives*, the product of intrinsic, expansive mental forces—a distinction, incidentally, latent in Ormond's deliberate substitution of the word *motive* for Constantia's word *cause* (p. 231).

Sophia, the narrator of *Ormond*, cannot easily reconcile cause and motive. She tends to assert the priority of natural cause, which she attributes to providential design as if God were the father of a family to which all humanity belongs. Because "our limited perceptions debar us from a thorough knowledge of any actions and motives" of others, she explains, "all that duty enjoins is to design and to execute nothing which may not be approved by a divine and omniscient Observer" (p. 217). One might suspect, however, that the reverse of Sophia's view could more plausibly be argued or, at least, that both human and divine purposes remain beyond the comprehension of the perceiving mind. Although she senses ambiguity at all levels of existence, as in her comment cited at the opening of this essay, Sophia prefers to assert a belief in "divine superintendence," in accord with which "all physical and moral agents are merely instrumental to the purpose that [God] wills" (p. 185). She relies on the concept of a deity as a parent surrogate originating all events and thereby providing a point of objective referentiality in accordance with which she can confidently believe in—albeit not scrutinize—a purpose behind Constantia's troubles. Whereas the reader dimly perceives Constantia's difficulties to emanate from the tangency of chance in the world and indefinite motives in the human mind, Sophia attributes them to her friend's lack of beliefs similar to her own:

> She was unguarded in a point where, if not her whole, yet, doubtless her principal, security and strongest bulwark would have existed. She was unacquainted with religion. She was unhabituated to conform herself to any standard but that connected with the *present* life. . . . She formed her estimate of good and evil on nothing but terrestrial and visible *consequences*. (p. 148; my emphasis)

Constantia lives in the present and behaves in terms of obscure *a posteriori* hints of causality or, more accurately, motive. Her lack of religious belief, in Sophia's opinion, leaves her bereft of a "felicity and excellence" which would aid her in "struggles with misfortune" (p. 149). Sophia, who may be a bastard and who was deserted (orphaned) by her mother on the day of her birth (p. 185)—later they are reunited—circumvents questions of origins by means of an *a priori* faith in divine causation, in predestination, and in a consequent delimiting dependence upon the past, when this providential regulation commenced.

Sophia's belief, however, is sorely tested by the seemingly malignant destiny of the characters in her story, and the incidents she recounts suggest that her notions amount to a protective fiction. The fact, for instance, that her prostitute mother becomes "maniacal" after she abandons her "mask of virtue" (p. 187), as a result of her religious conversion, undermines the reader's confidence in Sophia's view of religion.[8]

If *Ormond* intimates that religious explanations of origins constitute a mental aberration, it also suggests that attempts to fathom experience in the light of natural causality are similarly maddening. Ormond's conception of "the universe . . . [as] a series of events connected by an undesigning and inscrutable necessity, and an assemblage of forms to which no beginning or end can be conceived" (p. 149) comports with the world depicted in the romance—doubtless one reason for Brown's ambivalence toward Ormond[9]—yet he is demented, manifests perverse egocentric motives in response to the absence of purposeful divine or meaningful natural causality. Brown's romance fails to provide any norm, any middle ground between perverse motive and inscrutable causality; it merely portrays human experience as harrowing event in a world devoid of perceptible design.[10]

Ormond's example, then, reveals that *a posteriori* speculation about natural sources fails to answer the question "Whence?" as does an *a priori* belief in providence. Causality in nature is elusive; yellow fever, for instance, causes death, which in turn engenders a series of subsequent calamities, but the source of the disease—"what cause soever," in Sophia's words—in an immediate as well as in a metaphysical sense, remains unknown. Ormond perceives this aspect of existence all too well, describing it as "undesigning and inscrutable necessity." In the absence of knowledge about derivation—absence, as was earlier remarked, can paradoxically become causal—he emphasizes independent (in appearance at least), subjective human motives, or self-origination. Ormond maintains that "a man may reasonably hope to accomplish his end, when he proposes nothing but his own good" (p. 93); and his "mind of uncommon energy" originates, or "give[s] birth to[,] innumerable incidents" (p. 96). Lacking (actually or virtually) perceptible anterior, extrinsic cause, Ormond becomes, as it were, his own deity enjoying the impression he gives of possessing "something like omniscience" (p. 96), evincing "a freedom and originality" in the genesis of ideas (p. 130), disregarding the past as well as the consequences of his actions (pp. 122–123), and employing "instruments and not partakers of his authority—one whose mind was equal and not superior to the cogent apprehension and punctual performance of his will" (p. 105). Since Ormond manifests such deific qualities, it is appropriate that Constantia should confront him with the very dilemma that he, she, and the reader contemplate concerning life as depicted in the romance: "What your purpose is, or whether you have any purpose, I am at a loss to conjecture" (p. 227). In fact, Ormond's deity-like, "powerful" motives, similar to the cause which might inform creation, remain by his own admission quite "indefinite" (p. 237); so that for Ormond, and by implication for everyone, self-origination evinces a freedom which is, paradoxically, restricted because it is necessitated by the absence of cause in fact or in effect and because it always elicits unanswerable questions concerning cause in creation as well as in the mind.

Movement from dependence upon natural causality, whether providential or familial, to *seeming* independence of motive comprises Brown's variation of the fall-from-innocence theme in *Ormond*. The fall from innocence, or more accurately the birth out of ignorance, occurs when a character loses a familiar identity defined *a priori* by natural causality (providence, family) and discovers a tenuous selfhood informed *a posteriori* by vexing experience in a world of inscrutable, indefinite human motives. This metamorphosis is central to Constantia's development and it is epitomized in her murder of Ormond, an action indicative of her assertion of will in explicit response to Ormond's motives. It is central as well to Helena's behavior. Helena, who "scarcely comprehends the principle that governs the world," attempts to exchange her independent orphan condition for dependence as Ormond's mistress and, as a consequence, remains (in the opinion of both Ormond and Constantia, and in contrast to society's view of her as a "fallen" woman) "to a certain degree, innocent," as "ignorant and helpless as a child" (p. 117; cf. p. 127). When Ormond tells Helena of his decision to modify their arrangement, she must again confront her orphan status. Rather than assume responsibility for her life, she commits suicide; and since Ormond had promised to look after her physical welfare, the problem for Helena is clearly one of psychological dependence. Helena eschews facing a world in which, as Martinette (who was an orphan as a child) tells Constantia, independence or "liberty without peril can never exist" (p. 170).

Helena may be as "ignorant and helpless as a child," but her "fall" could have amounted to a second birth. Detailed at the very opening of the romance, the experience of Stephen Dudley, Constantia's father, is representative. During his early adult years Dudley lived in Europe, his career as a painter supported by his parents in America. In fact, "the liberality of his father relieved him from all pecuniary cares" (p. 5). The death of his father, however, "introduce[s] an important change in his situation" (p. 5). Dependence upon familial origin dissolves as "orphaned" Dudley assumes a new degree of financial and philosophical responsibility for himself. His father's death is followed by Craig's duplicity resulting in the forfeiture of Dudley's inheritance, by the demise of his wife, and by the loss of his sight. Dudley suffers an increasing diminishment of outer referentiality, until he is, we are told, reduced to "the helplessness of infancy" (p. 17), as if having undergone a second birth. In this new infancy, as distinct from Helena's attachment for the biological one, he encounters the intrinsic powers of the self; for his experience "restored him to himself" so that his "genius" (the generative power of the mind) was "undiverted from its purpose by the intrusion of visible objects" (pp. 23, 24). Dudley apprehends what Ormond, Craig, and Martinette know, what Constantia progressively learns, and what Sophia struggles to counter: that the human mind is, for no apparent reason, in some inscrutable sense self-originating; that *a posteriori* recognition of the indefinite motives engendered by that mind to some uncertain degree more accurately defines human experience of reality than does *a priori* belief in divine or natural causality.

Consider Craig. He appears suddenly and relates a fabricated story of "his birthplace and origin," remarking as well that he came "to America, in search of the means of independent subsistence" (p. 7). Because he creates a story of his origins, his identity is self-originated; he even forges letters pertaining to his past, thereby defining the present moment by sheer force of will. He is as skillful as Ormond in appearing or disappearing at will as well as in converting his motives into causal influences in human affairs. The ease with which he exerts his mental powers upon others is exemplified when, to a proposal by Dudley, he expresses reluctance "with certain tokens which sufficiently showed whence it arose" (p. 10). But the seemingly covert motive Craig deliberately reveals to Dudley deceives, the causal linkage between it and Craig's real motive disguised by "the arts of [the] subtle impostor" (p. 14). This capacity for inventing one's identity and for creating events through the power of the will underlies Craig's usefulness to Ormond, who, it should be recalled, employs people whose mind is equal to his own.

Herein too lies a clue to Ormond's attraction to Constantia. By the time Ormond meets Constantia, she has braved a distressing sequence of events eradicating her dependence upon her father and stimulating her genius for responding to circumstance. At this time, Sophia remarks, Constantia "stood alone in the world" (p. 26). Soon Constantia will surrender a final remnant of family-like dependence, a locket with Sophia's picture which, if Sophia is to be believed, is given up "as if she [Constantia] could have endured the loss of eyes with less reluctance than the loss of this inestimable relic" (p. 61).[11] The equation of the deprivation of the locket to the loss of sight signifies (like her father's blindness) the complete end of Constantia's dependence upon extrinsic referentiality for identity.

In *Ormond* blindness defines the human condition, for "human events are conjoined by links imperceptible to keenest eyes" (p. 215). Like Martinette, Craig, and Ormond, Constantia learns to harken to the genius of her own mind, to give birth to her own motives, in short to become self-originating. Powerful motives, however indefinite and oblique, provide their own reference. As Sophia observes, "In no case, perhaps, is the decision of a human being impartial, or totally uninfluenced by sinister and selfish motives. If Constantia surpassed others, it was not because her motives were pure, but because they possessed more purity than those of others. Sinister considerations flow in upon us through imperceptible channels, and modify our thoughts in numberless ways" (p. 130). By her own admission Sophia is prejudiced in Constantia's favor. Yet on the basis of her own unwittingly deepening awareness of the prevalence of human motives as active principals supplanting her protective predilection for a more traditional notion of divinely ordained natural causality, the best she can do is separate her friend from Ormond by degree. In short, Sophia cannot evade the fact of Ormond's attraction to Constantia. When relating the episode in which Ormond rejects Constantia's arguments as bad and confutable yet allows her "position [as] incontrovertibly proved by them" (p. 132), Sophia intimates an identification of both of them through a mutually shared mental procedure which stresses subjective assertion without regard for alleged objectivity or for consequences. Like Ormond, Constantia displaces emotional tumults with "steadfast purposes" of her own (p. 17), in the process asserting an independent, self-originated identity based on the standard of the present moment (p. 148).

In *Ormond* a self-originated identity is essentially reflexive, that is to say, self-enclosing and self-defining. The result of an absence (in fact or in effect) of precedent, exterior cause, it reflects an "assemblage of forms to which no beginning or end can be conceived" coincident with that manifested in the world for Ormond; for nature seems to reply to the question "Whence?" only with cyclic repetition. This pattern is suggested when Constantia reflects upon Ormond's "imperfect" disclosures:

> What knowledge was imparted, instead of appeasing, only tended to inflame, her curiosity. His answers to her inquiries were prompt, and, at first sight, sufficiently explicit; but, upon reconsideration, an obscurity seemed to gather round them, to be dispelled by new interrogatories. These, in like manner, effected a momentary purpose, but were sure speedily to lead into new conjectures and reimmerse her in doubts. The task was always new, was always in the point of being finished, and always to be recommenced. (p. 147)

In other words, the search for the source of human motives is as circular as is the pursuit of causality in nature, a fact perhaps reflected in the "endless tautologies" and "circuitous" language of laws (pp. 16, 75) produced by the human mind. Concerning the reflexiveness of human motives, who can say where they begin or end; or who can speak of them in terms of cause and effect? In *Ormond* this circularity serves a dual function: on the one hand, it performs as a traditional image for closure, reflecting how the human mind achieves an illusion of self-containment and identity; on the other hand, it reveals what it seems to conceal, that self-referentiality is fundamentally a "locked-in" condition resulting from the inability of the mind to ascertain whether there be exterior causality for what it knows and how it behaves.

The circularity characteristic of Ormond's explanations applies as well to Sophia's narrative manner. Sophia's revelations frequently clarify little for the reader; rather they generate other questions. Although she admonishes the reader that "to scrutinize and ascertain our own principles are abundantly difficult" and that "to portray the motives and relate the actions of another appears utterly impossible" (p. 92), Sophia recounts incidents as if their source could be identified. Often, she brings the reader to the verge of understanding, only to distract his attention by the urgency of a new present moment, leaving his comprehension of event incomplete and, shortly thereafter, once more in pursuit of meaning.

Consider, for instance, how many times Sophia doubles back to the same events.[12] Besides her periodic application of the image of the orphan, Sophia actually repeats, as early as the second chapter, the same details presented in her opening chapter, with the alleged difference that they are now seen from Constantia's point of view. In one way or another this pattern recurs throughout Sophia's narrative: to cite but two more instances, Constantia's account of her life related to Melbourne, who repeats it to Ormond (pp. 89–90); Sophia's final summary of the story (pp. 193–207). This pattern may owe something to Brown's possible desire to pad his work, but in manner and effect it comports perfectly with the problem of origination in forming the theme of the book. Repetition of event conveys to the reader, and perhaps to the speaker as well, an impression of concreteness, of reality; for when the details of something recur a number of times, we tend to credit them with validity, with a "being-ness" here and now, with a signified presence supplanting inquiries into their origin.

Repetition of event is reinforced in *Ormond* by doubling of character features and circumstances. Sarah Baxter and Constantia are alike: "Immersed in poverty, friendless, burdened with the maintenance and nurture of her father, their circumstances were nearly parallel" (p. 59). Constantia sees herself in Martinette (alias Ursula Monrose): "She was probably unconscious of this resemblance, but this circumstance may be supposed to influence her in discovering such attractive properties in a form thus vaguely seen" (pp. 63–64). And Craig creates an imaginary double of himself when he tells Ormond of the betrayal of Constantia by his (Craig's) "brother" (p. 82), a story which results in the defamation of Constantia's character, thereby duplicating an earlier episode when Balfour's sister spread fictitious gossip, to the same end, about Constantia.[13]

Most interesting is the doubling implied in characteristics shared by Constantia and Ormond. Several similarities between them have been remarked earlier in this essay. One should also note that, like Constantia, Ormond moves from New York to Philadelphia, where both live in relation to the present rather than to the past. She rouses Ormond "from his lethargy, to furnish him with powerful excitements, and the time spent in her company seemed like a doubling of existence" (p. 131). Ormond experiences a doubling of his own being because his attraction to Constantia is fundamentally narcissistic, as is her's to Sarah and Martinette.[14] Ormond admires those of his own attributes reflected in Constantia.

Doubling of character traits, like repetition of event, intensifies the reader's sense of reality in Sophia's narrative. At a subliminal level of the mind the reader registers that indeed something must *really* be there for it to be duplicated. Doubling quantifies identity. But an ominous dimension emerges as well, for doubling paradoxically denies the very identity it seems to quantify. It diminishes the quality of the posited identity by implying a lack of originality and by obscuring the original, or causal first, in the set. In *Ormond* "unvaried repetition" is "an evil which it [is] the tendency of time to increase" (p. 6). Doubling, like repetition, signifies a locked-in condition; it provides the self with a sense of reality through reflection and closure, but at the same time it denies any ground for such identity by contravening the originality and by obscuring the origin of that identity. The basic question remains: Whence this mind, or self, which appears *to be* when it is circularly reflected in others and when its motives are mirrored in events?

This crucial uncertainty of identity is also suggested in the management of names in *Ormond*. Surnames, for instance, are often withheld from the reader until long after their bearers have become active agents in the story. This pattern applies not only to major characters but also to such minor figures as Malcolm M'Crea and Mary Ridgeley (pp. 88, 197). Even the narrator's name is not divulged until the story is nearly finished. The reader is denied a familiar sense of confidence in the identity of a character whose complete name remains undisclosed. The reader consequently suspects that something more than a name has been withheld, a sense especially acute when at some later irrelevant moment in the story the full name is indifferently revealed.

In *Ormond* names never provide an index to identity; they are fictions. Constantia's name, to remark a most pertinent illustration, invites the reader to entertain conventional allegorical implications, but it (like Sophia's name, suggesting wisdom) fails to define her character, which evinces *vicissitudes*—Sophia's final word describing her friend (p. 242). One instance should suffice: Constantia's revelation of Craig's secret to Melbourne, though she promised otherwise; certainly she has been provoked, but her inconstancy is nonetheless evident. How can Constantia be steadfast when life in the romance is comprised of "entire and incredible reverses" (p. 89)? In such a world identities fluctuate, cannot be fixed. Ursula Monrose is Martinette de Beauvois, Ormond is her brother as well as a master of disguise and impersonation, Craig is whoever his imagination invents, Helena Cleves adopts the ironic alias of Mrs. Eden, and even the Dudleys have changed their name (p. 87), a detail of no importance to the plot of the romance but of significance to its thematic concern with origination and identity. In *Ormond* naming is like masking, disguise, and impersonation—prevalent motifs in the work; with a typical ambiguity as old as the Renaissance each reflects not only the deceptions of the human mind but also the protean, creative capacity of the human will.[15]

Ambiguity in identity based on names (masking, disguise, impersonation) is reinforced by reader uncertainty over who is the protagonist in the work. The title announces Ormond as the focal center, but the epistolary introduction points to Constantia. The narrative itself includes several possibilities. It commences with a portrait of Stephen Dudley, shifts to Constantia, turns to Ormond, devotes a chapter to Helena, then focuses on the narrator. In general the progress of the romance evinces a stop-and-go effect appropriate to the lack of "unity of design" announced by Sophia at the outset (p. 3); and it is indeed understandable that one critic should decry the imbalance of episodes and another should complain, Brown "breaks camp so often that the reader cannot become oriented."[16] This diffusion of narrative focus, in combination with the management of repetition, character trait doubling, and naming, makes the reader respond to the text in the same way Constantia reacts to Ormond: "the task [of comprehension is] always new, [is] always in the point of being finished, and always to be recommenced." Any "artificial and elaborate order"—any "harmonious congruity" (p. 3) of linear plot development anticipated by the reader—is replaced by seemingly inchoate, random and circuitous eventuation in the narrative; fixity gives way to flux in the narrative as a whole, even as do the named identities of its characters.[17]

Narrative management of the sort so far remarked includes framing devices in *Ormond*. A noteworthy illustration of this technique occurs when Sophia relates second hand an episode told to her by Constantia, in the course of which is recounted (at third remove) Sarah Baxter's account to Constantia, in the course of which is divulged (at fourth remove) Mr. Baxter's comments to Sarah (pp. 52–58). At a later point in the work Sophia similarly tells us what Courtland told her of what Martinette related to him (p. 190). Sometimes this manner of framing is employed to facilitate the plot; for example, when Craig gives Melbourne a fabricated account of Constantia, and in turn the Judge conveys this information to Ormond (pp. 81–91). This technique contributes to a "redundance and obscurity in the style of the narrative" (pp. 50–51) similar to that of Sarah Baxter's account. Its Chinese-box effect of regression makes reality problematic for the reader, who is distanced farther and farther from the center or origin of the events reported, a psychological distancing equivalent to Sophia's physical separation from most of the occurrences dramatized in her narrative (p. 22).

The distancing effect of framing tends to obscure the fact that Sophia's voice is the originating center of the narrative. Sophia assures the reader that she writes only of real incidents and so will avoid the manner of fiction (p. 3), though the reflective reader knows in fact that her voice, as Brown's impersonation, is a fiction; yet, in accordance with its concern with the problem of origination, the romance does indeed define reality, a reality unknowable save in terms of self-origination, or "fictional" perception of one's self-generating mind. Just as in human experience events participate in an expanding sequence of reactions to an uncertain cause, the human mind generates out of itself layers or series of meaning similar to the framing technique of Sophia's narrative. This creative expansiveness of self, the result of one's second birth, opposes the seemingly contracting limits of nature, or fate; and even Ormond, who is likened to God and to a deity-like artist (pp. 96, 111),[18] protests under pressure, "I make not myself; I am molded by circumstances" (p. 134). This is true insofar as "life [is] a struggle with malignant destiny" (p. 177), with the natural fate of a finitude and mortality defining humanity without disclosing anterior, extrinsic purpose. Paradoxically it is also true insofar as this condition provokes an illusory antithesis to it in the human mind; Ormond, Craig, and Constantia, like the deity-like creative artist, assert will, deriving from it a self-generated identity (mask, disguise) similar in effect to fictional expansive framing devices distancing one from inscrutable origins. The limits of nature and the reactive expansiveness of

the human will are best objectified in *Ormond* when Constantia's sequen-
tial development of independence of self is coupled with a simultaneous
contraction of living space. The four early moves by the Dudleys involve
successively smaller living quarters, leaving (as her father found earlier in
life) "little *room* for choice" (p. 6; my emphasis). Self-origination, the illusion of independent identity, is a *necessitated* fiction; but it is a fiction
which is, in the absence (in fact or in effect) of extrinsic origins, real for
the human mind, whence that fiction is derived.

So Sophia's narrative is as real as it is fictive, and her words are as
evasive concerning the origins of her account as is the world defined in it.
Not only does she conceal her own identity until very late in the account,
in which she has been a decisive presence from the start, but often she
deliberately obscures the sources of her information. Speaking of Ormond, for example, she says, "I shall omit to mention the means by which
I became acquainted with his character" (p. 92). Moreover, she implicitly confesses to a capacity for deviousness rather similar to that of Ormond when she remarks that her knowledge of his schemes was obtained
"surreptitiously, or, at least, by means of which he was not apprised" (p.
92). This remark echoes a comment in her epistolary introduction: "It was
not prudent to unfold *all* the means by which I gained a knowledge of his
actions" (p. 3). And indeed the reader remains in the dark regarding the
subject. This pattern also tellingly occurs at the end of the book when
Sophia indicates that her husband possesses very complete information
about Martinette "but conceal[s] from her [Martinette, not Sophia] the
means by which he had procured the knowledge" (p. 241). Everything
about Sophia's report becomes problematic, perhaps most especially
when we recall that she describes herself as a "distant friend" who
enjoyed Constantia's "uninterrupted correspondence" (p. 22) when subsequent events in the narrative make clear that this correspondence was
interrupted and never could have provided the bulk of Sophia's
information.

Just as the sources of Sophia's information remain unclear, so too
does the immediate origin of the narrative. In fact Sophia's introduction
plays rather cruelly with the reader when, in its direct address to I. E.
Rosenberg, it seems to provide some explanation for the existence of the
book:

> You are anxious to obtain some knowledge of the history of
> Constantia Dudley. I am well acquainted with your motives,
> and allow that they justify your curiosity. I am willing, to the
> utmost of my power, to comply with your request, and will
> now dedicate what leisure I have to the composition of her
> story. (p. 3)

The reader, like Constantia in her encounter with Ormond's explanations, seems about to close with these remarks only to have further ques-

tions emerge. Just what has been revealed to us? Virtually nothing, as Sophia's comments raise more questions than they supply answers: Who is I. E. Rosenberg, a person never mentioned in the story proper? Why is he anxious to know Constantia's history? Just what are his motives? *Motives* are very much to the point, for Rosenberg's undisclosed motives at once cause and displace primary emphasis upon Sophia's motives for telling the story. When later in the romance Sophia indicates that "we are prompted to conceal and to feign . . . motives" (p. 92), the issue of the motives behind her narrative voice becomes even more vexing for the reader because, in a sense, she had, like Ormond, "conceal[ed] the author," allowing the "instruments [of her narrative] to act as if they were principals" (p. 83).

This problem looms throughout the book but is epitomized in its conclusion. By the end of the work a reader in Brown's time expected a work of fiction to conclude neatly in compliance with the norms of established social and fictional conventions. At first *Ormond* superficially seems to conform.[19] Its ending appears to close with its introduction when in the final paragraph of the work Sophia says that "sufficient explanation has been given of the *cause* that led" to Constantia's trouble (p. 240; my emphasis). Here are the final words of the book:

> In consideration of your merits and of your attachment to my friend, I have consented to devote my leisure to this task.
>
> It is now finished; and I have only to add my wishes that the perusal of this tale may afford you as much instruction as the contemplation of the sufferings and vicissitudes of Constantia Dudley have afforded me. Farewell. (p. 242)

The romance technically closes with itself, but the reader remains vague about its message (despite the conventional reference to "instruction") and ignorant concerning Rosenberg's identity and motives. From these undisclosed motives originates the entire narrative, and so Sophia's final words, like Ormond's explanations, convey merely a semblance of closure, "instead of appeasing, [they] only tend . . . to inflame . . . curiosity" (p. 147). Rosenberg may provide an extrinsic, anterior cause for the book, but the hidden nature of his motives renders that cause in effect an absence—and indeed he has nothing to do with the narrative proper—so that Sophia necessarily becomes the motivating agency, the originator of the account.

In summary, the entire narrative manner of *Ormond*—self-referentiality, framing, non-linear eventuation, doubling of character trait and circumstance, naming and repetition of plot elements—keeps the reader epistemologically uneasy, just as, (in terms of the story told by a friend who was at the time and is now at a distance from the place of the events) everyone stands at a distance from his origins; just as Sophia's creator, Brown, remains at a still farther distance, his position akin to Ormond's: both protean artists employing human agents to do their will and both authorially absent from the events they originate, as if they were some inscrutable deity behind the natural world portrayed in *Ormond*. By means of these devices fact and fiction transubstantiate in the romance, as unknown extrinsic natural causality transposes with indefinite, self-originated human motives. In response to these techniques the reader experiences the theme of the work: the human mind's bewilderment over the uncertain cause or origin—whether something or nothing—of its own reactive and somehow apparently circular knowledge of and activity in a world devoid of perceptible meaning or purpose. In other words, the world in *Ormond*, to borrow a description from Julio Cortázar's *Hopscotch* (1963), is a place where "man only is in that he searches to be, plans to be, thumbing through words and modes of behavior and joy sprinkled with blood."[20] Such a view of human existence, similar to that presented in the work of Edgar Allan Poe and Nathaniel Hawthorne,[21] accounts for the pervasive mystery—at once horrifying and sublime—sensed in *Ormond* as well as in Brown's other romances; and it suggests why modern critical attention has been devoted to his works in spite of their evident technical defects.

Notes

1. Charles Brockden Brown, *Ormond*, ed. Ernest Marchand (New York: Hafner, 1937), p. 59 (my emphasis). Subsequent page references for quotations from this edition are included parenthetically in the text.

2. A much discussed theme: see, for example, Patrick Brancaccio, "Studied Ambiguities: *Arthur Mervyn* and the Problem of the Unreliable Narrator," *AL*, 42 (1970), 18–27; John Cleman, "Ambiguous Evil: A Study of Villains and Heroes in Charles Brockden Brown's Major Novels," *EAL*, 10 (1975), 190–219.

3. The hasty composition of *Ormond* is not in doubt: Harry R. Warfel, *Charles Brockden Brown: American Gothic Novelist* (Gainesville: University of Florida Press, 1949), p. 100; David Lee Clark, *Charles Brockden Brown: Pioneer Voice of America* (Durham: Duke University Press, 1952), p. 171; and most notably Paul C. Rodgers, Jr., "Brown's *Ormond*: The Fruits of Improvisation," *AQ*, 26 (1974), 4–22. Rodgers's vehement assertion, however, that "Brown himself had no controlling thematic or symbolic end in view" (p. 21) is hyperbolic; it not only ignores significant recurring events, details and images in *Ormond*, but it also disregards the similar haste with which *Wieland*, Brown's most critically acclaimed work, was written as well as the many similarities between these two romances: e.g., depiction of an ambiguous universe, apology for narrative incoherence, confusion over who is the central character, dismissal of the importance of specific geographic place, suspicion of religion, failure to provide a norm, distancing of authorial voice, and involvement of the reader—all of which I shall discuss and a few of which have been *mentioned*, albeit in contexts quite different from mine, in Alexander Cowie's "Historical Essay" in the Bicentennial Edition of *Wieland* (Kent: Kent State University Press, 1977(, pp. 311–48. Whereas in *The Rise of the American Novel* (New York: American Book Co., 1950) Cowie curiously concludes that *Wieland* "does not even closely resemble the other novels of Brown" (p. 327), Mark Seltzer *implies* otherwise in an intelligent essay which appeared while mine was in manuscript and which argues that Clara's language becomes the central action as she strug-

gles to compensate for perceived broken causal sequences: "Saying So Makes It So: Language and Event in Brown's *Wieland*," *EAL*, 13 (1978), 81–91. See also Sydney J. Krause, "*Ormond*: How Rapidly and How Well 'Composed, Arranged and Developed,' " *EAL*, 13 (1978), 238–49.

4. See any modern edition of *An Essay Concerning Human Understanding*, Bk. II, ch. 21. Locke shared Hobbes's view of a mechanistic world, and to be consistent with the view he could admit the existence only of efficient causality in that world. But Locke modified the Hobbesian conviction by attributing a degree of freedom, or capacity for action, to the human mind. In the human mind the will "acts" originatively, and the intellect "thinks" by combining simple ideas into complex concepts, which comprise real effects of real *mental* activity.

5. "Seminar on 'The Purloined Letter,' " trans. Jeffrey Mehlman, *French Freud: Structural Studies in Psychoanalysis* (New Haven: Yale University Press, 1972), p. 92.

6. *The Order of Things: An Archaeology of the Human Sciences* (New York: Pantheon Books, 1971), p. 330.

7. See, for instance, Arthur G. Kimball, "Savages and Savagism: Brockden Brown's Dramatic Irony," *SIR*, 6 (1967), 214–25; Donald A. Ringe, "Charles Brockden Brown," *Major Writers of Early American Literature*, ed. Everett Emerson (Madison: University of Wisconsin Press, 1972), p. 277; and Sydney J. Krause, "Romanticism in *Wieland*: Brown and the Reconciliation of Opposites," *Artful Thunder: Versions of the Romantic Tradition in American Literature in Honor of Howard P. Vincent*, ed. Robert J. DeMott and Sanford E. Marovitz (Kent: Kent State University Press, 1975), 13–24.

8. Some critics, however, have identified Sophia's view of religion with that of Brown: Warfel, p. 136; Ringe, pp. 273–94.

9. On Brown's ambivalence toward Ormond, see, for example, Leslie A. Fiedler, *Love and Death in the American Novel* (Cleveland: World Pub. Co., 1962), p. 77; Kenneth Bernard, "Charles Brockden Brown," *Minor American Novelists*, ed. Charles Alva Hoyt (Carbondale: Southern Illinois University Press, 1970), pp. 1–9; and Sydney J. Krause, "*Ormond*: Seduction in a New Key," *AL*, 44 (1973), 570–84.

10. William L. Hedges has discussed the unclear world of false appearance and mystery in Brown's work: "Charles Brockden Brown and the Culture of Contradictions," *EAL*, 9 (1974), 107–42. J.V. Ridgely describes an even larger metaphysical void in another of Brown's works: "The Empty World of *Wieland*," *Individual and Community: Variations on a Theme in American Fiction*, ed. Kenneth H. Baldwin and David K. Kirby (Durham: Duke University Press, 1975), pp. 3–16. Ridgely's article implicitly deepens the implications of Cowie's observation that in spite of occasional local references in *Ormond*, "the story is grounded nowhere" (*The Rise of the American Novel*, p. 79).

11. For what it is worth, a hint of lesbianism in the relationship between Constantia and Sophia is discussed by Fiedler, pp. 78–80, 207.

12. From a different perspective Warner B. Berthoff has argued that disconnected incidents in Brown's work restate each other and are united by common themes: " 'A Lesson in Concealment': Brockden Brown's Method of Fiction," *PQ*, 37 (1958), 45–57. Whereas Kenneth Bernard has argued that duplication of narrative in another of Brown's works conveys a sense of the world as a place of unfathomable complexity ("*Arthur Mervyn*: The Ordeal of Innocence," *TSLL*, 6[1965], 441–59), Carl Nelson has observed that the shifting perspectives of Sophia's narrative indicates the limits of her viewpoint ("A Just Reading of Charles Brockden Brown's *Ormond*," *EAL*, 8 [1973], 163–78).

13. Such details are often repeated: for example, the early reference to Craig's forged letters from England is repeated later in the romance when we learn that Martynne (alias Ormond) "came from England, bringing with him forged recommendatory letters" (p. 183).

14. On the relation of doubling to narcissism, lack of clearly defined identity, and confining self-enclosure (the latter to be discussed), see Otto Rank, *The Double*, trans. Harry

Tucker, Jr. (Chapel Hill: University of North Carolina Press, 1971); Ralph Tymms, *Doubles in Literary Psychology* (Cambridge: Bowes and Bowes, 1949); Claire Rosenfield, "The Shadow Within: The Conscious and Unconscious Use of the Double," *Daedalus*, 42 (1965), 326–44; Robert Rogers, *A Psychoanalytic Study of the Double in Literature* (Detroit: Wayne State University Press, 1970); C.E. Keppler, *The Literature of the Second Self* (Tucson: University of Arizona Press, 1972); John O. Stark, *The Literature of Exhaustion: Borges, Nabokov, and Barth* (Durham: Duke University Press, 1974), and John T. Irwin, *Doubling and Incest/Repetition and Revenge: A Speculative Reading of Faulkner* (Baltimore: Johns Hopkins University Press, 1975). Krause refers to this technique, interpreting it as an objectification of Brown's divided allegiances ("Romanticism in *Wieland*," pp. 13–24).

15. On this feature of masking, see Wayne A. Rebhorn, *Courtly Performances: Masking and Festivity in Castiglione's "Book of the Courtier"* (Detroit: Wayne State University Press, 1978). pp 29–30.

16. Donald A. Ringe, *Charles Brockden Brown* (New York: Twayne, 1966), p. 62; Cowie, p. 102, respectively.

17. On non-linearity in fiction, see Barbara Babcock-Abrahams, "The Novel and the Carnival World," *MLN*, 89 (1974), 911–37.

18. Michael D. Bell has identified *Ormond* with the artist's need to achieve a balance between authenticity and literary order on the one hand, and falsehood and literary energy on the other hand: " 'The Double-Tongued Deceiver': Sincerity and Duplicity in the Novels of Charles Brockden Brown," *EAL*, 9 (1974), 143–63. See also Paul Witherington, "Benevolence and the 'Utmost Stretch': Charles Brockden Brown's Narrative Dilemma," *Criticism*, 14 (1972), 175–91, and especially Witherington, "Charles Brockden Brown's *Ormond*: The American Artist and His Masquerades," *SAF*, 4 (1976), 111–19.

19. Brown's distortion of convention in other works is remarked by R.W.B. Lewis, *The American Adam: Innocence, Tragedy, and Tradition in the Nineteenth Century* (Chicago: University of Chicago Press, 1955), pp. 94–95; Michael D. Butler, "Charles Brockden Brown's *Wieland*: Method and Meaning," *SAF*, 4 (1976), 127–42; William C. Spengemann, *The Adventurous Muse: The Poetics of American Fiction, 1789–1900* (New Haven: Yale University Press, 1977), pp. 97–106.

20. Cortázar, *Hopscotch*, trans. Gregory Rabassa (New York: Random House, 1966), p. 363.

21. On Brown's influence on Poe and Hawthorne, see Lulu Rumsey Wiley, *The Sources and Influences of the Novels of Charles Brockden Brown* (New York: Vantage Press, 1950), pp. 233–39. See also my "The Hieroglyphic Rock in Hawthorne's 'Roger Malvin's Burial,' " *ESQ*, 24 (1978), 72–76; "The Geometric Structure of Poe's 'The Oval Portrait,' " *Poe Studies*, 11 (1978), 6–8.

Narrative Unity and Moral Resolution in *Arthur Mervyn*

Emory Elliott

At one point in his narrative Arthur Mervyn pauses to reflect: "Nothing, indeed, more perplexes me than a review of my own conduct."[1] Indeed, and perplexes the readers of this novel as well. There is no issue in the criticism of Brown's work over which there is more disagreement than the question of Mervyn's character. Some view him as the prototype of the successful American Adam—a young innocent who receives a just reward for a life of virtue—while others see him as a scoundrel, an opportunist, "a double-tongued deceiver."[2] Brown's critics are as divided in their assessment of Mervyn as the members of the Philadelphia society in the novel to whom he presents his story. Of course, there is good reason for this debate, for Brown structured the entire narration as Arthur's defense of himself in the face of a legal warrant for his arrest. The reader overhears Mervyn's own testimony and the sympathetic arguments of his advocate, Dr. Stevens, as they appear to bury the prosecution and persuade Mervyn's most vehement opponents, Mr. Wortley and Mrs. Wentworth. The problem is that the issue of Arthur's guilt or innocence is never resolved: the charges are dropped or forgotten; Mervyn marries a rich widow; and readers are left with an uneasy feeling that there must be something more to this masquerade. Critics often attribute this unsatisfying resolution to careless writing or to a change of Brown's mind that occurred during the months separating the publication of the novel's two parts.[3] A more fruitful approach is to consider first Brown's own explicit theory of fiction.

When Brown began planning this novel, in 1793, he had recently abandoned the study of law and devoted himself to the calling of authorship. A serious novelist of ideas, Brown said that he sought to stir the intellects and imaginations of the best minds of his generation to "enchain the attention and ravish the souls of those who study and reflect" and to arouse "the curiosity and sympathy" of "the man of soaring passions and intellectual energy."[4] In setting these goals Brown was following Beattie and the moral philosophers of the period who argued that the best fiction would affect the understanding and the emotions of the intelligent reader so deeply that he would feel compelled to review the text carefully to seek

142

answers to the moral issues raised and to understand his own disturbed feelings.[5] During the following years Brown was deeply concerned with political, moral, and philosophical questions, and in his fiction he explored these issues as well as many facets of human psychology. Thus, it is not unreasonable to approach this culminating work with the assumption that Brown intended it to have precisely the unsettling effect that it has. If this book leaves the thoughtful reader somewhat perplexed and provokes a vigorous moral debate about Mervyn's character, then Brown may have come closer in this novel than in any other to achieving the highest standards set in his time for good fiction.

As the title indicates, *Arthur Mervyn, or the Memoirs of the Year 1793* explores a single character and a historical social setting. The interaction between Mervyn and his society has moral consequences that demand the reader's intellectual engagement. Yet, while appealing to the reader to arrive at moral judgments, the intricate plots, internal contradictions, and multiple narrators seem to deny the presence of a controlling moral vision. As a result, readers tend to concentrate entirely upon the conscious actions of Mervyn and to choose sides over the issue of his guilt or innocence. The consequence is that most interpretations of this novel miss part of the richness and meaning of Brown's most ambitious work. To see Mervyn as an innocent rewarded and thereby to ignore the elements of the con man in his character is to miss the novel's ironies and comic dimension.[6] But to view Arthur as a total villain is to flirt with anachronistic misreadings which present the novel as a cynical and nihilistic forerunner of *Pierre* or *The Confidence-Man*.[7]

The purpose of this essay is to achieve a balanced view of Mervyn's character and a more thorough understanding of the novel's central themes. In the first part, I have explored the most sinister possibilities of Mervyn's character by gathering all possible grounds for believing his story to be, as his accuser claims, "a tissue of ingenious and plausible lies" (p. 215). The second part is an attempt to place Mervyn within his world and to examine the stages of his conscious and unconscious development as he responds to his conditions. When viewed in this setting, the full complexity of Mervyn's character becomes apparent. Neither picaresque saint nor complete confidence man, Mervyn, a name suggestive of Everyman, is a symbol of the amoral, unschooled but intelligent individual struggling to survive in the social turmoil of the post-revolutionary age. Using every skill he can acquire and exploiting every advantage which nature may have given him, including the strengths and weaknesses of others, Mervyn struggles to create a role for himself in his society. Throughout this process of accommodation, Mervyn's motives, ends, and means are constantly changing, and a careful assessment of his psychological make-up and of his adjustment to those around him provide the only sound foundation on which to judge his character. In the end this analysis reveals that the moral resolution of the novel does not depend entirely upon a verdict of

Arthur's guilt or innocence. A deeper understanding of the novel's full meaning requires a recognition of the tragic limitations of his character and the complex nature of his response to the social order, rather *disorder*, in which he exists.

I

From Percy Shelly and William Dunlap to the most recent critics, even the most sympathetic defenders of Mervyn's character are bothered by his decision to marry Achsa Fielding.[8] After Brown has established the reader's fondness for Eliza Hadwin, a young, attractive, forthright American country girl, he surprises everyone, including Dr. Stevens and even Mervyn himself, by having Arthur marry an older European Jewess whom the usually moderate Dr. Stevens describes in most unfavorable terms: "unsightly as a night-hag, tawney as a moor, [having] less luxuriance than a sharred log, fewer elasticities than a sheet pebble" (p. 416). In spite of Arthur's raves about Achsa, whom he insists on calling his "new mama" to the point of annoyance, his decision to marry her so complicates the ending of the book that it forces the reader to reassess all of Arthur's previous narrative. If, as it seems, Arthur has chosen the financial security which Achsa's wealth offers over the life of social purpose, moral purity, and vigorous labors he has claimed to desire, then his earlier idealistic expressions are called into question. And it seems to be exactly the function of his choice to send the reader back, with a new skepticism, to the beginning of Arthur's testimony; for a retrospective look at Arthur's narrative provides ample reason to doubt his sincerity.

On first reading it is difficult to peek behind the mass of complicated events to determine how Arthur might be distorting the facts to suit his purposes. But Brown does provide the attentive reader hints along the way, such as the quick glimpse behind Mervyn's mask when he boasts about his skillful manipulation of his "rhetorick" (p. 292) in the argument with Philip Hadwin over the legitimacy of Hadwin's claim to Eliza's estate. Mervyn explains how he calculated each word and gesture to achieve the desired effect that would leave Hadwin with the impression that he was "*a queer sort of chap*" (p. 296), and he proudly declares: "the stuff that I was made of was damnably tough and devilishly pliant" (p. 295). Given his bias in Mervyn's favor, it is not surprising that Stevens fails to draw the logical conclusion that Mervyn may be deceiving him as well, but an alert reader cannot fail to catch that implication in this scene. In fact, the extraordinary faith of Stevens in the countenance of Mervyn rather than in his words is itself a cause for the reader's suspicion. At one point Stevens admits that if *he* were the reader he would not believe Mervyn's story: "Had I heard it from another or read it in a book, I might perhaps have found it possible to suspect the truth . . . but the face of Mervyn is the index of an honest mind" (p. 218). Yet for some reason which he never explains Stevens has chosen to make his faith in Mervyn's honesty the only thing between himself and total cynicism: "If Mervyn has deceived me, there is an end to my confidence in human nature" (p. 236). But Brown's reader, who need not be swayed by what Wortley calls Mervyn's "smooth features and fluent accents" (pp. 236–37), has the advantage of being able to reexamine his story in light of his later actions.

Certainly one reason to question Mervyn's honesty is that he is always entering people's homes without bothering to knock and is repeatedly caught in the act of taking someone's property. Of course, each time he has some excuse—he was lost, his mission was urgent or, as he says at one point, "being busy with other thoughts I forgot to knock at the door" (p. 339). The situation is repeated so often that it is prevented from becoming a running joke only by the moral questions raised by the nearly disastrous consequences which often result. At the opening of the tale he finds himself accidentally inside the Thetford bedroom where he learns useful secrets, and this situation serves as a paradigm for his relationship to all people in his society. He repeatedly barges into people's lives and seems to benefit from the intrusion. He even meets Achsa after forcing his way into Mrs. Villars's house, an act that he almost pays for with his life.[9] When Welbeck accuses Mervyn of being a thief, he has good reason, for Arthur steals the Lodi manuscript containing $20,000 and breaks into Welbeck's house; and, on another occasion unknown to Welbeck, Mervyn sneaks into his bedroom and reads his private letters. Admitting that he has no regard for legalities or for the rights of private property, Mervyn tries to justify his intrusions by a spurious theory of ends justifying means. In regard to his forcible entry into the Villars's house, Mervyn asserts:

> The satisfaction that I sought was only to be gained by searching the house. . . . Did I act illegally in passing from one story and one room to another? . . . My behavior, I well know was ambiguous and hazardous, and perhaps wanting in discretion, but my motives were unquestionably pure. . . . Good intentions, unaided by knowledge, will perhaps, produce more injury than benefit, and therefore, knowledge must be gained, but . . . we must not be inactive because we are ignorant. Our good purposes must hurry to performance, whether our knowledge be greater or less. (p. 309)

Although the twisted logic of this rationalization is not challenged by any character in the book, Mervyn's dubious argument from good intentions is likely to cause the reader to think of the road to hell rather than to arouse confidence in Mervyn's honesty and reliability.

In view of Mervyn's final end—which is apparently to live in the greatest comfort with the expenditure of the least energy—and his readiness to use any means to attain his goals, there is also good reason to review the exact nature of Mervyn's relationship to Welbeck. Mervyn admits that he had ample reason to flee Welbeck from quite early in the relationship. Welbeck's requirement that Arthur deceive Mrs. Wentworth and others about his own past, his obvious dissimulation at a party, and his seemingly incestuous relationship to Clemenza lead Arthur to conclude that Welbeck was guilty of "the blackest and most stupendous of all crimes" (p. 72). But Mervyn stays and even allows Welbeck to believe that his disturbed reactions to Welbeck's activities are the result of homesickness—a deception that contradicts his claim that "my lips [are] untainted by prevarication or falsehood" (p. 129). After he finally does intend to abandon Welbeck, Mervyn even returns to try to save him from Thetford's plot. As a result he becomes involved in the shooting of Watson, aids Welbeck in the victim's basement burial, and assists the killer in his escape across the Schuylkill. The only explanation Mervyn can give for this loyalty, which appears to make him a partner in crime, is that he acted out of a sense of duty and gratitude to his employer. It is no wonder that Wortley calls Mervyn's story "a tissue of ingenious and plausible lies" (p. 215).

Either Mervyn is a complete fool, which he gives little evidence of being, or he has other reasons for his attachment to Welbeck which he conceals from Stevens. Mervyn's own admission that his first thought was of marrying Clemenza and inheriting Welbeck's wealth lends strong support to Wortley's suspicion that Mervyn hoped to profit by his association with Welbeck. With his dying words Welbeck also accuses Mervyn of preying upon him in the hope of picking up chances for gain that the master villain might miss. Although there is nothing concrete to support Welbeck's charges, they do darken the shadow which Wortley casts over Mervyn's character.

Another reason for being suspicious of Mervyn is that there are many glaring contradictions in his tale and in his descriptions of his own nature. For example, early in the second part Arthur waxes philosophical. All men, he has decided, may be classified as either men of thought or men of action, and he asserts that he is of the first type: "If men be chiefly distinguished from each other by the modes in which attention is employed, either on external and sensible objects, or merely on abstract ideas and the creatures of reflection, I may justly claim to be enrolled in the second class. My existence is a series of thoughts rather than of motions" (p. 253). As a description of Mervyn, this statement is only true in a very literary sense—that he is a series of Brown's thoughts. As a description of Mervyn's character, however, nothing could be further from the truth, for his life is a series of actions. Again, either he is gravely self-deluded, or, what is more likely, he is posing as a man of ideas in order to convince his listeners of his social worthiness. An Arthur who can choose his words with Mr. Hadwin to leave the impression that he is "a queer sort of chap" is also capable of persuading his present company that he shares their love of learning and ideas. Even before beginning his story, Arthur takes the time to learn the predisposition of his listeners.[10]

Throughout his narrative Mervyn makes great claims for his love of books and his avid reading, and he insinuates that given a chance he would blossom into a man of letters. But while his assertions lead Stevens to become the patron of Mervyn's brief medical education, they will not stand up to scrutiny. His speech is bare of literary reference, and the only author he gives evidence of having read is perhaps Benjamin Franklin, who may be his "darling writer" whose "encomiums on rural life" (p. 44) are the foundation of Mervyn's philosophy and ethics.[11] Anticipating Franklin's *Autobiography*, Arthur wonders: "Will it not behoove me to cultivate all my virtues and eradicate all my defects?" (p. 54). Indeed, a wary reader may ask how much of Mervyn's entire self-description may spring from the Franklin model of the Do-good and Busy-Body essays. (It is tempting to think that Brown may have intended the novel partly as a critique of Franklin's rendition of the American hero). However, Mervyn's claims to learning are dubious, at best, and Mrs. Althorpe's claim that Arthur despised reading receives some support from the two somewhat comic episodes which involve his contact with books.

In the first case he is searching Welbeck's bedroom when he finds a copy of *The Dramas of Apostolo Zeno*. But the curiosity that leads him to open this book is not exactly intellectual, for the personal letter hidden inside is much more to Arthur's taste. But even this bit of reading is immediately interrupted when the shot which kills Watson rings out. Then there is his only real claim to literary interest: his alleged desire to translate the Lodi manuscript. After supposedly having learned Italian for this task, Mervyn recounts a story it contained. Interestingly enough, Brown makes it the tale of political turmoil, intrigue, and betrayal which has thematic relevance to Arthur's own narrative, but Arthur fails to find any meaning in it. The humor depends upon the fact that just at the point in the narrative that the hero finds a buried treasure, which offers him hope for escaping his certain death, Mervyn himself discovers $20,000 hidden in the manuscript pages. Finding money rather than meaning in this literary work, Arthur cries: "Twenty thousand dollars! They are mine and by such means!" (p. 121). In putting aside his uncompleted translation forever, Arthur does not give weight to his professed love of learning, abstraction, and reflection.

Mervyn's various claims that he has dreams of living as a Jeffersonian gentleman-farmer, a warm-hearted affection for humanity, and even a romantic nature, all fail to be supported by his actions and too often serve as convenient obfuscations. For example, when Mrs. Althorpe's account of Arthur's youth casts a shadow over his character, Mervyn explains that he had held back details because of his delicate sensibilities: "I cannot look upon the sufferings of those I love without exquisite pain. I cannot steel my heart by the force of reason and by the submission of necessity; and therefore, too frequently employ the cowardly expedient of endeavoring to forget what I cannot remember without agony" (p. 328). Yet he often seems impervious, as in the death of Susan Hadwin whom he abruptly buries without even bothering to awaken Eliza, who chastizes him for his callousness. Similarly, he endures other deaths and the sufferings of many close to him and reports the details with cool accuracy, as when he reasons that his father's death "was an event . . . not unfortunate" (p. 377) or when he curtly tells Welbeck of the death of his child (p. 322). Mervyn also seems to share the cruel indifference which the elder Thetford displays toward the cries of a servant girl who begs not to be sent to the public hospital to die, for he remarks that "the rank and education of the young woman, might be some apology for negligence" (p. 151).

Perhaps the most conspicuous contradictions between Mervyn's self-descriptions and his actions stem from his relationship with Eliza Hadwin. With pronouncements about his vulnerability to the charms of women, which are surely designed to help him win the sympathy of Mrs. Stevens, whose name incidentally is also Eliza, Mervyn explains how his "romantic and untutored disposition" made him "liable" to being captivated by Eliza who "stole insensibly upon my heart" (pp. 117–18). Yet again, his actions prove that these emotions are much more governable than his rhetorical effusions, for when he calculates the amount of her inheritance, he concludes that "to foster my passion was to foster a disease destructive of either my integrity or my existence" (p. 119). He then simply stops talking to Eliza and ignores her protests and pleas. Later, when Mr. Hadwin and Susan die and the property appears up for the taking, Mervyn's feelings for Eliza are aroused again, and he urges her to burn the will which appoints Philip Hadwin as her guardian, take the loose cash in the house, and run away with him. Next, when Hadwin establishes his claims to the property, Arthur undergoes another "change in my views with regard to my friend" (p. 297). He weighs the girl's depleted fortune against the opportunities for advancement he has found in the urban society and decides that Eliza would only hinder his rise in the world.

In view of Brown's well-known support of women's equality at the time that he wrote *Arthur Mervyn*, the allusions in this novel to the works of the liberal thinker William Godwin, and the sympathy which women readers were likely to feel for Eliza in the ensuing lovers' debate, Arthur's self-centered rejection of Eliza serves as another clue to the dubious nature of his character.[13] After Arthur tells Eliza that her immaturity and ignorance would only burden him during his "apprenticeship to fortitude and wisdom" (p. 280), Eliza makes a powerful argument from the position of women's rights for sharing in his years of learning and experience:

> What angers and distresses me is, that you think me unworthy to partake of your cares and labors; that you regard my company as an obstacle and incumbrance; that assistance and counsel must all proceed from you; and that no scene is fit for me, but what you regard as slothful and inglorious. Have I not the same claim to be wise, and active, and courageous as you are? . . . but you desire it all for yourself. Me, you think poor, weak, and contemptible; fit for nothing but to spin and churn.

Provided I exist, am screened from the weather, have enough
to eat and drink, you are satisfied. As to strengthening my
mind and enlarging my knowledge, these things are valuable
to you, but on me they are thrown away. I deserve not the gift.
(pp. 283–84)

The high-mindedness of Eliza's appeal certainly stands in sharp contrast
to the pettiness of Mervyn's continued concern with property and
finances. After admitting that he "had certainly considered her sex as utterly unfitting her for those scenes and pursuit, to which I had destined
myself" (p. 284), Mervyn immediately thinks again of her property and
whether marriage to her would compel him to "take up my abode in the
woods, to abide forever in one spot, to shackle my curiosity, or limit my
excursions" (p. 284). He finally decides against marriage on the grounds
that time would probably "unfold qualities in her which I did not at present suspect, and which would evince an incurable difference in our
minds" (p. 284). Surely part of the reason that the reversal involved in Arthur's decision to marry Ascha Fielding remains so disturbing to readers is
that Eliza emerges as such a strongly sympathetic character in spite of
Mervyn's efforts to suppress her with his self-serving rhetoric.

Even when there is no obvious contradiction in Mervyn's assertions,
his pious platitudes about his honesty and benevolence and his self-
righteous attacks on others are so hollow as to sound nearly comic.[14] As
Warner Berthoff has observed, the scene in which Mervyn "stands at the
door of a brothel waiting with appropriate trepidation to present himself
to some 'supercilious and voluptuous being' suggests an instinct for the
comic [in Brown] that would have been worth nourishing." Although
Berthoff "does not want to claim too much for Brown as a comic artist
manque," he does believe that the novel comes "close to a kind of laconic
social comedy."[15] Indeed, there is much in the novel to suggest the influence on the author of *Joseph Andrews* and *Tom Jones*, including the
name of Mervyn's unexpected bride.[16]

Yet while there is surely a bit of Blifil in Arthur, the comic dimension
of his character is still another mask which the reader must penetrate to
arrive at a thorough understanding of his motivations and meaning. The
strident tone of his sanctimonious utterings, such as his extraordinary condemnation of his revengeful feelings towards his sister's rapist, put into
sharp relief those rare statements of studied self-awareness which reflect
the real desperateness of Mervyn's situation in the world. One such
remark which has the ring of truth is Mrs. Althorpe's reiteration of Arthur's view of Betty Lawrence, the girl of doubtful virtue who married his
aging father: "But think not that I blame Betty. Place me in her situation
and I should have acted just so. I should have formed just such notions of
my interest, and pursued it by the same means" (p. 226). This judgment,
which may indeed be a prediction of his own marriage, reveals a side of
Mervyn that Mr. Stevens chooses not to see.

It is, however, a side of Mervyn that Welbeck believes he does see.

Mervyn and Welbeck have much in common—a mutual scorn for manual labor, the law, and the property rights of others. Also, Mervyn claims to have learned much from his master "on the principles of human nature; on the delusiveness of appearances; on the perviousness of fraud; and on the power with which nature has invested human beings over the thoughts and actions of each other" (pp. 130–31). Thus, it is significant that the strongest charges against Mervyn come from the man who knows him most intimately—and that it is Welbeck's conclusion that Mervyn has learned too well. When Arthur self-righteously condemns the imprisoned Welbeck, the dying sharper accuses Mervyn of being the greater villain: "Curses on thy lips, infernal messenger! Chant elsewhere thy rueful ditty! Vanish! If thou wouldst not feel in thy heart fangs red with blood less guilty than thine . . . you are the author of the scene that you describe" (p. 322). While Welbeck cannot be expected to be objective about Mervyn, only he can provide the reader insight into a relationship which Mervyn keeps carefully concealed. Welbeck truly believes that he has been a biter bit by a villain more artful than himself: "Thy qualities are marvelous. Every new act of thine outstrips the last, and belies the newest calculations . . . under that innocent guise there lurked a heart treacherous and cruel" (pp. 246–47).

Once the evidence begins to unfold, other aspects of the narrative appear as hints of Mervyn's duplicity. For example, the many similarities between Mervyn and Clavering take on new meaning with the recognition that Clavering's story to Arthur's mother is a lie designed to enable him to win asylum, alter his identity, and escape his past. He did not flee cruel parents in England but doting ones in Philadelphia.[17] Also, Mervyn's character assassination of Wallace may not be simply a plot device. To support his view that Wallace was a complete villain whose death he welcomes, Mervyn uses a stranger's report that the feverish, dying Wallace made obscene jokes and remarks about women, including his fiancée Susan. But there may be deeper motives for Mervyn's attack on Wallace than his declared fastidiousness and concern for Susan's honor. Mervyn has reason to be jealous of Wallace whose betrothal to Susan had assured him half of the Hadwin estate, whose ambition had enabled him to earn enough money in the city in two years to finance his marriage, and whose supposed duping of Mervyn was Arthur's initiation to the city. In the context of the novel's important theme of the sexual-financial competition among young men that economic conditions encourage,[18] it is not improbable that Mervyn would use Wallace as a foil in his narrative: a blackened Wallace, and for that matter a grotesque Welbeck, makes a useful contrast to a whitened, angelic Mervyn.

Indeed, to recognize the moral complexity of Mervyn is to understand how similar he is not only to Welbeck but to Brown's other villains, Ormond, Carwin, and even Wieland.[19] Like them he arises from a tragic family situation in which a failure of paternal authority is a key to an unbridaled recklessness in the son, and like them also he uses the opportunities of an open republican society to escape his background and fabricate a new identity. Willing to use any means to attain his ends, he also possesses the talent for imitating the manners, style, and dress of his social betters, and he has the rhetorical skills needed for persuading or deceiving others. The difference between Arthur and his destructive and defeated counterparts is that he is able to control his emotions and repress his passions. Without the lust of fame which destroys Welbeck, the irrational obsession of Wieland, the passion for a woman that ruins Ormond, and the unchecked curiosity of Carwin, Mervyn is able to steer his deliberate course among the gapping jaws of the new society. Only twice does he lose control of his emotions, and both times he pays with physical harm—in the basement of Welbeck's house when he is trapped with the body of Watson and again in Clemenza's bedroom at the Villars house. Otherwise, in all his social intercourse, including his relationships to women, Mervyn acts with an icy reserve and calculated restraint for which he is appropriately rewarded in his marriage to Ascha Fielding.

Although this view of Mervyn may lean a bit too far to the negative as a corrective to Stevens's excessive defense, Arthur is clearly not a simple innocent as he pretends to be in Philadelphia. His previous experiences have taught him much: from Betty Lawrence he has learned that the farm goes to the swift, and from his family he has learned the dangers of disease, human brutality, and irrationality. He may not be a scholar, but Arthur understands the power of language as his only tool of survival. So effective is he at concealing his deficiencies and creating an appealing identity that the characters who look at him most objectively are the most baffled: Mrs. Althorpe says of him, "take away his jacket and trowsers, and you have as spruce a fellow as ever came from dancing-school or college" (p. 221), while Mrs. Wentworth expresses bewilderment: "You may possibly be honest. Such a one as you, with your education and address, may possibly have passed all your life in a hovel; but it is scarcely credible, let me tell you" (p. 347). While Brown's readers may sometimes feel similar frustration, the novel does contain sufficient information about Mervyn's character not only to expose his most unattractive features but also to allow for an understanding of the social conditions and of his psychological composition which may account for, though perhaps not justify, his chameleon-like response to his world.

II

Although Mervyn is more skillful than he first appears, Brown has created great liabilities for him to surmount. Pursued by a reputation for being lazy and brash, a seducer of his stepmother and a thief of his father's savings, he has no education or marketable skill and has nothing in his real identity that will help him to survive in the world: no family, friends, or obvious personal talents. Because he had to protect his mother from the drunken rages of his father, he has a skewed attitude toward older men and women; and because his mother recently died and an inherited malady has claimed all of his siblings before their nineteenth birthdays, he is haunted by dark forebodings of his own impending death.[20] When his father dies, Mervyn says he has no traces of a past; and when he wanders the streets of Philadelphia, before meeting Welbeck, he is quite alone.[21] To survive his desperate situation, Mervyn must be able to transform every event that occurs to him into an opportunity and be able to re-create his own identity into a new personality which would engage the attention of others enough to allow him to gain access into society. In the back of Mervyn's mind there always seems to be Franklin's maxim that an ambitious man should write something worth reading or do something worth writing about. Arthur does both. Thus, every judgment which the reader makes about Mervyn must also consider the nature of the society to which he accommodates himself, and Brown never lets the reader forget the sordid state of that society.

Symbolized by the city hospital during the plague where victims cry for help to the indifferent and jesting attendants, the post-revolutionary society of Philadelphia is a place pervaded by a lack of authority and moral leadership. Disregard for law is not confined to criminals like Welbeck but is the rule. Even the good citizen Mr. Stevens does not think of seeking aid from authorities in the death of Watson because he does not trust the legal system. Stevens has seen his friend Carlton imprisoned for a minor debt of his father's (pp. 349–50) while real villains walk free, and he understands quite well the meaning of the lawyer Hemmings's explanation that it would be folly to resort to the courts to claim Mervyn's just reward from Mrs. Maurice (pp. 370–73). It is a world of failed fathers and ruined families. The fathers of Mervyn, Welbeck, and Achsa desert or abandon their children while those like Mr. Hadwin, Watson, and the elder Lodi die prematurely from disease, crime, and political havoc. So fragile are the ties that bind people together that under the pressure of the plague self-interest quickly prevailed over the most intimate of bonds: "Terror had exterminated all the sentiments of nature. Wives were deserted by husbands, and children by parents" (p. 122). At the novel's center two entire families are destroyed: Mervyn learns the moving story of the deaths of Mary Walpole, her seven daughters, and their adoptive father, Maravegli (pp. 143–46); and he witnesses the removal of the bodies of the younger Thetford, his wife, and child. This latter episode takes on additional significance because on his initial night in the city Mervyn happened to learn that Thetford had put this infant in his wife's bed in what proves to be a doomed effort to replace his deceased first child, save his wife's sanity, and hold his family together.

In this society corrupt businessmen, such as the elder Thetford, scheme the ruin of their competitors and wait to pick clean any new victims, as the innkeepers do to Mervyn on his trip to the city. A wagon load of coffins stands ready to cart off the victims even before they are quite dead, as the novel's recurrent image of premature burial takes on a poignant social dimension.[22] While honest and compassionate men, such as Mediicote, Estwick, Maravegli, and Stevens, remain weak and ineffectual, those like Phillip Hadwin who are guided by selfish aims wield power and authority. In the second part of the novel the scope of this social picture widens into a panorama in which the manipulation of stocks in Frankfort leads to the ruin and suicide of Achsa's father in England, and the maneuverings of Robespierre and Pitt affect the lives of millions. Money, power, and capriciousness even at the highest levels affect the lives of individuals no less fatally than the contagion of the yellow fever.

In the context of this social corruption, Mervyn's most redeeming characteristic, as it is in all of Brown's villains, is his revolutionary impulse. Like Carwin and Ormond especially, Mervyn is an outsider who is disturbed by the cruelty and injustice of the social system and is inclined to want to initiate change. From early in his narrative he expresses shock at the opulence and luxury of the social elite, and he echoes Godwin's *Political Justice* in his observations on the function of inherited wealth: "Wealth had ever been capriciously distributed. The mere physical relation of birth is all that entitles us to the manor or thrones" (p. 54).[23] His first protests against the luxury of the few are motivated by his recognition of his own lowly place on the ladder of wealth, as when he first looks into Welbeck's enclosed garden: "The enclosure was a charming green, which I saw opened into a house of the loftiest and most stately order. . . . My father's dwelling did not equal the height of one story. . . . My heart dictated a comparison between my one condition and that of proprietors of this domain. How wide an impasse was the gulf by which we are separated!" (pp. 43–44).

After his initial reaction, which is to find a way to share this garden, Mervyn undergoes a series of what he calls "revolutions which had taken place in my mind" that lead him in new directions.[24] The high point of his revolutionary fervor occurs when he learns of the cruelty of the public hospital. Mervyn reports Wallace's description of the conditions and his cry: "O! how poor are the conceptions which are formed, by the fortunate few, of the sufferings to which millions of their fellow beings are condemned" (p. 166). While moved by this heightened awareness of injustice, Mervyn concludes that the problem lies "in the governor of such an institution," and he is ready to "hasten to City hall . . . to offer myself as a superintendent of the hospital" (pp. 68–71). But this readiness for public service is not the last revolution to occur in Arthur's mind, and experience teaches him to contain his reforming impulses. Unlike Brown's other rebels turned criminals, Mervyn is not overwhelmed by frustration and passion. He has learned from the example of Welbeck's ruin that the prudent course for one without resources is to keep up the appearance of honesty, accommodation, and humility. In the wake of Welbeck's misguided course of independence and lust, Mervyn fashions for himself a vocation as the healer of the villain's victims. Thereby, Mervyn leads a self-serving reform movement that allows one person, himself, to rise from the poverty of the farm to the comforts of his lady's drawing room.[25]

Mervyn's failure to become a genuine social reformer should not necessarily lead to a final condemnation of his character. What separates Mervyn from his violent and self-destructive counterparts, Welbeck, Ormond, and Wieland, is that he acts in accord with, and perhaps out of a dim awareness of his own psychological limitations. In shifting his goals and settling for less than the romantic ideals of independence and social action which Stevens and Eliza pose for him, Mervyn succumbs not only to social restraints but, more importantly, to the formidable obstacles which lie within himself. Certainly not Brown's most complete psychological study, Mervyn is more psychologically complex than he at first appears. His conspicuous oedipal dream of being stabbed by the father-like husband of Achsa usually arouses embarrassment among Brown's post-Freudian readers; however, this scene does serve as an unmistakable signal of the importance of Mervyn's inner life. In fact, in this novel Brown achieves a delicate balance of conscious and unconscious motivations in his central character by presenting his psychological inducements more subtly than in his other works.

Suspicious of the unconscious and of the inner forces which guide him, Mervyn often expresses his bewilderment about what really directs his life. Typically, he asks: "Why, said I as I hasted forward, is my fortune so abundant in unforeseen occurrences? Is every man, who leaves his cottage and the impressions of his infancy behind him, ushered into such a world of revolutions and perils as have trammelled my steps" (p. 317). While Arthur is not certain of whether he is Everyman or a unique individual, Brown provides enough detail about Mervyn's unconscious mind for the reader to understand the restraints which ultimately prevent him from escaping his particular past. Because of Mervyn's fear of dreams, imagination, and the inner life, he tries to repress all evidence of his unconscious drives: he derides the value of dreams and attributes his decision to marry Achsa to conscious motives such as her wealth and his poverty (p. 416).[26] But a careful examination of the stages of his psychological development reveals that ultimately his choices may not be as conscious as he would like to believe.

The four stages of Mervyn's psychological development are somewhat blurred by the narrative structure. When the novel opens and Arthur enters the Stevens's house, he is embarking upon the third phase of his psychological growth. The formative experiences which he had in his family have occurred before his arrival in Philadelphia, and the reader must piece together the fragmented descriptions of his early life presented throughout the narrative. Mervyn himself is aware of the impact of some of his family experience upon his nature: he understands that the pattern of early death underlies his bouts of morbid fatalism and that his economic deprivation has made him irrationally jealous of the rich. Still there are important aspects of his nature of which Arthur is ignorant but Brown's reader is aware. His antagonistic relationship with his father has left him with an ambivalent attitude toward other men, especially those in authority over him or in competition with him.[27] This tendency partially accounts for his hatred of Wallace and his tormenting of Welbeck and Philip Hadwin. In addition, the special intimacy between him and his mother has left Mervyn with an inclination toward the company of older women, such as Mrs. Wentworth, Mrs. Stevens, and Carlton's sister, which culminates in his marriage to his "new mama." Through the subsequent stages of Mervyn's development, Brown presents a series of responses which are remarkably consistent with these broad proclivities.

During his employment with Welbeck, Mervyn passes into his second phase. In this relationship Mervyn alternates between feelings of superiority and defiance toward Welbeck and a yearning to be martyred and vicitimized by him. Mervyn reveals this tendency toward self-destruction first when he talks about his fascination for the plague. "The rumour was of a nature to absorb and suspend the whole soul. A certain sublimity is connected with enormous dangers, that imparts to our consternation or our pity, a tincture of the pleasing. . . . I had leisure to conjure up terrific images, and . . . this employment was not enjoined upon me by necessity, but was ardently pursued, and must therefore have been recommended by some nameless charm" (p. 123). Because he is himself obsessed with the knowledge that "seeds of early and lingering death are sewn in my own constitution" (p. 128), he begins to identify with his projection of what he imagines to be the loneliness and desperateness of Susan's fiancé, Wallace: "My imagination was incessantly pursued by the image of this youth, perishing alone, and in obscurity" (p. 127). Thus, he journeys to the city to save Wallace and is so excited by the risk involved that he stops several people escaping the city to hear of their gruesome experiences: "Hitherto distress had been contemplated at a distance, and through the medium of fancy delighting to be startled by the wonderful, transported by sublimity" (p. 127). While in the city, Mervyn repeatedly and intentionally endangers himself by staying to listen to the tales of Estwick and Medlicote about the sufferings of the victims.

Like the irrational desire to court destruction which Clara Wieland described in herself,[28] Mervyn's underlying hunger for danger explains Mervyn's prolonged attachment to Welbeck, even against the dictates of reason. Brown makes Mervyn's unconscious motivation explicit in the scene which illustrates the association in Mervyn's mind between Welbeck and Colvill, the fatherly schoolmaster turned rapist who destroyed Mervyn's sister. As Mervyn lies at the feet of Welbeck who imitates the voice of Colvill, Arthur expresses the highest transports of martyrdom. With near delight he imagines Colvill driving a dagger into his heart, an image that will spring forth from his unconscious again in his dream about Achsa's husband. This connection in Mervyn's mind between Welbeck and Colvill only strengthens Mervyn's longing to provoke his employer's wrath, a tendency which had been evident quite early in his violation of Welbeck's instructions regarding Mrs. Wentworth. With the threatening figure of Welbeck looming above him, the sick and helpless Mervyn drives the villain into a rage by flaunting the Lodi banknotes before his eyes. Mervyn's otherwise misguided act of burning the banknotes may also be unconsciously movitated by his desire to defy Welbeck and incur his wrath even at the risk of losing a potential fortune.[29]

Arthur's description of his feelings during the moments after this defiant act is a key to understanding his psychological make-up. As he awaits what he thinks will be certain death at the hands of Welbeck, he experienced a certain self-satisfied pleasure: "all was frenzy and storm in the countenance and features of Welbeck. Nothing less could be expected than that the scene would terminate in some bloody catastrophe. . . . What remained, but to encounter or endure its consequences with unshrinking firmness?" (p. 202). Arthur displays a similar combination of self-pity and calm acceptance of expected punishment in the scenes in which he incites the anger of Philip Hadwin. This psychological pattern is not surprising in view of Mervyn's curious position as the family mediator who incurred his father's drunken rages: "As to my personal strength, it was nothing; yet my mother's person was rescued from brutal violence: he was checked, in the midst of his ferocious career, by a single look or exclamation from me" (p. 329).

The nature of Mervyn's relationship to Welbeck, which finally results in his chastizing the criminal and repairing the damage he has done to a series of women, suggests that Arthur is driven to repeat the ambivalent relationship he had with his father. Thus, to balance the possibility that Mervyn remains close to Welbeck because Arthur himself is either a villain or a fool, Brown's psychological material provides another possible explanation: that Mervyn's attachment to Welbeck is not completely rational but is also the result of his unconscious desire to recapitulate experiences of his childhood. His ultimate triumph over this adversary frees him to pass into the next phase of his development which begins with his rebirth in the arms of Stevens into a world of beneficent fathers and of economic, social, and sexual opportunities.

Mervyn's period in the security of the Stevens's household is really the continuation of the domestic calm which he enjoyed in the Hadwin home. Under the protection of these two benign fathers, Mervyn starts life anew. He begins his romantic relationship with Eliza, his education for a career as a physician, and his role as the benevolent reformer who transforms Welbeck's evil into good. As a conscious self-seeker, Mervyn embraces the opportunities to make social contacts which Welbeck's web of crimes conveniently provided for him. Assured of the love of Eliza and the support and influence of Stevens, Mervyn appears in this phase to have shaped a new identity whereby he can be socially useful and personally rewarded for his efforts. With the tone of a young Franklin or Cotton Mather, Mervyn embarks on a vocation of doing good: "My spirits were high, and I saw nothing in the world before me but sunshine and prosperity. I was conscious that my happiness depended not on the revolutions of nature or the caprice of man. All without was, indeed, vicissitude and uncertainty; but within my bosom was a center not to be shaken or removed" (p. 298).

Significantly, it is in this phase of promise that Mervyn takes up the profession of authorship. While it is Stevens who begins the narrative for him, Arthur comes to relish the role of storyteller. Finding that his captivating tale of his sufferings and triumph wins him the attention and admiration of others, especially of women like Mrs. Wentworth, Fanny Maurice, and Achsa Fielding, Mervyn never misses an opportunity to repeat his tale and is eager to take up the writing himself when Stevens loses interest.[30] Mervyn also finds that writing serves for a time as a means of holding his turbulent psychological life under control. In spite of his new career, Mervyn fears his inner life and tries to repress his unconscious. As he rides in a stagecoach to Baltimore to aid the destitute Watson family, Mervyn has a few moments of repose when his "imagination" shows him what he calls "the pictures which my wayward fancy had depicted," but he so distrusts his imagination that he quickly suppresses this experience: "I will not describe my dreams. My proper task is to relate the truth" (p. 355). Later when Achsa is frightened by the implications of his oedipal dream, he again denies the relevance of unconscious experience to conscious life: "Why you surely place no confidence in dreams" (p. 429). Indeed, he uses his writing as a means of controlling his inner turmoil: "The pen is a pacifier. It checks the mind's career; it circumscribes her wanderings. It traces out, and compels us to adhere to one path. It ever was my friend. Often it has blunted my vexations; hushed my stormy passions; turned my peevishness into soothing; my fierce revenge to heart-dissolving pity" (pp. 396–97).

To the disappointment of Stevens and many of Brown's readers, Mervyn does not continue in his promising life as a writer and medical student, but his motives for abandoning his new identity, as well as fleeing Eliza, are finally not rational.[31] The conscious attractions of his new life are simply not strong enough to overcome his psychological immaturity, and he retreats from potential adulthood into a prolonged, and perhaps permanent, adolescence. A close examination of the fourth and final phase of Arthur's psychological development reveals that Brown provides important verbal clues to Mervyn's unconscious gravitation towards the psychological security which Achsa symbolizes. On the surface, of course, the relationship between Arthur and Achsa has the appearance of a somewhat comic love match in a sentimental romance. Arthur needs money and Achsa wants a husband, and it is difficult to tell who catches whom. While Arthur appears to have cleverly assured himself of Achsa's affection by sitting admiringly at her feet and engaging her in conversation about love, it is she who initiates a socratic dialogue through which she shows him that he does not really love Eliza—at which point Achsa blushes and, in what is practically an aside to the reader, cries with near delight, "Poor Bess! This will be sad news to thee!" (p. 389). Once she has vanquished her competition, Achsa needs only, according to Dr. Stevens, to arouse Arthur's jealousy. To Arthur's expression of concern about the propriety of his love, Stevens shrewdly assures him: "How quickly would this tranquility vanish, and the true state of your heart be evinced, if a rival should enter the scene and be entertained for preference; then . . . would you be awakened to terror and anguish" (p. 418). Predictably, when she embarks with another youth for the country the next day, Arthur goes into a jealous rage, flies to her, and their love is sealed.

As with so many other aspects of this novel, however, things are more complex than they seem and understanding them is essential for judging Arthur's character. Besides the obvious oedipal dream and Arthur's repeated references to his "new mamma," Brown gives even greater emphasis to the psychological importance of this relationship through the extensive use of the pattern and language of religious conversion to describe Arthur's crisis of love. Because Arthur's search for identity, meaning, and authority is so spiritually empty, it is significant that Brown invests his devotion to Achsa with religious feeling. Describing her attraction as "mystical" (p. 348), Arthur is at a loss to explain "the secret of her power to entrance the soul of the listener and beholder" which "will best account for that zeal almost to idolatry with which she has . . . been regarded by me" (p. 397). When Stevens expresses surprise at the "idolatry which this woman has inspired," Arthur declares that his love is not sexual but spiritual: "Love her I do, as I love my God; as I love virtue" (p. 415). In response to Stevens's verbal attack upon her as unworthy, Arthur cries out "Hush! Hush! blasphemer!" (p. 416). Like a Puritan asking "what, Lord, may I do to be saved," Arthur pleads with Achsa: "Tell me how I shall serve you? What can I do to make you happier? Poor am I in every thing but zeal, but still I may do something. What pray tell me what can I do?" (p. 412). He yearns to submit his will completely to hers and become totally dependent upon her authority: "I had vowed to love her and serve her" (p. 397); "I was wax in her hand. Without design and without effort, I was always the form she wished me to assume. My own happiness became a secondary passion. . . . I thought not of myself. I had scarcely a separate or independent existence" (pp. 411–12).

At the culmination of his conversion to the religion of Achsa, Arthur experiences a kind of spiritual crisis which includes a dream and a night of wandering in the forest. Again, the language which Brown uses in both of these episodes strengthens the psychological and religious implications of Mervyn's devotion:

> I was roused as by a divine voice that said—Sleep, no more,
> Mervyn shall sleep no more. . . . What chiefly occupied me
> was a nameless sort of terror. What shall I compare it to?
> Methinks that one falling from a tree overhanging a torrent,
> plunged into a whirling eddy, and gasping and struggling
> while he sinks to rise no more, could feel just as I did
> then. . . . I stretched my hand, and caught the arm of a chair.
> This act called me back to reason, or rather gave my soul an
> opportunity to roam into a new track equally wild. Was it the
> abruptness of this vision that thus confounded me! was it a la-
> tent error in my moral constitution, which this new conjunc-
> ture drew forth into influence? These were all the tokens of a
> mind lost to itself; bewildered; unhinged; plunged into a drear
> insanity. (pp. 419–20)

With his inner life in such complete turmoil Mervyn first dreams that he seeks Achsa at her house where he finds the door locked—suggestively, this door in his unconscious mind is the only one in the novel which Mervyn cannot open. In the last of Mervyn's symbolic deaths into new life, he imagines himself destroyed by the dagger of Ascha's husband and awakens to spend the next night actually wandering in the woods. This experience of being lost in the forest is a recapitulation of an earlier parallel scene in which Mervyn becomes lost on his return to Welbeck. This time he appears to have found a more worthy object of his faith in a protecting mother figure who will provide him psychological asylum and a form of spiritual fulfillment.[32]

While there is much evidence that Arthur's rhetoric of benevolence was never sincere and that he was only seeking the smoothest way to wealth, the psychological development which leads him to marry Achsa belies other less rational motives. While his marriage may represent a financial and social victory, it also symbolizes his ultimate failure to form an independent sense of self and a personal identity. It is also meaningful that, in marrying his Achsa, Arthur also abandons his role as author of his own narrative, and the terms in which he casts off this most recent calling suggest a kind of psychic dismemberment: "But why do I indulge in this pen-prattle? The hour she fixed for my return to her is come, and now take thyself away quill. Lie there, snug in thy leathern case, till I call for thee, and that will not be very soon. . . . I *will* adjure thee, so let this be thy last office" (pp. 429–30). Along with this statement of self-abasement, the uncertainty of Mervyn's achievement is also underscored by the couple's plan to depart America and Arthur's rather tentative description of the anticipated life with Achsa: "Our household . . . should be *thus* composed. Fidelity and skill and pure morals should be sought out, and enticed, by generous recompenses, into our domestic service. Duties should be light and regular.—Such and such should be our amusements and employments abroad and at home, and would not this be true happiness?" (p. 429). The superciliousness of this projected scene and the possible dramatic irony of Mervyn's question only contribute to the conclusion that in his struggle for survival Arthur has achieved only a Pyrrhic victory.[33]

In this view *Arthur Mervyn* is neither a depiction of virtue rewarded, nor a study of unscrupulous deviousness, but is an anatomy of social and psychological survival which demands from the reader a systematic character analysis. In the mercenary world of post-revolutionary America and Europe which Brown depicts in these "memoirs of the year 1793," the absence of moral imperatives or shared spiritual values, symbolized so vividly by the city in plague, makes the determination of the guilt or innocence of an individual extremely difficult. Personal and societal revolutions are the order of the day, and it is Mervyn's struggle to plot his own course that makes him at once exploitive and open to exploitation. Just as Stevens needs to believe in Arthur in order to maintain his faith in humanity, so too Arthur relies upon the honesty of Achsa. When he first meets her, he says "Be not a deceiver, I entreat you. I depend only on your looks and professions and these may be dissembled" (p. 313). And indeed they may, for Arthur has no better grounds for believing this woman whom he meets in a house of prostitution than Stevens has for trusting Mervyn. Achsa's moving tale of her past—a story which perhaps surpasses Arthur's own for sensationalism—may also be a tissue of lies. But Arthur needs to believe her. Arthur is neither a hero nor a villain, for he lacks the force of will to be either. He is one young American who is not prepared to embrace a life of individualism and social freedom with the accompanying risks and responsibilities. Though he can acquire the education and possesses the necessary wit and personality for success, Arthur cannot overcome his psychological limitations, his feelings of inadequacy, insecurity, and dependency. Thus, he retreats from America and from the vision of his future which it offers and seeks safety and comfort in the arms of his Judeo-European mother.

Notes

1. All references to the novel, hereafter cited in the text, are to the edition of Warner Berthoff, *Arthur Mervyn or Memoirs of the Year 1793* (New York: Holt, Rinehart, and Winston, 1962).

2. Compare the sympathetic interpretations of Mervyn in R. W. B. Lewis, *The American Adam: Innocence, Tragedy, and Tradition in the Nineteenth Century* (Chicago: University of Chicago Press, 1955), p. 97 ff., and Henry Petter, *The Early American Novel* (Columbus: Ohio State University Press, 1971), pp. 337 ff., with those inclined to view the novel as presenting ironic condemnation of his character: Michael Davitt Bell, " 'The Double-Tongued Deceiver': Sincerity and Duplicity in the Novels of Charles Brockden Brown," *Early American Literature*, 9 (1974), esp. 155–58, and Warner Berthoff, "Adventures of the Young Man: An Approach to Charles Brockden Brown," *American Quarterly*, 9 (1957), 421–54 and

the "Introduction" to his edition. Though Berthoff is more restrained, both agree that Mervyn may be the "wily imposter" of Wortley's charges.

3. Both David Lee Clark, *Charles Brockden Brown: Pioneer Voice of America* (Durham: Duke University Press, 1952), pp. 179 ff., and Lewis, pp. 94–98, practically ignore the second part. For discussion of this problem, see Donald A. Ringe, *Charles Brockden Brown* (New York: Twayne, 1966), pp. 24 and 65–66) and Harry R. Warfel, *Charles Brockden Brown: American Gothic Novelist* (Gainesville: University of Florida Press, 1949), pp. 145 and 243. On the structure of the novel see Kenneth Bernard, "Arthur Mervyn: The Ordeal of Innocence," *Texas Studies in Literature and Language*, 6, (1965), 441–59. I believe that Bernard errs in seeing Stevens as a "negligible factor" in the novel (442).

4. "Advertisement for *Sky Walk*," in Harry R. Warfel, ed., *The Rhapsodist and Other Collected Writings by Charles Brockden Brown* (New York, 1943), p. 136. In agreement on this issue are Ringe, pp. 22–23, and William Hedges, "Charles Brockden Brown and the Culture of Contradictions," *Early American Literature*, 9 (1974), 112–14, although Hedges also recommends restraint in viewing Brown as a sophisticated craftsman, 109.

5. Especially relevant is John Butt, *The Oxford History of English Literature: The Mid-Eighteenth Century*, ed. and completed by Geoffrey Carnall (Oxford: Clarendon Press, 1979), pp. 449–513. Also see, Terence Martin, *The Instructed Vision: Scottish Common Sense Philosophy and the Origins of American Fiction* (Bloomington: 1961), and William Charvat, *The Origins of American Critical Thought, 1810–1835* (Philadelphia, 1936), esp. pp. 134–63.

6. Berthoff notes this comic tendency in his "Introduction," p. xviii.

7. Bell ventures far in this direction, while more balanced readings are presented by Berthoff and by James H. Justus in "Arthur Mervyn, American," *American Literature*, 42 (1970), 304–24.

8. Dunlap called the change "as unsuspected as disgusting" in *The Life of Charles Brockden Brown* (Philadelphia: James P. Parke, 1815), II, 40. It was reported that Shelley was "extremely displeased"—see *Peacock's Memoirs of Shelley*, ed. H. F. B. Brett-Smith (London: Henry Frowde, 1909), pp. 35 ff. For recent comment on these attitudes, see Berthoff, "Young Man," 432, and Ringe, p. 77.

9. The misappropriation of money and goods is a central theme of the novel discussed in Justus, 314–16. Just as Arthur intrudes into rooms he also insinuates himself into the lives of others who can help him financially (see Ringe, p. 77).

10. While the length of his narrative testifies to his loquaciousness, he "was far from talkative" (p. 7) in the Stevens's house until he has tested their interests, and he requires a night to prepare his answer to Wortley's charges (p. 11).

11. Both Hedges, 123, 136–38, and Justus, 306–22, have noted the thematic importance of Franklin. Also, pertinent to Mervyn's career perhaps is Franklin's *Reasons for Preferring an Old Mistress to a Young One* (Philadelphia, 1745) where he recommends that young men marry older women. While the *Autobiography* had not yet been published, its existence and content were known among Philadelphia intellectuals who had read the section completed before 1789 and had urged Franklin to print it. See Mary E. Rucker, "Benjamin Franklin," in *American Literature: 1764–1789, The Revolutionary Years*, ed. Everett Emerson (Madison: University of Wisconsin, 1977), 105–08. During the 1790s Franklin was seen by some as a master of self-promotion; see Richard D. Miles, "The American Image of Benjamin Franklin, *American Quarterly*, 9 (1957), 118 ff. Brown's well-known admiration of Franklin (Warfel, pp. 32–33, and Clark, p. 242) would not preclude his ironic use of the Franklin image or moral teachings.

12. Mervyn's language is filled with terms from the national-agrarian rhetoric: he seeks "asylum"; he wants a life of "competence"; the city offers only "pollution." He is so convincing that V. L. Parrington praised the work as an illustration of Jeffersonian dogma; see *The Romantic Revolution in America* (New York, 1927), p. 190. A germane study is Charles C. Cole, Jr., "Brockden Brown and the Jefferson Administration," *Pennsylvania Magazine of*

History and Biography (July, 1948), which traces Brown's shift from a Jeffersonian to a Federalist philosophy. Mervyn changes his mind on the question of the city vs. the country, and he abandons the Jeffersonian themes and catchwords as he gravitates toward Achsa. Justus sees this shift as an awakening, 309–13, while Ringe (pp. 70–85) views it as possibly ironic.

13. See Brown's *Alcuin: A Dialogue* in Dunlap's biography and in a new edition edited by Lee Edwards (Northampton: 1970). The influence of Godwin's *Caleb Williams* (1794) upon *Arthur Mervyn* has been frequently discussed, as in Bernard, 456–59 and Bell, 155–56.

14. Hedges explains this false ring as the result of Arthur's alternating among available cultural styles of discourse which include those of Jonathan Edwards, John Woolman and Franklin, See his "Culture of Contradictions," 135–38.

15. "Introduction," p. xviii and Hedges, 123.

16. Bernard, 444, notes a similarity between Mervyn and Joseph Andrews.

17. This conclusion can be drawn from the various reports about Clavering: the version Clavering gave to the Mervyns (p. 27); the tale Mrs. Wentworth tells about Clavering (pp. 63–64); the version told to Stevens by Wortley and his friends (pp. 238–39); and Mervyn's account to Mrs. Wentworth (pp. 340–41). The only conclusion is that on his suicidal path Clavering deceived the Mervyns as well as his friends and relatives. Bernard has also noticed similarities between Mervyn and Clavering in his "Ordeal of Innocence," 459.

18. This theme also underlies Achsa's story about her first marriage and is illustrated in the fate of Wortley whose plans and years of labor to save money for marriage are thwarted by Welbeck's financial schemes (p. 216). In his essay "Walstein's School of History," Brown stresses the close connection between property and sex in relation to human happiness (in *The Rhapsodist*, p. 152).

19. Bernard, 457, views Welbeck and Mervyn as complementary opposites; Hedges, 127–29, and Petter, 334–35, see them drawn together to torment one another; and Patrick Bracaccio sees them as doubles—see his "Studied Ambiguities: *Arthur Mervyn* and the Problem of the Unreliable Narrator," *American Literature*, 42 (1970), 21.

20. All of the children in Arthur's "numerous family" died before the age of nineteen, including his sister who committed suicide (p. 15). The suicides in the novel include Mervyn's sister, Clavering, and Achsa's father; Welbeck supposedly makes several attempts.

21. Mervyn is most terrified when he is alone, whether wandering the streets during the plague (pp. 122–39), trapped in Welbeck's basement (pp. 104–06), hiding in Welbeck's attic (p. 204), or lost in the forest (p. 74 and again p. 423).

22. In addition to the episode in which Arthur himself is placed in a coffin while still alive (p. 141), there are suggestions that the young Thetford is still alive when carried in a coffin from his home (pp. 133–34), and that Watson is still alive when Welbeck and Mervyn bury him (p. 104). There is also a hint that Mervyn might have rushed Susan Hadwin into her grave prematurely (pp. 268–69). Also important here is the recurrent image of the destruction of the family which Brown may intend as a challenge to the standard projection of family solidarity in the popular sentimental novel. On the latter see Terence Martin, "Social Institutions in the Early American Novel," *American Quarterly*, 9 (1957), esp. 77–80.

23. See Godwin on property, *Political Justice*, ed. H. S. Salt (London: George Allen and Unwin, 1890), chapters I and II.

24. The frequent repetition of this phrase and Mervyn's own awareness of being in a world of political revolutions and, in Stevens's phrase "mercantile revolutions" (p. 219), suggests a relationship between individual and corporate turmoils. On the function of social and political ideas in the novel, see David H. Hirsh, "Charles Brockden Brown as a Novelist of Ideas," *Books at Brown* 20 (1965), 165–84, and Hedges, passim.

25. On Mervyn's exploitation of Welbeck's sins, see Berthoff, "Introduction," p. xvii, and Ringe, p. 75.

26. On Mervyn's unconscious motives see Brancaccio, 22–27, and on the function of the irrational in Brown in general, see Arthur Kimball, *Rational Fictions: A Study of Charles Brockden Brown* (McMinnville: Linfield Research Institute, 1968), and his "Savages and Savagism: Brockden Brown's Dramatic Irony," *Studies in Romanticism*, 6 (1967), 214–15.

27. Hedges, 127, also notes a suggested father-son relationship between Welbeck and Mervyn.

28. Clara makes similar comments about the lure of death in *Wieland or the Transformation: An American Tale*, ed. Sydney J. Krause and S. W. Reid (Kent, Ohio: Kent State University Press, 1977), pp. 193 and 234. She also shares Mervyn's attitude toward the emotionally pacifying effect of writing, pp. 221–23 and 234–35.

29. There are no rational grounds for Mervyn's revealing his possession of the money or his burning of it after hearing Welbeck's transparent story. But as Welbeck goes into a rage, Mervyn is clearly the ready martyr.

30. Although Brown does make one error by having Arthur refer to Stevens as a third party when he is supposedly the audience of the narrative (see Bernard, 442), the shift that makes Arthur the writer-narrator serves to emphasize his break with Stevens and to highlight his new role as Arthur-author.

31. For commentary on the importance of Mervyn's calling as a writer, see Bell, 158–60, and Paul Witherington, "Benevolence and the 'Utmost Stretch': Charles Brockden Brown's Narrative Dilemma," *Criticism*, 14 (1972), 175–91.

32. This language suggests that Mervyn's spiritual emptiness and moral confusion lead him, and others like Welbeck and Stevens, to invest a religious-like faith in objects and other persons.

33. In Arthur's closing comment about his future "happiness" are the seeds of Albee's *American Dream* where a young man like Arthur brings "satisfaction" to his new parents. The play closes with Grandma's ironic observation: "So, let's leave things as they are right now . . . while everybody's happy . . . or while everybody's got what he thinks he wants." Edward Albee, *The American Dream* (New York: Coward, 1961).

"Not My Tongue Only": Form and Language in Brown's *Edgar Huntly*

Paul Witherington

Interpreters of *Edgar Huntly* have been kind in recent years, but condescending. While praising the novel's ideas and psychic images, they have damned its artwork by handsomely tolerating Brown's thick style and his lumbering narrative, or by sweeping them under layers of meaning. *Edgar Huntly* is most often read as an initiation story which stumbles a bit, hedges a bit, and then moves rather directly toward resolution and theme. Edgar learns, like Clara in *Wieland*, that private convictions will not always solve complex "interpersonal" problems. Like Arthur Mervyn, he finds that good intentions are not always productive of good, that benevolence is an awkward and sometimes ugly affair, and that the New World is all too likely to repeat the follies of the Old. The psychological equivalent of these movements from near-sighted individual concerns to social maturity may be stated as Edgar's quest to exchange a splintered ego for psychic wholeness and a more complex Self by acknowledging Clithero, his daemonic double and the projection of Edgar's own unconscious hatred and avoidance.

These ideological and archetypal interpretations have left us some valuable keys to Brown and a methodology for dealing with some of the more abstruse works of early American literature. In their preoccupation with closure and conclusion, however, such approaches have often neglected both the literary conventions Brown is starting from and the formal variations he is attempting: his rhythmically episodic structure which resists any particular "statement," and his use of language to create what Richard Poirier has called "a world elsewhere."[1] *Edgar Huntly* is a surprisingly modern work in its self-conscious attack on the very assumptions and structures and language that make fiction possible, and it calls for a criticism that illuminates not only Edgar's initiation but that of the reader into new forms and voices. We should now grant Brown the license he claimed as an experimental novelist, and we should slip him some of the linguistic affection we currently lavish on Melville and John Barth.

Recent criticism seems to slight or misunderstand Brown's kinship with gothic tradition. A by-product of gothic literature's revolutionary

164

tendencies is its wariness of conventional plot logic, and the resulting "carelessness" may disturb both the unreformed New Critic and the sort of psychological or myth critic who insists on matching bizarre effect with common cause, however far he must abstract to make them jibe. In Brown and his predecessors, for example, there is a strong sense of infection by proximity, the sort of uncaused misfortune that seems closer to early social realism than to psychological allegory. Gothic novelists were often less concerned with guilt by dissociation than with guilt by association, evil being transferred through confession with all the randomness of a plague. Thus Edgar is blasted by Clithero's story as is the young man by Falkland's story in Godwin's *Caleb Williams*, the shared secret having become the shared sin. Even those historical critics who categorize Brown as a gothic novelist sometimes then deny him the prerogatives of that genre. William L. Hedges calls *Edgar Huntly* "the most baffling of all Brown's novels, a botched gothic thriller."[2] "Botched," presumably, because it lacks the authority of later writers (Poe, specifically) and because matters like Waldegrave's murder are left anti-climactically and unsatisfactorily resolved. But surely the gothic tradition is noted as much for works containing supernatural or psychic loopholes as for the kind of thriller that slides back to solid reason at the end.

In truth, Brown both uses and alters traditional gothic to his narrative purposes. For him it works like a dream related by a key character—obviously relevant but not to be taken definitively. The European tradition of "castles and chimeras" referred to by Brown in his introduction is Americanized, but not necessarily made more rational; and despite Brown's social realism and his objective treatment of scientific curiosities such as ventriloquism and somnambulism, his dramas of tangled inner landscapes tend to resist analysis. Even when his plots are laid bare, mysteries remain that beg for the kind of sequel Brown provided to *Wieland* in *Carwin the Biloquist*. *Edgar Huntly* flaunts these loose ends, or as they would be termed in the language usually reserved for calculating modern novels, "open ends," and in burying them, or binding them with the knots of critical hindsight, we do no favor to Brown's intellect or his art.

One touchstone of the problem raised with genre and critical method is the motif of guilt. In their enthusiasm for correspondences, myth critics tend to reduce all guilt to the same level, all moral conflict to a contest between consciousness and unconsciousness. When they insist too much on the parallels between Edgar and Clithero, they obscure the distinctions Brown is making and ironically repeat Edgar's fault, an indiscriminate rush to sympathy.

In the most recent and ambitious of these psychic shadow studies, Philip Russell Hughes links Edgar and Clithero by their "standard revolt against parental authority" and their unconscious fascination with "father-murder."[3] To his credit, Hughes is more flexible than most of the earlier myth critics, and he admits that Clithero and Edgar are separate characters as well as variations of the same character. When Hughes concentrates on his thesis, however, he falls back on the formulas and vocabulary of mythopoeic criticism, even going so far as to call Clithero's crimes "imaginary" (p. 176). But Clithero's sleepwalking serves as mental compensation for very real crimes: he kills Wiatte in a street brawl and tries to kill Wiatte's twin sister, Mrs. Lorimer, under the delusion that he can thereby save her from lingering pain. Although Edgar approaches Clithero's behavior by killing Indians and jeopardizing Mrs. Lorimer's life further under the guise of benevolence, these non-criminal actions come *after* his sleepwalking pattern is already established, and they would seem to be efforts to find a cause, retroactively, for the anxiety Edgar already feels—a problem far different from Clithero's more conventional guilt. In the few lapses of propriety that precede Edgar's sleepwalking, there is no action adequate to his reaction unless we accept Kenneth Bernard's rather thin theory that Edgar, and not a hostile Indian, murdered Waldegrave.[4]

Hughes's "father-murder" thesis is worth entertaining, but it requires severe qualification because of the ambiguity with which Brown always depicts authority. One of his most typical characters is a real or symbolic orphan who searches for the security of home and a stable benefactor even as he exhibits the very eccentricities that would make that home uninhabitable. Moreover, to adopt the view of Hughes and other myth critics that the hero quest necessarily includes a separation from the smothering mother (Mrs. Lorimer) is to ignore Brown's own divided nature: on the one hand, his tendency to liberality and experimentation in politics and fiction; on the other hand, his systematic retreat to the security of editorship as illustrated in *Arthur Mervyn* and *Jane Talbot* where liberal writer-narrators, the "orphans" of the raw new American society, seek out the bosoms of conservative matrons in a Philistine society, thus seeming to betray the very fiction that has given them life.

Hughes does suggest that "Mother Captor" and "Mother Bountiful" are one and the same (p. 182), but the way he speaks of rebellion makes Edgar seem closer to Lizzie Borden than to his more benign fictional descendents, Irving's Rip Van Winkle and Ichabod Crane. Insistence on formula leads Hughes to complain that "the reader finds it difficult to resolve the madness in the novel into proper parts of Gothic fantasy, overwriting, symbolism, and myth" (p. 178). I suggest that Brown is experimenting with approaches rather than following a recipe, and that his character doublings and plot parallels are often formal or aesthetic gambits rather than psychic inevitabilities.

The subject of guilt itself may be part of Brown's experiment, Clithero's real worries played off against Edgar's more insubstantial anxieties. Edgar's problem resembles the existential guilt and alienation of the "modern" condition which of course is as old as irrationality and cosmic unfairness in early Greek drama. Causation loses its way in a world overcome by madness, this novel seems to be saying, as if in refutation of the detailed analysis of causes in that more conventional detective story, *Wieland.*

A good antidote to the tendency of some critics to oversimplify guilt is John Cleman's article, the thesis of which is pretty much summed up in its title: "Ambiguous Evil: A Study of Villains and Heroes in Charles Brockden Brown's Major Novels."[5] Cleman discusses in commendable detail Brown's dramatization of "moral complicity," the idea we associate with Howells and Crane in the late nineteenth century. But Cleman's antidote, like the potion in Hawthorne's famous tale, has the effect of removing some of the body along with the birthmark. Like Hughes, he ignores gothic and sentimental traditions. He seems mystified by Wiatte's unmixed evil (he finds it unparalleled in Brown) but accepts easily Mrs. Lorimer's unmixed goodness, though both are readily explained either by the extreme dissociation of Clitherto's mental state or by the gothic convention of exaggeration or even by the rhythm of extremes in American frontier "brag." As archetypal criticism tends to level guilt, so the minute character analysis of which Cleman's essay is an excellent example tends to parse guilt (and all other feelings) mercilessly until the abstractions and figures of literary convention become real people and all sense of art, as well as all sense of humor, is lost.

Brown's humor has been downgraded rather consistently since Dunlap's ponderous biography except for recent criticism of *Arthur Mervyn* which has generally agreed that Brown's approach to Arthur's monstrous predicaments is satiric. But those who remember that *Edgar Huntly* was written between the writing of Parts I and II of *Arthur Mervyn* (in 1799) would quite naturally expect some crosscurrents. I find them most obviously in the episodic and picaresque Indian adventures, scenes that are quite different from earlier ones and take up four to five times more space in the novel than the celebrated cave scene where Edgar wakes from sleepwalking. The mountain wilderness has been regarded as merely an extension of that earlier scene, further evidence of Edgar's ego in conflict with his id (the savages) and of the vertical hazards of the psyche. There is little personalizing of violence and gore in the Indian sections, however; they seem at times a tedious walk-through of cardboard savages and rescued maiden, a rehearsal for all the mediocre wilderness literature to follow Brown. "I was weary of contemplating these rueful objects," Edgar says late in the narrative. "I was grown callous and immovable,"[6] Yet what is very much alive in these sections, and humorously so, is the rhythm and the changing character of Edgar's voice, the sharply modulated discrepancies between superman and bumbling fool, experienced woodsman and tenderfoot, unique adventurer and everyman.

Even before the cave scene, this rhythm of inflation and deflation begins. "My perserverance surmounted every impediment," Edgar says as he follows Clithero's progress through Norwalk (p. 104). Suddenly he is expert with a tomahawk, having often in the past "severed an oak-branch, and cut the sinews of a catamount, at the distance of sixty feet" (p. 119). Soon afterward, though, he admits the limitations of a "constitution by no means distinguished for its force"(p. 132) and seems to have returned again to what he once called his "ancient sobriety" (p. 5).

After he dispatches his first Indian, Edgar says he "felt prepared to undergo the labours of Hercules" (p. 173), but he seems to have inherited that superhero's ineptness along with his strength. At one point he jumps into the river, after remarking that he finds water "almost as congenial an element as air" (p. 206), and almost immediately goes numb with the cold. Only a few pages later, though, water has become "not only my field of sport but my sofa and my bed" (p. 214). Even his injuries have a comic composition: the "thousand wounds" on his legs turn out to be the scratches of brambles (p. 187).

If Edgar's confidence in himself were the only issue in these scenes, his vacillation would be merely humorous, like the situation in *Life on the Mississippi* where the young Twain, in quest for an elusive pilot's license, must memorize a new river every day. But there is also the question of which set of facts we are to believe about Edgar's past. In an inflated moment, he says: "I had delighted, from my childhood, in feats of agility and perseverance. . . . I disdained to be outdone in perspicacity by the lynx, in his sure-footed instinct by the roe, or in patience under hardship, and contention with fatigue, by the Mohawk" (p. 202). Not long before this, however, he admits: "All my education and the habits of my life tended to unfit me for a contest and a scene like this" (p. 184). These voices invite us to speculate about Edgar's "history" but warn us not to trust our conclusions.

Richard Slotkin, one of the few critics to deal with the discrepancies in Edgar's voice, has argued that they arise from guilt, Edgar's inability to admit to himself that he is an experienced hunter and therefore potentially a violent killer.[7] Tension becomes extreme when Edgar shoots and then reluctantly bayonets the last of the pursuing Indians. Whereas he usually stresses the uniqueness of his experience, Edgar now chooses to play the role of everyman: "Such are the deeds which perverse nature compels thousands of rational beings to perform and to witness! Such is the spectacle, endlessly prolonged and diversified, which is exhibited in every field of battle" (p. 193). It seems necessary for him to feel, at this heart of violence, the common pulse of humanity. Soon afterward, he is back to hyperbole: "Surely my fate has never been paralleled!" (p. 213).

Without denying the psychological motifs behind such discrepancies, I would suggest that the Indian episodes are far too extroverted to be explained only by subtleties of guilt. These sections were published before the novel as "Edgar Huntly: A Fragment" (in Brown's *The Monthly Magazine*, April, 1799), and they stand quite well on their own. Their primary tension is not between conscious and unconscious levels of awareness but between two external aspects of Edgar, the voice of romantic aspiration and the voice of realistic qualification. It is odd that Slotkin, who has a long, excellent analysis of the episodic adventures of Daniel Boone (from John Filson's *The Discovery, Settlement and Present State of Kentucke*, published just fifteen years before *Edgar Huntly*) and who mentions many times the connections between the hunters Boone and Huntly, does not seem to have recognized Brown's tendencies toward ironic humor.

Nor does Hedges, despite his thorough comments on *Arthur Mervyn* as part of a tradition of picaresque humor. Yet the rhythms of *Edgar Huntly* are quite comparable to those of Melville's *Typee* (the laborious and sometimes mock-heroic descent into the valley of the headhunters) or *Pierre*, and especially to that tongue-in-cheek serial of remarkable rebirths in Poe's *The Narrative of Arthur Gordon Pym*. Early twentieth-century critics were right about *Edgar Huntly* splitting into parts, but they were wrong about the aesthetics of that split. In his experimentation with the voices of hero and clown, Brown is working in the tradition of Cervantes, Fielding and Brackenridge, but also anticipating the modern revival of picaresque by Bellow, Donleavy and Barth.

Humor may serve more domestic purposes, though. We must not forget that the immediate recipient of Edgar's bumptious and self-effacing tale is Mary Waldegrave, and that he may be spinning out his story to avoid as long as possible the end of the letter and of their relationship, the marriage plans having foundered on the issue of money. Psychological approaches suggest just the opposite, that Edgar's delay in "sterile" Norwalk and the letter itself constitute an elaborate foreplay to avoid deeper sexual relations. But perhaps Edgar's posturing is simply the swagger of the male humorously preening before the female.

Then again, humor in these sections may have been Brown's own antidote to the terrible journey toward nihilism he was taking with Edgar, and it may have functioned like the ventriloquist's uneasy laugh at the dummy's verbal outrages; behind the performers is the fear that appearances cannot be trusted any more than inclinations, and that no one truly knows himself or anyone else, or even the carefully constructed characters of fiction.

II

In his "Advertisement for *Sky-Walk*," a lost early novel, Brown complains that the popular novels of his time appeal to unthinking readers: "By a string of well connected incidents, they amuse the idle and thoughtless; but are spurned at by those who are satisfied with nothing but stories of lofty eloquence, the exhibition of powerful motives, and a sort of audaciousness of character." He goes on to speak of "souring passions and intellectual energy," by displaying which "we hope to enchain the attention and ravish the souls of those who study and reflect."[8] It is doubtful that the more mature Brown would so glibly have associated writing with sadism and rape ("enchain" and "ravish"), but he does follow through with the "audaciousness of character" as far as Edgar, and as he implies in the quotation above, when one large character with several voices dominates, the work may happily lose its narrative smoothness.

Much potentially good archetypal and ideological criticism has hardened into a formula stressing either an arrival at wholeness, the hero returned from his journey (as outlined by Joseph Campbell in his *Hero with a Thousand Faces*) to show "mastery of two worlds," or else the refusal of wholeness, the hero regressed interminably. In ideological terms, the hero either embraces the dialectic of which experience is composed, or retreats into provincialism. The implication of the episodic structure of *Edgar Huntly*, however, is that wholeness and closure themselves are to be challenged. To work with Edgar's several attempts at initiation more closely it is convenient to divide the novel into seven parts: the introductory section, Clithero's confession, Edgar's later detective work, the Waldegrave-Weymouth interlude, the cave scene, the Indian adventures, and scenes of attempted reunion. Each section tests Edgar in a slightly different way as he tries out a new identity; from the writer's perspective, each section is Brown's attempt to find a literary form compatible with Edgar's distress. Both efforts fall short. Brown seems at times to stand not so much on the borderland of Romanticism as on the edge of a far more recent world of fragmentation, paranoia and loss of faith in the very process by which that world can be described. This inconclusiveness is only barely mitigated by the hero's persistence, his naive faith that space and time are on his side.

The motifs established in the introductory section (Chapters 1–3) set the tone and action for the rest: First, there is a pretended involvement with another person or situation, usually under the banner of benevolence or duty, during which Edgar's ego expands as if his mind could contain all experience and all remedies for distress. Barriers are broken, and nothing is separate or impossible. The antithesis of this voice is retraction, a movement toward isolation, a humbling; more negatively, it is a diminishment of relationships by false restrictions, false reasonings, artificial separations. Sometimes these aspects of Edgar alternate, as if they were only moods, and other times we see that the roles are complementary and the cosmic busybody mask is simply another form of avoidance of one's true identity. Anticipating Clithero's confession late in Chapter 3, for example, Edgar goes "in fancy" to the place of Waldegrave's murder where he imagines they will meet. "My soul was big with expectation," he says, admitting that the scene had "more in it of pleasure than of pain" (p. 32). The way he brings about that confession is revealing because it is similar to Montressor's deception of Fortunato in Poe's "The Cask of Amontillado." To confront Clithero on favorable ground, Edgar invites him to the Huntly house (the home of Edgar's uncle). "I was fashioning an implement, I told him, with respect to which I could not wholly depend upon my own skill. I was acquainted with the dexterity of his contrivances, and the neatness of his workmanship" (p. 28). Clithero, like Fortunato, is taken in by vanity and the narrator's pose of humility, along with the prospects of communion with a comrade, but he is "walled off" just as surely as Poe's character by what Edgar calls his "experiment" (p. 31).

Earlier, Edgar says of Clithero, seen at a distance: "I beheld, in this man, nothing but an object of compassion" (p. 11). "Nothing" aims at inclusiveness, but its effect is negative, limiting and demeaning, as is "object" which takes the humanity out of "compassion." From the beginning, each step toward wholeness turns ironically toward fragmentation.

So it goes with the following sections, most of which have been too closely explicated to need more than a note here. In the second, Clithero exudes humility in the tale he tells Edgar. He is not worthy to be adopted by Mrs. Lorimer, much less to marry her daughter. On the other hand, the Lorimers become little more than playthings in his drama of good and evil as he undertakes, godlike, to alter their situation. In the third section, Edgar who has vowed to observe and yet "to elude observation" (p. 10) leaves food for the sleepwalker in an almost inaccessible area of the wilderness, hoping that Clithero will wake and interpret the gift as "heavenly condemnation of his purpose" (p. 107). This is a clear parallel to Carwin's playing God to stay Wieland's hand in Brown's first novel. Benevolence is tagged with a strangely flamboyant anonymity.

The Waldegrave-Weymouth chapters (13–15) have been slighted by most critics except Bernard even though they come structurally at the very center of the book and introduce Edgar's sleepwalking. Chapter 13 begins with Edgar saying that as a temporary relief from his search for Clithero, he will take up the problem of transcribing Waldegrave's early letters which he, Mary's brother, had forbidden anyone to publish because they contained his former materialistic and atheistic views. Edgar resolves to go ahead with the transcription, but he will show Mary only a few of the letters she has asked to see. By editing them against Waldegrave's wishes and by refusing some of them to Mary under the guise of benevolence (in this case, woman's delicacy), Edgar is again playing God, pretending to break barriers while actually he creates more dangerous ones between himself and his fiancée and between both of them and the memory of the brother.

In the next two chapters, a strange horseman, Weymouth, comes to claim the fortune that Waldegrave had left to Mary. "Honest" Edgar vows that justice will be done and renounces marriage with Mary, finishing what he had symbolically initiated earlier by his very separation from her to investigate the murder. What follows is a variation of the quest imposed by the king on the hero as prerequisite for marrying the princess, with Edgar inflating to fill both male roles, and one suspects that his protestations of poverty (he will not marry Mary without proper means of support) is in line with other avoidances throughout. From an artistic point of view, Edgar's waiting until midway through the long, long letter to reveal to his fiancée that he is breaking their engagement seems plausible, though contrived. Morally viewed, his delay becomes just another barrier drawn between people who are pledged to breaking down barriers.

Brown's realism in the cave scene is intense. Edgar, deprived of sight and memory and sustenance, reverts to a primitive state: imagines cutting a vein and drinking his own blood even as he dies; kills a panther with a tomahawk and eats part of the creature raw; sucks his own sweat. Poe has no better scenes than this in *Pym*. But realism, even ironical realism, is not necessarily the stuff of psychic paradox. If Edgar establishes any contact with the collective unconscious here, any "penetration to the center," it is quickly forgotten in passages that follow, and looking back, he calls his most savage moment "some freak of insanity" (pp. 159–60). Even his stilted language, after so graphic an experience, serves only to mock it: "I bitterly lamented my inordinate avidity," Edgar writes. The potential for mental expansion through physical reduction is not developed or sustained, and Brown, discouraged by comments about his morbidity, never again wrote in so intense a vein.[9]

If there is any mythological analogy in operation in this famous chapter, it may be more on the order of Plato's cave than of the Belly of the Whale. During his ordeal, Edgar sees terror for the first time from the inside out as if he, suddenly, had become Clithero. But without the memory of that outer world, without grounds for comparison or analysis of causes, the experience becomes simply an exercise in visual perception; it cannot be remembered once it is finished any more than it could be imagined before it began. What seems an expansion is once more a kind of reduction. It is not that Edgar alone fails to know the "other"; we are all powerless to see into, or out of, the cave of man.

We have already distinguished the two "voices" of Edgar in his forest adventure: his pretended involvement in larger social and literary contexts through the medium of the seasoned frontiersman revenging his family's tragedy and rescuing the young girl from Indian captivity, and his actual isolation and retreat into self-effacement that apparently belies his numerous miracles and "rebirths." The introduction to his story of talkative Old Deb, or Queen Mab as Edgar dubs the old Indian woman he remembers from his youth, raises the possibility of Edgar's advancement to higher levels of consciousness incorporating the savage and the civilized, the wise old woman and naive young man, but Edgar's true companion in the wilderness is the farmer's daughter he saves from the savages, and she is mute and listless throughout. From the introspection suggested by the cave scene and then denied, we come to an almost completely external rhythm of heroism and anti-heroism in which the adventurer is disencumbered by nourishing inner voices. Edgar returns home sadder, and no wiser.

Richard Slotkin has this to say about the process of mythmaking in America:

> The evolution of the American myth was a synthetic process of reconciling the romantic-conventional myths of Europe to American experience—a process which, by an almost revolutionary turn, became an analytical attempt to destroy or cut through the conventionalized mythology to get back to the primary source of blood-knowledge of the wilderness, the "Indian" mind, the basic, moiratic, myth-generating psychology of man.[10]

This generalization seems applicable to Brown's initial success with the American myth as a synthesis of old world values and new world forms, and his later discovery that cutting through the old forms could in fact create frightening new values. Edgar's voices of expansion and reduction, in short, are not only Brown's but those of the new American culture; synthesis is invited, belabored, and rationalized, but the actual "analysis" that comes is the source of mental and political revolutions, and for some writers it creates anxiety and a pulling back from conflict.

In the final, ironic scenes of reunion, Edgar tries to bring himself and Clithero into a favorable relationship again with Sarsefield and Mrs. Lorimer. The medium for his matchmaking seems to be the tale of woe and joy, a recapitulation of what has already happened. We recall that the unbosoming of oneself to a bosom friend from whom one has been sorely separated is a signature of the sentimental novel where stories are given from one to another like house gifts. But at the end of *Edgar Huntly* communication alienates rather than unifies, and the past repeats itself as Mrs. Lorimer, hearing of Clithero's attempts to find her after all this time, suffers a miscarriage. We are not told of any reunion between Edgar and Mary, nor of any solution to the financial problem that has kept them apart.

Edgar's control of the narrative breaks in the final letter which is Sarsefield's. We are somewhat prepared for this because the two short letters preceding the final one are Edgar's letters to Sarsefield, but the effect is not only to end the Edgar-Mary relationship which has lasted throughout the one long letter of the novel, but to cast Edgar's final voice into doubt by turning the whole novel at the last moment into another kind of novel. At the end, even though we are closer to the actual events in time (since the letters are shorter), the account of them has become distanced, objectified, and the personality we glimpsed earlier, the "implied author" whose narrative we became so immersed in that we forgot we were reading a letter, has been dissolved.

Brown alters narrative focus in earlier novels with mixed results. In *Wieland*, stories within stories seem to preclude any one interpretation of the central events. Sophia, the shadowy narrator of *Ormond*, suddenly appears in the flesh to add her "wisdom" to Constantia's "constancy." The frame in *Arthur Mervyn*, in which Arthur's story is narrated by a Dr. Stevens, dissolves suddenly in Chapter 39 and Arthur, grown up and ready for love, begins to tell his story more directly. The change in *Edgar Huntly*, though, seems to recast the novel at its last moment into one of the two epistolary novels which ended Brown's fictional career. If the narrator "dissolved" to become an actor with Mary in some meta-fictional drama of love, this turn would seem more typical, but there is no indication that the lovers are still lovers, and Edgar simply vanishes.

Saying this suggests that whatever problem there is in the ending must be owing to Brown's ineptness, but in fact it would have been easy to end the novel happily, and such an ending would have been easier for its audience to digest structurally. Instead, we are left with loose ends, doubts, and lack of a definitive closure. Looking back at the other parts of the novel, however, we see that each begins with the promise of Edgar's enlightened and enlightening involvement with others, and each ends with his doubts and a denial of the very fabric of initiation. The last is consistent with the first.

What is sometimes not stressed in otherwise excellent articles on Brown's ideas is the fact that Brown's fiction is not seeking solutions to ontological and ethical problems so much as open-ended debate, and that he often speaks with two voices elucidating and not apologizing for the central ambiguities of his culture and his profession. Hedges, for example, who wants to document the debilitating effect of conflict on Brown, quotes from *Ormond* to show Brown's distaste for the law's "endless tautologies, its impertinent circuities, its lying assertions and hateful artifices."[11] But these words belong to Constantia's father who has just been betrayed out of his fortune. A more reliable spokesman might be the narrator, Sophia, who speaks directly to the reader: "Every thing is progressive in the human mind. When there is leisure to reflect, ideas will succeed each other in a long train, before the ultimate point be gained. The attention must shift from one side to the other of a given question many times before it settles" (*Ormond*, p. 142). This is similar to Clara Wieland's comment that a certain amount of "agitation and concussion" is necessary to the attainment of truth (*Wieland*, p. 43), and most critics would agree that these comments reflect a notion common to Brown's major works. The question might be how far Brown was willing to suspend judgment, how long a "train" of fictional conflicts he could sustain before resolution, considering that the "leisure to reflect" is limited to the duration of the novel. Could he allow the novel itself to share the unresolved fate of his protagonist? Perhaps, if we can show that for Brown the novel was not merely a device aimed at the truth, and if we can show that despite the goal-orientation of Brown's protagonists, Brown himself could conceive of the novel as an aesthetic, apart from a moralistic, structure.

Brown's views about fiction are difficult to establish, for many of his pronouncements come either in prefaces which tend to serve tradition and the marketplace, or in the editorials he wrote after he was done with fiction, and these often have the flavor of sour grapes. In the "Advertisement for *Sky-Walk*," Brown says he will endeavor to "amuse the imagination and improve the heart," and this neo-classical piety is repeated in later prefaces which stress "moral instruction." But in a letter to his brother, about the time of *Edgar Huntly's* publication, Brown says his aim in realism is "to excite and baffle curiosity, without shocking belief."[12] The wording here reveals a subtle shift in the relationship between art and morality and what may be Brown's more candid view of literature. Fiction aims not at "improving the heart" but at leaving its values undisturbed. Such "realism" may not need to be taken as real at all, not "shocking" because, like fantasy and myth and ultimately all art, it is somewhat irrelevant to the actual world. Brown of course did not develop this "anti-realistic" implication which would have linked him more to the world of Poe and our tormented moderns than to Hawthorne's conscience-stricken artist. Nor could he have afforded to develop it, given the climate in America at the turn of the century.

Brown's choice of narrative technique illustrates his notion that writing can be a testing out of ideas, as Warner Berthoff noted a number of years ago,[13] but few critics have dealt with Brown's writing as a testing out of forms. The opposition to such approaches is sometimes adamant. Hedges recently warns that apologists for Brown have gone too far either in "making him out to be a highly conscious and sophisticated craftsman" or in arguing that "structural disjointedness and incoherence are appropriate in his work because the novels are *about* irrationality." He says that we are in danger of having Brown "palmed off as one of the pre-eminent American writers because his work is so full of contradictions."[14] In the uncertain light of the present Brown "revival," no critic should ignore Hedge's warning. But surely there is some middle ground between the positions of, on the one hand, those myth critics who believe that Brown's works are unconscious productions, implicitly denying any part Brown's craft may have played, and on the other hand, those ideological critics who limit conscious production to social motivation and rarely give Brown credit for writing better than he knew. Middle ground is also needed between critics who refuse to admit that "structural disjointedness" can exist (all things presumably coming together in the collective psyche) and critics like Hedges who deny Brown his due because he lived too soon to profit from the modern favor into which "formal discontinuity" has come. If Brown lived in what Hedges calls a "culture of contradictions," similar in many ways to our culture of the 1960's and 1970's, there may be further similarities between Brown's narrative technique and that of the novelists who are lionized in our time.

III

Critics have not yet accredited Brown's experiments with language, and few have admitted that they were anything out of the ordinary. The voices in *Edgar Huntly* are stretched between the traditional pose of a narrator verbally enfeebled by an overwhelming situation ("words cannot tell") and a narrator who is on the way to forging a new language. One remembers the scene where Edgar imagines sitting by Clithero in silence because "words were impotent, and arguments were nugatory" (p. 101), or Edgar's hesitation about writing of his cave adventure because "one image runs into another" and because of "a kind of complex sentiment of distress and forlornness that cannot be perfectly portrayed by words" (pp. 151–52). But later, of his impassioned communication with Sarsefield, Edgar says: "No wonder that my eloquence was vivid and pathetic; that I portrayed the past as if it were the present scene; and that not my tongue only, but every muscle and limb, spoke" (pp. 235–36).

The difference between Edgar's early reservations about language and this later burst of enthusiasm is partly a stock sentimental dramatization of the fact that nothing can compete with the direct oral communication of old friends, especially when it is aided by "body language." Brown seems conscious in these words, though, of his position as a pioneer novelist who can transcribe the stories of the past into new language as well as new forms. And consciousness breeds doubt. On the one hand, Brown holds back with Edgar's initial reserve, "In proportion as I gain power over words, shall I lose dominion over sentiments" (p. 5), fearing perhaps that the writer by nature of his craft violates some of the heart's sanctities, or anticipating a dilemma more often expounded in our times, that inherent in any effort of creation is some new prohibition or confinement;[15] on the other, he plunges forward, like Edgar, into a polymorphous language that transcends time and genre and even the dialectical rhythm that characterizes his prose.

Brown's language is basically one of classical parallelisms, the doubling of noun or adjective or verb phrases, and a carefully modulated reinforcement of ideas through contrasts or similarities. Many years ago, Barrett Wendell called it "an instinctive sense of formal phrasing."[16] Consider the novel's opening paragraph:

> I sit down, my friend, to comply with thy request. At length does the impetuosity of my fears, the transports of my wonder, permit me to recollect my promise and perform it. At length am I somewhat delivered from suspense and from tremors. At length the drama is brought to an imperfect close, and the series of events that absorbed my faculties, that hurried away my attention, has terminated in repose.

Notice the balanced pairs: "the impetuosity of my fears, the transports of my wonder," and "recollect my promise and perform it," for example. In the last sentence, however, the parallel constructions "is brought to an imperfect close" and "has terminated in repose" are separated from each other by another pair of verbals, "absorbed my faculties" and "hurried away my attention." "Close" and "repose" are linked by syntax and by rhyme, but they are separated by the action verbs "absorbed" and "hurried away." In one sentence Brown forecasts the cyclical course of the entire novel: We begin with Edgar writing, we flash back to episodes that have come between him and his "repose," and after proceeding "at length" we end in what seems to be a state of bliss, one which is heavily and ironically qualified however by our memory of the "imperfect" which modifies "close." There may be resolution, this sentence warns, but it will not be satisfying except to the extent that the balanced prose itself offers finish and aesthetic repose.

I am not implying that all of Brown's rhetorical efforts are equally effective. Some sentences contain lamentable excesses: "Time and reason seemed to have dissolved the spell which made me deaf to the dictates of duty and discretion" (p. 8). Here the sense is obscured by alliteration and wordiness, and this example makes one wonder if the deafness Edgar claims to have cast aside might not have been absorbed by Brown. Even such crudities cast their spell, though, and Brown seems at times to be luring the reader into the kind of hypnagogic state Poe later exploited. The style is strongly cumulative, building by odd and even pairs, by qualification and intensification, and at its best it suggests the way Melville and more recently Faulkner and Mailer work to illustrate, through labyrinthine prose, the complexity of their worlds, to show the impossibility of telling anything finally even as they proceed to give it a good try.

Doubleness in Brown's narrative must be considered in its philosophical and aesthetic dimensions, not merely as evidence of psychic fragmentation. As it occurs in a character's internal deliberations, in plot and sub-plot, in scenes which are never sustained with more than two characters, and in language, this doubleness reflects Brown's love of debate and his striving for euphony and balance in even the smallest details of his writing. In his novels, the name of almost every character, first and last, is composed of two syllables, and when there are exceptions, like "Clithero" and "Euphemia Lorimer," these elongations seem to call for special attention.[17] Likewise, when a third element is added to the more normal paired words, it sticks out like a clue—complicating and transcending. Edgar writes to Mary about her brother's death: "His bloody and mysterious catastrophe equally awakened thy grief, thy revenge, and thy curiosity" (p. 6). This statement ends anticlimactically until we realize Edgar's pointed and paradoxical concern with curiosity: its power to include another in sympathy and its power to isolate oneself from that other who is being observed. The weapon that saves Edgar's life during his forest adventures is a double-barrelled fusil, a perfect "congeries of tubes and springs" (p. 179), but in killing the last Indian he meets, Edgar empties both barrels and then must dispatch the wounded man with the third part of the weapon, its attached bayonet.

A minute form of doubleness is set up within words themselves by Brown's use of prefixes indicating negation: *un-* and *in-*. By far the most instances of this sort of negation come in sections where a character's internal debate is rendered as soliloquy. These loaded words become the rhetorical counterpart to mental tension. The negative prefix suggests Brown's awareness of the discrepancy between what can and cannot be done, overcome, or even expressed, and yet the very weight of the words suggests a cumulative transcendence of oppositions.

Early critics often regarded this kind of heavy texturing as clumsy, and more recent critics have not significantly altered that opinion. Some who defend Brown's style, on the other hand, are quite vague. Says Richard Chase: "Brown's elevated rhetoric and his melodramatic effects forecast much that is admirable in Poe, Hawthorne, Melville, Faulkner, and even James."[18] George Snell has linked Brown's "luxurient, involuted prose" with a "school" of American writers concerned with apocalyptical vision which he traces from *Wieland* to *Absalom, Absalom!*[19]

"Apocalyptic" may seem a strange adjective to use of Brown, and perhaps Snell's lumping together of writers on the basis of general stylistic similarities is as condescending as the ignoring of stylistic distinctions by archetypal critics. What Brown is trying out with his prose may not be the visionary so much as vision itself—perception. Brown's concern with perception is first stated fictionally in the ventriloquism motif of *Wieland* where the characters who are terrified by the discrepancy between what they see and what they hear are invited to break through to a new awareness of the illusory nature of truth and the vanity of appearances. In *Wieland*, Brown was trying out his voices, along with Carwin's, and as he continued to do so in the later novels, they began to sound more and more ominous. The voice of nihilism, for instance, slouches through *Edgar Huntly* along with the voice of the frontier hero, the humble pose of the distanced lover, the dark rhetoric of the man buried alive. Brown does not always succeed in rendering these voices in different styles, of course, and probably he paid no more attention to doing so than did the more famous authors who followed him, Poe, Hawthorne and Melville.

The ventriloquism analogy proves useful in showing that no particular voice need reflect the final view of the author who can easily disavow, as in our more modern context of the stage performance, what the dummy has just said, though the voice that is "thrown" is never completely thrown away. Brown plays with nihilism, then tells us in a sense to disregard: one way writers then and now can have their say and not say at the same time. Yet the implications of nihilism are serious, so serious that Brown gave up fiction because it seemed to him a less expedient and certainly more dangerous means for expressing his divided views than editorial writing, and because at times the techniques of fiction seemed opposed to the virtues of benevolence and direct expression. What Clara says of Carwin, "He is able to speak where he is not" (*Wieland*, p. 237), sums up the frightening and seemingly immoral approach that is the fiction writer's by nature of his craft.

Another feature of Brown's style is the large number of questions asked by the narrator, sometimes four or five in a row. Some are matters of fact, but most are rhetorical as we would expect in a letter of justification to one's fiancée, the pose of a man who knows his mind but is trying to talk himself or someone else into it. The real questions are not asked because they can't be. Edgar's behavior operates, Sarsefield says, "as if to set the limits of nature at defiance, to sport with human penetration" (p. 232). Edgar speaks of his experience as "passage into new forms, overleaping the bars of time and space, reversal of the laws of inanimate and intelligent existence" (p. 228). Such "polymorphous perversity" is humorous in terms of an anti-hero, but in linguistic terms it signals an attempted break through the restraints of ordinary rhetoric.

What happens with language happens on a larger scale with the imagery patterns and larger technical forms Brown employs. Kenneth Bernard discusses in good detail Brown's images of light and dark, understanding and confusion, and height and depth.[20] To these should be added circles and circularity, and the related phenomenon of coincidence. Circles, like literary doubles, have a comfortable, predictable quality, as does coincidence. Edgar's wandering in the circular wilderness of Norwalk is counterpointed by the travels of the double-barrelled fusil, which makes a bizarre circle from Sarsefield, its original owner, to Edgar, to Edgar's uncle, to an Indian, to Edgar, and back to Sarsefield. Circumference brings the persistent one back home, and coincidence assures us that life is inclusive, that the new faces we meet are not new at all. Depth psychology tells us further that all we meet is really a part of ourself. Comforting, but not the way things are, Brown's novel seems to be saying. Circles become increasingly a kind of circularity which ends in a question that cannot be framed. Late in the novel, Edgar despairs of interrogating directly a man he has just met who may have news of his family: "I could deal only in circuities and hints" (p. 223). Edgar's old self has returned, seemingly, but not his old voice; thus a momentary confusing of the tongue, a prelude to the more expansive communication which uses all of one's senses. Coincidence too loses its comforting sense of *déjà vu* and takes on the randomness of picaresque literature. There is finally no solution to the matters of Waldegrave's murder, Weymouth's money, or Edgar and Mary's marriage. There is no satisfactory explanation for Mrs. Lorimer's irrational fears of Clithero and her refusal to understand his motives when she had so easily understood, or at least defended, the more consummate evils of her brother and so quickly diagnosed Clithero's love for her niece. Ordinary solutions and causes become irrelevant to a world of madness and to Brown's world of art.

Consider Clithero's marvelously constructed box: its sides "solid and smooth," its secrets guarded by a hidden spring which governs the lid. It is not to be opened by reason or by employing the primary sense of sight. When finally Edgar touches it open, he gets by accident what "a hundred hands might have sought in vain" (p. 112). And then it will not close. Some myth critics read the box as analogue for Clithero's (and therefore Edgar's) innermost being which he has rigged to remain inviolate. But the box is also a microcosm of the novel and the tales within the novel going back to Clithero's confession, a sequence planned and yet accidental like a hall of mirrors or Barth's funhouse that is never ended once it is truly begun. Or form itself (one remembers Brown's lifelong fascination with architecture). The inside has "numerous compartments, none of which contained any thing of moment" (p. 112). Or art itself which unifies the planes of experience but alienates personal affections: Pandora's box, with the one hope being the many mansions of the imagination.

In Brown's fiction, as in the literature of our time, there is a movement toward silence, though the interpretation of that silence varies considerably. We know that Brown ended his creative writing career at odds with his art, and that this disillusion came when he was only thirty, nine years before his death. The process of a young man putting away the pen is dramatized in *Arthur Mervyn* and *Jane Talbot*, and it is hinted at in *Edgar Huntly* where the narrator stops writing before the end of his own story. I have suggested elsewhere that Brown's growing conservatism and prejudices against "wild narratives of the imagination" were part of a more general American reaction, in Brown's time, against fiction, a reaction participated in even by such advocates of the arts as Thomas Jefferson.[21]

It might be argued that Brown's retreat is not to silence, but to anonymity, the position of the "secret witness" forecast by so many of his characters, and that editorship offered Brown the opportunity to see without being seen. Edgar likes to play anonymous benefactor to Clithero, and both Sarsefield and Clithero refer to Edgar's "invisibility," his tendency to change shapes in the wilderness where "passage into new forms" becomes possible. Tony Tanner has written about this metaphorical wilderness in modern fiction, "some 'border area' where author and hero alike attempt to create themselves and come into the meaning of their experience."[22] Classical American novelists of the nineteenth century, Tanner says, develop the idea of the hero as both "an editor, a philologist, a librarian, a supervisor of the house of custom—in a word, the guardian of language," and an experimenter with language, "a voyager, hunter and explorer."[23] The struggle between these ways of valuing language may be Brown's most important link with the American "Renaissance."

Movement toward silence in art is far from reactionary, as we have seen in minimal artists like Beckett and critics such as Susan Sontag and Richard Poirier. Sontag speaks of two theories or myths of art, one in which art is an expression of human consciousness seeking to know itself, and the other, more modern notion that art is not consciousness per se, but rather its antidote evolved from within consciousness itself. In this second myth, the tools of the artist become his trap and "art becomes the enemy of the artist, for it denies him the realization—the transcendence—he desires."[24] I believe that we can see Brown's movement, through his writing, from the first of these theories to the frontier of the second, with all the accompanying angst that we are used to attributing only to much more modern writers.

Cleman's study of ambiguity in Brown's characters leads him to this conclusion: that both virtue and vice are "short-circuited" in the novels: "Rather than drawing the lines too narrowly between self and other, Brown's purpose seems to be thoroughly and purposely reductionist, to create final situations of moral blankness or paralysis."[25] Cleman is right in calling Brown a "reductionist," but wrong in attributing this reduction to the ambiguity in Brown's characters. Rather, it comes from Brown's inability to fashion complexity in his work. He was not, I think, a complex person. He had intellectual depth, a broad sense of conflict and even paradox, and he was in tune with the more bizarre aspects of his society, of contemporary science, and of his own psyche. He could even accept the bizarre in small, properly distanced doses. But he was never happy with nuance, with fine distinctions of character and meaning. He had the debater's axe of overstatement, not the novelist of manner's scalpel, and this is why *Clara Howard* and *Jane Talbot*, though successful in a minor way on their own terms, are not successful on Brown's terms. He could not continue in that vein either.

Brown could not follow through with the philosophical and aesthetic paradoxes of silence any more than Edgar, in the cave, could fully appreciate the descent into Self, but then the awful interchanges of art and self-knowledge have driven much more sophisticated and self-conscious writers into chaos. How can one create when the ultimate creation begs to be the obliteration of the evils and falsities of consciousness itself? Toward the end of *Edgar Huntly*, Sarsefield notes, "Consciousness itself is the malady, the pest, of which he only is cured who ceases to think," and Edgar reluctantly agrees (p. 266), but this is no more than Clithero was saying earlier in the novel: "Till consciousness itself be extinct, the worm that gnaws me will never perish" (p. 35). For once, all three of the major characters are agreed; it may be their only point of rapport, and it is Brown's single voice.

Poe solved the dilemma of the consciousness-stricken artist by a neat juxtaposition of decay and death with the recovery of an original cosmic unity, and he learned to dramatize the split between artist's ideal and mundane survival, as in "The Fall of the House of Usher." Brown has no cosmic scheme and no such tolerance of psychic split. He not only returns his characters to the prison of their everyday consciousness, the reaction

Poirier suggests is typical of classical American writers after they have given their heroes a new kind of freedom through "stylistic ingenuity,"[26] he returns himself to that prison, which for him was unambiguous silence. In effect, Edgar is both Usher and the narrator of Poe's story, and soon there was no one left to tell the tale.

Notes

1. Richard Poirier, *A World Elsewhere* (New York: Oxford University Press, 1966).

2. William L. Hedges, "Charles Brockden Brown and the Culture of Contradictions," *Early American Literature*, 9 (1974), 122.

3. Philip Russell Hughes, "Archetypal Patterns in *Edgar Huntly*," *Studies in the Novel*, 5 (1973), 180 and 184 respectively.

4. Kenneth Bernard, "*Edgar Huntly*: Charles Brockden Brown's Unsolved Murder," *The Library Chronicle*, 33 (1967), 30–53.

5. *Early American Literature*, 10 (1975), 190–219.

6. *Edgar Huntly*, p. 221. The text of this novel and others discussed will be that of the 1887 edition of *The Novels of Charles Brockden Brown*, 6 vols. (Philadelphia: David McKay). Subsequent references to the works will appear in parentheses in my text. References to *Wieland* have been collated with the Kent State edition.

7. Richard Slotkin, *Regeneration Through Violence: The Mythology of the American Frontier*, 1600–1860 (Middletown: Wesleyan University Press, 1973), pp. 384 ff.

8. "Advertisement to *Sky-Walk: The Man Unknown to Himself*," *The Weekly Magazine*, I (March 17, 1798), 202.

9. See Brown's letter of April, 1800, to his brother James, quoted in William Dunlap, *The Life of Charles Brockden Brown*, II (Philadelphia: James P. Parke, 1815), p. 100. Brown vows henceforth to assume a cheerful tone, to drop the "prodigious or the singular."

10. Slotkin, p. 17.

11. Hedges, p. 115.

12. Letter of February 15, 1799, to James Brown, quoted in Dunlap, II, 97.

13. Warner Berthoff, " 'A Lesson on Concealment': Charles Brockden Brown's Method in Fiction," *Philological Quarterly*, 37 (1958), 45–57.

14. Hedges, p. 107.

15. See Tony Tanner, *City of Words: American Fiction 1950–1970* (New York: Harper & Row, 1971), p. 60.

16. *A Literary History of America* (New York: Charles Scribner's Sons, 1901), p. 167.

17. In an 1807 letter to W. Keese, Esq., Brown says "I heartily wish *Brown* had a little more music and dignity in it. It has ever been an irksome and unwelcome sound to my ears" (Quoted in Dunlap, II, 120).

18. *The American Novel and its Tradition* (Garden City: Doubleday, 1957), p. 37.

19. *The Shapers of American Fiction, 1798–1947* (New York: E.P. Dutton & Co, 1947), pp. 32–33.

20. Bernard, pp. 42–46.

21. See my "Benevolence and the 'Utmost Stretch': Charles Brockden Brown's Narrative Dilemma," *Criticism*, 14 (1972), 175–91, and Michael Davitt Bell's "'The Double-Tongued Deceiver'; Sincerity and Duplicity in the Novels of Charles Brockden Brown," *Early American Literature*, 9 (1974), 143–63.

22. Tanner, p. 63.

23. Tanner, p. 27.

24. "The Aesthetics of Silence," *Styles of Radical Will* (New York: Farrar, Straus and Giroux, 1969), p. 5.

25. Cleman, p. 216.

26. Poirier, p. 29.

Clara Howard and Jane Talbot: Godwin on Trial

Sydney J. Krause

I

In the entire history of Brown criticism, now a generation shy of two centuries old, there has been only one fully concerted attempt to come to terms with his last two novels, the consensus losers, *Clara Howard* and *Jane Talbot*. And this one analysis, a quite recent article by Paul Witherington, strikes so totally sanguine a note as to suggest it is time we went back to see what these novels are really about—or at least, what has been missed, which is one objective of this paper.[1]

From the beginning, *Clara* and *Jane* have had a bad rap. Paul Allen, Brown's first biographer, was so out of sorts with the unnaturalness of motivation in *Clara* that he saw it as the equivalent of Brown's taking "a monster for his model."[2] (Clara cannot love Edward Hartley and still enjoin him to prove his love for her by marrying Mary Wilmot whom he does not love.) William Dunlap, who took over the biography from Allen, declared *Jane* so void of interest that he could not so much as abide doing the summary of it he had written for the other novels.[3] Nor were the early reviewers much help. When noticed at all, which was not often, *Clara* and *Jane* were seen as wholly lacking in distinction, which obviously made it a little difficult for anything of distinction to be said about them. Typically cited were dullness, tediousness, and humorlessness, a superfluity of argument and lack of incident. The most that could be conceded on the positive side was a certain "knowledge of human nature," assumedly reflected in the psychological component of the love-duty conflict.[4] As one reads reviews of the collective editions, or the more recent broadscale studies of Brown (Warfel, Clark, Ringe), it is apparent that *Clara* and *Jane* are the stepchildren, the novels that get touched upon only because they are there. A common tack is to find them representing the new, the regrettably "cheerful" mood promised after the "doleful tone" of *Edgar Huntly*.[5] Who can quarrel with Donald A. Ringe's assessment that Brown "turned his back upon the kind of fiction in which he achieved his greatest success"[6]; that, indeed—to put the case in its severest

184

terms—Brown betrayed his own best instincts as writer in tossing aside, as Harry Warfel and others have observed, his obsession with the abnormal, the diabolic, the doomed, the whole murky world of terror and guilt that we identify with the psychology of the gothic?[7] *Clara* is no *Wieland*, *Jane* no *Edgar Huntly*; and gone as well is the at once brilliant and debasing disintegration of an Ormond, the nightmarish wanderings through a plague-wracked city or a harsh and hostile wilderness filled with black pits, savage beasts, and warring Indians. We can go further (and might as well for the moment, to better appreciate what was accomplished in spite of shortcomings), and say that Brown abandoned the "gloominess" mode not out of artistic conviction, but out of artistic cowardice, since he plainly stated that he did so because "most readers" objected to it (Dunlap, *Life*, II, p. 100). *Clara* and *Jane*, in other words, were his last-gasp efforts to cultivate a following, a matter over which he became deeply disillusioned. In April, 1799, while feverishly at work on finishing *Edgar Huntly* and putting together copy for the first issue of his *Monthly Magazine*, he openly complained that while some of our writers were read in Europe, they got short shrift at home: they have to "pay the expense of their own publications, reaping no rewards from their countrymen, but neglect or reproach."[8] Some see in the last novels a sell-out to the tender bias of his women readers.[9] Certainly, Brown would seem to have been making embarrassing concessions to convention and conservatism in *Clara* and *Jane* (consider how Hartley and Colden capitulate), and throwing in the sop of a happy ending to boot. He somehow loses his intellectual fire, runs out of venturesome ideas, or no longer finds them interesting. So it would seem, anyway.

But there is a more serious consideration. It was beginning to become both apparent and depressing to Brown that novel writing—especially *his*—did not pay; and as it was also unremunerative in other than tangible ways, this could be expected to have an effect on his writing. One sign of flagging inspiration shows up in the fact that Brown's invention seems to have gone flat. For, while there was nothing new about his cribbing from his own works, where it occurred in *Clara* and *Jane*, it became blatant. The most startling example is Mary Wilmot's unexpectedly discovering $5,000 in her dead brother's estate, which first serves as the "competence" needed for an engagement to marry Edward Hartley, and is then claimed by Morton. One instantly notices that Brown is replicating the situation in *Edgar Huntly* where Mary Waldegrave's brother had similarly left a large sum on his death ($8,000) which was to be the basis for her marrying Huntly, only to have the money claimed by Weymouth. Both brothers were impoverished teachers, both Edgar Huntly and Edward Hartley have two younger sisters and an uncle on a farm, both men have an indulgent preceptor and patron, who comes to their aid (Sarsefield and Howard).[10] If this tells us something about Brown's tiring invention, it also suggests, as I shall be indicating, that his concentration in the last two novels lay in other areas than in plotting (he could have used any of a variety of incidents to make his point), and that it is in these that we have to look for his meaning.

Perhaps the first thing to be said to redress the balance is that *Clara* and *Jane* need not compete with the first four for their viability. Minimally, they need only do reasonably well what they set out to do; and, maximally, there should be some inherent significance in what is done. This "what" is of course the matter to be clarified, which is not difficult. For when one determines Brown's purpose in the last two novels, one finds it is an extension of the same basic investigation of the "moral constitution of man" that concerned him in the first four. The terms are different, certainly the geography—physical and psychic—is changed, but if he was returning us to the sphere of the normal, of such "daily incidents" as love with and without marriage, marriage without and with love, the protocols of obligation, filial and personal, he was doing so with the idea of philosophically re-examining the tenets by which we are motivated to virtue in these relationships. Brown, in fact, suggested when renouncing the "prodigious" that he would be better off "substituting moral causes" (Dunlap, *Life*, II, p. 100). What he actually got into was moral causation, using as his base the dominant thesis of the most widely read treatise on the subject published in the 1790's—of which more very shortly. The point is Brown was surely continuing to do what he did best as a literary ideologist. In addition, *Clara* and *Jane*, far from representing a deviation in form, both confirm and consummate the tendency of the earlier novels. As Warner Berthoff observed some time ago, the key facet of Brown's fictional method is that narrative becomes "an instrument for *discovering* ideas, for exploring and testing them out." Central to a comprehension of what happens in *Clara* and *Jane* is the fact that, as Berthoff continues, Brown does not simply "expound moral ideas, Godwin's or his own, in his fiction; he investigates them, tests them, exposes them to the risks of human nature and conduct. Rather than repeating or discursively qualifying the Godwinian doctrines of sincerity, candor, truthfulness, and natural perfectability, Brown's imagination turned to creating characters who try to live by these doctrines."[11]

Testing out Godwin, to be sure. This is exactly what takes place in *Clara* and *Jane*. Yes, literally, for in them even more than in "Carwin," *Arthur Mervyn*, or *Ormond*, Brown was putting on trial the moral and social ideals of the one writer who had the most pervasive influence on the intellectual content of his novels over all. And he was going to the core of his philosophy—basic Godwin—as set forth in *Political Justice* (1793), not to such collateral matters as the abuse of class privilege, as illustrated, e.g., in *Caleb Williams*. Brown must have assumed that his point would be recognized—however little it has been is not his fault—for *Political Justice* was a book you read if you had the slightest pretension to being intellectually up to date in the revolutionary '90's—an era in which the

French experiments in political radicalism were stimulating a radicalism of thought that had the English-speaking world on edge.

One cannot really understand *Clara Howard* without seeing Clara as a pillar of Godwinian moral theory, an adherent of "disinterest" de rigueur, who treats truth and virtue as universal, virtually Platonic, absolutes and selfless benevolence as the highest function of rational man. The gift of Godwin, Clara Howard—need one say—is the original Iron Maiden of American Literature. In fact, as will be seen, in the abiding dilemma which is the mainspring of crisis in the novel—Clara's insistence that Edward honor his prior commitment to Mary Wilmot—Brown is pitting one Godwinian good against another. The virtue of objectively denying all selfish gratification (evidence of the Puritan and Platonist in Godwin) for a true moral end, must, in this instance, override Godwin's utilitarian principle of avoiding blind adherence to prior promises, qua promises, which time and change might prove irrational. Much of what Allen was incensed about as unnatural inheres in this conflict; to deny it, out of hand, as a human possibility is of course to miss the point that there is an active tug of war going on here between checking virtues, which ironically exposes the fallacies on either side produced by their mutual source. As a further irony, the conflict reflects yet another Godwinian ethic: that in the free marketplace of ideas one principle must inevitably contend with another as we pursue the dialectic out of which hopefully truth may emerge. Thus, far from caving in to conventionalism, Brown was attacking the socially most conservative of the purportedly radical notions in *Political Justice*, and doing it by means of the epistemological liberalism Godwin was also advancing in that book. Out of the disparity between a given perceived truth and the permanent Truth we seek, but do not reach, evolve the ironies which give *Clara Howard* its intellectual substance and artistic subtleties. The novel is to be viewed as a drama of Godwinism being tested by Godwin.

In *Jane Talbot*, the complication goes up a notch, as both Jane and Colden, who are Clara's temperamental opposites, find themselves nevertheless leagued with a Godwinism to which both external and internal pressures have them vying for adherence, only to find themselves—especially Jane—continually falling out of line, until the self-corrective process begins to set in. The Godwinism is likewise ironic because Jane's Rousseauesque personality makes her so susceptible to the sorrows of sensibility, that they enhance her candidacy for a Godwinian benevolence which steadily demands that she act, as she says, "with no exclusive regard to my own pleasure, but as it flows from and is dependent on the happiness of others."[12] By the end of *Jane Talbot*, Godwin is not just tested, he is corrected; Jane and Colden dispense with theoretical obligations, as it becomes plain that one partner can in no way receive a happiness conferred at the expense of the other's happiness. Where it assumedly should work best, with persons in love, Godwinian benevolence fails abysmally. Moreover, it is largely through reflection—the search for truth internalized—that Colden, our reconstructed Godwinian, returns to the faith that Godwin's rationalism had previously driven him away from.[13]

II

What has somewhat confused the picture is the fact that in *Clara* and *Jane*, as almost everyone points out, Brown seems to owe a very substantial debt to the sentimental tradition, and very specifically to Richardson and Rousseau. Thus, the last two novels are in reality not so much a development away from shadowy gothicism into the sunshine of romance, as a reversion to the materials that preceded Brown's major phase, materials which to some extent nurtured the big four and then went dormant. He was going back to unfinished business, as he frequently did with each new work. Godwin, of course, also figured prominently in that pre-*Wieland* past, as we know from the fact that Brown's reading of *Caleb Williams* stimulated the attempt at a novel of similar extent in 1795.[14] But we must pause at this point to pick up the elements of Richardson and Rousseau that appear in *Clara* and *Jane*, because the road to Godwin proceeded first through them, and also because Brown's treatment of their motifs is of a piece with his treatment of Godwin's—i.e., one gets played off against another.

One construction of Brown's objective in returning to Richardson for *Clara* and *Jane*—Fiedler's—is that "by casting aside the seduction theme," he tried to write "a Richardsonian novel of sentimental analysis in a domestic setting, stripped of tragic and melodramatic elements alike"—but with results that create only the "inane" (*Love and Death*, p. 74). Paul Levine discerns the same reversion with a difference and even considers *Clara* and *Jane* less "a radical departure from Brown's early work than an extension in new terms of the dialectic of *Wieland* and *Ormond*," though for Levine, as well, Brown's innovation spelled failure.[15]

The failing, I would submit, lies more in what we don't see than in what we do. A brief inquiry into Brown's uses of the sentimental mode in *Clara* and *Jane* will show that he returned to its conventions in order to study how well the importunities of feeling (bread and butter of the sentimental) would withstand a philosophical determination. Could the Richardsonian, he asked, be Godwinized? With regard to Richardson in particular, whom Brown so greatly admired ("who is there who can stand in competition with the writer of *Clarissa*?"[16]) but who, for our purposes, is less germane than Rousseau, Brown was clearly drawing on several stock situations established in *Clarissa*, as that of the parent (Mr. Harlowe—Mrs. Fielder) intent on marrying a daughter (Clarissa—Jane Talbot) to a stable, older man, to whom she is indifferent (Mr. Solmes—Lewis Talbot). We also have the triangle of one man (Lovelace—Edward Hartley) involved with two women (Clarissa and Arabella—Clara

Howard and Mary Wilmot), one of whom he does not care for but who cares for him. He becomes attracted to the one he is not supposed to be falling in love with (Clarissa—Jane) and is objected to by the family as morally unreliable (Lovelace—Colden).[17] Also, of lesser importance, we find an evil, scheming brother (James Harlowe—Frank) balanced off against the avuncular, reconciling figure (Colonel Morden—Thomson).

On this level, Brown's borrowing is strictly formulaic. His meaningful variations are thematic. Richardson's concern with desire and sexual politics, guilt and recompense, becomes transformed with *Clara* and *Jane* into the characters' quite other desires to measure up to a standard they feel they must live by for self-respect. Playing Godwin, Brown intellectualizes his conflicts, making them morally purposive. Nowhere in Richardson are the issues between Clarissa and Lovelace debated as if the lovers belonged in a seminar on moral philosophy—though of morals, as such, there is sufficient mention. Moreover, Brown's female character is given the quite unorthodox position of moral preeminence in being arbiter of the standard. While Clara Howard is the arbiter par excellence, Jane Talbot, for her part, though a more feminine, more pliable, and even submissive, character, still has her own rigidities. She mediates the struggle between herself and Mrs. Fielder, on the one hand, and between both of them and Colden, on the other, with enough skill to eventually win over each.

Brown was not just trying to recast the conflict between passion and reason, the head and heart. He was trying to upgrade the level at which his characters would interact. In terms of human interest, Brown, of course, made the tactical error of failing to consider the fact that no amount of philosophy can take the place of seduction. It would be a mistake, however, to think the seduction game could not be played in another arena. Clara Howard's hegemony is such that *she* becomes the seductress; ironically it is she going after her lover's mind, rather than he going after her body. Not only is Clara calling all the shots, but, though Edward Hartley complains that her decision to send him in quest of Mary Wilmot is "absurd," he is compelled to swallow his objections and concede her "motives are disinterested and heroic" (the Godwinian compensation) and satisfy himself with railing against the all-regnant moral system which rational man cannot do other than espouse, even if he suffers for it: "it is the system of nature that deserves my hatred and my curses; that system which makes our very virtues instrumental to our misery."[18] Here and throughout Edward is put on the rack by hard-core Godwinism, which he ambivalently must both resist and obey, while bearing the righteous reproof of his uncompromising beloved. This is the lecture he gets for his pains; it could have come straight out of *Political Justice*: if he has "misconstrued" Clara's meaning,

> it affords a proof of a narrow and ungenerous heart, an heart
> incapable of perceiving the possibility of sacrificing my own

personal gratification to that of another, and of deriving from that very sacrifice, a purer and more lasting felicity. It shews you unable to comprehend that the welfare of another may demand self-denial from us, and that in bestowing benefits on others, there is a purer delight than in gratifications merely selfish and exclusive (pp. 39f.).

Brown's representation is dramatic (a structural bonus of the epistolary form); we are not being persuaded to approve or disapprove one attitude or the other, but to form our views from what is being presented on stage. Clara's Godwin is emphatically on trial. Convincing—indeed—irresistible—as Godwin may seem when Clara articulates his ideas, we—and Edward—are also inescapably aware that it is a *hard* philosophy, against which Edward gets ample opportunity to present his own arguments. The case is strenuously pressed on both sides, with human ramifications, and ultimately an implied verdict, of no small complexity—a matter which can be developed more fully after we have glanced at the role of Rousseau in all this.

III

Brown's major characters in *Clara* and *Jane* make a fetish of their altruism, at times to the point almost of perversity. Mary Wilmot tries to outdo even Clara in the renunciation of self. After all, she loved Hartley first, and it took something to give him up yet a second time out of deference to Clara's love. Jane and Colden become reconciled to their separation—much as it runs contre-coeur—on the basis that each is promoting the happiness of the other, as well as of their parents. When suffering is sublimated by the greater-good principle, that is one thing. When the suffering induces its own inherent pleasure, that is another. In the latter instance, rational morality has been stretched beyond its bounds, and one finds oneself in the camp of Rousseau, with whom exquisite sensibility becomes a delicate instrument on which one explores the reaches of virtuosity. But particularly savored is sacred sorrow; the lover finds an undeniable pleasure in lingering over the pangs of loss—what would become his Wertherian prerogative. If, however, Rousseau's characters seemed addicted to self-excruciation, this also has its own kind of uplift. Something of this ambivalence appears in Jane Talbot's prolonged bouts of pained emotionalism (her hurt seems proof of her goodness), and there even comes a moment of sweet anguish for Clara when Edward lies near death after rescuing the drowning girl from the raging Schuylkill. In the contest to see who can suffer the most, Mary Wilmot for a while seems the winner. She is so set on giving Edward up to a woman who is younger, more beautiful, and more wealthy than herself, that a mechanism has been set in motion over which she no longer has any control: "I cannot be yours," she tells Hartley, "because I am not my own." She could not accept him "even if all [her] wishes were in favour of it." It is not the mere "illusion of despair" she experiences: "I feel in my deepest vitals the progress of death" (*CH*, p. 24). Mary not only does not die, she continues to hang on in her languishing sadness. Should we imagine that it somehow keeps her alive—that she may even cherish it? Consider how Rousseau explains an effect of the torment Saint-Preux suffers in his separation from Julie (as described by Lord Bomston): "his heart . . . is made for struggling and conquering. Such love as his is not so much a weakness as a strength badly exerted. An ardent and unhappy passion is . . . itself proof of [the] excellence [of his faculties] and of the use he could make of them in cultivating wisdom; for the highest reason is only attained through the same power of the soul which gives rise to great passions, and we serve philosophy worthily only with the same ardor that we feel for a mistress."[19]

So, acute feelings are heuristic; through the acutest of them we learn virtue. That is the course of wisdom. In other words, if you were a Godwinian, Rousseau was not just the opposition, his was a competing system of morality. And Brown, as it turns out, was not alone conversant with Godwin; he had just prior to his infatuation with *Caleb Williams* and *Political Justice*, gone through his Rousseauesque phase. Furthermore, his own direct source for *Clara* comes from that period. But even if this were not known, it would still be apparent that the Clara Howard paradox (it is because she loves Edward that Clara compels him to do the right thing by Mary) has its parallel in *Julie*: after her marriage to Wolmar, Julie tells Saint-Preux to love her cousin Claire who loves him, but whom he does not love.

Godwin is certainly being tried in and for himself. But without an identifiable Rousseauist presence on the other side—particularly in *Jane Talbot*—there is no counter-theory, nothing very substantial that can be put up against Godwin—that is, beyond his own faults. It is a dialectic interaction. One mode of thought pulls against the other, and out of this tension other ideas emerge. On the simplest level, Godwin's is the voice of Reason, Rousseau's, the voice of Feeling in Brown's last novels.

But Rousseau came first. His ideas are, I have said, the prime source to which the beginnings of *Clara* and *Jane* can be tangibly traced. Brown's Rousseauism goes back to the early 1790's and his friendship with William Wood Wilkins. Their minds much heated by the vogue of the sentimental tradition, they exchanged letters containing hypothetical disquisitions on the quality of love, thwarted love, and melancholia—all derived from what they knew of *Julie, ou la Nouvelle Héloïse*, blended with Richardson. Their correspondence frequently turned into exercises in Rousseauesque gamesmanship. They wrote of imagined ardors indulged as if they had grown out of actual experience, Brown with "Henrietta," for example, his "luminous idea of a gracious beauty" (Clark, p. 26). In his typical "visionary" mood, Brown at one point suggested if he could not instruct his friend in other imposing matters ("literary glory," "ethereal science," "knowledge of thyself, of nature, or of God"), he can surely guide him in "the raptures and the agonies of love"; only to reverse himself when the reverie is gone, holding, on reconsideration, it is Wilkins, his "amorous friend," who can better instruct *him*, for "his concepts will be . . . the result of infinite sagacity and long experience" (Clark, p. 27). The highly volatile Wilkins—witty and mirthful in conversation, "pensive, sentimental and poetical" in letters (Clark, p. 25)—would present Brown, in turn, with the lover's conundrum which, as Paul Allen indicated, contains the basic story from which *Clara Howard* would later be germinated. Here, in part, is Allen's presentation of the story:

> Emilius [Wilkins] the friend of Charles, demands his opinion on the following question: He had reason to believe himself beloved by Arabella, a lady for whom he entertained every sentiment but that of love. . . . His connection with this lady was perfectly honourable. He had beguiled her with no promises, nor had he ever in a single instance encouraged her to cherish the belief, that he was bound by a stronger tie than that of friendship. . . . In short whatever motives she might have to persevere in her addresses, he had supplied her with none; and the blame if any must be attributed to the indulgence of an unfortunate passion, equally ardent and hopeless. . . . Now comes the delicate reverse of the story. It seems that this dispairing [sic] swain, who so nobly resisted the sway of female blandishments where he was sure of a conquest bec[a]me himself the slave of such blandishments where he was not. . . . He acknowledges that her [Ophelia's] connection with him was perfectly honourable, that she had neither beguiled him with promises, or had ever in a single instance confirmed his belief, that she was bound by a stronger cord than that of friendship. . . . Now the question submitted for the opinion of Charles was this, whether in the case of a lover thus pursuing and pursued, it was his duty to encourage the addresses of Arabella, or to persecute Ophelia with his own. . . . He stated the argument in his own favour so strongly, that he seemed rather to dictate than to ask the opinion of his friend. Probably to a man more zealous to preserve friendship than truth and justice, it would have been justifiable to have encouraged the addresses of his friend, and to have slighted those of his lady. To Charles however every argument urged by his friend in behalf of himself, was decided and convincing in favour of the adverse party. If Arabella, he answered, in the midst of so many embarrassments, still preserved her constancy in her affections, what might not be anticipated, when a passion at once so hopeless and so vivid, is suitably requited? . . . On the other hand, his friend's own example was urged to show that

the indulgence of his present passion would insure future vexa-
tion and disappointment. . . . Even if he had contemplated
nothing more than friendship, and had been innocently the
cause of such misapprehension on the part of Arabella, was he
not bound in honour to repair the injury? But if on the other
hand his friend . . . had in a single instance encouraged the
hopes of Arabella, there was an end of the argument. . . .
These arguments . . . were strong and forcible, but it will excite no surprise in the reader, to learn that they fell far short of
convincing a lover that he was bound in duty to renounce the
object of his love (Allen, *Life*, pp. 44–46).

If this provided the germ of his story, other statements Brown made
to Wilkins more nearly accent the thematic emphasis he would give it, as
"that the most perfect and refined misery is the price at which we buy just
conceptions of propriety and duty, by acting in opposition to them"
(ibid., p. 42). Allen gives no date for this correspondence with Wilkins,
but it was probably written around 1792, when he and Brown were law
clerks together, and at the time when Brown was writing his "Henrietta
Letters," for which, as Robert Hare has shown, Brown derived his
character relations, situations, ideas, style, and even parts of the text
itself, from Rousseau's *Julie*.[20]

By far the most popular novel of the late eighteenth century, *Julie*
went to seventy-two editions between the time of its original publication
in 1761 and 1800; and there were ten—perhaps as many as fourteen—editions of it in English in that time, all based on the William Kenrick
translation, which appeared in the same year as the original. It is believed
that Brown may have known the book in French, though the translation
could have served as well, as copies of it were being sold in Philadelphia by
the Library Society in 1771 and by Bradford in 1784.[21] In any event, his
allusions to the novel are made with the clear confidence of a person
drawing on a self-evident familiarity with it, as when, for example, in his
"Man at Home" series, the remark is made to Miss DeMoivre, "You . . .
have dipped into the very soul of St. Preux, but have escaped the voluptuous contagion."[22]

The major explicitly Rousseauistic piece Brown wrote in this period
has been brought to light with the recent publication of a May 20, 1792,
letter that Brown wrote to Joseph Bringhurst.[23] Two weeks earlier, Brown
had written, "I have been conversing with Rousseau. I have since ten
o'clock been plying with rapturous attention through his impassioned and
illumined pages. . . . What a model of pathetical eloquence" (ibid., p.
37). This directly inspired him to write a sketch which was to be the
beginning of his own *Julie*, "The Story of Julius," sent to Bringhurst in the
letter of May 20. The frame that occasions his writing "Julius" is Henrietta's outrage at his having enjoyed reading the first two volumes of *Eloisa*
(the title given the English translation of *Julie*), which to her is moral con-

traband, "the most pernicious and seductive book that she had ever read."[24] When he contests her view that it is a "dangerous" work, she makes forgiveness contingent on his writing a similar work supporting "different maxims" in which virtue and duty must triumph "over the most lawless and impetuous passions" (ibid., p. 39). He is free to fight fire with fire, using Rousseau himself, or Richardson, as his model. In the first section of the story, Julius Brownlow forms "a most tender and inviolable union" with his twin sister, Julietta. It offers an altogether too heavy-handed antidote to Rousseau in tracing "the effects of friendship of the purest and most exalted kind" between siblings. But in portraying this inviolable love, Brown does fulfill his penance; for the "danger" which so intimidated the popular mind with regard to *Julie* was an intensely sympathetic treatment of unmarried lovers (Julie and Saint-Preux) finding their happiness in a tender union, which, though not immune to judgment, would be judged only in the wrong quarters—i.e., among those who equated their relationship with sexual anarchism.

The Julius-Julietta relationship is, however, a mere blind; for the next sequence is straight Rousseau—not in his most subversive vein, perhaps, but agitating enough to depict innocently feeling persons being made the pawns of parental opportunism and social hypocrisy. And, as we shall see, not only does the plotting begin to resemble that in *Julie*, but, beyond that, in the sanctification of sentiment, the dilemmas of love, and the indictment of a system wherein feelings are sacrificed to duty, we come close to the position from which one aspect of Godwinian morality will be challenged in *Jane Talbot* and get a clear prelude to matters that will be replayed in *Clara* as well.

While recovering from an illness at the home of the Reverend Mr. Wentworth, the formerly "studious, philosophical Julius" becomes the "passionate," languishing lover of the Reverend's daughter, Sophia. He persuades her to confess her love for him, and his proposal of marriage is accepted by her father. But not so with Julius's mother. Motivated by money and position, she has picked another girl for him, Caroline, who has both. On a return home, Julius met Caroline "and made an impression on her tender and susceptible heart, which gradually grew stronger," but which he could not reciprocate, though he treated her "with the utmost politeness and respect." Her condition being hopeless, Caroline declines in health to the point of alarming her father, who hastily negotiates with Mrs. Brownlow to have his daughter rescued through marriage. Mrs. Brownlow falls ill, and, while she is directing Julietta to write her brother what has transpired with Caroline, a letter arrives from him relating his intention to marry Sophia. Julius is told of his mother's "total disapprobation" and is instructed to break off all connections with Sophia and return home. His mother dies before Julius arrives, but not before preparing a statement for him that he "solemnly" honor "all sacred obligations of filial piety to forsake the one and wed the other." "After many conflicts," he determines to obey. The sensitive Caroline refuses his offer, because she knows "his heart is devoted to another," and she tries to persuade him to marry Sophia in spite of his mother's "exhortations." Julius remains resolute and is "torn by all the violence of conflicting passions." As his health declines, he is prevailed upon by Julietta and Caroline to take a trip to the continent, where he falls sick and, after writing pathetic letters to Julietta, Sophia, and Caroline, dies ("Julius," pp. 45–48).

Having dropped the subterfuge that he was doing a counter-Rousseauist piece, Brown has Henrietta forget her own prior objections and give way to the exact type of response that had gained Rousseau his enthusiastic following: "how often were her bright eyes suffused with tears, at the perusal of it! how many sighs did it draw from the bottom of her heart!" (p. 49). While Brown gives us a sampling of the Clara Howard-Edward Hartley-Mary Wilmot magnanimity syndrome, "Julius" more nearly anticipates the mediating relationship that *Julie* will have on Jane Talbot. Again, as with Richardson (by whom Rousseau himself was much influenced) *Julie* exploits the set conflicts of parent versus child in choosing a mate. The overbearing Baron L'Etrange, like Mrs. Fielder, callously insists that the daughter follow parental preference in marrying a man, Baron de Wolmar, the daughter is not interested in (Lewis Talbot's prototype), and blocks any connection with the likes of a Saint-Preux whom she has fallen in love with (Colden), but who is socially unacceptable and must eventually set out on a journey of self-exile.

Various specific parallels come to mind, as the irony of Saint-Preux's citing the need to part in the interest of Julie's happiness, much as Colden does with Jane, and Saint-Preux's being honorably alone with Julie during Wolmar's absence, as Jane and Colden are in Talbot's absence—sequences in which both couples are thrown temptingly together by storms. But the point of thematic affinity between *Julie* and *Jane Talbot* which is important for our purposes has to do with the demonstration in both books that the moral life is less likely to be achieved through the traditional restraints of reason and obedience to custom than by following the noble call of the psyche within—of the passions, if need be, these being obviously more answerable to the needs of our humanity.

Instances of Jane's finding herself, à la Julie, so helplessly in love as to fear for her well-being are too numerous to cite, but it is interesting to note that Brown sets this special tone in Jane's opening letter, where it seems very much as if, with Jane's "excess of love" (p. 5), he were trying to cue us as to the unmistakable ambience of this romance. In spite of conscience and shame, which move her to subdue her "overflowing heart," Jane is unable to stem its promptings: she freely admits that "vanity" relieves her by "insinuating that all happiness springs from affection; that nature ordains no tie so strong as that between the sexes; that to love without bounds is to confer bliss not only on ourselves but on another;

that conjugal affection is the genuine sphere not only of happiness but duty" (p. 4). *Duty?* one asks. It is in her building to this last assertion that Jane's embracing an implicit Rousseauism is clearly established and that the contrary—should one say morally normal?—view of duty is being put on the defensive.

Literary historians tend to say it was in giving such free sway to passion as a natural good that Rousseau made his chief contribution to the course of Romanticism. If there is a direct effect of Rousseau on Brown in this area, it surely lies—as we see—in Jane Talbot's being the most effusively passional character (male or female) in all of his fiction. She openly confesses to an inherent "impetuosity of . . . temper" (p. 8), and cannot have it otherwise and be herself. Thus, Brown is not so much committed to an unquestioning acceptance of the rightness of feeling, as in having a Rousseauist motivation serve as a check on the unfeeling of an obdurate rationalism. Which brings us back to Godwin.

IV

First, just as there is Rousseau and Rousseauism, so is there a difference between Godwin and Godwinism. In Mrs. Fielder's oft-quoted complaint against Colden, it is not so much Godwin who is being arraigned as the anti-social radicalism which was synonymous with his name.

According to Mrs. Fielder, Godwin uses the art of Satan himself in "disguising all that is impious or blasphemous or licentious under the guise and sanctions of virtue" (*JT*, p. 100). Taking up the litany of sins she connected with Colden's reading of *Political Justice*, one may concede that Godwin considered suicide a feasible alternative under given circumstances, but he was not its categorical "advocate"; and while he questioned slavish adherence to promises (rational man has no need to be *bound*), he was not properly a "scoffer" at them.[25] Certainly, he did not write as a "despiser of revelation, of providence and a future state" (p. 99). *Political Justice* was a completely secular book, and while Godwin was known to have gone through a period of atheism (from which he said Coleridge eventually redeemed him, "Intro.," p. 106), a number of his remarks clearly assume acceptance of a higher spiritual power—and namely, God.[26] He did, as Mrs. Fielder charges, take exception to marriage, as socially constituted, (Priestly, *PJ*, II, pp. 499–514). However, when she says Colden "denied . . . that any thing but mere habit and positive law, stood in the way of marriage; nay, of intercourse without marriage, between brother and sister, parent and child" (*JT*, p. 99), any implication that this can be remotely connected with *Political Justice* is pure fantasy.

Both Mrs. Fielder and Colden—insofar as he actually held these views—show the prevailing confusion over what "radical" Godwinism stood for, which illustrates a point. However, the real thrust of Brown's last two novels turns not so much on that as on the doctrinal mainstream of *Political Justice*. The whole tenor of Godwin's argument—both in itself and as Brown represented it—is, as I have already noted, heavily weighted toward an individualistic (as opposed to statist) conservatism, containing, as it does, strains of the Greek classical philosophy (Platonism and stoicism) and dissenting Puritanism, which were large elements in Godwin's education and background, and quite alien to the radicalism, for example, of a d'Holbach and the French materialists (See "Intro.," e.g., pp. 13, 16, 20, et passim). His Platonism (gained directly and by his reading of Richard Price) and Puritanism (he had been a dissenting minister) are fused in Godwin's implicit faith in the character of truth as a fixed and independently subsistent value, which needs only to be comprehended by the individual intelligence to receive its unaided acceptance. In full and open discussion, "errors . . . will combat each other," but truth, once discovered, "cannot be overthrown" (*PJ*, I, p. 22). Hence, in the political sphere, a "good government" will remove all restraints on the "enquiring mind" and a "bad one by its patronage of error [will] procrastinate the discovery and establishment of truth" (ibid., p. 4). Particularly offensive to Godwin were the political and religious superintendence of thought. "Truth and virtue are competent to fight their own battles" (*PJ*, II, p. 223). In his preface, Godwin indicated that he wanted his book to have a direct impact on moral improvement; he wanted readers to take it to heart and act on it. Brown and his close friend Elihu Hubbard Smith were two such readers. Smith spoke openly of the strong impression Godwin made on him, and he noted Godwin's influence on Brown, too, in dispelling his well-nigh disabling infatuation with Rousseau.[27]

It is in the area of morality and its practical effects that the operation of characteristic premises out of *Political Justice* is most apparent in Brown's last two novels. For Godwin, true virtue defines itself by "benevolent intention." It cannot be personalized, but must rather always apply to what benefits another human being (*PJ*, I, p. 78). This "disinterested benevolence" means that persons must lose "the feeling of their personal existence in the pursuit of general advantage" (*PJ*, I, pp. 333f.). Disinterest, disinterest! Godwin hammers home his undeviating theme that "The true perfection of mind consists in disinterestedness" (*PJ*, I, p. 334). Without it, man is a moral void; with it, both he and society are redeemable—perfectable (Priestly, *PJ*, II, p. 244). The moral legislator "should gradually wean men from contemplating their own benefit in all that they do, and induce them to view . . . the advantage that is to result to others" (*PJ*, I, pp. 334f.). Moreover, the virtue of benevolence is not only self-attracting, but it compels action. "Can a man have a clear discernment," Godwin asks, that a certain virtuous action "most conducive to his own interest, and to the general good" ought to be performed, "and refrain from performing it?" (Priestley, *PJ*, II, p. 244). Benevolence is not theoretic. Only in the realization does it mean anything—which is of the highest importance for Brown's use of it; he was doing precisely what Godwin prescribed. A corollary of this can be seen in the significance Godwin attaches to sincerity (a quality, by the way, that figures in all of Brown's novels, and that, with the foregoing, has special application to the last two). It means, among other things, that one must tell the truth regardless of personal danger or injury to personal interests. We are under obligation that nothing be suppressed. "Real sincerity deposes me from all authority over the statement of the facts." They must be stated, whether one wants to have them out or not. Sincerity "annihilates the bastard prudence." "It extirpates the low and selfish principle, which would induce me to utter nothing to the disadvantage of him from whom I have received no injury." The "energy" of a sincere person is such that "nothing human can resist [him]" (*PJ*, I, pp. 219, 220, 223).

The relevance of these facets of Godwinian morality to the central situation in *Clara Howard* does much to clarify and deepen its meaning. They are the entire rationale for Clara's insisting that Edward make Mary Wilmot happy at her (Clara's) own expense—and at his. Clara could not more clearly demonstrate her Godwinian position than by adhering as she does to the principle of "disinterest" prescribed by "reason" (p. 32). (This is stated several times; in fact, at almost every instance of Edward's wavering.) He seems in the early stages "to have strangely misconstrued [her] meaning" (p. 39). This is apt because her message is not easily understood (lacking Godwin) and also because it affords Clara the chance to elucidate for the reader's benefit the moral that (as previously cited) one must sacrifice one's "own personal gratification" to achieve "a purer and more lasting felicity" (pp. 39f.).

If one wants to ask where Clara gets the right to exercise this sort of force over another person (especially as it seems inconsistent with Godwin's ideas about obedience versus "unforced . . . assent" [*PJ*, I, pp. 154–57]), the answer lies, first, in the fact that it is the duty of persons to *act* on their benevolent perceptions, and, secondly, in the logic that follows from Godwin's condemnation of "moral independence." While he approves of "natural independence," its moral counterpart is "always injurious." And the reason for this goes back, in part, to the role of sincerity. How can one remain silent in the face of error and vice? Godwin therefore recognizes the obligation of "a censure to be exercised by every individual over the actions of another, a promptness to enquire into and to judge them. Why should we shrink from this?" (Priestley, *PJ*, II, p. 496). Rather than rely on political control, which Godwin abhors, each of us must freely act as one another's moral policeman. Clara's keeping Edward in line is not an imposition; on the contrary, it is her duty, avoidance of which would be morally injurious. She could not stand aside if she wanted to. So Clara is not acting at all unnaturally. The Godwinian ethic requires that the affections of the heart be stilled so that one's larger obligation to unselfish virtue may be fulfilled. And to repel the anarchy of moral independence—to which we are prone—individuals must see to it that a perceived ethic is enforced. Such, then, is Clara's position. That it should nevertheless—in spite of philosophic backing—be productive of moral conflict is exactly what Brown was trying to dramatize in *Clara* and *Jane*. He was taking Godwin at his word and trying to effectualize his morality in order to see what the consequences might be. Indeed, Godwin himself had had some second thoughts; he had to acknowledge, for example, that he underestimated the role of the emotions in human affairs and took cognizance of this failing in his revision of *Political Justice* ("Intro.," p. 90).

V

Just as Brown had shown the limits of Reason in the breakdown of Ormond, his most obviously Godwinian character, so in *Clara Howard* was he revealing what it would be like to write the Enlightenment's courtesy book, with a Godwinite Iron Maiden as instructress in love. (She can even remedy love sickness.) The ramifications are—to say the least— quite ironic; a tone that is set forth at the outset. For one thing, Clara is such a Prussian that not only is she insistent on Edward's finding Mary, but once found he must *compel* her, he is told, "to accept your vows" (p. 8). (That Mary may want to choose what she does with her life is of no moment.) Clara has given Edward half her fortune on which to get the job done—another nice gesture. Edward rightfully—but fruitlessly—bemoans the irony: "I am still beloved by Clara; but that passion produces nothing but her misery and mine" (p. 9). He sees that these proceedings yield nothing but evil, and that the "truth, whatever it be, will avail me nothing" (p. 10). Actually, he is too frail-minded to grasp her concept, just as she is too doctrinaire to see the impossibility of dealing with human beings in the abstract, in which case her very wrong lies in her intellectual rightness. Edward does catch the Godwinian keynote—temporarily—that her "motives are disinterested and heroic" (p. 28); except that such argument fails to win the assent of feeling, and he backslides.

Known for his "rashness" (p. 19), Edward seems to need some chastening. It was inexplicably foolish of him to have agreed to marry Mary in the first place and to have pressured her to consent. He is unwise, inconsistent, and the evidence seems to support Clara's charge that he is also myopic. To this extent is she correct in trying to shape him up by telling him she cannot respect a man who deserves her "contempt" and that her "esteem can be secured only by a just and disinterested conduct" (p. 31). He could use more of Godwin, she less.

At the end, when their problem is solved by Mary's marrying Sedley, Clara's determination to enlighten Edward seems to have its worthy side:

as he is "deficient" in "moral discernment," she plans to be his counselor and guide, but—unhappy thought—she will also "assume some of the prerogatives of an elder sister." But the arbitrariness of her means seems to cancel out the benefit of her end. She is going to see to it that, come what may, their "modes of judging and . . . maxims shall be the same"; and, she continues, "this resemblance shall be purchased at the cost of all my patience, my skill, and my love" (p. 265). Irony of ironies, to bring him around will cost her her love! (So much for a happy ending.[28]) The damage comes from the absolutist side of Godwin's dissenting morality. One tyranny over the mind is gotten rid of and is replaced with another. In this, as in everything else, Clara Howard consistently follows the book, and in so doing, dooms the system on behalf of which she follows it.

This sort of resolution was typical for Brown. From his beginnings as published author, in *Alcuin*, he had shown himself to be more interested in keeping alive the dialectic by which the intelligence groped for truth than in advocating a point of view that proposed to preempt it. Related to what seems to have been an ingrained suspicion of pat solutions was Brown's fondness for paradox, the irresolvable. Thus, part of the problem with Clara and Edward lies in the fact that one never enters the dialectic process with a clean slate. The point Edward has to start from boxes him into a contradiction. He has said he loves Clara for her "own sake," which means he must desire her "happiness above all things" (p. 32). Yet to retain her love, he must violate it; or, at least, on his fulfilling Clara's terms, it must become a different kind of love. The challenge is comparable to that which Wieland poses for himself; to show his unqualified love of God, he had to be prepared to make himself undeserving of divine love. Or, there is Huntly, whose persistence in trying to save Edny drives the poor soul to the fate he hated most, suicide. Paradoxically, the only way out for Edward is the one that got him into his fix: to allow Clara to make a Godwinian of him.

On the other hand, Brown does not fail to do justice to the paradoxes Clara's Godwinism creates for *her*. Can she become Edward's wife just to save his life? she asks. That would be giving in "to humiliating and painful necessity," for Godwin, as for anyone, the worst consequence, when one is free to choose. Clara would be binding herself "beyond the power of loosening [her] bonds to one whom [she] *despised*" (p. 33). (Shades of Godwin's argument against marriage.) For her to respect him enough to marry him, he must first marry someone else so she can't.

As can be seen, *Clara Howard* is primarily an intellectual novel. The course it takes is a continuous back and forth debate, point and counterpoint, which in its variation, takes on aspects of the baroque. One person casts his meaning into emotive terms (love, pity, compassion, misery), the other into judgmental terms (sincerity, esteem, rectitude, injustice); and both are talking about the same things. Baroque-like, too, they even exchange positions for a while. Consumed with guilt over Edward's near-death illness (from the river plunge) after she had sent him away, Clara uncharacteristically begs forgiveness: "O! . . . that I could pour out the tears of my remorse . . . of my love upon your hand" (p. 57). She is even willing to renounce her injunction (p. 58), though, when calm returns, the thought of it displeases her (p. 59). Meanwhile, Edward, in response, jumps to the side of reason. He could not urge her "to the commission of what [he] deemed wrong." Does she think he could accept her hand "unattended with the fullest concurrence of [her] reason?" (p. 62).

There are even variations within variations. When Clara attributes to Edward the thought that she is purposely degrading herself in her own estimation for the purpose of raising herself in his (p. 41), that is merely her construction of an inference to be drawn from her assuming his viewpoint. She likewise finds preposterous his attributing "*anguish* and *suffering*" to her performance of a duty she takes pleasure in. She is being "upbraided," she exclaims—all on the basis of her recasting his ill-advised appeal to her feelings on behalf of his own—"in proportion to the fulness of that enjoyment, which, the approbation of conscience, the sense of doing right myself, and conferring good on others, has given me!" (p. 42).

And on it goes. But it does lead somewhere. The stronger Clara is in argument, the weaker she gets not just in appeal, but—final irony—in reason, as well. In fact, before the novel is over, her position will be fairly well devastated—and from several directions. Whence, for example, came Edward's original, uncalled-for proposal of marriage to Mary—whence, but from the same stand of benevolence that Clara was disastrously using to force him into that marriage? "Wedlock [to Mary] had been desired by me, more from zeal for the happiness of another, than for my own" (p. 109). His lament that "destiny" was thereby making "the affections of three persons merely the instruments of their misery" (p. 109) may be hindsight, but it is also rational *in*sight, and reason being used differently from Clara's use of it. His indictment of Clara's reasoning is further underscored by his saying that his vows to Mary were dictated by his "understanding," not by his "heart" (p. 127).

By a great thematic irony, the most damaging blow to Clara's Godwinism comes when Edward makes his plea to Mary and is turned down because "she was too blind an admirer, and assiduous a follower of Clara Howard, to accept [his] proffers" (p. 212). Mary will not be outdone. She insists *she* must have the privilege of benevolence, of self-denial; Edward must be free to marry Clara (p. 230). To clinch her point, she fights Godwinism with Godwinism: Clara's are "prayers which counteract their own purpose, since they exhibit an example of disinterestedness and self-oblivion which I cannot fail to admire and to imitate" (pp. 243f.). Mary's is the last word. Indeed Mary—unlike Clara—is capable of change, and growth. Having taken this course of giving up the man she loves, she is going to sustain herself by conquering her "perverse affections" (p. 244). Clara's happiness—contrary to all she has said—will, according to Mary's rational light, have to depend on an "incompliance with her wishes" (p. 243).

But, as we have seen, reasonableness—as opposed to reason—does not evidently make much of a dent in the Iron Maiden's armor; for, to the end, she remains frozen in her prior philosophy in spite of its failure. It is one thing for Edward to speak of Clara's "narrow heart," to call her "resolutions . . . absurd" (p. 132), her "judgment . . . misguided" (p. 198). However, Mary Wilmot's soft reproach of her absolutist mentality is perhaps the most telling critique of Clara Howard that one is to take away from a reading of this epistolary novel: "Your letters," Mary tells her, "are void of that extenuating spirit, that reluctance to inflict suffering, which, perhaps, the wisest inflexibility will not be slow to feel, or unwilling to express . . ." (p. 249).

Regardless of whether Clara loses more than she gains it would seem that in her applying Godwin's philosphy of benevolence to life, humanity (hers and ours) stands mainly to lose.

VI

As indicated, Godwin's moral philosophy seems somewhat less involved in *Jane Talbot*, where it is explicity referred to, than in *Clara Howard*, where it is not. In the one book it would appear we are getting the letter of *Political Justice*, and in the other—where its presence has not been recognized—the intent. Actually, once one disposes of the pseudo-Godwinism (as we have in dealing with Mrs. Fielder's accusations against Colden), and sets aside, as well, the fact that what little the presumed Godwinite tells us about his convictions does not seem especially relevant to Godwin,[29] a simple analysis of motives reveals that the last two novels are indeed counterparts, which have to be read together, in sequence, as they were written, *Jane* in the context of *Clara*. Not only was *Jane* begun almost immediately after *Clara* was finished, but it is its intellectual complement suggesting a progression of where we go from *Clara*, and where we do not. From the negative analysis on which *Clara* ended, we move on to a consideration of alternatives.

For one thing, there is a decided change in Clara's role. At worst, she was the moral enforcer; at best, defender of principle over the merely personal. When this authority devolves upon Mrs. Fielder, we see that what at a higher level had been strained to autocracy, at the lowest becomes melodramatized and is made the servant of hardened conventionalism. So far down can the honorifics of disinterest filter that we find Mrs. Fielder complimenting Jane on the "force of understanding" she showed in obediently marrying Lewis Talbot (p. 93). Moreover, just as a virtuous person conquers selfishness, so had Jane "evinced more magnanimity" in overcoming her "scruples" than if she had never had them (p. 93). Here—for what it is worth—is Mrs. Fielder's version of self-denial on behalf of a larger good. It is all of a piece with her substituting a rationalized for a rational morality that Mrs. Fielder sees no hypocrisy in her saying she wanted to entrust Jane's happiness to "a man of merit," when she blandly admits that Talbot "had nothing that deserved to be called religion," and gave little thought to a "a governing diety" (pp. 94f.). (Irreligion was, of course, the basis for Colden's disqualification.)

Jane and Colden inhabit a middle ground between Clara and Mrs. Fielder. It produces conflicts both less and more onerous than Clara's. Clara had the problem of opposing her own love. There was no external coercion (as with Jane), which is simpler to cope with. Clara had to have more willpower, a stronger compulsion to adhere, because she alone was responsible for adherence. For Jane and Colden, on the other hand, there is the same informing Godwinian ethic that happiness is achieved through sacrificing one's own interests for the benefit of others. What makes this so difficult in their case is that the moral drama must be played out in the volatile arena of the "affections." So, while Jane believes that, contrary to conscience, "all happiness springs from affection," that one must love "without bounds," since in "conjugal affection" "happiness" and "duty" are one, she is also aware that her "passion" goes beyond the "bounds" which would counteract "its own purposes" (p. 4). In short, she is hopelessly in love, and hopeless to be other than a slave to it. Yet (as already instanced) Jane is just as forcefully inspired to promote the happiness of others at the expense of her own: "I think I act with no exclusive regard to my own pleasure, but as it flows from and is dependent on the happiness of others" (p. 88). Specifically, it is the happiness of [her] revered mama," Mrs. Fielder, "that is dearer to [her] than [her] own" (p. 82). Her chief conflict is that she has the same attitude toward Colden, and in far stronger measure. Thus, it is the love she prizes more than life itself that must be over-ridden for her to obey the call of "duty." Unlike Clara, this does not come easy to her, but she does it—conferring happiness by giving up her own. Moreover, as she goes back on herself, she must *re-do* it, several times.

Then, there is the further complication that Jane does not act in isolation. Although Colden is up to playing the game in all its niceties ("I should not deserve your love, if I did not . . . relinquish it with an anguish next to despair . . ." [p. 215]), he does so with a realization of the fix Jane is in: she cannot "forfeit" Mrs. Fielder's love and still preserve her own "integrity" (p. 122). Hence, he explores their options. First, since he is primarily concerned for her happiness, if it could be secured by her "abjuring" him to satisfy her stepmother, without having her "tranquillity . . . invaded by self-reproach," he would cheerfully persuade her to do so. But, seeing that the one will not follow from the other, he shifts to a common-sense appeal: since she must find her happiness in conferring it on another, why not on him? (p. 123). Yet this cannot work either because he could not find *his* happiness in causing her unhappiness.

As Colden's analysis proceeds, it becomes evident that there is a total break-down in the code of disinterest. Can happiness really be achieved for its intended beneficiary if that person knows it is at the expense of someone else's happiness? As Colden pointedly remarks to Jane: "I ask not for proofs of love; for the sacrifice of others to me. My happiness demands it not. It only requires you *to seek your own good*" (p. 123, my italics).

Clearly, Godwinian benevolence cannot work well where it should above all work best, among persons who have only one another's interest at heart. Who could be more disinterested? This would be fine; they could disown disinterest and find happiness. But the sad irony is that they *cannot*; and things come apart again. Clara and Edward were victims of blind compliance, which is bad, but it is surely worse for Jane and Henry to comply with a full knowledge of the moral defect of compliance. Regardless, Colden sees he must give her up. Their impoverishment, her ingratitude to Mrs. Fielder, can only make everyone unhappy. Jane is peeved at how easily he can do it. Her preference is that *she* be essential to *his* happiness (p. 129). Moreover, in pleasing Mrs. Fielder she intolerably displeases herself because she cannot please Colden, and having already gone that route too, she cries out in frustration, "I have nothing but evil to chuse" (p. 244). When Jane decides to renege on Mrs. Fielder, fly into Colden's arms and take the consequences, Colden is put on the spot, for, having solemnly pledged himself to Mrs. Fielder's happiness, he is honor bound to stand fast. He finds himself defending the Godwinian stance he had already exposed as fallacious; and he plays for a doubling of its effect (a tripling, if placating his father be indirectly included), all of which proves that his critique had been fully as theoretic as the theory he criticized. "The happiness of one or another must be sacrificed," he had written Mrs. Fielder, "and shall I not rather offer, than demand the sacrifice! and how poor and selfish should I be if I did not strive to lessen the difficulties of [Jane's] choice, and persuade her that in gratifying her mother, she inflicts no lasting misery on me?" (p. 222).

It is precisely this argument which determines Jane to break her vows, plus her sense that she had acted selfishly with regard to Colden in breaking off with him (p. 256)—in spite of which, she allows herself to be sat on yet again.

Brown pushes his paradox to the point that only circumstances can help his characters out of it. There is Colden's departure for the Far East with Stephen Montford, Mrs. Fielder's death and death-bed forgiveness, Colden's chance meeting of Cartright in England after his four-year ordeal (he did not want to return to America having heard that Jane had remarried) and Colden's learning from Cartright that she would not marry him till she had proof of Colden's death.

When Colden took the type of escape that Hartley had planned before him, in assuming the life of a voyager to remote parts of the globe, careless of what might happen to him, Jane ironically iterates the discredited justification for her responsibility in it: "What I did, was in oblivion of self; was from a duteous regard to his genuine and lasting happiness" (p. 307). Too late does she have to admit that she has "mistaken the means"—which is the crux of the problem with the Godwinian ethic. Its means do not bring about the end that is proposed. When there is a mistake in theory, nobody gets hurt, except those who have tried to live by it. For them, Jane confesses, the "penalty of . . . error" is "cruel" (p. 307). To have seen a way to correct the flawed ethic and to have lamely returned to it anyway is no consolation, but it does seem to say something about the perversity of its attractiveness. Also, it was plain another direction had to be tried; one that, as it turns out, completely reverses Godwin's. The movement I allude to goes from Reason to Faith, from a closed to an open mentality; on this last point, Godwin notwithstanding, and, in one respect, Godwin also assisting.

No one is more aware than Jane herself that she gives in too readily. But being "an April girl," as she calls herself (p. 53), is not without certain advantages; it makes her flexible in a good, as well as a bad way. She had thought she could not love a man lacking in religion; however, in addition to finding out that she can, because of him, she tests a faith she had been accepting without inquiry and strengthens it. She acquires a "new clearness of [her] own convictions" (p. 194), and is indebted to him for everything in her faith that is "permanent and rational" (p. 194). Without having had to subject her faith to doubt and justification, what, she notes, "would have been [her] claims to religious knowledge?" (p. 195). She has grown both in depth and breadth; secure in her own reaffirmation, she no longer abhors those who differ from her (p. 195). The upshot is she has come to understand herself better (p. 196). Thus are we unexpectedly returned to the central Godwinian nexus, though with a critical difference. Godwin's certainly is Jane's liberalism of attitude, and, more significantly, her epistemology—conviction hammered out through open inquiry—which, however, leads to a non-Godwinian end.

Nor does the process stop there. Indeed, Jane's revisionism induces another version of benevolence. She will do good for the person she loves by saving him from error. To be faced with doubt and be indifferent to it would be "criminal." "What becomes of our obligation to do good to others, if we do not extend ourselves, when all the means are in our power, to confer the most valuable of all benefits: to remove the greatest of all ills?" (p. 191). Reversing the terms by which a solely rational conviction is achieved, she notes that it is merely Colden's "understanding" that "dissents"; his "heart is not yet persuaded to refuse" (p. 190). Piety that comes from "the study of homilies and creeds [alone] . . . without *rational* activity for others [sic] good, is not religion" (p. 192). While her love had been a source of discord (where presumably reason would have produced accord), it has the greater compensation of harmonizing her feelings and actions; she is filled with "unconquerable zeal" to rescue the man she loves from the calamities of doubt. The important thing about Jane's zeal is that—unlike Clara's with Edward—it involves no duress—only the intellectual necessity of reasoning things through.

Colden is receptive to the extent that he embraces the obligation—also out of Godwin—of total objectivity: the one "unequivocal merit," he claims, is, "I stick to the truth" (p. 142), and he maintains he will only be convinced by it (p. 182).

The person who makes the biggest impact on Colden in this regard is not Jane, but Harriet Thomson, sister of the friend to whom he had written those radical letters which Mrs. Fielder used against him. Harriet (a name Brown had also given the adulated "Henrietta") picks up Jane's line of reasoning. Unbelief is not so serious a fault as doubt. "A state of doubt and indecision was in every view, hurtful, criminal and ignominious" (p. 296). And the way to resolve it (Godwin simply will not go away), is by the familiar dialect of open inquiry: by his entering on "regular discussions" out of a "love of truth" and confidence in this method of finding it (p. 296). Let unbelief be contested by belief and whichever won out, that should he adhere to. A religious conviction earned in this way would clearly insure "happiness." But equally acceptable would be an "irreligious conviction," so long as it had been established by one's "enquiries" (p. 296).

The proselytizing element seems—if anything—a bit less strenuous than it is with Godwin. He had advocated that change be realized through active persuasion (as against revolution), and sincerity, it will be recalled, demanded that the truth when found had to be vigorously promulgated regardless of consequences to persons. It is in keeping with this aspect of the Godwinian formulation that Harriet urges that, whatever his final belief, "the love of truth and the consciousness of that certainty would raise [Colden] above hatred and slander" (p. 296). And, as it turns out, a necessary consequence of Colden's having learned "true piety" is the feeling that he must "exemplify and . . . teach" it (p. 342).

Between them, Jane and Harriet started Colden (supposedly the more venturesome spirit) on the mission of rethinking his views, but it would obviously have been cliché for either of them to have been the final catalyst for Colden's conversion. That he had to do on his own. Already given to enlightenment through "meditation; severe, intense, candid and dispassionate" (p. 293), and having been "far from principled against religion" (pp. 298f.), Colden recovered his faith naturally, through his own "reflection," (p. 342) and the "vicissitudes" he had experienced during the Far Eastern voyaging, the mutiny, his being deserted on the "inhospitable" Japanese island, and the wandering thereafter (p. 341).

The final reward that Jane and Colden realize is not just marriage, but the firmest basis for it, a whole-hearted concurrence of minds—or exactly the sort of harmony which Godwin, in his diatribe against matrimony, felt it was impossible to expect and inadvisable to strive for, since whatever accommodation was reached had to mean a subjugation of the individuality of both persons (Priestly, *PJ*, II, pp. 501–07).

The pursuit of happiness by following the virtue of a "duteous regard" for the "genuine and lasting happiness" of one another (p. 307) out of Godwinian disinterest is where the whole moral process had begun. In the mind, selflessness seemed an infallible guide toward human perfectibility. On the other hand, living by it had brought Jane and Colden nothing of what they sought for each other and had resulted only in their unabating misery. Thus, it seemed inevitable that experience should bring about an inversion of Godwin; and, to be sure, it worked with beautiful simplicity: once they dispensed with self-denial, they did indeed find that in practice the *happiness* of one creates the happiness of the other.

VII

The romantic susceptibilities ascribed to the youthful Jane Talbot rather closely image the Rousseauist Charles Brockden Brown of the early nineties, as glimpsed, for example, in his letters of the time to Joseph Bringhurst and William Wood Wilkins. There is a direct autobiographical link to that correspondence in Mrs. Fielder's reminding Jane: "I . . . remembered that impetuosity of feeling which distinguished your early age: those notions of kindred among souls: of friendship and harmony of feelings which, in your juvenile age, you loved to indulge" (p. 97). These "chimeras" were temporarily set to rest by Jane's marriage to Talbot; for them to be reawakened it was only "requisite to meet with one [i.e., Colden], contemplative, bookish and romantic as yourself" (p. 98). Since, in the course of the novel, Jane and Colden surmount a variety of inhibiting circumstances, in addition to the rather stringent Godwinism they impose on themselves, Brown was with one part of his psyche paying private—if not outright nostalgic—tribute to the early belletristic sensibility he shared with his friends. *Jane Talbot* also shows Brown reexamining another chief interest of his in the nineties, and with a critical discernment that suggested he was ready to move on from it. In an important letter to Brown in May, 1796, Elihu Hubbard Smith recorded what he saw as the crucial transition from Rousseau to Godwin. Commenting on Brown's habit of affecting the "mysterious" and making "ambiguity" his "delight," Smith wrote, "The example of J. J. Rousseau had too many charms in your eyes, not to captivate you, & incite you to imitate him . . ." (*Diary*, p. 171). Much given to fantasizing and representing the imagined as real, Brown, it seemed to Smith, "wandered in a world of [his] own creation," except when an occasional "ray of truth broke in." Suddenly, there was a break in the clouds: "*Godwin came, & all was light*" (*Diary*, p. 171).

Brown never had a more solicitous or more genuinely helpful friend than Smith. In Henry Colden, he paid at least partial homage to his

memory. For, like Colden, Smith was, among other things, an intellectual and admitted disbeliever, a poet and devotee of literature. He also
kept up a regular correspondence with his sister Mary who was married to
Thomas Munford (Colden's sister Mary, with whom he corresponds, is
married to James Montford); but above all, Smith had an intense affinity
for Godwin, and especially for the moral precepts of *Political Justice*,
which he felt confirmed his own, even before he had read the book in
full.[30]

Since it was at the height of Smith's enthusiasm for Godwin (1796)
that he and Brown were engaging in "multifarious & interesting conversations" (*Diary*, p. 297), and since Smith talked about him with almost
everyone else, Godwin had to have been discussed with Brown as well,
and on a more than occasional basis. In any case, Brown seems to have
picked up from Smith an emphasis that came into play in his characterization of Colden; and it is also possible that something of the criticism of
Godwin that appeared in *Clara* and *Jane* may have originated in his conversations with Smith. Citing Godwin's idea that "it is the duty of every
human being . . . to inquire for himself" in matters of religion (as with
any other belief) and "to rest his faith on his own convictions only," Smith
noted the Godwinian process seemed to work better at proving what was
"false" with "other systems" than in unfolding "the true one" itself
(*Diary*, p. 123). Smith regarded Godwin as anything but a dogmatist; he
saw him presenting *Political Justice* to the world in the spirit that we "examine it attentively" and "adopt" its views only if they prove themselves
to us as "true" (pp. 123f.).

In *Clara Howard* and *Jane Talbot*, Brown did this much and more.
He gave Godwinian morality the ultimate trial of proving its effectiveness
at achieving its own ends, and found it wanting. To put Brown's findings
in their simplest terms, the experience of his characters with Godwin
seems to suggest that his moral philosophy was as easy to believe as it was
impossible to live by, which, considering the various irrelevant criticisms
of Godwin in his day, at least has the virtue of meeting him on his own
grounds.

Notes

1. For Witherington, these are Brown's "most mature novels," "remarkably tight" in
plotting, excellent in "structure, point of view, and characterization." "Brockden Brown's
Other Novels: *Clara Howard* and *Jane Talbot*," *Nineteenth Century Fiction*, 29 (1974), pp.
257–58, 267.

2. *The Life of Charles Brockden Brown*, ed. Charles E. Bennett (Delmar: Scholars'
Facsimiles & Reprints, 1975), pp. 47f. Hereafter cited as Allen, *Life*.

3. *The Life of Charles Brockden Brown* (Philadelphia: James P. Parke, 1815), II, p. 67.
Hereafter cited as Dunlap, *Life*.

4. Anon. Review of Brown's Novels, *British Critic*, 3rd Ser., 2 (April, 1826), p. 61.

5. Brown's comment on the need of a shift was given in a letter to his brother James in
April, 1800. Dunlap, *Life*, II, p. 100.

6. *Charles Brockden Brown* (New York: Twayne Publishers, 1966), p. 112.

7. *Charles Brockden Brown: American Gothic Novelist* (Gainesville: Univ. of Florida Press, 1949), p. 193.

8. "On the State of American Literature," *Monthly Magazine*, 1 (April, 1799), p. 18.

9. The English writer, John Davis, whom Brown had reason to envy and dislike as a successful competitor, suggested that *Jane Talbot* was an attempt to win favor with ladies. (*Travels of Four Years and a Half in the United States of America . . .* , ed. A. J. Morrison (New York: Henry Holt, 1909), p. 222. [Original publication, London, 1803.])

Leslie Fiedler finds Brown crassly trying to capture the female audience that had made Susannah Rowson rich (*Love and Death in the American Novel* [New York: World Publishing Co., 1960], p. 74).

Presumably, it is also possible to suppose that his falling in love with Elizabeth Linn in 1800 (his wife to be) had something to do with his new departure. His letters to her in 1801, published by David Lee Clark seem suggestive of this. (*Charles Brockden Brown: Pioneer Voice of America* [Durham: Duke Univ. Press, 1952], pp. 199–209. Hereafter, Clark.)

10. Another such correspondence occurs in Jane Talbot's ambivalent relationship with her devious brother Frank, which repeats the Mrs. Lorimer-Arthur Wiatte relationship in *Edgar Huntly*.

11. " 'A Lesson on Concealment': Brockden Brown's Method in Fiction," *Philological Quarterly*, 37 (1958), pp. 46f.

12. *Jane Talbot, A Novel* (Philadelphia: John Conrad & Co., 1801), p. 88. Hereafter all references will be to this, the first edition, presently the most reliable available text.

13. A clarification. I am saying the doctrine of benevolence that appears in *Clara* and *Jane* derives from Godwin. This is not to deny that benevolence as such had been around for quite a while in eighteenth-century thought. An important ethic of the Enlightenment at large, it was also prevalent in America, and very early in the century, as in such disparate, though related, works as Cotton Mather's *Bonifacius* (1710, reissued as *Essays to do Good*) and Franklin's *Dogood Papers* (1722). Brown himself had of course used the concept before, as with the selfless concern of Constantia Dudley and Arthur Mervyn during the pestilence experience, and in depicting the acute solicitousness of Clithero Edny and Edgar Huntly. The distinction with regard to Godwin is that he made benevolent intention the moral cornerstone of *Political Justice*; it assured personal virtue and was the corrective of social injustice, as in the process of benefitting others, we improved both ourselves and mankind collectively. In *Clara* and *Jane*, Brown made a special and persistent application of this definitively Godwinian treatment of benevolence. He was showing, in a thorough-going way, how it might not work in given life situations where it was proposed as the standard of conduct. And this is essentially different from his use of the doctrine in its more general form in his other works.

14. William Dunlap, "Charles Brockden Brown," in *The National Portrait Gallery of Distinguished Americans*, ed. James Herring and James B. Langacre (New York: Henry Perkins, 1836), III, p. 3.

15. "The American Novel Begins," *American Scholar*, 35 (1965–66), p. 144.

16. Brown's letter to Joseph Bringhurst May 5, 1792, quoted by Herbert R. Brown, "Charles Brockden Brown's 'The Story of Julius': Rosseau and Richardson 'Improved,' " in *Essays Mostly on Periodical Publishing in America*, ed. James L. Woodress (Durham: Duke Univ. Press, 1973), p. 37. Hereafter, "Julius."

17. The Richardsonian triangle of one man—two women, Brown used elsewhere (as in *Ormond, Arthur Mervyn*, and "Stephen Calvert"), occasionally changing it to one woman—two men (as in *Wieland* and "Mary Selwyn"). The fact that he paired his couples in *Clara* and *Jane* was not simply to give himself the "cheerful" option at the end. That was quite secondary. Rather it is that his conflicts are not wholly dependent on a third-party mechanism—though it is used in *Clara*—so much as on a clash of irreconcilable values.

18. *Clara Howard; in a Series of Letters* (Philadelphia: Asbury Dickins, 1801), p. 28. As

with *Jane Talbot* all references to *Clara* will be to this, the first edition, which is likewise the only reliable text available. This means that I use the name, Edward Hartley, for the protagonist, rather than Philip Stanley, the one substituted for it in the 1807 British Edition, which also re-titled the novel *Philip Stanley; or, The Enthusiasm of Love.*

19. *La Nouvelle Héloïse; Julie or the New Eloise . . .*by Jean Jacques Rousseau, tr. Judith H. McDowell (University Park: Pennsylvania State Univ. Press, 1968), pp. 162f.

20. Citing chapter and verse of direct parallels, even of specific details, as with the voyeur closet scene, in which Brown imagines himself secreted in Henrietta's dressing room, Hare convincingly describes the "Henrietta Letters" as a "free adaptation of Rousseau's material transposed into a Philadelphia setting," offering "a sort of amalgamation of Rousseauist phrases, attitudes and ideas." "Charles Brockden Brown's *Ormond*: The Influence of Rousseau, Godwin and Mary Wollstonecraft," Diss. (Univ. of Maryland, 1967), pp. 67, 69.

21. He presumably began learning the language at around the age of sixteen (1787), either on his own or in Proud's Latin School, where it was taught; and what he learned was reinforced by his associations with the French émigrés who began coming to Philadelphia in considerable numbers in the early nineties (Dunlap, *Life*, I, p. 14, Clark, pp. 19f.).

22. *The Rhapsodist and Other Uncollected Writings by Charles Brockden Brown*, ed. Harry R. Warfel, (New York: Scholars' Facsimiles & Reprints, 1943), p. 71.

23. Herbert Brown, "Julius," op. cit., pp. 38–50.

24. "Julius," p. 38. It is worth noting that the term "pernicious" was also used by Mrs. Fielder with regard to Colden's attachment to Godwin (*JT*, p. 98).

25. William Godwin, *An Enquiry Concerning Political Justice and Its Influence on General Virtue and Happiness* (Dublin: Luke White, 1793), I, pp. 138–40; 142–50. These sections cover suicide and promises. I have also consulted F. E. L. Priestley's facsimile of Godwin's revised third edition (1797) (Toronto: Univ. of Toronto Press, 1946). My citations of text are mainly to the first edition, hereafter *PJ*. But when I cite the third edition, usually because of a certain change, or cogency of phrasing, this is noted as Priestley, *PJ*. Priestley's Introductory Essay (in Volume II of his edition) is cited as "Intro."

26. For example: "God, according to the ideas usually conceived of that being, is more benevolent than man, because he has a constant and clear perception of the nature of that end which his providence pursues" (Priestley, *PJ*, I, p. 318). What Godwin most urgently opposes is Established Religion and its enforced conformity.

27. *The Diary of Elihu Hubbard Smith (1771–1798)*, ed. James Cronin (Philadelphia: American Philosophical Society, 1973), pp. 164, 171, 248–50. (Hereafter, *Diary*.) I return to this subject in the last section of my paper.

28. Actually, if one discounts the irony for a moment, and sticks with Godwin, the best case to be made for the ending is not so much that it is happy as lucky; for without Mary's finally accepting Sedley, there could only have been a permanent stand-off between Clara, Edward, and Mary, with each of the women pleading for the primacy of the other's happiness.

Another matter. In the prefatory letter, Edward, in looking back, tells us that he was supremely happy in his marriage. Since the letter is set in a different type size from that used for the body of the text, and is in a separate gathering (which means it was imposed independently of the rest of the text), it probably was written, as well as printed, after the text had been done. If Brown was thereby trying to leave no doubt that for Edward the ending was happy, this would still be entirely consonant with what goes on in the novel proper. For Edward's euphoria is but a consistent extension of his shallowness (he puts his happiness on a level with being "rich," which is listed first, p. iv); and it suggests the further irony of his incomplete understanding of the Godwinism he submitted himself to.

29. Colden remains rather vague about where he stands intellectually. (We do not get to see his letters to Thomson.) At best, he comes across as a sort of unaffiliated eighteenth-

century pre-existentialist: " . . .Though less sordid than the epicure, the voluptuary, or the sportsman, the principle that governs them and me, is the same: equally limited to self; equally void of any basis in morals or religion" (*JT*, p. 145).

30. In a long letter to Timothy Dwight (of November 1796), Smith staunchly defended Godwin's moral system, saying his "disbelief" and "conviction of the truth of several doctrines whose advocate he is" were well "fixed" before he had so much as heard of Godwin (*Diary*, p. 249). Godwin gave weighty support to Smith's opinions and greatly strengthened his love of virtue and desire to practice it in the manner Godwin proposed. Godwin's views were well known and often alluded to among Smith's circle of friends. William Dunlap, in fact, was in personal correspondence with Godwin (*Diary of William Dunlap* [New York: New York Historical Society, 1930], III, p. 650).

Charles Brockden Brown: Man of Letters

Charles E. Bennett

When Charles Brockden Brown left New York for Philadelphia in the autumn of 1800, he no doubt carried in his baggage copies of the half dozen novels he had written in the previous two years, and no doubt carried in his head the matter of numerous others, three certainly. If, in returning home, he was abandoning his hope of being able to support himself by literature, he certainly had no intention of abandoning literature. What he would write would be markedly different from what he had done before but not less ambitious.

As he rode he may have been thinking of "Jessika," a novel about an American heiress abroad, which he had begun to plan the previous spring. And he may also have been thinking of how he would complete his epistolary novel of Julia and Jessica, fragments of which he had published in the July and August issues of the *Monthly Magazine*.[1] But foremost in his mind may have been the tale of those star-crossed lovers, Jane Talbot and Henry Colden, for it was to their story that he would first address himself when able to spare time from his mercantile and legal studies. *Jane Talbot* finished, he began *Clara Howard*. Within a little more than six months of his return, Brown wrote and published two novels—his seventh and eighth—proof, were it wanted, that whatever the motives that had called him home, a disgust with literature was no consideration.

Brown continued a prolific, even a profligate author throughout the new century's first and his final decade. He wrote poems and polemics, essays and reviews, travelogues and translations, biography and geography, even a play. Not in succession, but continually and all at once.

Much of what he wrote he published in one or another of the magazines with which he was associated. On the demise of Brown's own *Monthly Magazine* in 1800 and his departure from New York, several of his friends in that city resolved to carry on the most highly regarded feature of that magazine, its "American Review." This they launched and kept afloat through 1802. Though Brown has sometimes been thought to have been its editor, he was by his own account merely a contributor, a reviewer chiefly.[2] Unfortunately there seems no way of knowing which reviews are his.

212

When that magazine too failed, Brown determined to venture once more into the field, this time with the *Literary Magazine and American Register*. It would, he advised the public, be "an American Review, in which the history of our native literature shall be carefully detailed."[3] The *Literary Magazine* ran fifty-two issues (October 1803-January 1808), an extraordinary feat for a magazine in those times. Its eight volumes are replete with the editor's own contributions, most notably his memoir of Carwin, the biloquist, which was serialized in ten irregularly spaced installments.[4] Of those, the first seven installments had been written in New York in 1798; the final three however were written specifically for the *Literary Magazine*.[5] There is, in addition, conclusive evidence for Brown's authorship of some four dozen essays.[6] A far greater number remain unidentified.

As early as November 1806 Brown advised one of the magazine's contributors that it was time the *Literary Magazine* "should die"; it would, he wrote, be "metamorphosed" to a semi-annual register as the printer was confident such a change would improve its "vendability."[7] In fact, the transformation was deferred another year. The first issue of the *American Register, or General Repository of History, Politics, and Science* did not appear until the final weeks of 1807. His newest periodical was modeled, as Brown was the first to acknowledge, on the British annual registers and was, by his own description, of a kind "previously unattempted" in America: a chronicle of contemporary events, a review of current literature, a repository of public documents.[8] Much of the *American Register* was abstracted from the laws of the United States and from American and foreign state papers; much else was extracted from the press. What was neither abstracted nor extracted was Brown's own. The *American Register* was a solo performance. Far from being the "hack work" Frank Luther Mott thought it, the five volumes of the *American Register* constitute an impressive achievement.[9] "They make Brown," Fred Lewis Pattee has written, "unquestionably the pioneer American historian in the modern manner.[10]

Brown's return to Philadelphia coincided with the initiation in that city of the most successful periodical of its time: the *Port Folio*. Despite his chronic need for materials to fill his own periodicals, Brown was a frequent contributor to Dennie's magazine. After the *Literary Magazine* gave way to the *American Register*, the *Port Folio* became Brown's vehicle for the publication of compositions he could not appropriately include in his own more austere *Register*. Happily, John E. Hall—a fellow contributor and friend to both Brown and Dennie—left annotated copies that identify the *Port Folio* authors.[11] Perhaps the most interesting of Brown's contributions is an essay in which he considers the relative merits of Smollett, Fielding and Richardson. The two former, Brown declared, "will ever be valued by judicious readers, for their wit, their strong and vivid portraits of human characters, and the testimony which their ingenious narrations . . . afford to the beauty and the usefulness of virtue, but the approbation which, with regard to them, will be qualified and moderate, will soar into something like rapture, at the pathetic and varied elegance, the moral grandeur and sublimity of Richardson."[12]

Brown's purpose, he declared, was to provide his readers with "useful information and rational amusement."[13] He therefore went out of his way in the *Literary Magazine* and, later, the *American Register* to avoid political controversy. The success of these periodicals, as evidenced by their long life, may be attributed in part to Brown's ability to steer them clear of the reefs and shoals of contemporary politics. That is not to say Brown was without political opinions or took no part in the political combat of his time. For that he made use of a quite different vehicle—the ubiquitous pamphlet.

Long before, in December 1796, the members of the Friendly Club, Brown among them, had discussed President Washington's farewell address to the Congress. A week later Brown presented his friends with a "Reply which might have been made, by the Senate of the United States to the President."[14] This work, now lost, is the earliest indication of a serious concern with contemporary political issues.

Whatever his political sentiments, for the next half-dozen years Brown confined them to his conversation and correspondence. Only when the nation was brought to the brink of crisis by Spain's closure of the Mississippi and the impending cession of the Louisiana territory to France was Brown moved to public statement. He may have been prompted by a meeting of the merchants of Philadelphia—of whom he was now one—held the first week in January 1803 for the purpose of determining "what steps it would be proper to pursue to obtain redress for Spanish injuries."[15] That Brown was present is not certain, but that he shared the concerns of his fellow merchants one cannot doubt. The proof is the pamphlet he published on January 20, 1803: *An Address to the Government of the United States, on the Cession of Louisiana to the French; and on the Late Breach of Treaty by the Spaniards: Including the Translation of a Memorial, on the War of St. Domingo, and Cession of the Missisippi* [sic] *to France, Drawn Up by a French Counsellor of State.*[16] This address was so immediate a success that a second, abridged edition was published a month later.[17]

Brown made a forceful, cogent case for the immediate acquisition, by war if necessary, of the Louisiana territory. Espousing the argument of America's manifest destiny, he declared that "we have looked on with stupid apathy, while European powers toss about among themselves the property which God and Nature have made ours." Not only has America a right to Louisiana, it has a duty to mankind to bring that vast territory under its benign and civilizing jurisdiction. "We have a right to the possession. The interests of the human race demand from us the exertion of this right. These interests demand that the reign of peace and concord should be diffused as widely and prolonged as much as possible. By unity of manners, laws and government is concord preserved, and this unity will be maintained . . . by the gradual extension of our own settlements, by erecting new communities as fast as the increase of these settlements requires it, and by sheltering them all under the pacific wing of a federal government" (p. 49). America's failure to seize Louisiana, moreover, would not merely emplace a hostile power on its western frontier and astride its southern trade routes but would very probably result in the rebellion and seccession of the inhabitants of transmontane America. "The western people will not be trifled with. They will not bear that injuries to their dearest rights should excite no emotion in that government whose claim to their regard is founded on the equality and efficacy of its protection. There never was a time when this government might gain the hearts of that important portion of its citizens more effectually than now. To let the opportunity pass unimproved will be a deadly wound to its popularity. It will probably be followed by some immediate act of rebellion. The loss of the affection of the western states will be the certain consequence." Therefore, the one-time Quaker argues, "The iron is now hot! . . . rise as one man and STRIKE!" (p. 49).

The *New York Evening Post* declared that "if anything can arouse the government and the people of this country to a proper sense of the dangers which menace their peace from the magnificent and alarming projects of a towering, ambitious foreigner, it will be the perusal of this pamphlet. . . . It is eloquent and ingenious. That the views of the writer are comprehensive and the maxims of policy which he inculcates just and dignified, few American readers will be disposed to deny."[18]

More than a few actually. Jefferson's supporters attacked the pamphlet at its most vulnerable point: the authenticity of the supposed counsellor's memoir, actually a fictional device Brown had employed to expose what he took to be the devious designs of France. For weeks the *Aurora*—the principal editorial supporter of Jefferson and his policies—attempted to flush out the author or, as it preferred to describe him, that "rank literary character."[19]

Pleased with the sensation created by his *Address to the Government*, Brown took his own advice—"strike while the iron is hot!"—and published a second pamphlet a few months later: *Monroe's Embassy, or, the Conduct of the Government, in Relation to Our Claims to the Navigation of the Missisippi [sic], Considered.*[20]

Outraged by what he took to be Jefferson's "cowardly and dilatory measures" in sending Monroe to Paris to negotiate a peaceable purchase of Louisiana, Brown, in his second address on the subject, renewed the arguments he had made in his first, but where the earlier had been couched in the language of a public-spirited citizen, this was steeped in partisan venom. Not that Brown asserted that Monroe's mission could not succeed. It may, he wrote, but "if the French . . . should be willing to sell the province for a sum far inferior to the cost of invading and preserving it, that man is a silly calculator, as to the value either of money or of honour, who should think the purchase cheaper than the seizure." Brown seems, indeed, to have feared that Monroe would succeed and the occasion for war be lost. "Seasonable war," he wrote, "is . . . the surest way to peace."

Brown's warmongering in these pamphlets of 1803 had its origin not in a passion for blood but in a belief that the vital interests, indeed the survival of the United States would be at hazard were French forts to close the western frontier and French imposts to strangle trade on the Mississippi. What is more, Brown feared that twenty years after the successful conclusion of the revolutionary struggle, the nation was in danger of being split asunder by irreconcilable interests and virulent factions. He was not the first to see in war the means of rallying a divided and distracted people. War with France, like the earlier conflict with England, would remind Americans of their common interests and thus help forge a national identity, while at the same time necessarily expanding the role and strengthening the powers of the federal government.

With the happy, and bloodless, resolution of the Louisiana crisis, Brown withdrew temporarily from the political wars. He returned to the affray in 1807 exasperated by Jefferson's maritime policies, policies that worked great harm to his, his brothers' and their friends' mercantile interests. The *British Treaty* was, like *Monroe's Embassy*, a vituperative attack upon Jefferson and his policies.[21] Not only did the new treaty (1806) make damaging concessions to the British, according to Brown, but the government's policies discouraged trade and commerce. Since the strength and well-being of the nation depend upon these, Jefferson's policies were sapping the nation's strength and endangering its well being.

Eighteen months later, in January 1809, Brown published a fourth pamphlet, not another polemic however but a reasoned and far-reaching statement of principles. *An Address to the Congress of the United States, on the Utility and Justice of Restrictions upon Foreign Commerce. With Reflections on Foreign Trade in General, and the Future Prospects of America* is one of the most remarkable political documents to have appeared in the early years of the republic.[22] Intended to expose the Embargo Act of 1807 as a political error and an economic calamity, Brown's address was and remains a devastating criticism of the isolationist view of a self-sufficient America.

The embargo, Brown argued, is a failure. It is unenforceable, has failed to moderate the conduct of the belligerents, has done more harm to America than to its enemies, and has increased the risk that America will be drawn into the war. Worse yet, by setting region against region, interest against interest, it has exacerbated factional divisions that threaten to rend the federal union.

What should American policy be? By studying the conduct of nations Brown established certain first principles: "The examples of all ages and nations justify us in preferring the smallest good of our own to the greatest of other states." "The real law of nations," he continued, "the sole law which all of them recognize is that they must enrich and aggrandize themselves by all the means in their power." America's conduct, then, "should originate . . . in no desire but the sole advantage of the natîon" (p. 36).

Where then is America's advantage in the present instance: in maintaining the embargo or in resuming trade? Those who support the embargo would like to believe that Americans can sit "quiet spectators of the storms that shake the rest of the world, secure in our solitude and in the waste that rolls between them and us, employing all our vigour in building up an empire here in the West and in cementing the members of our vast and growing nation into one body." There is something "charming" Brown allowed in such a notion, but it is specious and naively utopian (pp. 77–78).

"We are a nation of farmers, traders and artisans, but our wants are not entirely supplied by our artisans. . . . We are clothed, and adorned, and supplied with tools, in a great degree, by artisans beyond the ocean. Our principal employment is to catch fish, to cut timber, to reap corn, to feed cattle, and to carry what we do not consume of these away in exchange for the viands of foreign climates, or those articles of foreign manufacture which they will buy, which we want" (p. 81). It will not always be so: "The period will inevitably arrive when most of our own wants will be supplied by our own hands. . . . We shall become the manufacturers of other nations. Such we are, even now, to a certain degree, but our manufacturers will multiply to a larger proportion than our husbandmen. Less and less of the produce of mere handicraft will be imported from abroad, and more and more will be exported. . . . It will even be our lot to import the raw material of our manufactures. . ." (p. 83). "All this will come," Brown insisted presciently. "Eternal and immutable causes will bring us finally to this point, without the aid of government to push us forward, and in spite of all its efforts to hold us back. . . . The impossibility of any internal regulation to suspend our commercial intercourse with foreigners will be as evident when that intercourse consists in carrying cloths and fetching flour and cotton, as now when it consists of carrying cotton and fetching cloths" (p. 84). Trade, then, is not only desirable and necessary but inevitable, a law of nature. Addressing the Congress directly, Brown summarized his argument thus: "The constitution has not denied you the power of perpetually suspending commercial intercourse with Asia or Europe, nor that of maintaining it with the hither side of the moon. Nature has denied you both the one and the other" (pp. 73–74).

Clearly, America's economic advantage is to be sought in trade. But not just economic advantage. "Commerce, or the intercourse of buying and selling, is itself manifestly beneficial, and necessarily implies and creates all the more liberal kinds of intercourse. . . . One of the consequences . . . is to pull down the barriers which separate mankind from each other; to enlarge that circle which each man calls his country; to take away the grounds of dissension and rivalship; to create one nation out of many; to blend into one system of friendly, and especially of commercial intercourse, tribes that formerly looked upon each other as natural and hereditary enemies" (p. 84). Thus, where the embargo has wrought commercial stagnation, political dissension and an increased risk of war, free and unrestricted trade may be expected to contribute not only to the nation's prosperity but to its political stability and its cultural enrichment. Furthermore, as trade expands to the mutual benefit of all peoples, war with its attendant disruption of international trade will be recognized as inimical to a nation's true interests. Trade, not war, will hereafter offer the most advantageous (and, happily, a mutually advantageous) avenue to national self-aggrandizement.

Here, in his *Address to the Congress*, published just a year before his death, Brown evidenced once again his life-long affinity for utopian prospects. No longer however does he expect the transformation of the world to be wrought by a romantic brotherhood of illuminati (as in "Signor Adini"); it will instead be the work of men of practical good sense, merchants and traders like himself and his brothers.

Brown's political writings have not received their due. Nothing else he wrote during his brief life had so profound and immediate an effect upon his contemporaries. These few pamphlets, superior to all but a few of that breed, entitle Brown to a place not among the crowd of polemicists whose writings troubled the time but to an honored place among the select company of political theorists intent on endowing the infant republic with an informing political philosophy.

Brown's love of his country manifested itself not only in his political concerns but in a fascination with its varied topography and climate. He prided himself on his knowledge of geography. Asked by Samuel Miller to comment on that gentleman's manuscript of *A Brief Retrospect of the Eighteenth Century*, Brown apologized for the paucity of his comments by alleging that "geography was the only subject in which I was at all qualified to correct any mistakes you have committed, and, on this I have not been sparing, as you will find."[23] It was, no doubt, this fascination with geography that prompted Brown to translate Volney's *A View of the Soil and Climate of the United States of America* (1804).[24] Though the title page announced, rather modestly, that the work had been "Translated, with Occasional Remarks, by C. B. Brown," those remarks are a good deal more frequent and extensive than that caption would suggest. M. Volney's work was, in fact, escorted into English by a fleet of miniature essays camouflaged as footnotes.

Five years later (1809) Brown had "nearly finished" his own "System of General Geography; Containing a Topographical, Statistical, and Descriptive Survey of the Earth." A prospectus was published.[25] Failing health prevented him from completing the work however and it was left to his wife to engage Paul Allen to complete the twelve-hundred-page work for posthumous publication. Allen failed Elizabeth in this as he did in the matter of the "Life."[26] Someone though must have completed the "Geography," then or later, for "the full original manuscript . . . *since perfected*" was said to be in the possession of Brown's son, William Linn Brown, in 1827.[27] Though he too promised that his father's perfected work would soon be presented to the public, it never was. The whereabouts of the manuscript, if it survives, is unknown to Brown's living descendants. Its disappearance is much to be regretted for the erudite footnotes with which Brown adorned his translation of Volney suggest that his own geography might have proved a monumental work and gained for Brown precedence among American geographers.

History, too, fascinated Brown. While still in New York, he had evidenced an interest in the fictional portrayal of historical events. "The Death of Cicero" and "Thessalonica," both written in 1799, bear witness to that interest.[28] In 1803 he determined to try that vein again, but this time he would write a play.[29] For his subject he chose "an imaginary incident of Egyptian history, the interest turning on the intellectual sway of a magician over a young Persian, and the attachment of the latter to a Greek girl, who attempted to combat the magician's influence. Thus between the powers of love and superstition, the disciplines of Art and Nature, the magician and the girl, a contest ensued which terminated with the triumph of the sorcerer and the death of the lovers." Brown burned the manuscript.[30]

These exercises in historical fiction were as nothing in comparison to the work Brown began at about that same time and at which he appears to have labored through the remainder of his life. His "History of the Carrils" is one of the most ambitious and one of the most eccentric works to have come from the pen of an American author.[31]

The extent and nature of this strange and remarkable work have yet to be appreciated. Over 100,000 words survive in at least ten printed fragments.[32] Several of these are themselves composed of improperly articulated segments.[33] Nevertheless, when correctly assembled, these many fragments form a coherent, if incomplete, narrative. That no one has recognized this is due to Paul Allen and William Dunlap. Allen, apparently unable to make head or tail of Brown's unwieldy manuscript, began the process of obfuscation by selecting random fragments for inclusion in the "Life," a felony he then compounded by intermingling other fragments from wholly unrelated works.[34] When Dunlap assumed editorial responsibility for the *Life*, he discarded the extraneous materials Allen had introduced. The first of Allen's fragments—"Sketches of

Carsol"—Dunlap extended greatly, amending its title to "Sketches of a History of Carsol." The second of Allen's fragments he suppressed.[35] The third, fourth and fifth he preserved unchanged and himself added a sixth. Though Dunlap's editing was an improvement upon Allen's, he did not restore the fragments to their proper order. In another respect he contributed to the confusion: while recognizing the kinship among four of the fragments, he set off a fifth—the Carsol fragment—as if it were an unrelated work. In truth, the Carsol fragment is as much a part of the saga of the Carrils as any other.

Warner Berthoff was the first to recognize two essays which had appeared in the *Literary Magazine* in 1805—"A Specimen of Agricultural Improvement" and "Specimen of Political Improvement"—as additional fragments of the saga. "The Romance of Real Life," also in the *Literary Magazine*, is another. A manuscript fragment entitled "Don Manuel" may be still another.[36]

Taken together and properly ordered these many fragments tell the history of one family from the conversion of its patriarch by St. Paul in 67 A.D. until the time of writing. "No family," Brown wrote, "has made a more conspicuous and illustrious place in British annals than this."[37] Whether we have all of the "History" that Brown wrote is uncertain. There appears to be at least one important lacuna in the text: the story of "the great Arthur," "the British hero," "Arthur the king," who is often referred to but whose story is never told. Certainly the work is without a conclusion. Whether Brown had finished it, abandoned it, or was working on the Carrils's history still when he died seems impossible to know.

William Dunlap, Brown's friend and biographer, seems to have known nothing of the work prior to examining his friend's manuscripts. "Of the intention of the author of these Sketches," he declared, "I have no definite idea."[38] He could only marvel at his friend's "great work."[39]

In 1806, Brown had mentioned to Susan Linn, his sister-in-law, "a great book" on which he was then engaged. He had, he wrote, "undertaken to compose a great book, and have limited myself in my engagements with a bookseller, to one year, within which to complete it."[40] Whether Brown was referring to his history of the Carrils or, as seems more likely, his "Geography" one cannot know. Either, surely, would qualify.

Or perhaps he was referring to "a work on 'Rome during the Age of the Antonies,' similar to 'Anarcharsis' Travels in Greece," on which, according to one report, he had made "considerable progress" prior to his being taken ill.[41] There is no evidence to support this claim, but knowing Brown's interests and ambitions, it is not implausible.

With or without the "Age of the Antonies," those ten years following Brown's return to Philadelphia in 1800 were years of almost frenetic literary activity. The widely held belief that Brown's achievement as an author and his contribution to American letters began and ended with the two incredibly productive years he spent in New York in 1798-1800 is a consequence of a failure to see in Brown anything more than a popular novelist. Brown was more than that; he was a man of letters.

His *American Register* entitles him to a place among our pioneer historians, his political pamphlets ("An Address to the Congress" especially) qualify him as one of the early republic's most articulate political theorists. His translation of Volney suggests that his own "Geography" might have proved a monumental work. And there were, of course, the numerous essays and reviews—hundreds probably—he wrote for the *American Review* and the *Literary Magazine*. And then, too, there was that strange and eccentric history of the Carrils nothing like which had been attempted in English. In conception as bold as it was odd, it testifies to Brown's willingness to experiment with literary forms and thus gives new meaning to the description of Brown as a pioneer American novelist.

"A Sketch of the Life of General Horatio Gates" began in the November 1809 issue of the *Port Folio*. The editor acknowledged that "for the biography of General Gates . . . we are indebted to the splendid genius and indefatigable industry of a gentleman who, in our rivetted opinion, is in the very first rank of our authors. . . ."[42] The Sketch was continued, as promised, in the December issue. Instead of the final installment the January issue contained an announcement that "owing to the violent indisposition of one of our most valued correspondents, the conclusion of the interesting biography of General Gates is unavoidably postponed. . . ."[43] The Sketch was finally concluded in the February issue where the author appended the following apology: "Respect for the reader obliges the writer of the above performance to mention as an apology for some of its defects, that a greater part was written when sickness disabled him from consulting books or holding the pen."[44] Brown did not live to see it published. He died February 21, 1810, at the age of 39.

Notes

1. (1800), 37-39, 101-11. See also Charles E. Bennett, "The Charles Brockden Brown Canon," Diss. University of North Carolina, 1974, pp. 214-23.

2. MS ltr (July 8, 1802), Berg Collection, NYPL.

3. *Literary Magazine*, 1 (October 1803), 3-4.

4. 1 (1803-04), 100-04, 181-84, 255-59, 332-35, 412-16; 2(1804), 3-7, 89-93, 243-52; 3 (1804-05), 110-14, 210-14.

5. Bennett, "Brown Canon," p. 198.

6. Bennett, "Brown Canon," pp. 98-107.

7. MS ltr (November 21, 1806), Virginia.

8. *American Register*, 5(1808), iii.

9. *History of American Magazines, 1714-1850* (New York: Appleton, 1930), p. 222.

10. "Introduction," *Wieland* (New York: Harcourt, Brace, 1926), p. xxiv.

11. Randolph C. Randall, "Authors of the *Port Folio* Revealed by the Hall Files," *American Literature*, 11 (1940), 389.

12. 2 (June 19, 1802), 185–86.

13. *Literary Magazine*, 1 (October 1803), 3.

14. James E. Cronin, ed., *Diary of Elihu Hubbard Smith* (Philadelphia: American Philosophical Society, 1973), pp. 271–72.

15. *New York Evening Post* (January 8, 1803). Cited by Harry Warfel, *Charles Brockden Brown* (Gainesville: University of Florida Press, 1949), p. 206.

16. Jacob Blanck, *Bibliography of American Literature* (New Haven: Yale University Press, 1955), I, #1504. Blanck is cited here and elsewhere in notes to indicate location of Brown's work.

17. Blanck, #1505.

18. *New York Evening Post* (January 24, 1803).

19. *Aurora* (February 2, 1803).

20. Blanck, #1506.

21. Blanck, #1511. David Lee Clark (*Charles Brockden Brown* (Durham: Duke University Press, 1952), p. 261.) questioned Brown's authorship of the *British Treaty* on three grounds. The only one which might be considered to have any merit is his discovery of a copy of the pamphlet owned by Oliver Wolcott bearing the handwritten ascription "By Gouv. Morris, Esq." One is left to choose between an ascription perhaps by Wolcott of the pamphlet to Morris and one by Dunlap to Brown. Dunlap wrote less than eight years after the event; he wrote with Brown's journals, manuscripts and papers before him. He had been moreover in regular communication with Brown throughout the period. His attribution must therefore carry the greater weight.

22. Blanck, #1513.

23. MS ltr (March 16, 1803), Princeton.

24. Blanck, #1508.

25. Blanck, #1514.

26. For an account of the dealings between Elizabeth Brown and Paul Allen see Charles E. Bennett, "Introduction" to Paul Allen's *Life of Charles Brockden Brown* (Delmar: Scholars' Facsimiles and Reprints, 1975).

27. "Memoir of Charles Brockden Brown," *Wieland* (Boston: S. G. Goodrich, 1827), p. 19.

28. "Death of Cicero," in *Edgar Huntly*, III (Second Edition). See Blanck, #1499, 1500; "Thessalonica," *Monthly Magazine*, 1 (1799), 99–117.

29. This was not Brown's first attempt at a play. In 1799 he had attempted a dramatic adaptation of Bage's *Hermsprong*.

30. John Bernard, *Retrospections of America, 1797–1811* (New York: Harper and Brothers, 1887), pp. 254–55.

31. The name Brown intended is almost certainly Carrol not Carril. Paul Allen had transcribed Brown's MS for inclusion in his abortive biography. If he transcribed the MS fragments in the same order in which he printed them, and nothing else will account for their order, his first encounter with the name came in this passage: "By the marriage of this heiress to Arthur Carrol, a third son of Carrol, lord of Halloway, and Lodowick in England, a new line was established" (Allen, p. 173). Carrol. That Allen had difficulty in reading Brown's vowels is attested by the fact that on the next two occurrences of the name he wrote it Carrel (Allen, pp. 179, 188.). Only on its fourth occurrence, and thereafter, did he spell it Carril. He also spelt the name of the Breton family with whom the Carrils are allied as Martil but then allowed that they were descended from Charles Martel. Brown then intended to relate the

history of the Carrols and their kin the Martels—not, as Allen would have it, the Carrils and Martils. Rather than generate additional confusion I have continued to use the spellings now commonly accepted.

32. The fragments appear in:
  I Allen/Dunlap *Life*, pp. 170–222.
  II William Dunlap, *The Life of Charles Brockden Brown* (Philadelphia: James P. Parke, 1815) pp. 223–58.
  III Allen *Life*, pp. 242–62.
  IV Allen/Dunlap *Life*, pp. 262–99.
  V Allen/Dunlap *Life*, pp. 299–322.
  VI Allen/Dunlap *Life*, pp. 322–58.
  VII Dunlap *Life*, pp. 359–96.
  VIII "Specimen of Agricultural Improvement," *Literary Magazine*, 3 (1805), 86–93.
  IX "Specimen of Political Improvement," *Literary Magazine*, 3 (1805), 120–28, 201–05, 214–25.
  X "Romance of Real Life," *Literary Magazine*, 4 (1805), 392–96.

33. Fragment III, for example, appears to consist of five separate and incorrectly articulated segments: pp. 222–46, 246–49, 249–51, 251–52, 252–62.

34. The fragments given on pp. 222–42 and 359–87 are actually portions of Brown's "Ellendale" novel written in 1795–97.

35. For the reasons Dunlap did so see the "Introduction" to Paul Allen's *Life of Charles Brockden Brown*, edited by Charles E. Bennett (Delmar: Scholars' Facsimiles & Reprints, 1975).

36. "Don Manuel" is the title of a 32-page MS among the Brown papers in the collection of the Humanities Research Center at the University of Texas. It forms part of the collection that David Lee Clark had obtained from Brown's descendants. There is a difference of opinion as to whether the handwriting is Brown's. I think it is. "Don Manuel," moreover, tells the story of Victoria, countess of Modena. According to the Dunlap text (*Life*, I, 374), "Ferrara, Modina and Reggio have continued, with little permanent alteration in this branch of the Carril family till the beginning of the nineteenth century." The lady being the countess of Modena and Modena being a principality of the Carrils, the Countess of Modena ought to be a Carril. The work, then, must be Brown's. The narrative thread cannot however be otherwise tied to the known fragments of the Carril history. The narrative voice, too, it should be noted, is quite different.

37. *Life*, I, 346.

38. *Life*, I, 169.

39. *Life*, I, 169.

40. *Life*, II, 115–16.

41. "Memoir of Charles Brockden Brown," *Wieland* (Boston: S. G. Goodrich, 1827), p. 19.

42. 3rd Ser., 2 (1809), 577.

43. 3rd Ser., 3 (1810), 80.

44. 3rd Ser., 3 (1810), 108.

Selective Bibliography of Writings about Charles Brockden Brown

Charles A. Carpenter

The following checklist of commentary on Charles Brockden Brown is intended for the use of everyone embarking on a study of Brown's life and work. As far as I have been able to determine, here are the books, articles, chapters, and (rarely) passages that discuss Brown in a substantial, significant, or at least highly interesting manner.

The bibliography is at once comprehensive and selective. That is, it derives from a full-fledged search for material about Brown and a scrutiny of that material to decide what not to include. The search has been aided considerably by the 1966 checklist of Robert E. Hemenway and Dean H. Keller (see I), the only previous attempt at a full secondary bibliography prior to the very recently published annotated work by Patricia Parker, *Charles Brockden Brown: A Reference Guide* (Boston: G. K. Hall & Co., 1980). The deliberately non-selective list of Hemenway and Keller includes many items—over half of the 278, in fact—which seemed too sketchy or remote to repeat here. But their work still served as the indispensable basis for the present selective list. I have supplemented and updated it by consulting a wide range of bibliographical tools. In an attempt to cover the ground (it is of course impossible to leave no stone unturned), I have checked all the standard sources of literary bibliography, including several of foreign origin, plus a great many indexes to periodicals and parts of books that are little known and less used.[1] I have also combed likely areas of the bookshelves in the Yale, Cornell, and Texas libraries. Finally, I checked my preliminary list against the opulent file of offprints at Kent State University, maintained by Sydney J. Krause. Though an appalling omission or two will no doubt turn up, the list represents a concerted effort at genuine comprehensiveness.

The process of deciding what not to include involved a not-too-

Notes

1. Three examples: The WPA project entitled *Literary Writings in America: A Bibliography* (see I), the *Index to Writings on American History 1902-1940*, and the *Bibliographie der fremdsprachigen Zeitschriftenliteratur*, 1911-1962.

stringent application of two main criteria: Is the commentary of interest and value to more than advanced Brown specialists, and does it say something distinctive? Virtually all short reviews, summaries, and overviews of Brown therefore do not appear (Hemenway and Keller list most of them), but virtually all items that merit the terms "criticism" or "scholarship" (whatever their quality) do appear. Also included are the relatively insubstantial but fascinating utterances of such people as Keats, Shelley, Cooper, Poe, and Margaret Fuller. A few items escaped exclusion mainly because they did not appear in Hemenway-Keller or in any standard literary bibliography. A much more selective treatment of the literature on Brown, and an excellent springboard for Brown studies, is Paul Witherington's bibliographical essay in *Early American Literature* for 1974 (See I).

The ensuing checklist is arranged for the convenience of the user. After a bibliographical section, it lists biographical material in part II and critical material in parts III and IV. Part III: Critical Works, General and Miscellaneous has three subdivisions, roughly marking the chief phases of Brown studies: Nineteenth Century Commentaries; Critical Studies, 1900–1944; and Critical Studies, 1945–1979. Part IV: Studies of Individual Works has subdivisions for each novel (alphabetically ordered) and a final section, Other Works. Unlike Hemenway-Keller, I have tried to give enough bibliographical information—chapter titles, paging, clarifying annotations—for the user to decide whether to pursue an item further. Virtually every item has been verified.

Abbreviations of Journals

AL   *American Literature*
DA   *Dissertation Abstracts*
DAI   *Dissertation Abstracts International*
EAL   *Early American Literature*
ESQ   *Emerson Society Quarterly*
PMLA   *Publications of the Modern Language Association*

I. Bibliographical Works (an asterisk denotes "most valuable")

*Bennett, Charles E. "The Charles Brockden Brown Canon." *DAI*, 35 (1974), 3670A

*———. "The Letters of Charles Brockden Brown: An Annotated Census." *Resources for American Literary Study*, 6 (1976), 164–90

Blakey, Dorothy. *The Minerva Press, 1790–1820*. London: Bibliographical Society, Oxford Univ. Press, 1939 [for 1935]. 339 pp. (passim)

Blanck, Jacob. "Charles Brockden Brown, 1771–1810." *Bibliography of American Literature*. New Haven: Yale Univ. Press, 1955, I, 302–9

Frank, Frederick S. "The Gothic Novel: A Checklist of Modern Criticism." *Bulletin of Bibliography*, 30 (1973), 45–54

*Hemenway, Robert E., and Dean H. Keller. "Charles Brockden Brown, America's First Important Novelist: A Check List of Biography and Criticism." *Papers of the Bibliographical Society of America*, 60 (1966), 349–62

Howard, Patsy C. *Theses in American Literature 1896–1971.* Ann Arbor, Mich.: Pierian Press, 1973, 15–16 (lists 26 M.A. theses)

Katz, Joseph. "Analytical Bibliography and Literary History: The Writing and Printing of *Wieland.*" *Proof,* 1 (1971), 8–34

Kimball, Leroy Elwood. "An Account of Hocquet Caritat, XVIII Century New York Circulating Librarian, Bookseller, and Publisher of the First Two Novels of Charles Brockden Brown, 'America's First Professional Man of Letters.' " *Colophon,* 18 (1934), n.p. (12-page article; 3 pages on CBB)

*Krause, Sydney J., with the assistance of Jane Nieset. "A Census of the Works of Charles Brockden Brown." *Serif,* 3, iv (1966), 27–55 (locates editions in American libraries)

———. "Charles Brockden Brown." *Center for Editions of American Authors Newsletter,* 1 (1968), 13–14 (available editions and manuscripts)

Literary History of the United States: Bibliography, ed. Robert E. Spiller et al. 4th ed. rev. New York: Macmillan, 1974, 417–19, 879, 1153

Literary Writings in America: A Bibliography. Millwood, N.Y.: KTO Press, 1977, 1427–33 (items by and about CBB to 1940)

Parma, V. Valta. "The Rare Book Collection of the Library of Congress." *Colophon,* 7 (1931), n.p. (one page describes its CBB holdings)

Raddin, George G. "Charles Brockden Brown." *Hocquet Caritat and the Early New York Literary Scene.* Dover, N.J.: Dover Advance Press, 1953, 50–60; see also Raddin, *The New York of Hocquet Caritat and His Associates, 1797–1817.* Dover, N.J.: Dover Advance Press, 1953

Reid, S. W. "Brockden Brown in England: Notes on Henry Colburn's 1822 Editions of His Novels." *EAL,* 9 (1974), 188–95

Schneider, Evelyn S. ". . . II. The Changing Image of Charles Brockden Brown as Seen by American Critics from 1815 to the Present. . . ." *DAI,* 32 (1972), 6943A (second part of a three-part diss.)

Ward, William S. "American Authors and British Reviewers 1798–1826: A Bibliography." *AL,* 49 (1977), 1–21 (CBB reviews, 5–6)

———. "Charles Brockden Brown, His Contemporary British Reviewers, and Two Minor Bibliographical Problems." *Papers of the Bibliographical Society of America,* 65 (1971), 399–402

Wells, Daniel A. "An Index to American Writers and Selected British Writers in Duyckinck's *Literary World,* 1847–1853." Pp. 259–78 of *Studies in the American Renaissance, 1978,* ed. Joel Myerson. Boston: Twayne, 1978 (7 references to CBB on p. 262)

*Witherington, Paul. "Charles Brockden Brown: A Bibliographical Essay." *EAL,* 9 (1974) 164–87

II. Biographical Works

Allen, Paul. *The Life of Charles Brockden Brown: A Facsimile Reproduction,* ed. Charles E. Bennett. Delmar, N.Y.: Scholars' Facsimiles and Reprints, 1975. 391 pp. (introduction, v–xxxiv)

———. *The Late Charles Brockden Brown,* ed. Robert E. Hemenway and Joseph Katz. Columbia, S.C.: Faust, 1976. 396 pp. (introduction, xiii–lx; both editions reproduce the unique copy of this work, entitled simply *Biography,* housed at the Pennsylvania Historical Society)

Bernard, John. *Retrospections of America, 1797–1811.* New York: Harper, 1887, 250–55 (not 350–55 as in index)

Charvat, William. "The Beginnings of Professionalism." *The Profession of Authorship in America, 1800–1870,* ed. Matthew J. Bruccoli. Columbus: Ohio State Univ. Press, 1968, 5–28; on CBB, 24–28

Clark, David Lee. *Charles Brockden Brown, Pioneer Voice of America.* Durham: Duke Univ. Press, 1952. 363 pp.; reprint, AMS Press, 1966 (pp. 162–85 discuss the novels)

————, ed. "Unpublished Letters of Charles Brockden Brown and W. W. Wilkens." *Studies in English, Univ. of Texas,* 27, i (1948), 75–107

Cole, Charles C. "Brockden Brown and the Jefferson Administration." *Pennsylvania Magazine of History and Biography,* 72 (1948), 253–63

Dunlap, William. *The Life of Charles Brockden Brown: Together with Selections from the Rarest of His Printed Works, from His Original Letters, and from His Manuscripts Before Unpublished.* Phila.: James P. Parke, 1815. 2 vols.; abridged as *Memoirs of Charles Brockden Brown, the American Novelist.* London: Colburn, 1822

————. *Diary of William Dunlap (1766–1839).* New York: New York Historical Society, 1930. 3 vols. (see index)

Ellis, Harold Milton. *Joseph Dennie and His Circle: A Study in American Literature from 1792 to 1812.* New York: AMS Press, 1971. 285 pp.; reprint of *Bulletin of the Univ. of Texas: Studies in English,* No. 3, 1915 (see index)

Hemenway, Robert E. "Charles Brockden Brown's Law Study: Some New Documents." *AL,* 39 (1967), 199–204 (a letter and a page from a diary)

[Kennedy, Daniel Edwards.] Robert E. Hemenway. "Daniel Edwards Kennedy's Manuscript Biography of Charles Brockden Brown." *Serif,* 3, iv (1966), 16–18; see also Roger E. Stoddard. "Daniel Edwards Kennedy, a Forgotten Collector of Charles Brockden Brown and Early American Literature." *Serif,* 3, iv (1966), 11–16

"Memoir of Charles Brockden Brown." Pp. 3–22 of CBB *Wieland, or the Transformation.* Phila.: McKay, 1887

Mott, Frank Luther. "*The Monthly Magazine, and American Review,* and Its Successors Under the Editorship of Charles Brockden Brown." *A History of American Magazines, 1741–1850.* New York: Appleton, 1930, 218–22; see also index

Oberholtzer, Ellis P. *The Literary History of Philadelphia.* Phila.: Jacobs, 1906, 157–67; see also Joseph Jackson. "Charles Brockden Brown, 1771–1810." *Literary Landmarks of Philadelphia.* Phila.: McKay, 1939, 41–44

Peden, William. "Thomas Jefferson and Charles Brockden Brown." *Maryland Quarterly* (Briarcliff Manor), 2 (1944), 65–68 (correspondence)

Prescott, William Hickling. "Memoir of Charles Brockden Brown, the American Novelist." *Biographical and Critical Miscellanies.* New York: Harper, 1845, 1–56; reprinted from *The Library of American Biography,* ed. Jared Sparks, Vol. I [first series]. Boston: Hilliard, Gray, 1838, 117–80

Smith, Elihu Hubbard. *The Diary of Elihu Hubbard Smith (1771–1798),* ed. James E. Cronin. Phila.: American Philosophical Society, 1973. 481 pp.; see also Cronin. "Elihu Hubbard Smith and the New York Friendly Club." *PMLA,* 64 (1949), 471–79

Smyth, Albert H. *The Philadelphia Magazines and Their Contributors 1741–1850.* Phila.: Lindsay, 1892, 152–70 (pp. 154–63 print the text of "The Editor's Address to the Public," from the *Literary Magazine and American Register*)

Stearns, Bertha Monica. "A Speculation Concerning Charles Brockden Brown." *Pennsylvania Magazine of History and Biography,* 59 (1935), 99–105 (did he help launch two ladies' magazines?)

Warfel, Harry R. *Charles Brockden Brown, American Gothic Novelist.* Gainesville: Univ. of

Florida Press, 1949. 255 pp.; Warfel has also issued "Footnotes to *Charles Brockden Brown* . . . ," 12 sheets annotating and sometimes correcting statements in his book

Woodberry, George Edward. "Charles Brockden Brown." *Literary Memoirs of the Nineteenth Century*. New York: Harcourt, Brace, 1921, 275–82

III. Critical Works: General and Miscellaneous

A. Nineteenth Century Commentaries

"American Novels [Review of CBB's major novels]." *British Critic*, 2 (1826), 53–78

Beers, Henry A. *An Outline Sketch of American Literature*. New York: Hunt & Eaton, 1896, 79–82; also in his *Initial Studies in American Letters* (1895) and its reprint, *Studies in American Letters* (1900), 64–66

"The British Treaty." *Monthly Anthology and Boston Review*, 4 (1807), 563–70 (retort to CBB's pamphlet)

"Charles Brockden Brown." *American Review: A Whig Journal Devoted to Politics and Literature*, 7 (1848), 260–74 (on *Wieland*)

Cooper, James Fenimore. "Preface." *The Spy*. 2nd ed. New York: Wiley and Halstead, 1822, v–x (refers to *Edgar Huntly* on vi)

Dana, Richard Henry. "The Novels of Charles Brockden Brown." *Poems and Prose Writings*. New York: Baker and Scribner, 1850, II, 325–43; reprinted from *United States Review and Literary Gazette*, 2 (1827), 321–33

Fuller [Ossoli], Margaret. "Charles Brockden Brown." *The Writings of Margaret Fuller*, ed. Mason Wade. New York: Viking, 1941, 377–80; a review of *Ormond* reprinted from *Papers on Literature and Art* (1846), reprinted as *Literature and Art* (1852)

Griswold, Rufus Wilmot. "Charles Brockden Brown." *The Prose Writers of America*. Phila.: Carey and Hart, 1849, 107–20

Hazlitt, William. [Review of William Ellery Channing's *Sermons and Tracts*.] *Edinburgh Review*, 50 (Oct. 1829), 125–44 (125–28 on CBB); reprinted in Hazlitt. *Complete Works, Volume 16: Contributions to the Edinburgh Review*, ed. P. P. Howe. London: Dent, 1933; reprint, AMS Press, 1967 (318–20 on CBB)

[Irving, Washington.] Stanley T. Williams. *The Life of Washington Irving*. New York: Oxford Univ. Press, 1935. 2 vols. (see index)

Keats, John. *Letters, 1814–1821*, ed. Hyder Edward Rollins. Cambridge, Mass.: Harvard Univ. Press, 1958, II, 173

"The Life of Charles Brockden Brown . . . by William Dunlap. . . ." *North American Review*, 9 (1819), 58–77. *Poole's Index to Periodical Literature, 1802–81* (1891) cites Gulian C. Verplanck as the review's author, but it has also been ascribed to E. T. Channing. The latter is cited as the author by William Cushing, *Index to the North American Review* (Cambridge, Mass.: Press of John Wilson and Son, 1878), reprinted in *Research Keys to the American Renaissance*, ed. Kenneth Walter Cameron (Hartford: Transcendental Books, 1967). p. 91. Both Channing and Verplanck are plausible candidates for authorship, and on the basis of evidence available I refrain from choosing between them.

Lippard, George. "The Heart-Broken." *Nineteenth Century* (Phila.), 1 (Jan. 1848), 19–27 (tribute to the neglected CBB)

[Longfellow, Henry Wadsworth.] Lawrance Thompson. *Young Longfellow (1807–1843)*. New York: Macmillan, 1938, 44–45 (his reaction to *Arthur Mervyn*)

McCowan, Jo. S. "Our First Novelist." *Sewanee Review*, 4 (1896), 174–80

Mitchell, Donald G. *American Lands and Letters: The Mayflower to Rip-Van-Winkle.* New York: Scribner's, 1897, 179–90

Neal, John. *American Writers: A Series of Papers Contributed to Blackwood's Magazine (1824–1825),* ed. Fred Lewis Pattee. Durham: Duke Univ. Press, 1937, 56–68 (from *Bl. Mag.,* 16 [Oct. 1824], 415–28), 213–15, 238–41

Nichol, John. *American Literature: An Historical Sketch, 1620–1880.* Edinburgh: Adam and Charles Black, 1882, 157–62

"The Novels of Charles Brockden Brown." *American Quarterly Review,* 8 (1830), 312–37

"The Novels of Charles Brockden Brown. . . ." *Western Monthly Review,* 1 (1827), 483–94

"On the Writings of Charles Brown, the American Novelist." *New Monthly Magazine and Universal Register,* 14 (1820), 609–17

Phillips, E. L. "The Earliest American Novelist." *Cornell Magazine,* 2 (1890), 200–204

Poe, Edgar Allan. "Marginalia." *Complete Works,* ed. James A. Harrison. New York: G. D. Sproul, 1902, XVI, 41

R., A. "Critique on the Writings of Charles B. Brown." *Port Folio,* 6 (1811), 30–35

[Review of *Jane Talbot.*] *Imperial Review, or London and Dublin Literary Journal,* 3 (1804), 392–401

[Scott, Walter.] Tremaine McDowell. "Scott on Cooper and Brockden Brown." *Modern Language Notes,* 45 (1930), 18–20

[Shelley, Percy Bysshe.] Thomas Love Peacock. *Memoirs of Shelley,* ed. H. F. B. Brett-Smith. London: Henry Frowde, 1909, 35–37

Smith, George Barnett. "Brockden Brown." *Fortnightly Review,* 30 (1878), 399–421

Tuckerman, Henry T. "The Supernaturalist: Charles Brockden Brown." *Mental Portraits.* London: Bentley, 1853, 271–86; also in his *Essays, Biographical and Critical.* Boston: Phillips, Sampson, 1857, 369–78; reprinted, pp. 58–66 of *American Romanticism: A Shape for Fiction,* ed. Stanley Bank. New York: Putnam's, 1969

Vail, Eugène A. *De la littérature et des hommes de lettres des États-Unis d'Amérique.* Paris: Charles Gosselin, 1841, 478–89

Warner, Charles Dudley. *Washington Irving.* Boston: Houghton, Mifflin, 1881, 10–16

Whittier, John Greenleaf. "Fanaticism." *Writings,* Vol. VIII. Cambridge, Mass.: Riverside Press, 1888, 391–95 (on *Wieland*)

"*Wieland, or the Transformation . . .*" *American Review and Literary Journal,* 1 (1801), 333–39; 2 (1802), 28–38

B. Critical Studies, 1900–1944

"American Pioneer Prose Masters: Charles Brockden Brown." *Mentor,* 4 (1 May 1916), 16–34 (not verified)

Angoff, Charles. "Charles Brockden Brown." *A Literary History of the American People. Volume Two: From 1750 to 1815.* New York: Knopf, 1931, 319–25

Birkhead, Edith. *The Tale of Terror: A Study of the Gothic Romance.* London: Constable, 1921, 197–200

Blake, Warren Barton. "Brockden Brown and the Novel." *Sewanee Review,* 18 (1910), 431–43

Boynton, Percy H. "Charles Brockden Brown." *A History of American Literature.* Boston: Ginn, 1919, 100–108

Bronson, Walter C. *A Short History of American Literature.* Boston: Heath, 1900, 94–101

Brooks, Van Wyck. *The World of Washington Irving.* Phila.: Blakiston, 1944, 22–26 and passim

Clark, David Lee. *Brockden Brown and the Rights of Women.* Austin: Univ. of Texas Bulletin, No. 2212, 1922. 48 pp.; reprint, Folcroft Library Editions, 1973

Coad, Oral Sumner. "The Gothic Element in American Literature Before 1835." *Journal of English and Germanic Philology,* 24 (1925), 72–93 (80–82 on CBB)

Erskine, John. "Charles Brockden Brown." *Leading American Novelists.* New York: Holt, 1910, 3–49

Fricke, Max. *Charles Brockden Brown's Leben und Werke.* Hamburg: Meissner, 1911. 95 pp. (diss.)

Haviland, Thomas P. "Preciosité Crosses the Atlantic." *PMLA,* 59 (1944), 131–41 (the indebtedness of William Hill Brown and CBB to French Heroic Romance)

Higginson, Thomas Wentworth. "Charles Brockden Brown." *Carlyle's Laugh, and Other Surprises.* Boston: Houghton Mifflin, 1909, 57–64; derived from *A Reader's History of American Literature,* by Higginson and Henry W. Boynton. Boston: Houghton Mifflin, 1903, 69–78

Hintz, Howard W. "Charles Brockden Brown." *The Quaker Influence in American Literature.* New York: Revell, 1940, 33–40

Just, Walter. *Die romantische Bewegung in der amerikanischen Literatur: Brown, Poe, Hawthorne: Ein Beitrag zur Geschichte der Romantik.* Berlin: Mayer & Müller, 1910. 93 pp. (passim)

Keiser, Albert. "Fiction Discovers the Native." *The Indian in American Literature.* New York: Oxford Univ. Press, 1933, 33–37

Loshe, Lillie Deming. *The Early American Novel.* New York: Columbia Univ. Press, 1907, 29–51

Marble, Annie. "Charles Brockden Brown and Pioneers in Fiction." *Heralds of American Literature.* Chicago: Univ. of Chicago Press, 1907, 279–318; see also her "The Centenary of America's First Novelist." *Dial,* 48 (16 Feb. 1910), 109–10

Marchand, Ernest. "The Literary Opinions of Charles Brockden Brown." *Studies in Philology,* 31 (1934), 541–66

Oberholtzer, Ellis Paxson. "The First American Novelist." *Journal of American History* (New Haven), 1 (1907), 236–40

Pattee, Fred Lewis. "Charles Brockden Brown." *The First Century of American Literature, 1770–1870.* New York: Appleton-Century, 1935, 96–106

Quinn, Arthur Hobson. "Charles Brockden Brown and the Establishment of Romance." *American Fiction: An Historical and Critical Survey.* New York: Appleton-Century, 1936, 25–39

Sickels, Eleanor. "Shelley and Charles Brockden Brown." *PMLA,* 45 (1930), 1116–28 (Shelley's specific indebtedness to CBB)

Smith, Bernard. *Forces in American Criticism: A Study in the History of American Literary Thought.* New York: Harcourt, Brace, 1939, 14–18

Snell, George. "Charles Brockden Brown: Apocalyptic." *The Shapers of American Fiction, 1798–1947.* 2nd ed. New York: Cooper Square, 1961, 32–45 (essay same as in 1947 edition; derived from *University of Kansas City Review,* 4 [1944], 131–38)

Solve, Melvin T. "Shelley and the Novels of Brown." Pp. 141–56 of *Fred Newton Scott Anniversary Papers.* Chicago: Univ. of Chicago Press, 1929

Van Doren, Carl. *The American Novel, 1789–1939.* Rev. ed. New York: Macmillan, 1940, 10–14

———. "Fiction I: Brown, Cooper." Pp. 284–306 of *The Cambridge History of American Literature,* Vol. I. New York: Putnam's, 1917 (pp. 287–92 on CBB)

Vilas, Martin Samuel. *Charles Brockden Brown: A Study of Early American Fiction.* Burlington, Vt.: Free Press Association, 1904. 66 pp.; reprints, Folcroft Library Editions, 1973; Norwood Editions, 1976; R. West, 1977

Warfel, Harry R. "Charles Brockden Brown's German Sources." *Modern Language Quarterly*, 1 (1940), 357–65

Wendell, Barrett. "Charles Brockden Brown." *A Literary History of America*. New York: Scribner's, 1931, 157–68

C. Critical Studies, 1945–1979

Bell, Michael Davitt. " 'The Double-Tongued Deceiver': Sincerity and Duplicity in the Novels of Charles Brockden Brown." *EAL*, 9 (1974), 143–63

Bernard, Kenneth. "Charles Brockden Brown." Pp. 1–9 of *Minor American Novelists*, ed. Charles A. Hoyt. Carbondale: Southern Illinois Univ. Press, 1971

–––––. "Charles Brockden Brown and the Sublime." *Personalist*, 45 (1964), 235–49 (*Edgar Huntly* is the chief example)

–––––. "The Novels of Charles Brockden Brown: Studies in Meaning." *DA*, 23 (1962), 1008

Berthoff, Warner B. "Brockden Brown: The Politics of the Man of Letters." *Serif*, 3, iv (1966), 3–11

Bulgheroni, Marisa. *La tentazione della chimera: Charles Brockden Brown e le origini del romanzo americano*. Rome: Storia e Letteratura, 1965. 275 pp.

Butler, David L. *Dissecting a Human Heart: A Study of Style in the Novels of Charles Brockden Brown*. Washington, D.C.: Univ. Press of America, 1978. 130 pp.

Chase, Richard. "Brockden Brown's Melodramas." *The American Novel and Its Tradition*. Garden City, N.Y.: Doubleday, 1957, 29–41

Clark, David Lee. *Charles Brockden Brown* [see II, above], 162–85

Cleman, John. "Ambiguous Evil: A Study of Villains and Heroes in Charles Brockden Brown's Major Novels." *EAL*, 10 (1975), 190–219

Cowie, Alexander. "Vaulting Ambition: Brockden Brown and Others." *The Rise of the American Novel*. New York: American Book Co., 1948, 69–114 (69–104 on CBB); see also his "The Beginnings of Fiction and Drama." Pp. 177–91 of *Literary History of the United States*, ed. Robert E. Spiller et al. 4th ed. rev. New York: Macmillan, 1974 (181–84 on CBB)

Coyle, James John. "The Problem of Evil in the Major Novels of Charles Brockden Brown." *DA*, 21 (1961), 3780

Craft, Commodore. "A Study of the Interaction of Good and Evil in the Four Major Novels of Charles Brockden Brown." *DAI*, 37 (1977), 6483A

Craft, Harvey Milton. "The Opposition of Mechanistic and Organic Thought in the Major Novels of Charles Brockden Brown." *DA*, 25 (1965), 5926

Cunningham, Judith A. "Charles Brockden Brown's Pursuit of a Realistic Feminism: A Study of His Writings as a Contribution to the Growth of Women's Rights in America." *DAI*, 32 (1972), 4558A

Elliott, Emory B. "Charles Brockden Brown." Pp. 124–49 of *American Writers: A Collection of Literary Biographies. Supplement I*. New York: Scribner's, 1979

Fiedler, Leslie A. *Love and Death in the American Novel*. Rev. ed. New York: Stein and Day, 1966, 98–104, 145–61

Flanders, Jane Townend. "Charles Brockden Brown and William Godwin: Parallels and Divergences." *DA*, 26 (1965), 3334–35

Frank, Frederick S. "Perverse Pilgrimage: The Role of the Gothic in the Works of Charles

Brockden Brown, Edgar Allan Poe, and Nathaniel Hawthorne." *DA*, 29 (1968), 1866A–67A

Harap, Louis. *The Image of the Jew in American Literature from Early Republic to Mass Immigration*. Phila.: Jewish Publication Society of America, 1974, 40–44

Hayne, Barrie Stewart. "The Divided Self: The Alter Ego as Theme and Device in Brockden Brown, Hawthorne and James." Diss., Harvard Univ., 1964 (not in *DA*)

Hedges, William. "Charles Brockden Brown and the Culture of Contradictions." *EAL*, 9 (1974), 107–42

Hemenway, Robert E. "Fiction in the Age of Jefferson: The Early American Novel as Intellectual Document." *Midcontinent American Studies Journal*, 9 (Spring 1968), 91–102

―――. "The Novels of Charles Brockden Brown: A Critical Study." *DA*, 28 (1967), 676A

Hilton, William C. "The Triumph of the Conservative Unconscious in the Novels of Charles Brockden Brown." *DA*, 29 (1968), 230A

Hirsch, David H. "Brown: Ideas and Ideologies." *Reality and Idea in the Early American Novel*. The Hague: Mouton, 1971, 74–100

Hoekstra, Ellen L. J. "The Characterization of Women in the Novels of Charles Brockden Brown." *DAI*, 36 (1976), 8059A

Hume, Robert D. "Charles Brockden Brown and the Uses of Gothicism: A Reassessment." *ESQ*, no. 66 (1972), 10–18

Izzo, Carlo. "Charles Brockden Brown: Un maestro di brividi settecentesco." *Civiltà americana*. Rome: Storia e Letteratura, 1967, I, 13–22; rev. version of an essay in his *Storia della letteratura nord-americana*. Milan: Nuova Accademia, 1957, 165–71

Keshian, Charles G. "The Political Character of the Novels of Charles Brockden Brown." Diss., Univ. of California at Berkeley, 1973 (not in *DAI*)

Kimball, Arthur G. *Rational Fictions: A Study of Charles Brockden Brown*. McMinnville, Ore.: Linfield Research Institute, 1968. 238 pp. (on the four major novels, especially *Wieland*)

―――. "Savages and Savagism: Brockden Brown's Dramatic Irony." *Studies in Romanticism*, 6 (1967), 214–25 (stresses *Edgar Huntly*)

Kinslow, Kenneth J. "Quaker Doctrines and Ideas in the Novels of Charles Brockden Brown." *DAI*, 39 (1978), 2938A–39A

Levine, Paul. "The American Novel Begins." *American Scholar*, 35 (1966), 134–48

Limprecht, Nancy S. "Repudiating the Self-Justifying Fiction: C. B. Brown, N. Hawthorne, and H. Melville as Anti-Romancers." *DAI*, 39 (1978), 886A

McAlexander, Patricia J. "Sexual Morality in the Fiction of Charles Brockden Brown: Index to a Personal and Cultural Debate Regarding Passion and Reason." *DAI*, 34 (1974), 6597A

McCay, Mary Ann D. "Women in the Novels of Charles Brockden Brown: A Study." *DAI*, 35 (1974), 3692A

Nelson, Carl W. "The Novels of Charles Brockden Brown: Irony and Illusion." *DAI*, 32 (1971), 392A

Nye, Russel B. "The Early Novel: Charles Brockden Brown's American Gothic." *American Literary History: 1607–1830*. New York: Knopf, 1970, 241–44

Pease, Marilyn T. "The Novels of Charles Brockden Brown: Studies in the Rise of Consciousness." *DA*, 28 (1968), 4140A

Petter, Henri. *The Early American Novel*. Columbus: Ohio State Univ. Press, 1971, 174–77, 192–96, 334–60

Riese, Teut. "Charles Brockden Brown." *Das englische Erbe in der amerikanischen Literatur:*

Studien zur Entstehungsgeschichte des amerikanischen Selbstbewusstseins im Zietalter Washingtons und Jeffersons. Bochum-Langendreer: Pöppinghaus, 1958, 118–38

Ringe, Donald A. *Charles Brockden Brown.* New York: Twayne, 1966. 158 pp.

———. "Charles Brockden Brown." Pp. 273–94 of *Major Writers of Early American Literature*, ed. Everett Emerson. Madison: Univ. of Wisconsin Press, 1972

———. "Early American Gothic: Brown, Dana and Allston." *American Transcendental Quarterly*, 19, i–ii (1973), 3–8 (mostly on CBB)

Schulz, Max F. "Brockden Brown: An Early Casualty of the American Experience." Pp. 81–90 of *Americana-Austriaca: Beiträge zur Amerikakunde*, ed. Klaus Lanzinger. Vienna: Braumüller, 1970, II, 81–90

Shapiro, Morton. "Sentimentalism in the Novels of Charles Brockden Brown." *DA*, 27 (1966), 1384A–85A

Slanina, Ann M. "The Development of Charles Brockden Brown's Literary Ideas: A Study of His Major Novels." *DAI*, 37 (1976), 2187A–88A

Smith, Allan Gardner. "Nineteenth-Century Psychology in the Fiction of Charles Brockden Brown, Edgar Allan Poe and Nathaniel Hawthorne." *DAI*, 35 (1975), 7880A–81A

Tomlinson, David Otis. "Women in the Writing of Charles Brockden Brown: A Study in the Development of an Author's Thought." *DAI*, 35 (1975), 5431A

Tricomi, Elizabeth T. "The Search for Knowledge in the Major Novels of Charles Brockden Brown." *DAI*, 31 (1971), 5430A

Ullmer, R. John. "The Quaker Influence in the Novels of Charles Brockden Brown." *DAI*, 30 (1969), 1577A–78A

Warfel, Harry R. *Charles Brockden Brown* [see II, above], 78–164

Weber, Alfred. "Charles Brockden Browns Theorie der Geschichtsschreibung und des Romans." Pp. 15–41 of *Geschichte und Fiktion: Amerikanische Prosa im 19. Jahrhundert*, ed. Alfred Weber and Hartmut Grandel. Göttingen: Vandenhoeck & Ruprecht, 1972

Wiley, Lulu R. *Sources and Influence of the Novels of Charles Brockden Brown.* New York: Vantage Press, 1950. 381 pp.

Witherington, Paul. "Benevolence and the 'Utmost Stretch': Charles Brockden Brown's Narrative Dilemma." *Criticism*, 14 (1972), 175–91

———. "Narrative Technique in the Novels of Charles Brockden Brown." *DA*, 25 (1964), 2992

IV. Studies of Individual Works

A. *Alcuin*

Edwards, Lee R. "Afterword." Pp. 92–104 of CBB. *Alcuin: A Dialogue*, ed. Edwards. New York: Grossman, 1971

Kimball, LeRoy Elwood. "Introduction." Pp. vii–xxi of CBB. *Alcuin: A Dialogue: A Type-Facsimile Reprint of the First Edition Printed in 1798.* New Haven, Conn.: C. and M. Rollins, 1935

Rice, Nancy. "*Alcuin.*" *Massachusetts Review*, 14 (1973), 802–14

Violette, Augusta Genevieve. "Charles Brockden Brown: The Dialogues of Alcuin, 1798." *Economic Feminism in American Literature Prior to 1848.* Orono, Me.: Univ. Press, 1925; reprint, Burt Franklin, 1971, 38–50

Warfel, Harry R. *Charles Brockden Brown* [see II, above], 78–95

B. Arthur Mervyn

Bernard, Kenneth. "*Arthur Mervyn:* The Ordeal of Innocence." *Texas Studies in Literature and Language*, 6 (1965), 441–59

Berthoff, Warner B. "Adventures of the Young Man: An Approach to Charles Brockden Brown." *American Quarterly*, 9 (1957), 421–34 (focuses on *Arthur Mervyn*)

———. "Introduction." Pp. vii-xviii of CBB. *Arthur Mervyn, or Memoirs of the Year 1793*, ed. Berthoff. New York: Holt, Rinehart & Winston, 1962

Brancaccio, Patrick. "Studied Ambiguities: *Arthur Mervyn* and the Problem of the Unreliable Narrator." *AL*, 42 (1970), 18–27

Harap, Louis. "Fracture of a Stereotype: Charles Brockden Brown's Achsa Fielding." *American Jewish Archives*, 24 (1972), 187–95

Hedges, William L. "Benjamin Rush, Charles Brockden Brown, and the American Plague Year." *EAL*, 7 (1972), 295–311 ("the relation of the yellow fever to character" in Rush's letters and in *Ormond* and *Arthur Mervyn*)

Justus, James H. "Arthur Mervyn, American." *AL*, 42 (1970), 304–24

Lewis, R[ichard] W. B. "The Hero in Space: Brown, Cooper, Bird." *The American Adam: Innocence, Tragedy and Tradition in the Nineteenth Century*. Chicago: Univ. of Chicago Press, 1955, 90–109 (92–98 on *Arthur Mervyn*)

McAlexander, Patricia J. "*Arthur Mervyn* and the Sentimental Love Tradition." *Studies in the Literary Imagination*, 9, ii (1976), 31–41

Nelson, Carl W. "A Method for Madness: The Symbolic Patterns in *Arthur Mervyn*." *West Virginia Univ. Philological Papers*, 22 (1975), 29–50

Ringe, Donald A. *Charles Brockden Brown* [see III.C, above], 65–85

Rose, Alan Henry. "Sin and the City: The Uses of Disorder in the Urban Novel." *Centennial Review*, 16 (1972), 203–20 (204–7 on *Arthur Mervyn*)

Rose, Harriet. "The First-Person Narrator as Artist in the Works of Charles Brockden Brown, Nathaniel Hawthorne, and Henry James." *DAI*, 33 (1973), 6373A

Spengemann, William C. *The Adventurous Muse: The Poetics of American Fiction, 1789-1900*. New Haven: Yale Univ. Press, 1977, 98–106 (the "poetics of domesticity" in *Arthur Mervyn*)

Stout, Janis P. "Urban Gothicists: Brown [etc.]." *Sodoms in Eden: The City in American Fiction Before 1860*. Westport, Conn.: Greenwood Press, 1976, 44–50 (on *Arthur Mervyn* and *Ormond*)

VanDerBeets, Richard, and Paul Witherington. "My Kinsman, Brockden Brown: Robin Molineux and Arthur Mervyn." *American Transcendental Quarterly*, 1 (1969), 13–15

Warfel, Harry R. *Charles Brockden Brown* [see II], 141–48

Wiley, Lulu R. *Sources and Influence* [see III.C], 141–54

SEE ALSO: Clark, D.L. [II]; Vilas, M.S. [III.B]; Butler, D.L. [III.C]; Petter, H. [III.C]

C. Clara Howard

Ringe, Donald A. *Charles Brockden Brown* [see III.C, above], 113–20

Wiley, Lulu R. *Sources and Influence* [see III.C], 172–76

Witherington, Paul. "Brockden Brown's Other Novels: *Clara Howard* and *Jane Talbot*." *Nineteenth-Century Fiction*, 29 (1974), 257–72

SEE ALSO: Clark, D.L. [II]; Warfel, H.R. [II]; Vilas, M.S. [III.B]; Butler, D.L. [III.C];

D. *Edgar Huntly*

Alderson, Evan. "To Reconcile with Common Maxims: Edgar Huntly's Ruses." *Pacific Coast Philology*, 10 (1975), 5–9

Bernard, Kenneth. "Charles Brockden Brown and the Sublime." *Personalist*, 45 (1964), 235–49

————. "*Edgar Huntly*: Charles Brockden Brown's Unsolved Murder." *Library Chronicle* (Univ. of Penna.), 33 (1967), 30–53

Carter, Boyd. "Poe's Debt to Charles Brockden Brown." *Prairie Schooner*, 27 (1953), 190–96 (*Edgar Huntly* and "Tale of the Ragged Mountains"); see also G. R. Thompson. "Is Poe's 'A Tale of the Ragged Mountains' a Hoax?" *Studies in Short Fiction*, 6 (1969), 454–60

Clark, David Lee. "Introduction." Pp. v–xxii of CBB. *Edgar Huntly, or Memoirs of a Sleep-Walker*, ed. Clark. New York: Macmillan, 1928

Davis, David Brion. *Homicide in American Fiction, 1798–1860: A Study in Social Values.* Ithaca, N.Y.: Cornell Univ. Press, 1957, 87–100 (the "disordered mind" in *Wieland* and *Edgar Huntly*); see also index

Fleck, Richard F. "Symbolic Landscapes in *Edgar Huntly*." *Research Studies* (Washington State Univ.), 39 (1971), 229–32

Hamilton, Wynette L. "The Correlation Between Societal Attitudes and Those of American Authors in the Depiction of American Indians, 1607–1860." *American Indian Quarterly*, 1 (1974), 1–26 (9–11 on *Edgar Huntly*)

Hughes, Philip Russell. "Archetypal Patterns in *Edgar Huntly*." *Studies in the Novel*, 5 (1973), 176–90

Kimball, Arthur G. "Savages and Savagism: Brockden Brown's Dramatic Irony." *Studies in Romanticism*, 6 (1967), 214–25

Morris, Mabel. "Charles Brockden Brown and the American Indian." *AL*, 18 (1946), 244–47

Ringe, Donald A. *Charles Brockden Brown* [see III.C, above], 120–28

Schulz, Dieter. "*Edgar Huntly* as Quest Romance." *AL*, 43 (1971), 323–35

Slotkin, Richard. *Regeneration Through Violence: The Mythology of the American Frontier, 1600–1860.* Middletown, Conn.: Wesleyan Univ. Press, 1973, 371–93 (*Edgar Huntly* and Chateaubriand's *Les Natchez*)

Stineback, David. "Introduction." Pp. 7–22 of CBB. *Edgar Huntly, or Memoirs of a Sleep-Walker*, ed. Stineback. New Haven, Conn.: College & Univ. Press, 1973

Toles, George Edward. "The Darkening Window: Four Problematic American Novels." *DAI*, 37 (1977), 4378A (*Edgar Huntly* and novels by Melville, Twain, and Faulkner)

Warfel, Harry R. *Charles Brockden Brown* [see II], 149–64

Wiley, Lulu R. *Sources and Influence* [see III.C], 155–71

Witherington, Paul. "Image and Idea in *Wieland* and *Edgar Huntly*." *Serif*, 3, iv (1966), 19–26

SEE ALSO: Clark, D.L. [II]; Vilas, M. S. [III.B]; Butler, D.L. [III.C]; Kimball, A.G. *Rational Fictions* [III.C]; Petter, H. [III.C]

E. *Jane Talbot*

Ringe, Donald A. *Charles Brockden Brown* [see III. C, above], 120–28

Wiley, Lulu R. *Sources and Influence* [see III.C], 176–88

Witherington, Paul. "Brockden Brown's Other Novels: *Clara Howard* and *Jane Talbot*." *Nineteenth-Century Fiction*, 29 (1974), 257–72

SEE ALSO: Clark, D.L. [II]; Warfel, H.R. [II]; [Review of *Jane Talbot*] [III.A]; Vilas, M. S. [III.B]; Butler, D. L. [III.C]; Petter, H. [III.C]

F.*Ormond*

Davies, Rosemary Reeves. "Charles Brockden Brown's *Ormond*: A Possible Influence upon Shelley's Conduct." *Philological Quarterly*, 43 (1964), 133–37 (the novel's plot and the Harriet-Mary-Percy Shelley triangle)

Hare, Robert R. "Charles Brockden Brown's *Ormond*: The Influence of Rousseau, Godwin, and Mary Wollstonecraft." *DA*, 28 (1968), 4599A

Hirsh, David H. "Charles Brockden Brown as a Novelist of Ideas." *Books at Brown*, 20 (1965), 165–84 (on *Ormond* and *Wieland*)

Krause, Sydney J. "*Ormond*: How Rapidly and How Well 'Composed, Arranged and Delivered.' " *EAL*, 13 (1978–79), 238–49

–––––. "*Ormond*: Seduction in a New Key." *AL*, 44 (1973), 570–84

Marchand, Ernest. "Introduction." Pp. ix–xliv of CBB. *Ormond*, ed. Marchand. New York: American Book Co., 1937

Nelson, Carl W. "Brown's Manichaean Mock-Heroic: The Ironic Self in a Hyperbolic World." *West Virginia Univ. Philological Papers*, 20 (1973), 26–42 (stresses *Ormond* and *Wieland*)

–––––. "A Just Reading of Charles Brockden Brown's *Ormond*." *EAL*, 8 (1973), 163–78

Ringe, Donald A. *Charles Brockden Brown* [see III.C, above], 49–64

Rodgers, Paul C. "Brown's *Ormond*: The Fruits of Improvisation." *American Quarterly*, 26 (1974), 4–22

Russo, James R. "The Tangled Web of Deception and Imposture in Charles Brockden Brown's *Ormond*." *EAL*, 14 (1979), 205–27

Warfel, Harry R. *Charles Brockden Brown* [see II], 125–40

Wiley, Lulu R. *Sources and Influence* [see III.C], 122–41

Witherington, Paul. "Charles Brockden Brown's *Ormond*: The American Artist and His Masquerades." *Studies in American Fiction*, 4 (1976), 111–19

SEE ALSO: Clark, D.L. [II]; Fuller, M. [III.A]; Stout, J.P. [III.B]; Vilas, M.S. [III.B]; Butler, D.L. [III.C]; Petter, H. [III.C]; Hedges, W.L. [IV.B]

G:*Wieland* (and *Carwin the Biloquist*)

Bredahl, A. Carl. "Transformation in *Wieland*." *EAL*, 12 (1977), 177–92

Butler, Michael D. "Charles Brockden Brown's *Wieland*: Method and Meaning." *Studies in American Fiction*, 4 (1976), 127–42

Christensen, Peter J. "The First Locked-Room Mystery? Charles Brockden Brown's *Wieland*." *Armchair Detective*, 10 (1977), 368–69

Cowie, Alexander. "Historical Essay." Pp. 311–48 of CBB.*The Novels and Related Works . . . : Bicentennial Edition*. Vol. I: *Wieland, or the Transformation: An American Tale; Memoirs of Carwin, the Biloquist*, ed. Sydney J. Krause, S. W. Reid, and Alexander Cowie. Kent, Ohio: Kent State Univ. Press, 1977

Ferguson, J. Delancey. "Death by Spontaneous Combustion." *Colophon*, 9 (1932), n.p. (12-page article; second page on *Wieland*)

Frank, John G. "The Wieland Family in Charles Brockden Brown's *Wieland*." *Monatshefte*, 42 (1950), 347–53

Franklin, Wayne. "Tragedy and Comedy in Brown's *Wieland*." *Novel*, 8 (1975), 147–63

Garrow, Scott. "Character Transformation in *Wieland*." *Southern Quarterly*, 4 (1966), 308–18

Gilmore, Michael T. "Calvinism and Gothicism: The Example of Brown's *Wieland*." *Studies in the Novel*, 9 (1977), 107–18

Gorlier, Claudio. "Due classici dissepolti: *Wieland* e *Clarel*." *L'Approdo Letterario*, 12 (Jan.-March 1966), 125–31

Greiner, Donald J. "Brown's Use of the Narrator in *Wieland*: An Indirect Plea for the Acceptance of Fiction." *C.L.A. Journal*, 13 (1969), 131–36

Hirsh, David H. "Charles Brockden Brown as a Novelist of Ideas." *Books at Brown*, 20 (1965), 165–84 (on *Wieland* and *Ormond*)

Hobson, Robert W. "Voices of Carwin and Other Mysteries in Charles Brockden Brown's *Wieland*." *EAL*, 10 (1975), 307–9

Jenkins, R. B. "Invulnerable Virtue in *Wieland* and *Comus*." *South Atlantic Bulletin*, 38, ii (1973), 72–75

Kable, William S. "Introduction." Pp. 1–14 of *Three Early American Novels*, ed. Kable. Columbus, Ohio: Merrill, 1970 (on *Carwin the Biloquist* as well as *Wieland*)

Katz, Joseph. "Analytical Bibliography and Literary History: The Writing and Printing of *Wieland*." *Proof*, 1 (1971), 8–34

Kirkham, E. Bruce. "A Note on *Wieland*." *American Notes & Queries*, 5 (1967), 86–87 (Wieland's Camisard doctrine)

Ketterer, David. "The Transformed World of Charles Brockden Brown's *Wieland*." *New Worlds for Old: The Apocalyptic Imagination, Science Fiction, and American Literature.* Bloomington: Indiana Univ. Press, 1974, 167–81

Kimball, Arthur G. *Rational Fictions* [see III.C, above], chapter 2 and passim

Krause, Sydney J. "Romanticism in *Wieland*: Brown and the Reconciliation of Opposites." Pp. 13–24 of *Artful Thunder: Versions of the Romantic Tradition in American Literature*, ed. Robert J. DeMott and Sanford E. Marovitz. Kent, Ohio: Kent State Univ. Press, 1975

———, and S. W. Reid. "Introduction." Pp. vii–xxv of CBB. *Wieland, or the Transformation: An American Tale; Memoirs of Carwin, the Biloquist*, ed. Krause and Reid. Kent, Ohio: Kent State Univ. Press, 1978 (edition reprints text of *The Novels and Related Works* [see IV.G: Cowie])

Lyttle, David. "The Case Against Carwin." *Nineteenth Century Fiction*, 26 (1971), 257–69

Manly, William M. "The Importance of Point of View in Brockden Brown's *Wieland*." *AL*, 35 (1963), 311–21

Mulqueen, James E. "The Plea for a Deistic Education in Charles Brockden Brown's *Wieland*." *Ball State Univ. Forum*, 10, ii (1969), 70–77

Pattee, Fred Lewis. "Introduction." Pp. ix–xlvi of CBB. *Wieland, or the Transformation, Together with Memoirs of Carwin the Biloquist: A Fragment*, ed. Pattee. New York: Harcourt, Brace, 1926; reprint, Harcourt, Brace & World, 1969

Prescott, F. C. "*Wieland* and *Frankenstein*." *AL*, 2 (1930), 172–73

Raneri, Marietta R. "The Self Behind the Self: The Americanization of the Gothic." *DAI*, 34 (1974), 5200A–01A

Reid, S. W. "Textual Essay." Pp. 349–70 of CBB. *The Novels and Related Works* [see IV.G: Cowie]

Ridgely, J. V. "The Empty World of *Wieland*." Pp. 3–16 of *Individual and Community: Variations on a Theme in American Fiction*, ed. Kenneth H. Baldwin and David K. Kirby. Durham: Duke Univ. Press, 1975

Ringe, Donald A. *Charles Brockden Brown* [see III.C], 25–48

Seltzer, Mark. "Saying Makes It So: Language and Event in Brown's *Wieland*." *EAL*, 13 (1978), 81–91

Shelden, Pamela J. "The Shock of Ambiguity: Brockden Brown's *Wieland* and the Gothic Tradition." *DeKalb Literary Arts Journal*, 10 (Sum. 1977), 17–26 (not verified)

Soldati, Joseph A. "The Americanization of Faust: A Study of Charles Brockden Brown's *Wieland*." *ESQ*, no. 74 (1974), 1–14; see also his "Configurations of Faust: Three Studies in the Gothic (1798–1820)." *DAI*, 32 (1972), 6945A

Strozier, Robert. "*Wieland* and Other Romances: Horror in Parentheses." *ESQ*, no. 50, Suppl. (1968), 24–29

Van Doren, Carl. "Early American Realism." *Nation*, 99 (12 Nov. 1914), 577–78; followed up in James C. Hendrickson. "A Note on *Wieland*." *AL*, 8 (1936), 305–6 (source of the murder plot)

Wagenknecht, Edward. "The Author of *Wieland*." *Cavalcade of the American Novel from the Birth of the Nation to the Middle of the Twentieth Century*. New York: Holt, 1952, 9–13

Warfel, Harry R. *Charles Brockden Brown* [see II], 96–115

Wiley, Elizabeth. "Four Strange Cases." *Dickensian*, 58 (1962), 120–25 (spontaneous combustion in novels by Brown, Marryat, Melville, and Dickens); see also George Perkins. "Death by Spontaneous Combustion in Marryat, Melville, Dickens, Zola, and Others." *Dickensian*, 60 (1964), 57–63

Wiley, Lulu R. *Sources and Influence* [see III.C], 96–121

Wilson, James D. "Incest and American Romantic Fiction." *Studies in the Literary Imagination*, 7, i (1974), 31–50 (37–40 on *Wieland*)

Witherington, Paul. "Image and Idea in *Wieland* and *Edgar Huntly*." *Serif*, 3, iv (1966), 19–26

Ziff, Larzer. "A Reading of *Wieland*." *PMLA*, 77 (1962), 51–57

SEE ALSO: Clark, D.L. [II]; "Charles Brockden Brown" [III.A]; Whittier, J.G. III.A]; "*Wieland*. . ." [III.A]; Vilas, M.S. [III.B]; Butler, D.L. [III.C]; Petter, H. [III.C]; Davis, D.B. [IV.D]; Nelson, C.W. [IV.F]

H. Other Works

Aldridge, A. Owen. "Charles Brockden Brown's Poem on Benjamin Franklin." *AL*, 38 (1966), 230–35 (its import in 1789)

Bennett, Charles E. "Charles Brockden Brown's 'Portrait of an Emigrant.' " *C.L.A. Journal*, 14 (1970), 87–90

———. "A Poetical Correspondence Among Elihu Hubbard Smith, Joseph Bringhurst, Jr., and Charles Brockden Brown in *The Gazette of the United States*." *EAL*, 12 (1977–78), 277–85

Berthoff, Warner B. "Charles Brockden Brown's Historical 'Sketches': A Consideration." *AL*, 28 (1956), 147–54

———. " 'A Lesson on Concealment': Brockden Brown's Method in Fiction." *Philological Quarterly*, 37 (1958), 45–57

Borchers, Hans. "Introduction." Pp. ix–xxvii (notes, 187–215) of CBB. *Memoirs of Stephen Calvert*, ed. Borchers. Frankfurt am Main and Las Vegas: Lang, 1978

Brown, Herbert. "Charles Brockden Brown's 'The Story of Julius': Rousseau and Richardson 'Improved.' " Pp. 35–53 of *Essays Mostly on Periodical Publishing in America*, ed. James Woodress. Durham: Duke Univ. Press, 1973

Clark, David Lee. "Brockden Brown's First Attempt at Journalism." *Univ. of Texas Studies in English*, 7 (1927), 155–74

Eitner, Walter H. "Samuel Miller's Nation 'Lately Become Literary': The *Brief Retrospect* in Brockden Brown's *Monthly Magazine*."*EAL*, 13 (1978), 213–16

Free, William J. *The Columbian Magazine and American Literary Nationalism*. The Hague: Mouton, 1968, 99–101 and passim

Garnett, Richard. "Alms for Oblivion, III: The Minor Writings of Charles Brockden Brown." *Cornhill Magazine*, 13 (1902), 494–506

Hemenway, Robert E. "Brockden Brown's Twice Told Insanity Tale." *AL*, 40 (1968), 211–15 (the 1798 "A Lesson on Sensibility" compared to its 1809 version, "Insanity: A Fragment")

Tichi, Cecelia. "Charles Brockden Brown, Translator." *AL*, 44 (1972), 1–12 (on his translation of Volney; see White, below)

Tilton, Eleanor M. " 'The Sorrows' of Charles Brockden Brown." *PMLA*, 69 (1954), 1304–08 (the "letters" of CBB and "Henrietta G.")

Warfel, Harry R. "Introduction." Pp. v–xii of CBB. *The Rhapsodist, and Other Uncollected Writings*, ed. Warfel. New York: Scholars' Facsimilies and Reprints, 1943

Weber, Alfred. "Eine neu entdeckte Kurzgeschichte C. B. Browns." *Jahrbuch für Amerikastudien*, 8 (1963), 280–96 (identifies an anonymous story, "Somnambulism. A Fragment," as Brown's and reprints it)

— — —, ed. "Essays und Rezensionen von Charles Brockden Brown." *Jahrbuch für Amerikastudien*, 6 (1961), 168–330 (reprints several essays and reviews [in English])

White, George W. "Introduction." Pp. xi–xii of Constantin François Volney. *A View of the Soil and Climate of the United States of America, Translated with Occasional Remarks by C. B. Brown*. New York: Hafner, 1968 (facsimile of Phila. edition of 1804)

Notes on Contributors

CATHY N. DAVIDSON, Assistant Professor of English at Michigan State University, has published numerous essays on the development of American fiction from William Hill Brown to Thomas Pynchon. She has also edited collections of scholarly essays and is currently writing a study of the social, cultural, and literary origins of the early American novel (1789–1815), for which she has received a grant from the National Endowment for the Humanities.

NINA BAYM is Director of the School of Humanities at the University of Illinois. She has held a Guggenheim Fellowship and is the author of *The Shape of Hawthorne's Career* and *Woman's Fiction: A Guide to Novels by and about Women in America, 1820–1870*. Her other publications include numerous articles on American writers such as Cooper, Emerson, Dickinson, Frost, Melville, Poe, and Thoreau.

BERNARD ROSENTHAL, Chairman of the Department of English at the State University of New York at Binghamton, is the author of *City of Nature: Journeys to Nature in the Age of American Romanticism*. He has edited various books, has published numerous essays on early American literature, and has been the recipient of a grant from the National Endowment for the Humanities.

WILLIAM J. SCHEICK is Professor of English at the University of Texas at Austin, where he also serves as editor of *Texas Studies in Literature and Language*. His wide-ranging work has appeared in numerous journals, and his books include *The Will and the Word: the Poetry of Edward Taylor; The Writings of Jonathan Edwards: Theme, Motif, and Style; The Slender Human Word: Emerson's Artistry in Prose;* and *The Half-Blood: A Cultural Symbol in Nineteenth-Century American Fiction*.

EMORY ELLIOTT is Chairman of the American Studies Program at Princeton University. He has edited *Puritan Influences in American Literature* and is the author of *Power and the Pulpit in Puritan New England*. His numerous essays have appeared in various journals and essay collections. He has been a Fellow at the National Humanities Center and is completing a study of literature and religion in the early national period.

PAUL WITHERINGTON, Professor of English at South Dakota State

University, has written several essays on Brown, including a major bibliographical essay on him. He has published widely on early and modern American writers, was a contributing editor to *College English*, and was a Fulbright lecturer at the University of Jordan.

SYDNEY J. KRAUSE, Professor of English at Kent State University, is General Editor of the CEAA-CSE Bicentennial Edition of the *Novels and Related Works of Charles Brockden Brown*. He is the author of *Mark Twain as Critic* and has published widely on nineteenth and twentieth-century American writers. He has held grants from the National Endowment for the Humanities and the American Philosophical Society.

CHARLES E. BENNETT is Dean of Faculty and Vice President for Academic Affairs at Dowling College. He has published several essays on Brown and has edited Paul Allen's unpublished *Life of Charles Brockden Brown*. He is preparing an edition of the letters of Charles Brockden Brown.

CHARLES A. CARPENTER, Associate Professor of English at State University of New York at Binghamton, specializes in literary bibliography and modern drama. He has published a book on Shaw's early plays, a Goldentree Bibliography of Modern British drama articles on Pinter and other dramatists, and annual bibliographies in the journal *Modern Drama* since 1974. Under a grant from the National Endowment for the Humanities he has recently visited numerous libraries in Europe to pursue his research for a forthcoming bibliography on modern drama studies.

INDEX